A JOURNEY THROUGH THE WORD OF GOD

The Study of The Four Gospels

A JOURNEY THROUGH THE WORD OF GOD

The Study of The Four Gospels

LADY FLORA E. WIGGINS

ARPress
45 Dan Road Suite 5
Canton MA 02021

Hotline: 1(888) 821-0229
Fax: 1(508) 545-7580

Ordering Information:

Quantity sales. Special discounts are available on quantity purchases by corporations, associations, and others. For details, contact the publisher at the address above.

Printed in the United States of America.

ISBN-13:	Softcover	979-8-89330-728-3
	eBook	979-8-89330-729-0

Library of Congress Control Number: 2022912690

DMWW INTERNATIONAL BIBLE INSTITUTE
A JOURNEY THROUGH THE WORD OF GOD
VOLUME I: THE FOUR GOSPELS

Study Guide Workbook Table of Contents

INTRODUCTION

WELCOME TO THE JOURNEY

PART 1 - MATTHEW

PART 2 - MARK

PART 3 - LUKE

PART 4 - JOHN

This Bible Study Workbook program has been tested in several countries. Here are a few testimonials from DMWW International Bible Institute students from overseas.

Pastor Gift Martin Chirwa

Malawi, Africa

Member Since 2020

Welcome to the winning team. These studies have been ordained by God to lead his people from all over the world, into the full knowledge of the truth as it is written in the Holy Bible. The members here are on assignment by God to follow his ordered steps to disciple all nations to Christ. DMWW International has set up this program so that you can choose to enroll in classes as an individual and follow along in a FREE class online or you can enroll your own home study group and teach it yourself. You can join a church group where your Pastor or a church leader teaches you. You can also coordinate a Prison Ministry group or a nursing home or homebound study ministry.

This workbook and program was created so students from other countries could understand it. This was so helpful for me and my fellow African classmates who have studied here, year after year. Try it for yourself. You will be so glad you did. It is set up in a very user-friendly manner that is simple to follow and understand. Many of us are now Administrators in our own various countries, discipling others with these same tools that we learned with.

Whatever way you decide to enroll and study, you will have access to DMWW Instructors, Administrators, and fellow students. DMWW also offers annual graduation opportunities to students who successfully complete required classes. We will be here to walk you through it, every step of the way.. #JOINTHEJOURNEYDMWW

Elder Ronald Mayanja

Uganda, Africa

Member Since 2018

The studies here at DMWW International Bible Institute have been a great blessing to me. I have studied the Bible for many years. But, the same things I have studied before are much clearer in these classes. We study everything "in context" which makes the stories and information in the chapters easier to understand and envision. My favorite study this far has been The Study of The Pentateuch. I learned the importance of obedience and following instructions closely from the story of Noah and the specifications of the building of the boat. Also with Moses and the children of Israel and seeing the results of disobedience. Learning the Bible in depth in such a simplistic format has been great. It's like experiencing a delicious meal. You can't quite describe it. You want others to taste and see. Well, come taste and see that this learning program is good. #JOINTHEJOURNEYDMWW

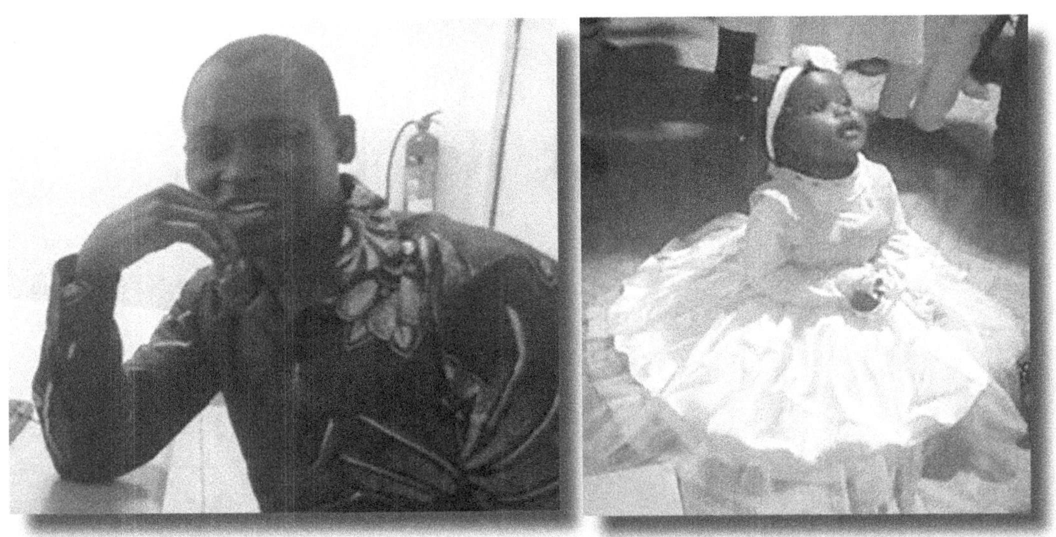

Pastor Remos Ngule

Nairobi, Kenya

Member Since 2017

I joined DMWW International in 2017. I was one of the original members who assisted Lady Flora by recording readings of the Bible and translating her work into the Swahili language. The translation helped people in my country learn about God even if they couldn't read. All they had to do was listen. This organization has introduced a pure, unadulterated study program that is good for use by anyone who believes in the Holy Bible.

My wife and I honor Lady Flora and the dedication to God's word and sharing it with the world. We had our first child December 26, 2020. This great woman of God is our baby's name sake. Meet Baby Flora

#JOINTHEJOURNEY

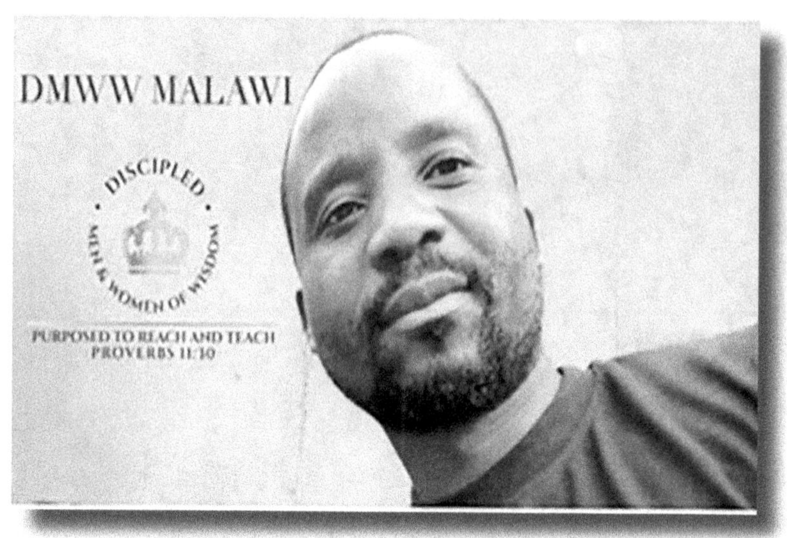

Apostle Sydney McLagen Kalipo

Malawi, Africa

Member Since 2018

The DMWW Bible Institute studies have been revelatory and intriguing enough to keep seasoned scholars of the Bible engaged, yet clear and concise enough for the newest born again Christians to understand. Order your book and join today. You won't regret it. I encourage you and your churches to #JOINTHEJOURNEYDMWW

Harrison Ambuko

Nairobi, Kenya

Member Since 2019

This Bible study program designed by the Discipled Men & Women of Wisdom has made the Bible clear and simple to understand more than ever before. The stories are interesting and they come alive as we study together. It is like you are in the story with the people we are reading about. We study difficult words with older meanings which helps us understand what we are reading much better.

I enjoyed learning and studying so much that I began teaching others in my country what I am learning. I can see them learning as well. This is true discipleship. It is amazing. #JOINTHEJOURNEYDMWW

Jacob Elavanyo

Ghana, Africa

Joined 2022

I am grateful to study with the people from other countries and even continents, other churches and religions, different races and economic backgrounds with a common goal to glorify the Lord. This must be what heaven looks like. I appreciate that Lady Flora, the President of this organization makes sure the students have what we need, from study guides and worksheets to graduation attire and certificates. But, she not only offers us a fish when we need it, more importantly she is teaching us to fish for ourselves.

We are all here because 1) we want to learn more about Jesus and 2) we want to share the good news with others. If you happen to have these things in common with us, you have come to the right place and you have found family. #JOINTHEJOURNEY

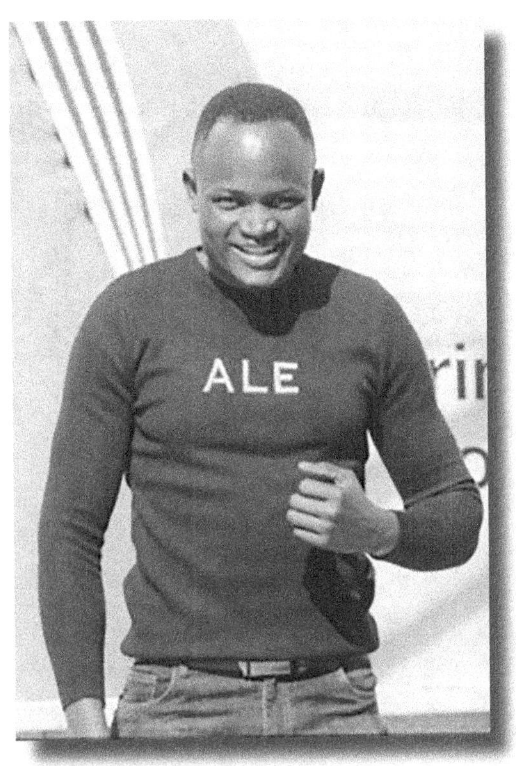

Chris Songwa

Brazil

I have followed the DMWW International Bible classes since 2019. I travel a lot. Sometimes internet access is great. Sometimes it is very bad. These classes are convenient because when data is out, instructors will email your assignments and assist you. I am grateful for this program that I can introduce to people who have little to no budget. This program is offered to anyone FREE. The only thing you will ever have to pay for is your books, which are very inexpensive. This study plan that Lady Flora has developed is very effective and efficient. It is very user friendly for those with an active lifestyle. You can get in your daily bread as it was intended, every day. Come

#JOINTHEJOURNEY

A Short Story About Our Author

God knew Flora Wiggins before she was formed in the womb, where she was sanctified and ordained by God (Jeremiah 1:5). The vision of "The Men & Women of Wisdom/Ladies in Waiting Support Group & Talk Show", that God has now given Flora was written upon her heart and into her life story before she ever knew her name. Satan got wind of this vision and the abundant life God had ordained for Flora's life. So, he set out to steal Flora from her mother's womb by killing Flora and destroying her mother with one fiery dart (St. John 10:10).

Flora's mother Margie, was hit by a train and thrown from her car while pregnant with Flora. What Satan did not know was that God had angels encamped around Margie. As the train approached and hit the car, Margie was thrown from her car. In the spirit realm, the angels actually lifted Margie from the car and swiftly placed her on the ground, so that she was not dashed against the stone (Psalms 91:11,12). Months later, Flora was born to Margie & her husband, Louis Wiggins.

This baby was miraculously healthy and completely whole (stunning the doctors and her parents). She came out with what her father described as, a smile that was spiritually connected to her heart. Her mother said her smile was created to draw people to Christ (who had just saved her life for a great purpose). Her mother, Margie dedicated and baptized her. She put Flora in Sunshine Band (a class that teaches small children about God), Purity Class (class that teaches teens about God), YPWW (Youth Class), Green Memorial Bible Institute & College (A college level class offered at our church) and everything possible to watch over the gift in Flora that she knew existed.

Filled with the word of God and adapting to the awesome feeling of classroom settings, Flora gained a love for education. She soon realized her gifted calling to teach. She began teaching Bible School and Sunday School. After graduating, she began teaching in Christian Schools. She began teaching in the Sikeston Public School system in 2010 in the state of Missouri where she was born. She later moved to Texas and began employment with the Round Rock Independent School District in Texas.

After graduating from high school, Flora wanted to get out from under (what she described as) the tedious rules and regulations of her parents who knew something she did not know.

The Devil had been out to kill Flora since before she was born. She moved twelve hours away. Satan lay in wait for her very soul.

Having been sheltered for seventeen years, Flora had gone out in a hurry as a (purpose filled) sheep for slaughter (Romans 8:36). She wanted to experience something she was not allowed to experience at home. A boyfriend to love her and share with her the beautiful thing she knew to be love. She had only seen this form of love through the eyes and heart of her parents who were together her whole life. What she experienced on her own journey was quite the opposite. She didn't understand what her parents were saying when they told her she wasn't ready to go out on her own. All her other brothers and sisters had moved the day they graduated. So, she wanted to do the same. She was of age. So, her parents reluctantly allowed her to move 12 hours away.

Naive, inexperienced, timid, shy, and ignorant of the devices of Satan (II Corinthians 2:11), she was spiritually torn to shreds. God came to rescue her and put the pieces back together... not once, twice, or three times. But, God came to her rescue time and time again. He never left her. He would never forsake her (Deuteronomy 31:6). She began to notice that no matter how many times she messed up, he still loved her. Every time she ran to him to cast her cares on him, he still cared for her (I Peter 5:7).

There was a particular relationship that stands out in her journey. This was not just any horrible and heart wrenching relationship. This was a relationship assigned to her straight from the pits of hell to kill her. She was consistently pursued and chased by this man and made to feel like she was loved, adored, wanted and needed. Inside, she knew something wasn't right. But, she had her spiritual guards down, looking for the true love she never had the opportunity to experience. Giving in and opening her heart to this man allowed the enemy to access a point of rejection inside of her that still existed from the very first failed relationship she had experienced. It had been growing like a cancer with each failed relationship she endured. It silently affected her self esteem and character. She settled for less than she knew she deserved in order to feel true love from someone...anyone. The familiar spirits within this man were released within forbidden, unhealthy soul ties. They began to wrap around the deep rooted rejection and build a stronghold of fear and rejection inside her. At that point she was in too deep and began to compromise her moral and spiritual values. When she tried to break loose, the man began to strike out in anger. He not only left her. But, he left her financially, spiritually, and emotionally broken.

She was lost. She felt alone, even in rooms full of people. She felt dead inside. Rejection was a familiar place for her. But, fortunately, the one thing she held dear and knew, was that the only place to run was to God. She didn't consider drugs, alcohol, meaningless sex, or anything but getting to a house filled with corporate praise and worship to fall on her face before her GOD. December 31, 2015, at a New Year's Eve watch meeting service, Flora was too ashamed to even pray. She found herself just crying to God in a heavenly language. Then she heard God speak in a resounding voice. He said, "Enough is Enough"! She felt the arms of the Holy Spirit embrace her and begin to minister to the purpose that was buried deep beneath her pain. As the spirit called out to the purpose that God put there when he created her, she began to breathe ruach (winds from the Holy Spirit). The spirit kept saying "New Year meet New Flora".

She went home as a new creature. God had changed her from the inside out. She was no longer the old Flora. So, when she left church and walked into her home, a spirit she had not recognized before, was very visible and apparent to her now. It was a spirit of depression. It was left in her home by the man with whom she had previously shared soul ties. She was not the same. So, the bad spirit could not access her spirit. But, the bad spirit didn't want to leave her home. She called on the elders, anointed her home and children and fasted and prayed for three days straight.

After three days, her home was filled with God's glory and an afterglow that still lingers there to this day. God began to minister to Flora daily. She fell in love with God and got to know God in a way she had never known existed. She had learned ABOUT God all her life. At the age of 46, she realized that she knew all about this God that she never got to KNOW personally. As she began to hunger and thirst after God, he filled her completely (Matthew 5:6). God began to share with her in the wee hours of the night and very early morning hours. Each time he ministered to her, he emphasized his love for her. He let her know the pain was never allowed as punishment. The pain was allowed because it was the only path to her purpose. She was filled with gratitude, praise, and a feeling of debt. She wanted to do something to say thanks for all he had done for her. He said, "Will you LIVE OUT LOUD for me?". She was honored at the request. It was not easy. But, she was always reminded of God's words that ministered to her about her purpose being beyond her pain. It gave her courage as she went forth and obeyed his every command closely year after year.

In the year of 2016, Flora began to give birth to several ministries that God had planted within her before she was born. She began to realize that all those men didn't hate her. She began to absorb the truth in the fact that we should love our neighbors purely and unconditionally, no matter what (Mark 12:31). Flora noticed that the pain was from the spiritual babies growing and moving and getting ready to come forth. The positioning of the first baby to crown was quite unfamiliar as it was her first spiritual birth. It was very painful. However, remaining mindful of the purpose behind the pain, Flora began to feel the new thing that God was doing within her as the well of living water began to flow from her belly (John 7:38). The intimacy with God had caused Flora's mind to be renewed and she began gradually transforming by the word of God, placed in her from her youth (Romans 12:2). As the words flowed from her, propelled by the ruach winds of the Holy Spirit, she pushed with all her might.

Flora found the will and strength to push in knowing that our fight is not with those who do evil against us. We all fight the same forces of evil against our own lives. Our fight is with the one who tries to plant the deeds in our hearts and who planted the evil they fell prey to, within them (Ephesians 6:12). In this revelation, Flora found the power within to forget the memories that would make her BITTER (Philippians 3:13) and embrace the GREATER within her to become BETTER! (I John 4:4).

One of the spiritual babies that came forth from Flora is the vision for a ***"Ladies in Waiting Support Group & Round Table Discussion Talk Show".*** **The vision** includes a talk show that includes interviews with ladies who are overcomers of physical, psychological, and emotional abuse.They are Ministers, Elders, Business Owners, ladies who specialize in fields of support in the areas of Psychology, Counseling, Self Help, and Motivational Speaking, who our audience can connect with for mentoring, assistance, referral and other help in their local areas.

The talk show began as a Facebook Production. Flora Says that this baby is much like a Jabez. It was born of pain and sorrow. It began small. But, its purpose that cried out from within it, has caused God to say to Flora, I will enlarge this baby's territory and bless it indeed for your obedience in enduring the pain to bring forth this purpose. The talk show and support group fall under the umbrella of another vision The Discipled Men & Women of Wisdom Outreach International.

This venture led us to a worldwide ministry to reach people everywhere and teach the word of God. In 2021, we officially registered and began the DMWW International Bible Institute that you are becoming a student of today. Welcome to the DMWW family.

Dear Future Student,

The purpose of me sharing this short story with you is to let you know that God can use Y-O-U! No matter what stage you are at, in life. God can use your story for his Glory. You may feel like giving up right now. But, do not. This is a perfect time for God to use you. God does his best work in times of despair.

At several stages in this story you can see I was a mess and Satan was after me. But God sent angels even before I was born, (up to and throughout my adult years) to protect me every time. He didn't do it because I deserved it.

He did it to protect the purpose he had placed inside of me to rightly divide, prepare and distribute these tools to help his people study his word.

By the same token, God is protecting you through dangers seen and unseen because of the purpose he has put in you. In the times that you may wonder why God keeps looking out for you, realize that he knows what is inside of you and he is protecting his investment in you, just like he did for me.

God sent me to feed his sheep and I am here to do that by spoon feeding you his word in context, word by word, and in a pure and unadulterated form, in these study guides and tools that I have prepared for you. As you join me on this journey to study his word in a very simple, user-friendly format, allow God's living water and daily bread to nourish and replenish you one day at a time. My team and I will be here for you every step of the way. Blessed Learning be unto you.

~Lady Flora

WRITE THE VISION AND MAKE IT PLAIN
Habakuk 2:2,3

OUR MISSION

The MISSION of The Discipled Men & Women of Wisdom International is to prepare and distribute teaching tools that are user-friendly, simple to understand, making learning engaging and inspirational, to REACH all nations through electronic means and to TEACH the word of God in a pure, unadulterated manner, reading and studying the King James Version of the Holy Bible, book by book, chapter by chapter, verse by verse and word for word to enlighten, encourage, and empower people to use their God given free will to make wise decisions for their life, as we disciple all nations to Christ according to ***Matthew 28:19, 20.***

OUR GOAL

We aspire to blaze new trails by offering free online study courses internationally, with the intention to inspire others to follow our example to deny conforming to this world and transforming according to ***Romans 12:2*** by the renewing of our minds. We desire to reach the nations by teaching men and women to teach teams in their own countries from models created in the United States of America.

OUR VISION

Our vision is to introduce a new way to study the word of God "in context" without regard to denomination, religion, color, sex, age, title or social status, focusing on God's rewards of obedience and punishments for disobedience, as well as his love for people and his desire to be loved by his people, leading to a renewed relationship between God and man and a spiritual healing of the land according to II ***Chrinicles 7:14.***

ABOUT OUR INSTITUTE

The Discipled Men & Women of Wisdom International Bible Institute Mascot is the lamb. It symbolizes the lamb of God (Jesus) who lives inside each of us.

Our school colors are red and white. The white is for the purity of the lamb. Red is for the blood of the lamb that was shed for our sins. We celebrate the completion of the study of each volume, or set of books of the bible with a commencement exercise where the students share what they have learned in class, by bringing a short message.

The reason DMWW International Bible Institute vows to reach and teach, is to inform everyone around the world that the lamb of God (Jesus) loves us so much that he bled and died to save us from our sins.

We obey his command in II Timothy 2:15 to study to show ourselves approved unto God workmen that need not be ashamed, rightly dividing the word of truth. We also follow his command to disciple all nations to Christ by teaching the pure, unadulterated gospel that you will find in this inspirational study guide workbook.

DMWW INTERNATIONAL CREED

*On my honor, I vow to love you Lord my God with all my heart, with all my soul and with all my mind, and love my neighbor as myself, realizing that my wrestle is not against flesh and blood, but against principalities, against powers, against the rulers of the darkness of this world, against spiritual wickedness in high places, according to Matthew 22:37, 39 and Ephesians 6:12

*I will continue to study to show myself approved unto you, a worker that will not need to be ashamed, rightly dividing the word of truth, as I hide your word in my heart that I might not sin against it. I will cry loud and spare not, lifting up my voice like a trumpet, showing your people transgressions, according to II Timothy 2:15, Psalm 119:11, and Isaiah 58:1

*I vow to walk in the spirit and not fulfill the lust of my flesh. I will allow you to create in me a clean heart and renew the right spirit within me, as I let this mind be in me, which was in you. I vow not to conform to this world, but I will allow your Holy Word to transform me by the renewing of my mind that I may prove your good, acceptable and perfect will of God, according to Galatians 5:16, Psalm 51:10, Philippians 2:5, and Romans 12:2

*This I vow on my honor, unto thee oh Lord my God

Student Signature ______________________________

The DMWW International Bible Institute ENROLLMENT

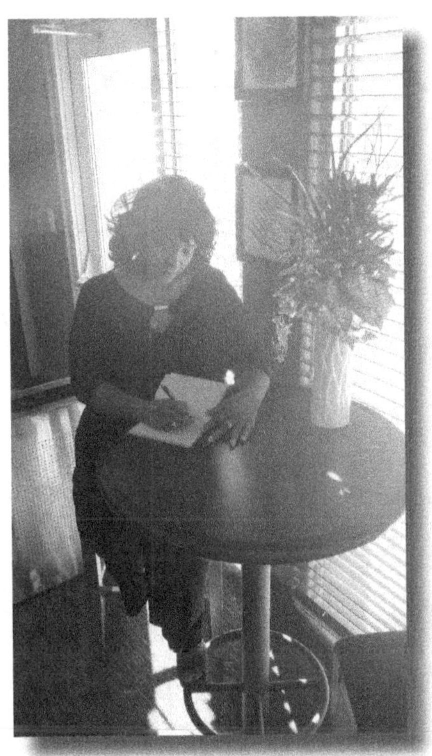

Please complete the following page and email it to ladyflora3g@gmail.com or send it to DMWW International Bible Institute 223 North Main street, Suite 143, Sikeston, Missouri 63801. If you would like to refer a friend, you may contact us at (573) 212-3813 Blessed learning be unto you.

DMWW INTERNATIONAL BIBLE INSTITUTE ENROLLMENT FORM

NAME____

EMAILADDRESS_______________________________________
(WE USE GMAIL FOR CLASS ASSIGNMENTS)

MAILING ADDRESS____________________________________
(FOR RECEIPT OF GRADUATION CERTIFICATES)

CITY__________STATE__________ZIP________COUNTRY_______________
COUNTRYCODE_________AREACODE_________PHONENUMBER_______________
TIME ZONE________________

****

The Founder of DMWW International Bible Institute wants you to know that you are our main priority here. We are offering these courses at no charge so that you may concentrate on your studies without worrying about whether or not you can afford it.

We, the members of DMWW International, are dedicated to ministering to the whole person, mind, body and soul. If you are in need of any basic necessities, please call the Ambassador in your local area and allow them to speak with you about our referral and resource programs. We would like to minister to your natural hunger first, so you can concentrate on receiving the spiritual nutrients that come from studying God's word.God is Love and we want to share him with you both naturally and spiritually. God cares about you and so do we.

****

What is your reason for taking this Bible Study Course? Please check one.

I am interested in becoming a DMWW Ambassador for my country__________________

I want to supervise a DMWW Study Space in my State (USA)__________________

Iwasreferredbymy Pastor/Counselor__________________

Iamanew Christian__________________

Ineedhelpunderstanding/studyingtheBible__________________

I have been a Christian for a while. I just want to study more__________________

I accepted my call to the ministry. I want to learn the Bible "in context"__________________

Would you like to be paired with a study partner?__________________

Will you be able to commit to at least 15 minutes per day to study the Bible and one hour per week for interactive class discussion on Saturdays?__________________

Whatisyourchurchaffiliation?__________________

If you are a new Christian, what is your religious preference?__________________

We believe ministry is about what you do, not just what you are called. If you are currently serving in the five-fold ministry, what do you do?__________________

____

If you are a Pastor, are you interested in enrolling a group?

This class is free of charge to you and anyone who would like to join. Would you like to refer a friend or family member to this class?
Please list their name and contact information below.

____

____

****

____
Applicant Signature

____
Date of Enrollment

____
Enrollment Counselor

____
Date of Acceptance

The Study of The Four Gospels Pre-Test

Students will take this quiz before and after studying in this class to determine what they know before and what they have learned after taking our course.

What is the name of our upcoming session of study? ______________________

How many weeks will it take to complete the class? ______________________

How many chapters will this study cover in all? ______________________

What four books of the bible are considered the Four Gospels? ______________________

How many chapters are in the book of Matthew? ______________________

How many chapters are in the book of Mark? ______________________

How many chapters are in the book of Luke? ______________________

How many chapters are in the book of John? ______________________

Which author(s) told about the step-daughter dancing and being rewarded with John's head on a platter for her mother? ______________________

What was her name? ______________________

Which author(s) told the people to repent and be baptized? ______________________

Which author(s) told in detail about fishermen's nets breaking full of fish after obeying God's instructions? ______________________

Which author(s) told about the woman with the issue of blood? ______________________

Which author(s) told about the demons being cast out of a man and into swine? ________

Which author(s) told about Jesus raising the dead man, Lazarus? ________

Which three (3) gospels are the most similar in their storyline? ________

Who is the most different? ________

What makes one author stand out from the rest in his particular gospel? ________

Where can you find our daily lessons online? ________

What day and time do we meet together each week for class discussion and participation grades? ________

What is the objective of this study of The Four Gospels? ________

Give a specific parable that you recall from the book of Matthew? ________

Tell of a lesson you learned in Mark that you did not learn in Matthew? ________

Tell a story or lesson that was given in Luke that is not given in Matthew or Mark. ________

Which particular parables were told by all four disciples, Matthew, Mark, Luke, and John.

What is something significant about the book of John that is very different from the books of Matthew, Mark, and Luke? ________

HOW TO WRITE A STANDARD SHORT ESSAY FOR DMWW INTERNATIONAL

Discipled Men and Women of Wisdom International practices formal essay writing to develop the art of informed persuasion, by combining two types of essay writings. They are the informative essay and the persuasive essay.

Our goal is to minister to others in a way that persuades them to walk in the truth as we know it, with fact based information from the Holy Bible and our personal experiences which relate to this information. You may also include outside sources that are credible as long as you cite anything you reference.

The element of persuasion according to Romans 8:38,39 ***"For I am persuaded that neither death, nor life, nor angels, nor principalities, nor powers,nor things present nor things to come, nor height, nor depth, nor any other creature shall beable to separate us from the Love of God, which is in Christ Jesus our Lord."*** is what takes place in the mind when one makes a conscious decision to follow Christ.

This week we will be learning to write standard short essays. We will keep it simple. Your essay will contain three parts.

PART 1	INTRODUCTION	Thesis Statement and Opening
PART 2	BODY	Supporting Statements
PART 3	CONCLUSION	Summary of the Information Given

The Study of
THE BOOK OF MATTHEW

Begin Date__________________________

Course End Date______________________________

Study Guide Prepared and Distributed by
The Discipled Men & Women of Wisdom, International

INTRODUCTION TO THE BOOK OF MATTHEW

Welcome to the study of the book of Matthew. This is the first book in the set of four books commonly known as The Four Gospels in the King James Version of the Holy Bible. As we begin our journey through the word of God in the book of Matthew, I want you to imagine yourself traveling through the places mentioned in the text and meeting the people that the disciples encountered.

Become a disciple in your mind and immerse yourself into the culture and ways of life in that time period. This wil help you to fully understand what the author, Matthew is portraying to you from his perspective. You will experience the things the disciples experienced when they travelled from town to town with Jesus as he healed, saved and delivered multitudes of people.

Your final assignment for the book of Matthew will ask you to write an essay telling about your journey through the places mentioned in this book. Blessed Learning be unto you.

STUDENT PRAYER JOURNAL

Please use this space to record your thoughts and feelings as you travel on this spirit led journey through the word of God with us. Please know that you have brothers and sisters in this organization from all over the world praying with and for you. My prayer for you is that you will begin to see the power of God resting in each set of your footprints. As you look back and examine your past in this journal, may you realize that you were never alone and according to Hebrews 13:5, God will never leave nor forsake you. ~LADY FLORA

The Study of Matthew Chapters 1-4
VOCABULARY DEFINITIONS

WORD	DEFINITIONS
1) GENERATION	
2) BEGAT	
3) ESPOUSED	
4) PRIVILY	
5) DILIGENT	
6) LAMENTATION	
7) LEATHERN	
8) PURGE	
9) LUNATIC(K)	
10) PALSY	

DMWW Daily Bible Reading
KJV MATTHEW CHAPTERS 1-4

CHAPTER 1

1. The book of the generation of Jesus Christ, the son of David, the son of Abraham.
2. Abraham begat Isaac; and Isaac begat Jacob; and Jacob begat Judas and his brethren;
3. And Judas begat Phares and Zara of Thamar; and Phares begat Esrom; and Esrom begat Aram;
4. And Aram begat Aminadab; and Aminadab begat Naasson; and Naasson begat Salmon;
5. And Salmon begat Booz of Rachab; and Booz begat Obed of Ruth; and Obed begat Jesse;
6. And Jesse begat David the king; and David the king begat Solomon of her that had been the wife of Urias;
7. And Solomon begat Roboam; and Roboam begat Abia; and Abia begat Asa;
8. And Asa begat Josaphat; and Josaphat begat Joram; and Joram begat Ozias;
9. And Ozias begat Joatham; and Joatham begat Achaz; and Achaz begat Ezekias;
10. And Ezekias begat Manasses; and Manasses begat Amon; and Amon begat Josias;
11. And Josias begat Jechonias and his brethren, about the time they were carried away to Babylon:
12. And after they were brought to Babylon, Jechonias begat Salathiel; and Salathiel begat Zorobabel;
13. And Zorobabel begat Abiud; and Abiud begat Eliakim; and Eliakim begat Azor;
14. And Azor begat Sadoc; and Sadoc begat Achim; and Achim begat Eliud;
15. And Eliud begat Eleazar; and Eleazar begat Matthan; and Matthan begat Jacob;
16. And Jacob begat Joseph the husband of Mary, of whom was born Jesus, who is called Christ.
17. So all the generations from Abraham to David are fourteen generations; and from David until the carrying away into Babylon are fourteen generations; and from the carrying away into Babylon unto Christ are fourteen generations.
18. Now the birth of Jesus Christ was on this wise: When as his mother Mary was espoused to Joseph, before they came together, she was found with child of the Holy Ghost.
19. Then Joseph her husband, being a just man, and not willing to make her a public example, was minded to put her away privily.

20. But while he thought on these things, behold, the angel of the Lord appeared unto him in a dream, saying, Joseph, thou son of David, fear not to take unto thee Mary thy wife: for that which is conceived in her is of the Holy Ghost.

21. And she shall bring forth a son, and thou shalt call his name Jesus: for he shall save his people from their sins.

22. Now all this was done, that it might be fulfilled which was spoken of the Lord by the prophet, saying,

23. Behold, a virgin shall be with child, and shall bring forth a son, and they shall call his name Emmanuel, which being interpreted is, God with us.

24. Then Joseph being raised from sleep did as the angel of the Lord had bidden him, and took unto him his wife:

25. And knew her not till she had brought forth her firstborn son: and he called his name Jesus.

CHAPTER 2

1. Now when Jesus was born in Bethlehem of Judaea in the days of Herod the king, behold, there came wise men from the east to Jerusalem,

2. Saying, Where is he that is born King of the Jews? for we have seen his star in the east, and are come to worship him.

3. When Herod the king had heard these things, he was troubled, and all Jerusalem with him.

4. And when he had gathered all the chief priests and scribes of the people together, he demanded of them where Christ should be born.

5. And they said unto him, In Bethlehem of Judaea: for thus it is written by the prophet,

6. And thou Bethlehem, in the land of Juda, art not the least among the princes of Juda: for out of thee shall come a Governor, that shall rule my people Israel.

7. Then Herod, when he had privily called the wise men, enquired of them diligently what time the star appeared.

8. And he sent them to Bethlehem, and said, Go and search diligently for the young child; and when ye have found him, bring me word again, that I may come and worship him also.

9. When they had heard the king, they departed; and, lo, the star, which they saw in the east, went before them, till it came and stood over where the young child was.

10. When they saw the star, they rejoiced with exceeding great joy.

11. And when they were come into the house, they saw the young child with Mary his mother, and fell down, and worshipped him: and when they had opened their treasures, they presented unto him gifts; gold, and frankincense and myrrh.

12. And being warned of God in a dream that they should not return to Herod, they departed into their own country another way.

13. And when they were departed, behold, the angel of the Lord appeareth to Joseph in a dream, saying, Arise, and take the young child and his mother, and flee into Egypt, and be thou there until I bring thee word: for Herod will seek the young child to destroy him.

14. When he arose, he took the young child and his mother by night, and departed into Egypt:

15. And was there until the death of Herod: that it might be fulfilled which was spoken of the Lord by the prophet, saying, Out of Egypt have I called my son.

16. Then Herod, when he saw that he was mocked of the wise men, was exceeding wroth, and sent forth, and slew all the children that were in Bethlehem, and in all the coasts thereof, from two years old and under, according to the time which he had diligently inquired of the wise men.

17. Then was fulfilled that which was spoken by Jeremiah the prophet, saying,

18. In Rama was there a voice heard, lamentation, and weeping, and great mourning, Rachel weeping for her children, and would not be comforted, because they are not.

19. But when Herod was dead, behold, an angel of the Lord appeareth in a dream to Joseph in Egypt,

20. Saying, Arise, and take the young child and his mother, and go into the land of Israel: for they are dead which sought the young child's life.

21. And he arose, and took the young child and his mother, and came into the land of Israel.

22. But when he heard that Archelaus did reign in Judaea in the room of his father Herod, he was afraid to go thither: notwithstanding, being warned of God in a dream, he turned aside into the parts of Galilee:

23. And he came and dwelt in a city called Nazareth: that it might be fulfilled which was spoken by the prophets, He shall be called a Nazarene.

CHAPTER 3

1. In those days came John the Baptist, preaching in the wilderness of Judaea,

2. And saying, Repent ye: for the kingdom of heaven is at hand.

3. For this is he that was spoken of by the prophet Esaias, saying, The voice of one crying in the wilderness, Prepare ye the way of the Lord, make his paths straight.

4. And the same John had his raiment of camel's hair, and a leathern girdle about his loins; and his meat was locusts and wild honey.

5. Then went out to him Jerusalem, and all Judaea, and all the region round about Jordan,

6. And were baptized of him in Jordan, confessing their sins.

7. But when he saw many of the Pharisees and Sadducees come to his baptism, he said unto them, O generation of vipers, who hath warned you to flee from the wrath to come?

8. Bring forth therefore fruits meet for repentance:

9. And think not to say within yourselves, We have Abraham to our father: for I say unto you, that God is able of these stones to raise up children unto Abraham.

10. And now also the axe is laid unto the root of the trees: therefore every tree which bringeth not forth good fruit is hewn down, and cast into the fire.

11. I indeed baptize you with water unto repentance. but he that cometh after me is mightier than I, whose shoes I am not worthy to bear: he shall baptize you with the Holy Ghost, and with fire:

12. Whose fan is in his hand, and he will throughly purge his floor, and gather his wheat into the garner; but he will burn up the chaff with unquenchable fire.

13. Then cometh Jesus from Galilee to Jordan unto John, to be baptized of him.

14. But John forbad him, saying, I have need to be baptized of thee, and comest thou to me?

15. And Jesus answering said unto him, Suffer it to be so now: for thus it becometh us to fulfil all righteousness. Then he suffered him.

16. And Jesus, when he was baptized, went up straightway out of the water: and, lo, the heavens were opened unto him, and he saw the Spirit of God descending like a dove, and lighting upon him:

17. And lo a voice from heaven, saying, This is my beloved Son, in whom I am well pleased.

CHAPTER 4

1. Then was Jesus led up of the Spirit into the wilderness to be tempted of the devil.

2. And when he had fasted forty days and forty nights, he was afterward an hungred.

3. And when the tempter came to him, he said, If thou be the Son of God, command that these stones be made bread.

4. But he answered and said, It is written, Man shall not live by bread alone, but by every word that proceedeth out of the mouth of God.

5. Then the devil taketh him up into the holy city, and setteth him on a pinnacle of the temple,

6. And saith unto him, If thou be the Son of God, cast thyself down: for it is written, He shall give his angels charge concerning thee: and in their hands they shall bear thee up, lest at any time thou dash thy foot against a stone.

7. Jesus said unto him, It is written again, Thou shalt not tempt the Lord thy God.

8. Again, the devil taketh him up into an exceeding high mountain, and sheweth him all the kingdoms of the world, and the glory of them;

9. And saith unto him, All these things will I give thee, if thou wilt fall down and worship me.

10. Then saith Jesus unto him, Get thee hence, Satan: for it is written, Thou shalt worship the Lord thy God, and him only shalt thou serve.

11. Then the devil leaveth him, and, behold, angels came and ministered unto him.

12. Now when Jesus had heard that John was cast into prison, he departed into Galilee;

13. And leaving Nazareth, he came and dwelt in Capernaum, which is upon the sea coast, in the borders of Zabulon and Nephthalim:

14. That it might be fulfilled which was spoken by Esaias the prophet, saying,

15. The land of Zabulon, and the land of Nephthalim, by the way of the sea, beyond Jordan, Galilee of the Gentiles;

16. The people which sat in darkness saw great light; and to them which sat in the region and shadow of death light is sprung up.

17. From that time Jesus began to preach, and to say, Repent: for the kingdom of heaven is at hand.

18. And Jesus, walking by the sea of Galilee, saw two brethren, Simon called Peter, and Andrew his brother, casting a net into the sea: for they were fishers.

19. And he saith unto them, Follow me, and I will make you fishers of men.

20. And they straightway left their nets, and followed him.

21. And going on from thence, he saw other two brethren, James the son of Zebedee, and John his brother, in a ship with Zebedee their father, mending their nets; and he called them.

22. And they immediately left the ship and their father, and followed him.

23. And Jesus went about all Galilee, teaching in their synagogues, and preaching the gospel of the kingdom, and healing all manner of sickness and all manner of disease among the people.

24. And his fame went throughout all Syria: and they brought unto him all sick people that were taken with divers diseases and torments, and those which were possessed with devils, and those which were lunatick, and those that had the palsy; and he healed them.

25. And there followed him great multitudes of people from Galilee, and from Decapolis, and from Jerusalem, and from Judaea, and from beyond Jordan.

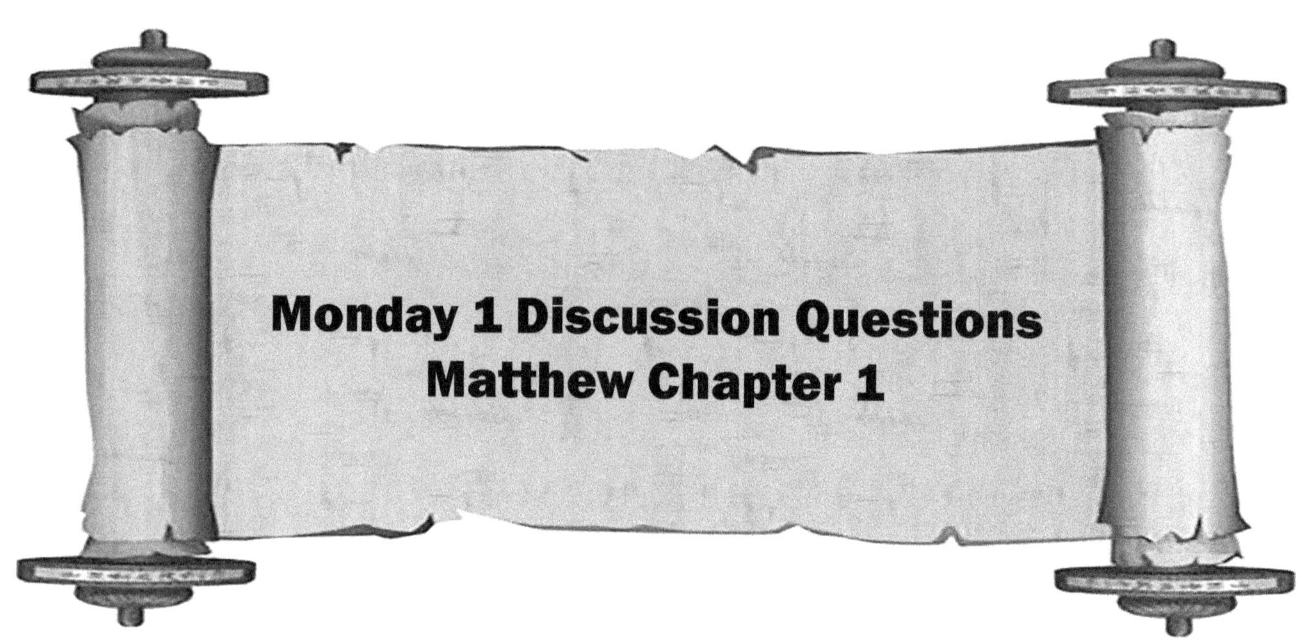

Monday 1 Discussion Questions
Matthew Chapter 1

1. Verse one of Matthew chapter one tells us that we will be learning the genealogy of Jesus and the sons of whom? ______________________________

2. List the lineage of Abraham, from his son Isaac to David's father, Jesse. ______________________________

3. Trace David's lineage from his son, Solomon to Josiah's son, Jeconiah. ______________________________

4. How many generations were there from Abraham to David? ______________________________

5. How many generations were there from the time David was born until the carrying away of Babylon? ______________________________

6. How many generations were there from the carrying away of Babylon unto Christ?
7. Who was espoused to Mary? ______________________________

8. Because Joseph did not want Mary to be a public example, what did he plan to do? ______________________________

9. What did he see in a dream? ______________________________

10. What did he do when he arose from his sleep? ______________________________

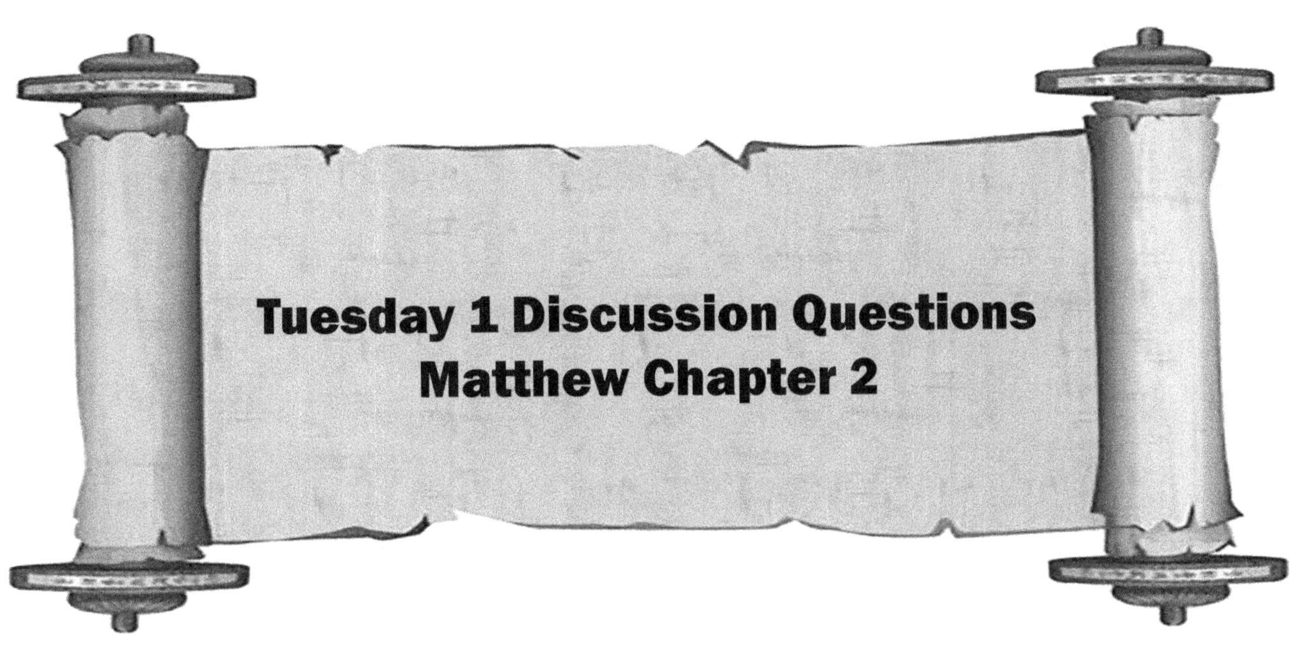

1. Where was Jesus born?

2. Who was the King when Jesus was born?

3. Who came from the East to Jerusalem, looking for Jesus?

4. Why were they looking for Jesus?

5. Where did they demand Jesus be born? Why?

6. What did the king tell the wise men to go back and do?

7. What did the king make the wise men think he wanted to do when they found the child?

8. What did the wise men do when they saw the child with his mother?

9. What did they do when God warned them in a dream not to go back to Herod?

10. What order did King Herod give when he heard that the wise men had mocked him?

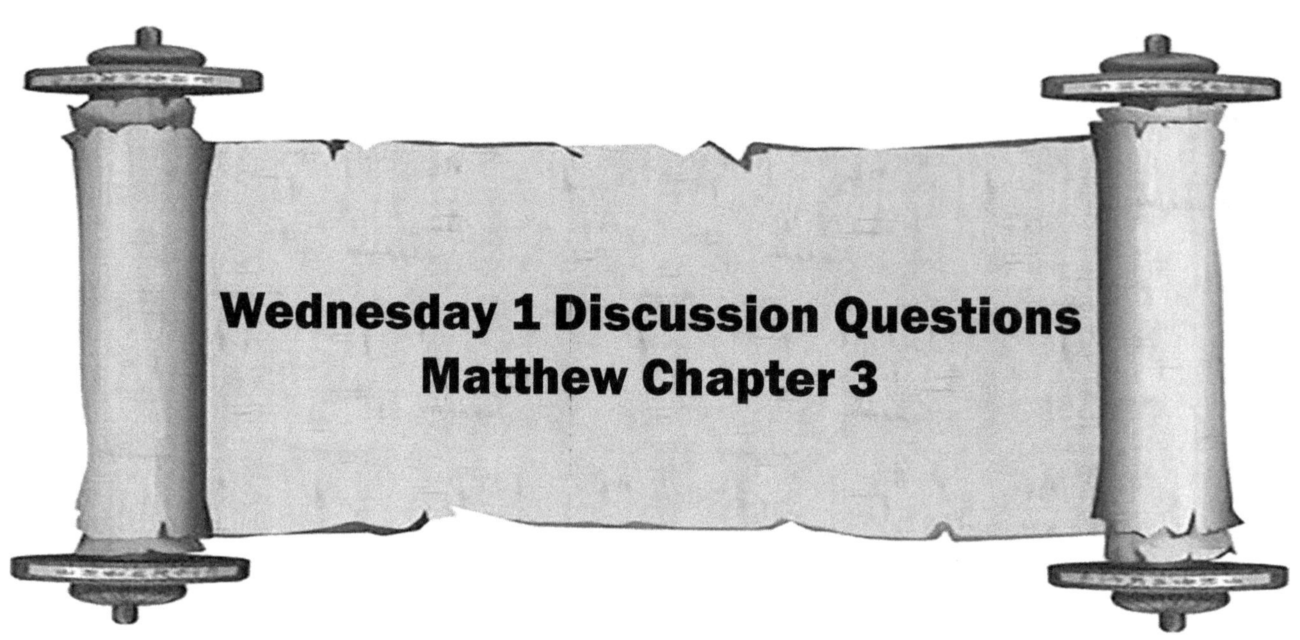

1. Who came in preaching in the beginning of chapter 3? ______

2. What was John saying in his message? ______

3. What was he crying out in the wilderness for them to prepare? ______

4. What was John wearing? ______

5. What did he eat for food? ______

6. Who went to confess their sins to John and be baptized by him? ______

7. What did John say to the Pharisees and Sadducees when he saw them coming to the baptism? ______

8. He said Jesus would come after him to baptize them with what? ______

9. What did John say when Jesus came and asked him to baptize him? What was Jesus' reply? ______

10. What Happened after Jesus was baptized? What did the voice from Heaven say? ______

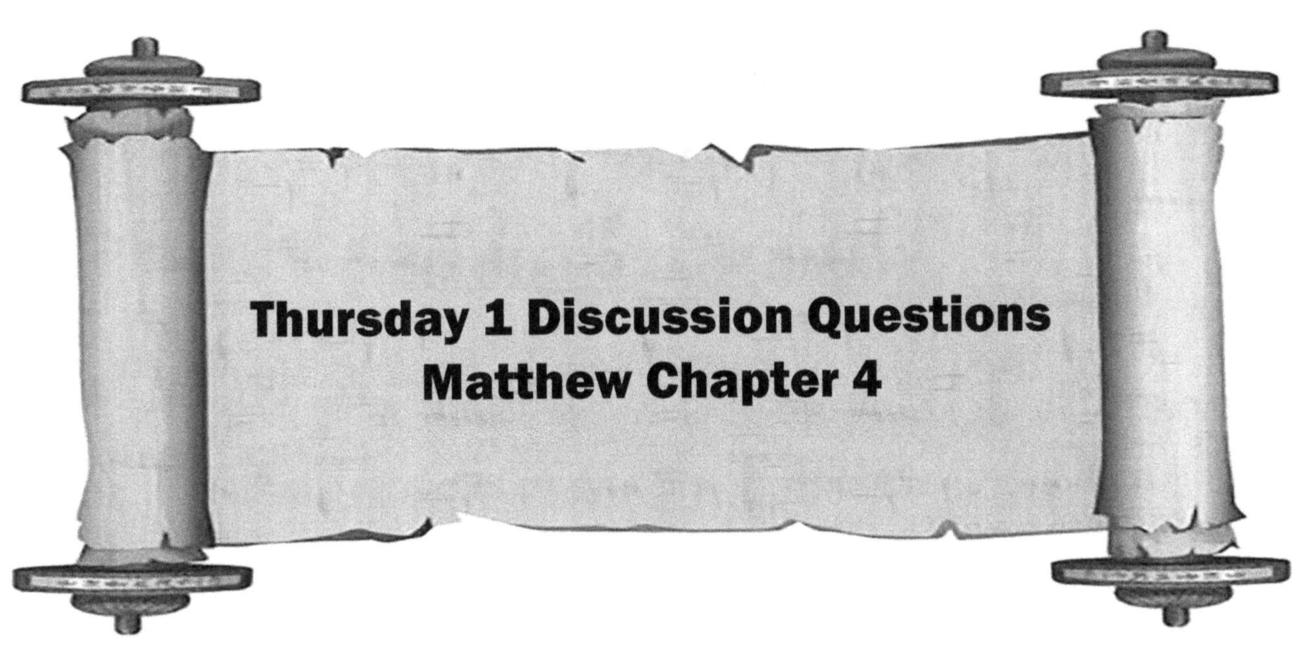

Thursday 1 Discussion Questions
Matthew Chapter 4

1. Who led Jesus into the wilderness to be tempted by the Devil? __________

2. How many days and nights had Jesus fasted? __________

3. What did the tempter challenge the son of God to do? __________

4. What was Jesus' reply? __________

5. Who took Jesus to the Holy City and set him upon a pinnacle? __________

6. What was the second thing the tempter told Jesus to do? __________

7. What was Jesus' reply? __________

8. What did the Devil take Jesus to the high mountain to show him? __________

9. What was the third thing the Devil told Jesus to do? __________

10. What was Jesus' response? Who came to minister to Jesus after the Devil left? __________

WEEKLY REVIEW
MATTHEW CHAPTERS 1-4

NAME THAT CHAPTER

1.____ IN THE BEGINNING OF THIS CHAPTER, JOHN THE BAPTIST CAME IN PREACHING. HE WORE CAMEL'S HAIR AND A LEATHER GIRDLE AROUND HIS LOINS AND HE ATE LOCUSTS AND HONEY. HE WAS PREACHING THAT MEN SHOULD REPENT AND BE BAPTIZED, FOR THE KINGDOM OF HEAVEN IS AT HAND. PREPARE YE THE WAY OF THE LORD.

2.____ THIS CHAPTER TEACHES US OF THE GENEALOGY OF JESUS AND THE SON OF DAVID AND THE SON OF ABRAHAM. THERE WERE 14 GENERATIONS FROM ABRAHAM TO DAVID. ALSO FROM THE TIME DAVID WAS BORN TO THE TIME THE CARRYING AWAY OF BABYLON WAS ANOTHER 14 GENERATIONS. THEN THERE WAS ANOTHER 14 GENERATIONS HERE THAT WERE BORN FROM THE CARRYING AWAY OF BABYLON UNTO CHRIST. WE LEARNED IN THIS CHAPTER THAT JOSEPH WAS ESPOUSED TO MARRY AND DID NOT WANT HER TO BE A PUBLIC EXAMPLE. AN ANGEL CAME TO JOSEPH IN A DREAM AND HE OBEYED THE ANGEL'S INSTRUCTIONS.

3.____ THE SPIRIT LED JESUS INTO THE WILDERNESS TO BE TEMPTED BY THE DEVIL. JESUS STAYED AND FASTED 40 DAYS AND 40 NIGHTS. SATAN TOLD THE DEVIL IF HE WAS THE SON OF GOD, HE SHOULD COMMAND THE STONES TO BE TURNED TO BREAD. JESUS REPLIED, "IT IS WRITTEN, MAN SHALL NOT LIVE BY BREAD ALONE. BUT BY EVERY WORD THAT PROCEEDETH OUT OF THE MOUTH OF GOD."

4.____ JESUS WAS BORN IN BETHLEHEM OF JUDEA WHEN HEROD WAS KING. WISE MEN WENT TO JERUSALEM LOOKING FOR JESUS. THEY SAW THE STAR IN THE EAST AND WENT TO WORSHIP HIM. KING HEROD MADE THE WISE MEN THINK HE WANTED TO KNOW WHERE JESUS WAS SO HE COULD GO WORSHIP HIM. GOD GAVE THE WISE MEN A DREAM NOT TO GO BACK TO HEROD AND THEY FLED. WHEN THE KING HEARD THEY MOCKED HIM, HE SENT AN ORDER TO SLAY ALL CHILDREN WHO WERE AGE TWO OR YOUNGER.

TRUE OR FALSE

5. The Lord appeared unto Joseph in a dream, saying, Joseph, thou son of David, fear not to take unto thee Mary thy wife: for that which is conceived in her is of the Holy Ghost.

____

6. The king sent the wise men to Bethlehem, and said, Go and search diligently for the young child; and when ye have found him, bring me word again, that I may kill him.

____

7. John was the one that was spoken of by the prophet Esaias, saying, The voice of one crying in the wilderness, Prepare ye the way of the Lord, make his paths straight.

____

FILL IN THE BLANKS

8. Then cometh________from_______to______unto________, to be baptized of him.
9. And lo a voice from _______, saying, This is my ______ Son, in whom I am well ______.
10. Now when_______had heard that______was cast into_______, he departed into _________.

STUDENT PRAYER JOURNAL

Please use this space to record your thoughts and feelings as you travel on this spirit led journey through the word of God with us. Please know that you have brothers and sisters in this organization from all over the world praying with and for you. My prayer for you is that you will begin to see the power of God resting in each set of your footprints. As you look back and examine your past in this journal, may you realize that you were never alone and according to Hebrews 13:5, God will never leave nor forsake you. ~LADY FLORA

THE STUDY OF THE FOUR GOSPELS VOCABULARY DEFINITIONS FOR MATTHEW CHAPTERS 5-8

WORD	DEFINITIONS
1) REVILE	
2) RACA	
3) OUGHT	
4) FORSWEAR	
5) TWAIN	
6) ALMS	
7) MAMMON	
8) METE	
9) MOTE	
10) SCRIBES	

DMWW Daily Bible Reading
KJV MATTHEW CHAPTERS 5-8

CHAPTER 5

1. And seeing the multitudes, he went up into a mountain: and when he was set, his disciples came unto him:
2. And he opened his mouth, and taught them, saying,
3. Blessed are the poor in spirit: for theirs is the kingdom of heaven.
4. Blessed are they that mourn: for they shall be comforted.
5. Blessed are the meek: for they shall inherit the earth.
6. Blessed are they which do hunger and thirst after righteousness: for they shall be filled.
7. Blessed are the merciful: for they shall obtain mercy.
8. Blessed are the pure in heart: for they shall see God.
9. Blessed are the peacemakers: for they shall be called the children of God.
10. Blessed are they which are persecuted for righteousness' sake: for theirs is the kingdom of heaven.
11. Blessed are ye, when men shall revile you, and persecute you, and shall say all manner of evil against you falsely, for my sake.
12. Rejoice, and be exceeding glad: for great is your reward in heaven: for so persecuted they the prophets which were before you.
13. Ye are the salt of the earth: but if the salt have lost his savour, wherewith shall it be salted? it is thenceforth good for nothing, but to be cast out, and to be trodden under foot of men.
14. Ye are the light of the world. A city that is set on an hill cannot be hid.
15. Neither do men light a candle, and put it under a bushel, but on a candlestick; and it giveth light unto all that are in the house.
16. Let your light so shine before men, that they may see your good works, and glorify your Father which is in heaven.
17. Think not that I am come to destroy the law, or the prophets: I am not come to destroy, but to fulfil.
18. For verily I say unto you, Till heaven and earth pass, one jot or one tittle shall in no wise pass from the law, till all be fulfilled.

19. Whosoever therefore shall break one of these least commandments, and shall teach men so, he shall be called the least in the kingdom of heaven: but whosoever shall do and teach them, the same shall be called great in the kingdom of heaven.

20. For I say unto you, That except your righteousness shall exceed the righteousness of the scribes and Pharisees, ye shall in no case enter into the kingdom of heaven.

21. Ye have heard that it was said of them of old time, Thou shalt not kill; and whosoever shall kill shall be in danger of the judgment:

22. But I say unto you, That whosoever is angry with his brother without a cause shall be in danger of the judgment: and whosoever shall say to his brother, Raca, shall be in danger of the council: but whosoever shall say, Thou fool, shall be in danger of hell fire.

23. Therefore if thou bring thy gift to the altar, and there rememberest that thy brother hath ought against thee;

24. Leave there thy gift before the altar, and go thy way; first be reconciled to thy brother, and then come and offer thy gift.

25. Agree with thine adversary quickly, whiles thou art in the way with him; lest at any time the adversary deliver thee to the judge, and the judge deliver thee to the officer, and thou be cast into prison.

26. Verily I say unto thee, Thou shalt by no means come out thence, till thou hast paid the uttermost farthing.

27. Ye have heard that it was said by them of old time, Thou shalt not commit adultery:

28. But I say unto you, That whosoever looketh on a woman to lust after her hath committed adultery with her already in his heart.

29. And if thy right eye offend thee, pluck it out, and cast it from thee: for it is profitable for thee that one of thy members should perish, and not that thy whole body should be cast into hell.

30. And if thy right hand offend thee, cut it off, and cast it from thee: for it is profitable for thee that one of thy members should perish, and not that thy whole body should be cast into hell.

31. It hath been said, Whosoever shall put away his wife, let him give her a writing of divorcement:

32. But I say unto you, That whosoever shall put away his wife, saving for the cause of fornication, causeth her to commit adultery: and whosoever shall marry her that is divorced committeth adultery.

33. Again, ye have heard that it hath been said by them of old time, Thou shalt not forswear thyself, but shalt perform unto the Lord thine oaths:

34. But I say unto you, Swear not at all; neither by heaven; for it is God's throne:

35. Nor by the earth; for it is his footstool: neither by Jerusalem; for it is the city of the great King.

36. Neither shalt thou swear by thy head, because thou canst not make one hair white or black.

37. But let your communication be, Yea, yea; Nay, nay: for whatsoever is more than these cometh of evil.

38. Ye have heard that it hath been said, An eye for an eye, and a tooth for a tooth:

39. But I say unto you, That ye resist not evil: but whosoever shall smite thee on thy right cheek, turn to him the other also.

40. And if any man will sue thee at the law, and take away thy coat, let him have thy cloak also.

41. And whosoever shall compel thee to go a mile, go with him twain.

42. Give to him that asketh thee, and from him that would borrow of thee turn not thou away.

43. Ye have heard that it hath been said, Thou shalt love thy neighbour, and hate thine enemy.

44. But I say unto you, Love your enemies, bless them that curse you, do good to them that hate you, and pray for them which despitefully use you, and persecute you;

45. That ye may be the children of your Father which is in heaven: for he maketh his sun to rise on the evil and on the good, and sendeth rain on the just and on the unjust.

46. For if ye love them which love you, what reward have ye? do not even the publicans the same?

47. And if ye salute your brethren only, what do ye more than others? do not even the publicans so?

48. Be ye therefore perfect, even as your Father which is in heaven is perfect.

CHAPTER 6

1. Take heed that ye do not your alms before men, to be seen of them: otherwise ye have no reward of your Father which is in heaven.

2. Therefore when thou doest thine alms, do not sound a trumpet before thee, as the hypocrites do in the synagogues and in the streets, that they may have glory of men. Verily I say unto you, They have their reward.

3. But when thou doest alms, let not thy left hand know what thy right hand doeth:

4. That thine alms may be in secret: and thy Father which seeth in secret himself shall reward thee openly.

5. And when thou prayest, thou shalt not be as the hypocrites are: for they love to pray standing in the synagogues and in the corners of the streets, that they may be seen of men. Verily I say unto you, They have their reward.
6. But thou, when thou prayest, enter into thy closet, and when thou hast shut thy door, pray to thy Father which is in secret; and thy Father which seeth in secret shall reward thee openly.
7. But when ye pray, use not vain repetitions, as the heathen do: for they think that they shall be heard for their much speaking.
8. Be not ye therefore like unto them: for your Father knoweth what things ye have need of, before ye ask him.
9. After this manner therefore pray ye: Our Father which art in heaven, Hallowed be thy name.
10. Thy kingdom come, Thy will be done in earth, as it is in heaven.
11. Give us this day our daily bread.
12. And forgive us our debts, as we forgive our debtors.
13. And lead us not into temptation, but deliver us from evil: For thine is the kingdom, and the power, and the glory, for ever. Amen.
14. For if ye forgive men their trespasses, your heavenly Father will also forgive you:
15. But if ye forgive not men their trespasses, neither will your Father forgive your trespasses.
16. Moreover when ye fast, be not, as the hypocrites, of a sad countenance: for they disfigure their faces, that they may appear unto men to fast. Verily I say unto you, They have their reward.
17. But thou, when thou fastest, anoint thine head, and wash thy face;
18. That thou appear not unto men to fast, but unto thy Father which is in secret: and thy Father, which seeth in secret, shall reward thee openly.
19. Lay not up for yourselves treasures upon earth, where moth and rust doth corrupt, and where thieves break through and steal:
20. But lay up for yourselves treasures in heaven, where neither moth nor rust doth corrupt, and where thieves do not break through nor steal:
21. For where your treasure is, there will your heart be also.
22. The light of the body is the eye: if therefore thine eye be single, thy whole body shall be full of light.
23. But if thine eye be evil, thy whole body shall be full of darkness. If therefore the light that is in thee be darkness, how great is that darkness!
24. No man can serve two masters: for either he will hate the one, and love the other; or else he will hold to the one, and despise the other. Ye cannot serve God and mammon.

25. Therefore I say unto you, Take no thought for your life, what ye shall eat, or what ye shall drink; nor yet for your body, what ye shall put on. Is not the life more than meat, and the body than raiment?

26. Behold the fowls of the air: for they sow not, neither do they reap, nor gather into barns; yet your heavenly Father feedeth them. Are ye not much better than they?

27. Which of you by taking thought can add one cubit unto his stature?

28. And why take ye thought for raiment? Consider the lilies of the field, how they grow; they toil not, neither do they spin:

29. And yet I say unto you, That even Solomon in all his glory was not arrayed like one of these.

30. Wherefore, if God so clothe the grass of the field, which to day is, and to morrow is cast into the oven, shall he not much more clothe you, O ye of little faith?

31. Therefore take no thought, saying, What shall we eat? or, What shall we drink? or, Wherewithal shall we be clothed?

32. (For after all these things do the Gentiles seek:) for your heavenly Father knoweth that ye have need of all these things.

33. But seek ye first the kingdom of God, and his righteousness; and all these things shall be added unto you.

34. Take therefore no thought for the morrow: for the morrow shall take thought for the things of itself. Sufficient unto the day is the evil thereof.

CHAPTER 7

1. Judge not, that ye be not judged.

2. For with what judgment ye judge, ye shall be judged: and with what measure ye mete, it shall be measured to you again.

3. And why beholdest thou the mote that is in thy brother's eye, but considerest not the beam that is in thine own eye?

4. Or how wilt thou say to thy brother, Let me pull out the mote out of thine eye; and, behold, a beam is in thine own eye?

5. Thou hypocrite, first cast out the beam out of thine own eye; and then shalt thou see clearly to cast out the mote out of thy brother's eye.

6. Give not that which is holy unto the dogs, neither cast ye your pearls before swine, lest they trample them under their feet, and turn again and rend you.

7. Ask, and it shall be given you; seek, and ye shall find; knock, and it shall be opened unto you:

8. For every one that asketh receiveth; and he that seeketh findeth; and to him that knocketh it shall be opened.

9. Or what man is there of you, whom if his son ask bread, will he give him a stone?

10. Or if he ask a fish, will he give him a serpent?

11. If ye then, being evil, know how to give good gifts unto your children, how much more shall your Father which is in heaven give good things to them that ask him?

12. Therefore all things whatsoever ye would that men should do to you, do ye even so to them: for this is the law and the prophets.

13. Enter ye in at the strait gate: for wide is the gate, and broad is the way, that leadeth to destruction, and many there be which go in thereat:

14. Because strait is the gate, and narrow is the way, which leadeth unto life, and few there be that find it.

15. Beware of false prophets, which come to you in sheep's clothing, but inwardly they are ravening wolves.

16. Ye shall know them by their fruits. Do men gather grapes of thorns, or figs of thistles?

17. Even so every good tree bringeth forth good fruit; but a corrupt tree bringeth forth evil fruit.

18. A good tree cannot bring forth evil fruit, neither can a corrupt tree bring forth good fruit.

19. Every tree that bringeth not forth good fruit is hewn down, and cast into the fire.

20. Wherefore by their fruits ye shall know them.

21. Not every one that saith unto me, Lord, Lord, shall enter into the kingdom of heaven; but he that doeth the will of my Father which is in heaven.

22. Many will say to me in that day, Lord, Lord, have we not prophesied in thy name? and in thy name have cast out devils? and in thy name done many wonderful works?

23. And then will I profess unto them, I never knew you: depart from me, ye that work iniquity.

24. Therefore whosoever heareth these sayings of mine, and doeth them, I will liken him unto a wise man, which built his house upon a rock:

25. And the rain descended, and the floods came, and the winds blew, and beat upon that house; and it fell not: for it was founded upon a rock.

26. And every one that heareth these sayings of mine, and doeth them not, shall be likened unto a foolish man, which built his house upon the sand:

27. And the rain descended, and the floods came, and the winds blew, and beat upon that house; and it fell: and great was the fall of it.

28. And it came to pass, when Jesus had ended these sayings, the people were astonished at his doctrine:

29. For he taught them as one having authority, and not as the scribes.

CHAPTER 8

1. When he was come down from the mountain, great multitudes followed him.

2. And, behold, there came a leper and worshipped him, saying, Lord, if thou wilt, thou canst make me clean.

3. And Jesus put forth his hand, and touched him, saying, I will; be thou clean. And immediately his leprosy was cleansed.

4. And Jesus saith unto him, See thou tell no man; but go thy way, shew thyself to the priest, and offer the gift that Moses commanded, for a testimony unto them.

5. And when Jesus was entered into Capernaum, there came unto him a centurion, beseeching him,

6. And saying, Lord, my servant lieth at home sick of the palsy, grievously tormented.

7. And Jesus saith unto him, I will come and heal him.

8. The centurion answered and said, Lord, I am not worthy that thou shouldest come under my roof: but speak the word only, and my servant shall be healed.

9. For I am a man under authority, having soldiers under me: and I say to this man, Go, and he goeth; and to another, Come, and he cometh; and to my servant, Do this, and he doeth it.

10. When Jesus heard it, he marvelled, and said to them that followed, Verily I say unto you, I have not found so great faith, no, not in Israel.

11. And I say unto you, That many shall come from the east and west, and shall sit down with Abraham, and Isaac, and Jacob, in the kingdom of heaven.

12. But the children of the kingdom shall be cast out into outer darkness: there shall be weeping and gnashing of teeth.

13. And Jesus said unto the centurion, Go thy way; and as thou hast believed, so be it done unto thee. And his servant was healed in the selfsame hour.

14. And when Jesus was come into Peter's house, he saw his wife's mother laid, and sick of a fever.

15. And he touched her hand, and the fever left her: and she arose, and ministered unto them.

16. When the even was come, they brought unto him many that were possessed with devils: and he cast out the spirits with his word, and healed all that were sick:

17. That it might be fulfilled which was spoken by Esaias the prophet, saying, Himself took our infirmities, and bare our sicknesses.

18. Now when Jesus saw great multitudes about him, he gave commandment to depart unto the other side.

19. And a certain scribe came, and said unto him, Master, I will follow thee whithersoever thou goest.

20. And Jesus saith unto him, The foxes have holes, and the birds of the air have nests; but the Son of man hath not where to lay his head.

21. And another of his disciples said unto him, Lord, suffer me first to go and bury my father.

22. But Jesus said unto him, Follow me; and let the dead bury their dead.

23. And when he was entered into a ship, his disciples followed him.

24. And, behold, there arose a great tempest in the sea, insomuch that the ship was covered with the waves: but he was asleep.

25. And his disciples came to him, and awoke him, saying, Lord, save us: we perish.

26. And he saith unto them, Why are ye fearful, O ye of little faith? Then he arose, and rebuked the winds and the sea; and there was a great calm.

27. But the men marvelled, saying, What manner of man is this, that even the winds and the sea obey him!

28. And when he was come to the other side into the country of the Gergesenes, there met him two possessed with devils, coming out of the tombs, exceeding fierce, so that no man might pass by that way.

29. And, behold, they cried out, saying, What have we to do with thee, Jesus, thou Son of God? art thou come hither to torment us before the time?

30. And there was a good way off from them an herd of many swine feeding.

31. So the devils besought him, saying, If thou cast us out, suffer us to go away into the herd of swine.

32. And he said unto them, Go. And when they were come out, they went into the herd of swine: and, behold, the whole herd of swine ran violently down a steep place into the sea, and perished in the waters.

33. And they that kept them fled, and went their ways into the city, and told every thing, and what was befallen to the possessed of the devils.

34. And, behold, the whole city came out to meet Jesus: and when they saw him, they besought him that he would depart out of their coasts.

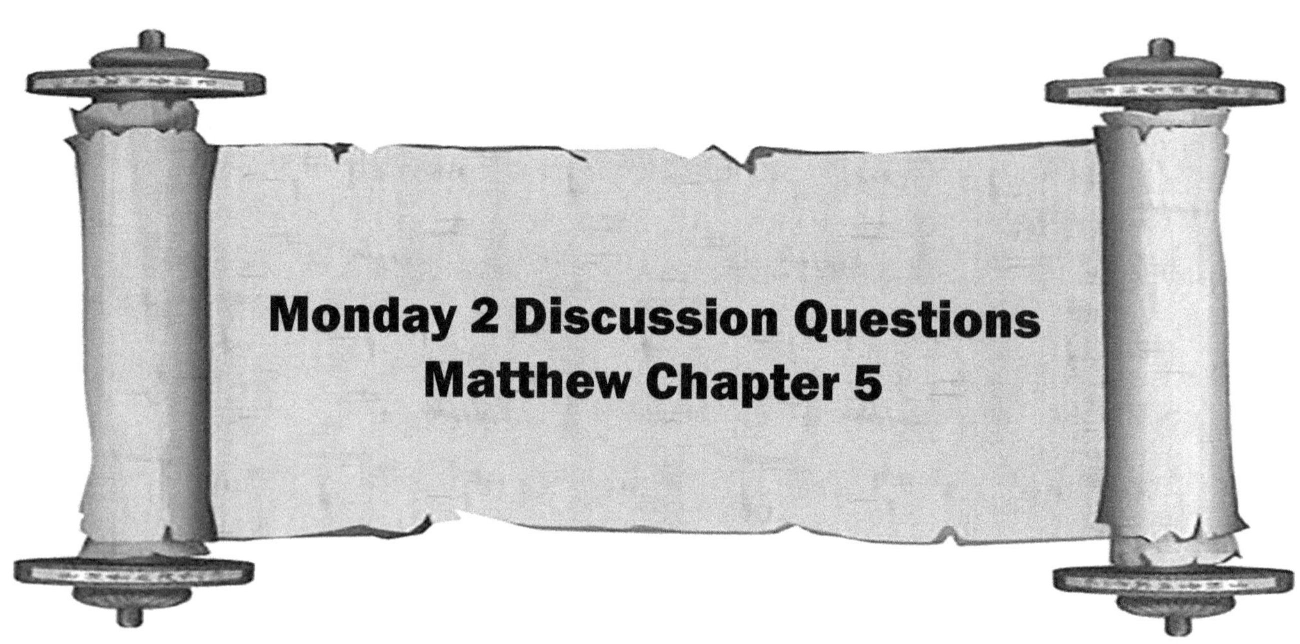

1. When Jesus saw the multitudes of people coming, where did he go?

2. When he was set, who came to him?

3. Jesus began to list people who are blessed. Who were the first three and why?

4. What did he say would happen to those who hunger and thirst after righteousness?

5. What did he say about the peacemakers?

6. What did he say belongs to those who are persecuted for righteousness sake?

7. What did Jesus say you should do when men revile you, persecute you, and shall say all manner of evil against you falsely, for his name sake?

8. What did he say about the salt of the earth?

9. What did Jesus say he did not come to do to the law? He came to do what?

10. What did he say to do if you bring a gift to the altar and remember your brother has an ought against you?

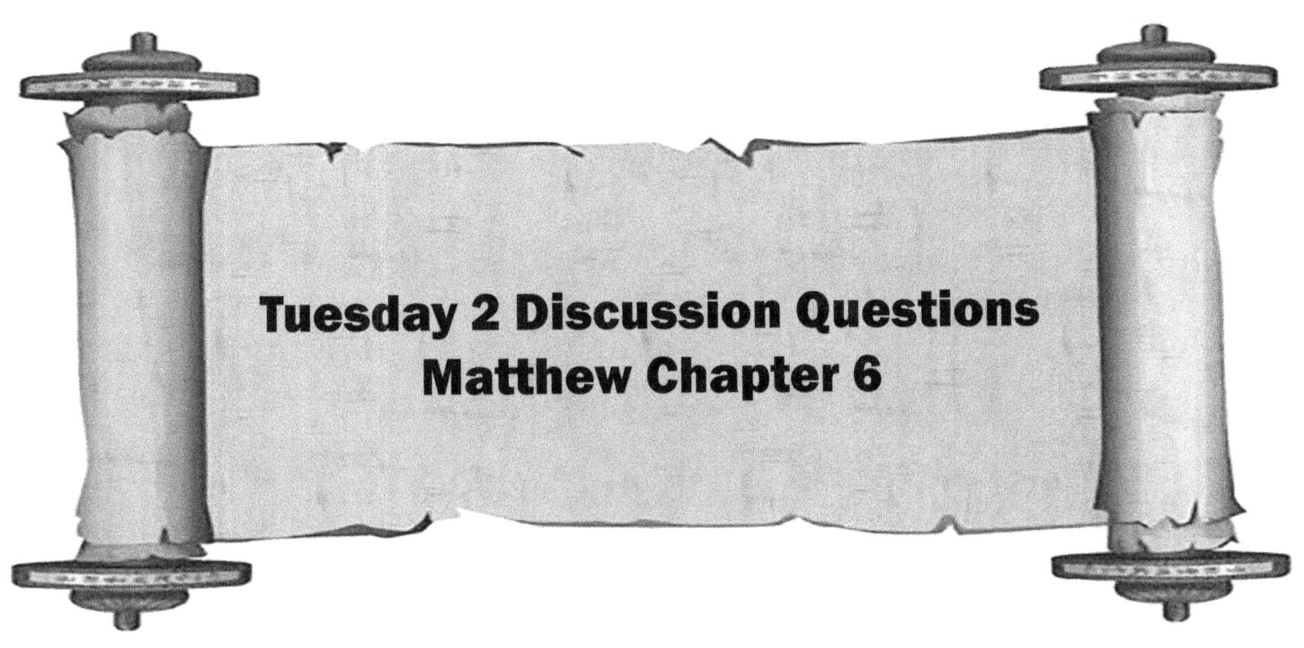

1. We should not do alms to be seen by men. If we do, what happens? ____________________

2. What does "do alms" mean? ____________________

3. How does the father reward us when we do alms in secret? ____________________

4. Where and how does this chapter tell us to pray? ____________________

5. What should we not use when we pray? ____________________

6. Who prays that way and why? ____________________

7. This chapter tells us how to pray. Quote the words given to us to pray? ____________________

8. What happens when you forgive men who commit trespasses against you? ____________________

9. What happens when you DO NOT forgive people who trespass against you? ____________________

10. What does this passage say about your treasures? Where should you store them and why? ____________________

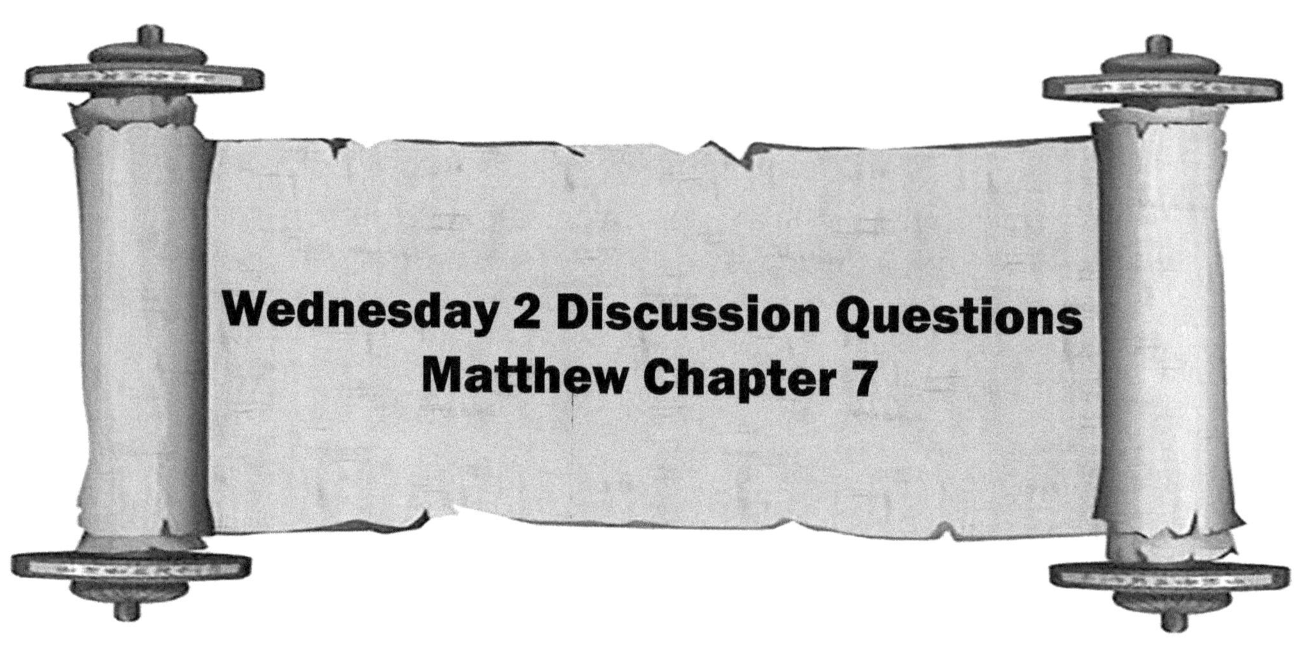

1. Why shouldn't we judge? ______________________________

2. How will we be judged and measured? ______________________________

3. What does this chapter call one who tries to remove the mote out of his neighbor's eye with a mote in his? ______________________________

4. What does it say we should do first? Why? ______________________________

5. What should we not give to the dogs and swine? ______________________________

6. Why shouldn't we cast them to the swine? ______________________________

7. What is the promise for those who ask? ______________________________

8. What is the promise for those who seek? ______________________________

9. What is the promise for those who knock? ______________________________

10. What happened when Jesus had ended his sayings? Why? ______________________________

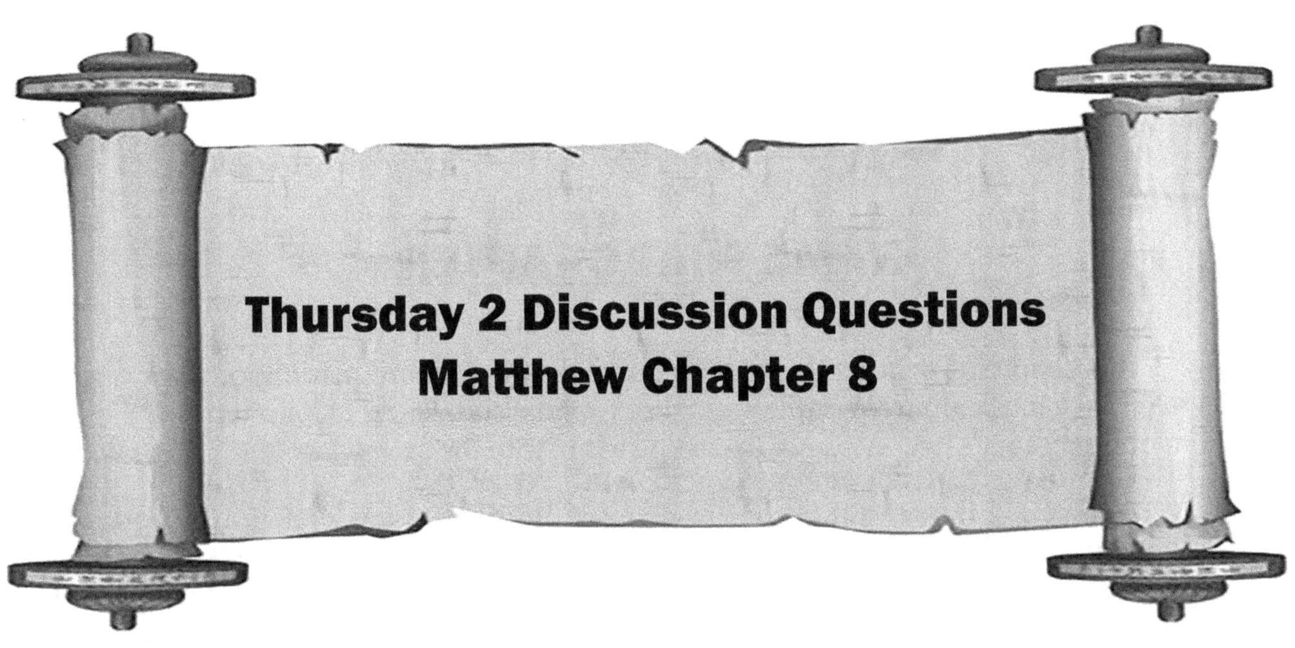

1. Who followed Jesus, when he came down from the mountain? ______________________

2. Who came to worship him? ______________________

3. What did the leper say to Jesus? ______________________

4. After healing the leper, what did Jesus tell him not to do? What did he tell him to do? ______________________

5. Who came to Jesus when he entered Capernaum? ______________________

6. Why was he beseeching Jesus? ______________________

7. What did Jesus offer to do for him? ______________________

8. What was the man's response to Jesus' offer? ______________________

9. What did Jesus see when he entered Peter's house? What happened when Jesus touched her hand? ______________________

10. What did Jesus say to the man who asked to go bury his father before following Jesus? ______________________

WEEKLY REVIEW
MATTHEW CHAPTERS 5-8

NAME THAT CHAPTER

1. _____ This chapter taught us to examine ourselves first before helping others by telling us to remove the beam from our eyes so that we may see clearly to help remove the mote from our neighbor's eye. Also not to cast pearls before the swine,

2. _____ We learned the beatitudes in this chapter. In this passage of scripture, Jesus tells us who he calls blessed and why he called them blessed. We also received instructions of what to do when people persecute us and say all manner of evil against us falsey, for his name sake. We are not to become bitter and angry and try to get revenge. We are instructed to Rejoice.

3. _____ We see Jesus traveling through Capernaum healing the sick in this passage of scriptures. We saw him heal a leper. Then he had a centurion who came to him and asked for healing for his sick servant. The centurion's faith pleased Jesus. Jesus told him he would come. But, the man said, if you only speak the word he will be healed. Jesus healed the servant for the centurion's great faith. This teaches us that we can believe for someone else to be healed.

4. _____ Jesus teaches us to do things with a focus and attention to glorify him and not to be praised by the people. He teaches us to feed the hungry, give money to the poor, and do good to people who need it, in secret. He teaches us not to pray just to be seen or with vain repetitions. He tells us that when we do that, it will be our only reward. We will not receive a reward for it in heaven. We also learn the very important lesson that if we do not forgive others, God will not forgive us.

TRUE OR FALSE

5. Jesus tells us not to worry about what we will eat, drink or wear tomorrow.

____

Matthew 6:34

6. Jesus tells us to pray that he curse people who persecute you, so he can avenge you.

____

Matthew 5:12
Matthew 5:44

7. Jesus tells us not to give what is holy to the dogs.

____

Matthew 7:6

FILL IN THE BLANKS

8. Ye are the________of the________: but if the salt have lost his________, wherewith shall it be salted?

Matthew 5:13

9. But the men________, saying, What________of man is this, that even the winds and the________obey him!

Matthew 8:27

10. Which of you by taking________can add one________unto his________?

Matthew 6:27

STUDENT PRAYER JOURNAL

Please use this space to record your thoughts and feelings as you travel on this spirit led journey through the word of God with us. Please know that you have brothers and sisters in this organization from all over the world praying with and for you. My prayer for you is that you will begin to see the power of God resting in each set of your footprints. As you look back and examine your past in this journal, may you realize that you were never alone and according to Hebrews 13:5, God will never leave nor forsake you. ~LADY FLORA

The Study of The Four Gospels
Matthew Chapters 9-12
VOCABULARY DEFINITIONS

Define the following words. This assignment is due by Friday at midnight. Be prepared to join us on FB LIVE for our class discussion participation grade of 200 points.

WORD	DEFINITIONS
1. BLASPHEMY	
2. MARVEL	
3. PUBLICANS	
4. BRIDECHAMBER	
5. SURNAME	
6. SCOURGE	
7. BEELZEBUB	
.8. FARTHING	
9. GLUTTONOUS	
10. FLAX	

DMWW Daily Bible Reading
KJV MATTHEW CHAPTERS 9-12

CHAPTER 9

1. And he entered into a ship, and passed over, and came into his own city.
2. And, behold, they brought to him a man sick of the palsy, lying on a bed: and Jesus seeing their faith said unto the sick of the palsy; Son, be of good cheer; thy sins be forgiven thee.
3. And, behold, certain of the scribes said within themselves, This man blasphemeth.
4. And Jesus knowing their thoughts said, Wherefore think ye evil in your hearts?
5. For whether is easier, to say, Thy sins be forgiven thee; or to say, Arise, and walk?
6. But that ye may know that the Son of man hath power on earth to forgive sins, (then saith he to the sick of the palsy,) Arise, take up thy bed, and go unto thine house.
7. And he arose, and departed to his house.
8. But when the multitudes saw it, they marvelled, and glorified God, which had given such power unto men.
9. And as Jesus passed forth from thence, he saw a man, named Matthew, sitting at the receipt of custom: and he saith unto him, Follow me. And he arose, and followed him.
10. And it came to pass, as Jesus sat at meat in the house, behold, many publicans and sinners came and sat down with him and his disciples.
11. And when the Pharisees saw it, they said unto his disciples, Why eateth your Master with publicans and sinners?
12. But when Jesus heard that, he said unto them, They that be whole need not a physician, but they that are sick.
13. But go ye and learn what that meaneth, I will have mercy, and not sacrifice: for I am not come to call the righteous, but sinners to repentance.
14. Then came to him the disciples of John, saying, Why do we and the Pharisees fast oft, but thy disciples fast not?
15. And Jesus said unto them, Can the children of the bridechamber mourn, as long as the bridegroom is with them? but the days will come, when the bridegroom shall be taken from them, and then shall they fast.
16. No man putteth a piece of new cloth unto an old garment, for that which is put in to fill it up taketh from the garment, and the rent is made worse.

17. Neither do men put new wine into old bottles: else the bottles break, and the wine runneth out, and the bottles perish: but they put new wine into new bottles, and both are preserved.

18. While he spake these things unto them, behold, there came a certain ruler, and worshipped him, saying, My daughter is even now dead: but come and lay thy hand upon her, and she shall live.

19. And Jesus arose, and followed him, and so did his disciples.

20. And, behold, a woman, which was diseased with an issue of blood twelve years, came behind him, and touched the hem of his garment:

21. For she said within herself, If I may but touch his garment, I shall be whole.

22. But Jesus turned him about, and when he saw her, he said, Daughter, be of good comfort; thy faith hath made thee whole. And the woman was made whole from that hour.

23. And when Jesus came into the ruler's house, and saw the minstrels and the people making a noise,

24. He said unto them, Give place: for the maid is not dead, but sleepeth. And they laughed him to scorn.

25. But when the people were put forth, he went in, and took her by the hand, and the maid arose.

26. And the fame hereof went abroad into all that land.

27. And when Jesus departed thence, two blind men followed him, crying, and saying, Thou son of David, have mercy on us.

28. And when he was come into the house, the blind men came to him: and Jesus saith unto them, Believe ye that I am able to do this? They said unto him, Yea, Lord.

29. Then touched he their eyes, saying, According to your faith be it unto you.

30. And their eyes were opened; and Jesus straitly charged them, saying, See that no man know it.

31. But they, when they were departed, spread abroad his fame in all that country.

32. As they went out, behold, they brought to him a dumb man possessed with a devil.

33. And when the devil was cast out, the dumb spake: and the multitudes marvelled, saying, It was never so seen in Israel.

34. But the Pharisees said, He casteth out devils through the prince of the devils.

35. And Jesus went about all the cities and villages, teaching in their synagogues, and preaching the gospel of the kingdom, and healing every sickness and every disease among the people.

36. But when he saw the multitudes, he was moved with compassion on them, because they fainted, and were scattered abroad, as sheep having no shepherd.

37. Then saith he unto his disciples, The harvest truly is plenteous, but the labourers are few;

38. Pray ye therefore the Lord of the harvest, that he will send forth labourers into his harvest.

CHAPTER 10

1. And when he had called unto him his twelve disciples, he gave them power against unclean spirits, to cast them out, and to heal all manner of sickness and all manner of disease.

2. Now the names of the twelve apostles are these; The first, Simon, who is called Peter, and Andrew his brother; James the son of Zebedee, and John his brother;

3. Philip, and Bartholomew; Thomas, and Matthew the publican; James the son of Alphaeus, and Lebbaeus, whose surname was Thaddaeus;

4. Simon the Canaanite, and Judas Iscariot, who also betrayed him.

5. These twelve Jesus sent forth, and commanded them, saying, Go not into the way of the Gentiles, and into any city of the Samaritans enter ye not:

6. But go rather to the lost sheep of the house of Israel.

7. And as ye go, preach, saying, The kingdom of heaven is at hand.

8. Heal the sick, cleanse the lepers, raise the dead, cast out devils: freely ye have received, freely give.

9. Provide neither gold, nor silver, nor brass in your purses,

10. Nor scrip for your journey, neither two coats, neither shoes, nor yet staves: for the workman is worthy of his meat.

11. And into whatsoever city or town ye shall enter, enquire who in it is worthy; and there abide till ye go thence.

12. And when ye come into an house, salute it.

13. And if the house be worthy, let your peace come upon it: but if it be not worthy, let your peace return to you.

14. And whosoever shall not receive you, nor hear your words, when ye depart out of that house or city, shake off the dust of your feet.

15. Verily I say unto you, It shall be more tolerable for the land of Sodom and Gomorrha in the day of judgment, than for that city.

16. Behold, I send you forth as sheep in the midst of wolves: be ye therefore wise as serpents, and harmless as doves.

17. But beware of men: for they will deliver you up to the councils, and they will scourge you in their synagogues;

18. And ye shall be brought before governors and kings for my sake, for a testimony against them and the Gentiles.

19. But when they deliver you up, take no thought how or what ye shall speak: for it shall be given you in that same hour what ye shall speak.

20. For it is not ye that speak, but the Spirit of your Father which speaketh in you.

21. And the brother shall deliver up the brother to death, and the father the child: and the children shall rise up against their parents, and cause them to be put to death.

22. And ye shall be hated of all men for my name's sake: but he that endureth to the end shall be saved.

23. But when they persecute you in this city, flee ye into another: for verily I say unto you, Ye shall not have gone over the cities of Israel, till the Son of man be come.

24. The disciple is not above his master, nor the servant above his lord.

25. It is enough for the disciple that he be as his master, and the servant as his lord. If they have called the master of the house Beelzebub, how much more shall they call them of his household?

26. Fear them not therefore: for there is nothing covered, that shall not be revealed; and hid, that shall not be known.

27. What I tell you in darkness, that speak ye in light: and what ye hear in the ear, that preach ye upon the housetops.

28. And fear not them which kill the body, but are not able to kill the soul: but rather fear him which is able to destroy both soul and body in hell.

29. Are not two sparrows sold for a farthing? and one of them shall not fall on the ground without your Father.

30. But the very hairs of your head are all numbered.

31. Fear ye not therefore, ye are of more value than many sparrows.

32. Whosoever therefore shall confess me before men, him will I confess also before my Father which is in heaven.

33. But whosoever shall deny me before men, him will I also deny before my Father which is in heaven.

34. Think not that I am come to send peace on earth: I came not to send peace, but a sword.

35. For I am come to set a man at variance against his father, and the daughter against her mother, and the daughter in law against her mother in law.

36. And a man's foes shall be they of his own household.

37. He that loveth father or mother more than me is not worthy of me: and he that loveth son or daughter more than me is not worthy of me.

38. And he that taketh not his cross, and followeth after me, is not worthy of me.

39. He that findeth his life shall lose it: and he that loseth his life for my sake shall find it.

40. He that receiveth you receiveth me, and he that receiveth me receiveth him that sent me.

41. He that receiveth a prophet in the name of a prophet shall receive a prophet's reward; and he that receiveth a righteous man in the name of a righteous man shall receive a righteous man's reward.

42. And whosoever shall give to drink unto one of these little ones a cup of cold water only in the name of a disciple, verily I say unto you, he shall in no wise lose his reward.

CHAPTER 11

1. And it came to pass, when Jesus had made an end of commanding his twelve disciples, he departed thence to teach and to preach in their cities.

2. Now when John had heard in the prison the works of Christ, he sent two of his disciples,

3. And said unto him, Art thou he that should come, or do we look for another?

4. Jesus answered and said unto them, Go and shew John again those things which ye do hear and see:

5. The blind receive their sight, and the lame walk, the lepers are cleansed, and the deaf hear, the dead are raised up, and the poor have the gospel preached to them.

6. And blessed is he, whosoever shall not be offended in me.

7. And as they departed, Jesus began to say unto the multitudes concerning John, What went ye out into the wilderness to see? A reed shaken with the wind?

8. But what went ye out for to see? A man clothed in soft raiment? behold, they that wear soft clothing are in kings' houses.

9. But what went ye out for to see? A prophet? yea, I say unto you, and more than a prophet.

10. For this is he, of whom it is written, Behold, I send my messenger before thy face, which shall prepare thy way before thee.

11. Verily I say unto you, Among them that are born of women there hath not risen a greater than John the Baptist: notwithstanding he that is least in the kingdom of heaven is greater than he.

12. And from the days of John the Baptist until now the kingdom of heaven suffereth violence, and the violent take it by force.

13. For all the prophets and the law prophesied until John.

14. And if ye will receive it, this is Elias, which was for to come.

15. He that hath ears to hear, let him hear.

16. But whereunto shall I liken this generation? It is like unto children sitting in the markets, and calling unto their fellows,

17. And saying, We have piped unto you, and ye have not danced; we have mourned unto you, and ye have not lamented.

18. For John came neither eating nor drinking, and they say, He hath a devil.

19. The Son of man came eating and drinking, and they say, Behold a man gluttonous, and a winebibber, a friend of publicans and sinners. But wisdom is justified of her children.

20. Then began he to upbraid the cities wherein most of his mighty works were done, because they repented not:

21. Woe unto thee, Chorazin! woe unto thee, Bethsaida! for if the mighty works, which were done in you, had been done in Tyre and Sidon, they would have repented long ago in sackcloth and ashes.

22. But I say unto you, It shall be more tolerable for Tyre and Sidon at the day of judgment, than for you.

23. And thou, Capernaum, which art exalted unto heaven, shalt be brought down to hell: for if the mighty works, which have been done in thee, had been done in Sodom, it would have remained until this day.

24. But I say unto you, That it shall be more tolerable for the land of Sodom in the day of judgment, than for thee.

25. At that time Jesus answered and said, I thank thee, O Father, Lord of heaven and earth, because thou hast hid these things from the wise and prudent, and hast revealed them unto babes.

26. Even so, Father: for so it seemed good in thy sight.

27. All things are delivered unto me of my Father: and no man knoweth the Son, but the Father; neither knoweth any man the Father, save the Son, and he to whomsoever the Son will reveal him.

28. Come unto me, all ye that labour and are heavy laden, and I will give you rest.

29. Take my yoke upon you, and learn of me; for I am meek and lowly in heart: and ye shall find rest unto your souls.

30. For my yoke is easy, and my burden is light.

CHAPTER 12

1. At that time Jesus went on the sabbath day through the corn; and his disciples were an hungred, and began to pluck the ears of corn and to eat.

2. But when the Pharisees saw it, they said unto him, Behold, thy disciples do that which is not lawful to do upon the sabbath day.

3. But he said unto them, Have ye not read what David did, when he was an hungred, and they that were with him;

4. How he entered into the house of God, and did eat the shewbread, which was not lawful for him to eat, neither for them which were with him, but only for the priests?

5. Or have ye not read in the law, how that on the sabbath days the priests in the temple profane the sabbath, and are blameless?

6. But I say unto you, That in this place is one greater than the temple.

7. But if ye had known what this meaneth, I will have mercy, and not sacrifice, ye would not have condemned the guiltless.

8. For the Son of man is Lord even of the sabbath day.

9. And when he was departed thence, he went into their synagogue:

10. And, behold, there was a man which had his hand withered. And they asked him, saying, Is it lawful to heal on the sabbath days? that they might accuse him.

11. And he said unto them, What man shall there be among you, that shall have one sheep, and if it fall into a pit on the sabbath day, will he not lay hold on it, and lift it out?

12. How much then is a man better than a sheep? Wherefore it is lawful to do well on the sabbath days.

13. Then saith he to the man, Stretch forth thine hand. And he stretched it forth; and it was restored whole, like as the other.

14. Then the Pharisees went out, and held a council against him, how they might destroy him.

15. But when Jesus knew it, he withdrew himself from thence: and great multitudes followed him, and he healed them all;

16. And charged them that they should not make him known:

17. That it might be fulfilled which was spoken by Esaias the prophet, saying,

18. Behold my servant, whom I have chosen; my beloved, in whom my soul is well pleased: I will put my spirit upon him, and he shall shew judgment to the Gentiles.

19. He shall not strive, nor cry; neither shall any man hear his voice in the streets.

20. A bruised reed shall he not break, and smoking flax shall he not quench, till he send forth judgment unto victory.

21. And in his name shall the Gentiles trust.

22. Then was brought unto him one possessed with a devil, blind, and dumb: and he healed him, insomuch that the blind and dumb both spake and saw.

23. And all the people were amazed, and said, Is not this the son of David?

24. But when the Pharisees heard it, they said, This fellow doth not cast out devils, but by Beelzebub the prince of the devils.

25. And Jesus knew their thoughts, and said unto them, Every kingdom divided against itself is brought to desolation; and every city or house divided against itself shall not stand:

26. And if Satan cast out Satan, he is divided against himself; how shall then his kingdom stand?

27. And if I by Beelzebub cast out devils, by whom do your children cast them out? therefore they shall be your judges.

28. But if I cast out devils by the Spirit of God, then the kingdom of God is come unto you.

29. Or else how can one enter into a strong man's house, and spoil his goods, except he first bind the strong man? and then he will spoil his house.

30. He that is not with me is against me; and he that gathereth not with me scattereth abroad.

31. Wherefore I say unto you, All manner of sin and blasphemy shall be forgiven unto men: but the blasphemy against the Holy Ghost shall not be forgiven unto men.

32. And whosoever speaketh a word against the Son of man, it shall be forgiven him: but whosoever speaketh against the Holy Ghost, it shall not be forgiven him, neither in this world, neither in the world to come.

33. Either make the tree good, and his fruit good; or else make the tree corrupt, and his fruit corrupt: for the tree is known by his fruit.

34. O generation of vipers, how can ye, being evil, speak good things? for out of the abundance of the heart the mouth speaketh.

35. A good man out of the good treasure of the heart bringeth forth good things: and an evil man out of the evil treasure bringeth forth evil things.

36. But I say unto you, That every idle word that men shall speak, they shall give account thereof in the day of judgment.

37. For by thy words thou shalt be justified, and by thy words thou shalt be condemned.

38. Then certain of the scribes and of the Pharisees answered, saying, Master, we would see a sign from thee.

39. But he answered and said unto them, An evil and adulterous generation seeketh after a sign; and there shall no sign be given to it, but the sign of the prophet Jonas:

40. For as Jonas was three days and three nights in the whale's belly; so shall the Son of man be three days and three nights in the heart of the earth.

41. The men of Nineveh shall rise in judgment with this generation, and shall condemn it: because they repented at the preaching of Jonas; and, behold, a greater than Jonas is here.

42. The queen of the south shall rise up in the judgment with this generation, and shall condemn it: for she came from the uttermost parts of the earth to hear the wisdom of Solomon; and, behold, a greater than Solomon is here.

43. When the unclean spirit is gone out of a man, he walketh through dry places, seeking rest, and findeth none.

44. Then he saith, I will return into my house from whence I came out; and when he is come, he findeth it empty, swept, and garnished.

45. Then goeth he, and taketh with himself seven other spirits more wicked than himself, and they enter in and dwell there: and the last state of that man is worse than the first. Even so shall it be also unto this wicked generation.

46. While he yet talked to the people, behold, his mother and his brethren stood without, desiring to speak with him.

47. Then one said unto him, Behold, thy mother and thy brethren stand without, desiring to speak with thee.

48. But he answered and said unto him that told him, Who is my mother? and who are my brethren?

49. And he stretched forth his hand toward his disciples, and said, Behold my mother and my brethren!

50. For whosoever shall do the will of my Father which is in heaven, the same is my brother, and sister, and mother.

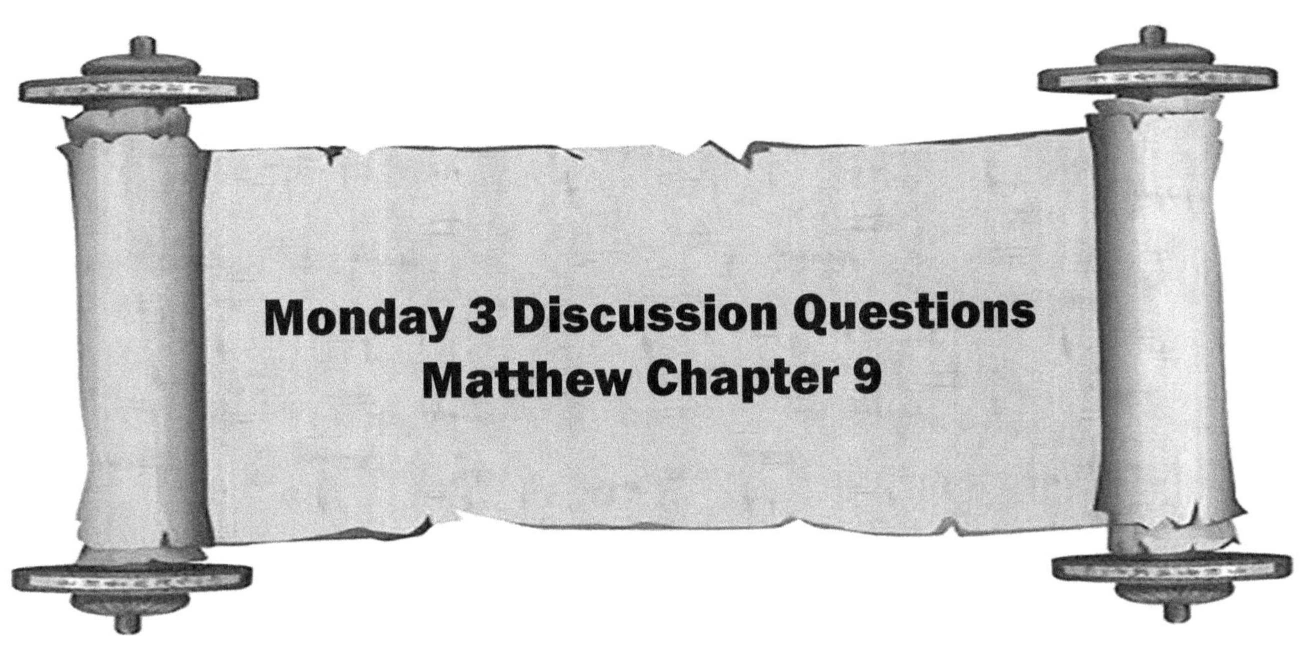

1. When Jesus entered the ship and passed over, where did he go? ______

2. Who was the first man they brought to Jesus? ______

3. What did Jesus say to the man laying on the bed? ______

4. What were the scribes thinking about the man Jesus healed? ______

5. What did Jesus ask them about their thoughts? ______

6. What did Jesus say he did, to show them he had power on earth to forgive sins? ______

7. Why did Jesus say that no one puts a new cloth on an old garment? ______

8. What did Jesus do for the man who came and said his daughter was dead and believed she would live again if Jesus laid his hands on her? ______

9. Why did the woman with the issue of blood say she wanted to touch the hem of Jesus' garment? ______

10. What did Jesus ask the blind men? What did they answer? What happened next. ______

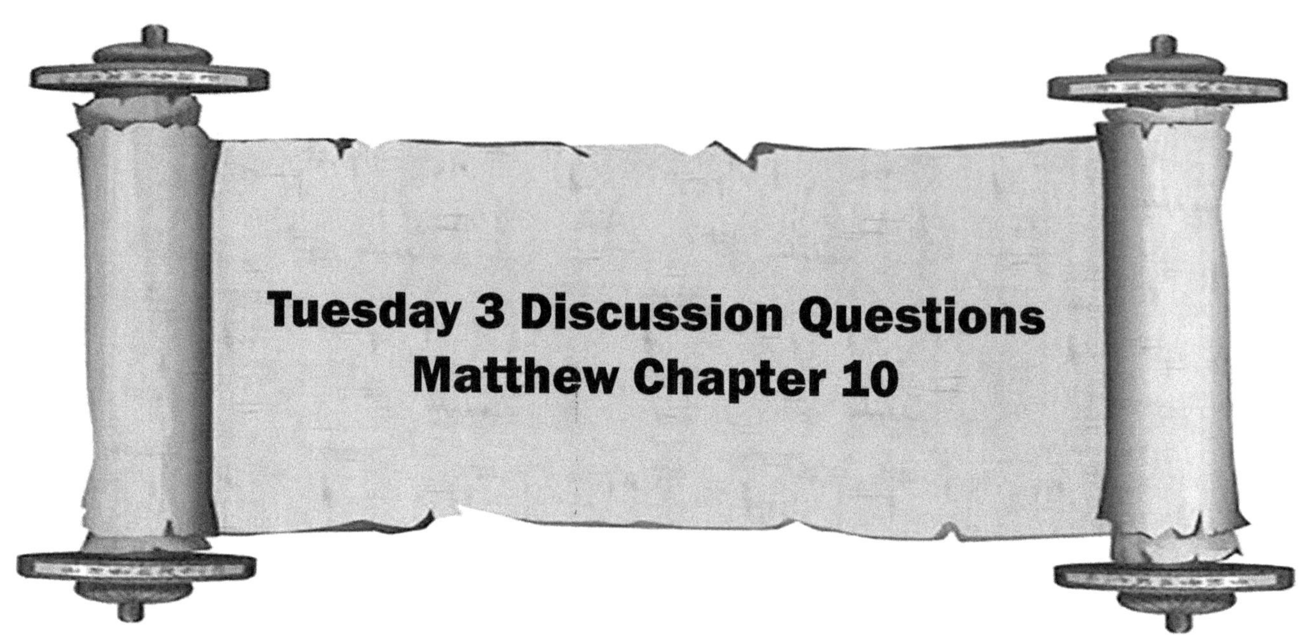

Tuesday 3 Discussion Questions
Matthew Chapter 10

1. When Jesus called the 12 disciples to him, what powers did he give them?

2. What is the name of the first disciple Jesus chose? What name did they call him?

3. What are the names of the 12 disciples he chose?

4. We see two Simons among the twelve. Where was the second Simon from?

5. There were also two James' among them. What was the first James' father's name? His brother was also a disciple. What was his brother's name?

6. What was the second James' father's name?

7. When Jesus sent the disciples forth, where did he tell them not to go? Where did Jesus command them to go?

8. What did he tell them to preach? What did he tell them to do?

9. What did Jesus command them not to provide? Why?

10. What did Jesus command the disciples to do if a house or city did not receive them? What did Jesus say would happen to that city on the day of judgment?

11. Because he was sending them as sheep in the midst of wolves, how were they to behave? What did Jesus tell them not to do when they were offered up? Why?

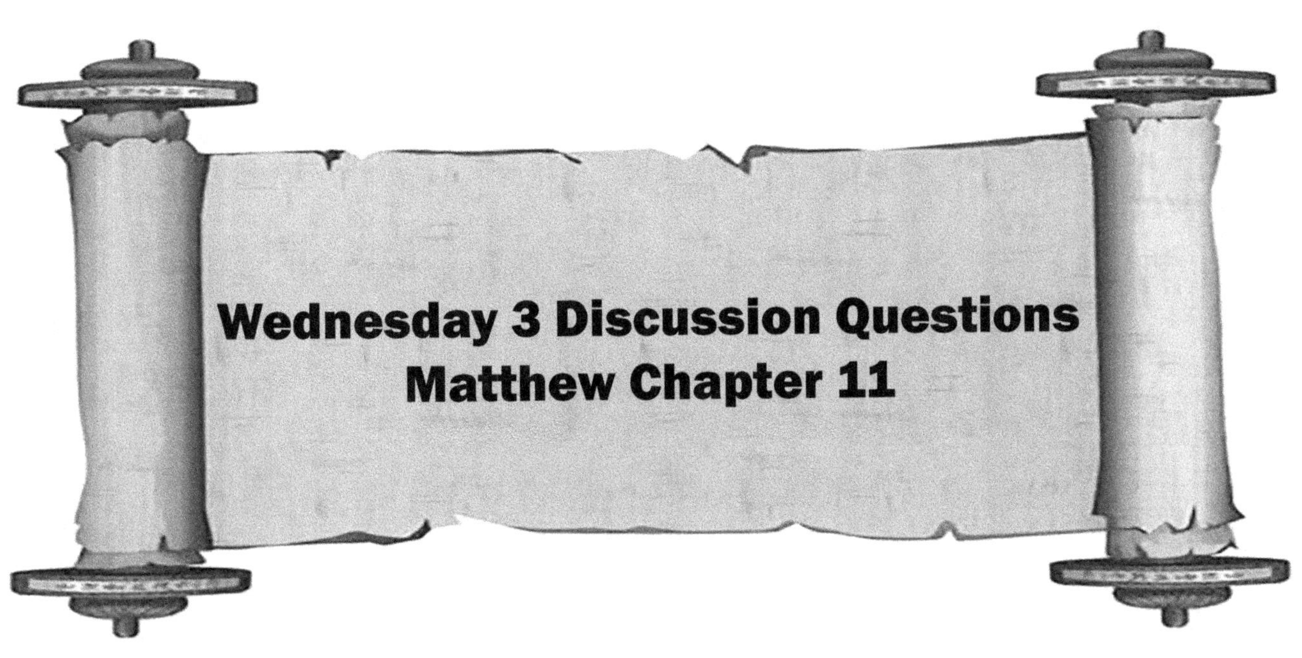

1. What did Jesus depart to do, after he had finished commanding the disciples?
2. What did John do when we heard the works of Christ, from prison?
3. List the things Jesus told the disciples to go back and show John they had seen?
4. What did Jesus ask the multitude concerning John?
5. What did Jesus say about John when he said It is written, Behold?
6. What did say when he compared John to anyone born of a woman?
7. From the days of John the Baptist to now, what happens when the kingdom suffers violence?
8. What did Jesus liken their generation to?
9. Why did Jesus say Woe unto Chorazin and Capernaum?
10. What did Jesus say to those who labored and were heavy laden?

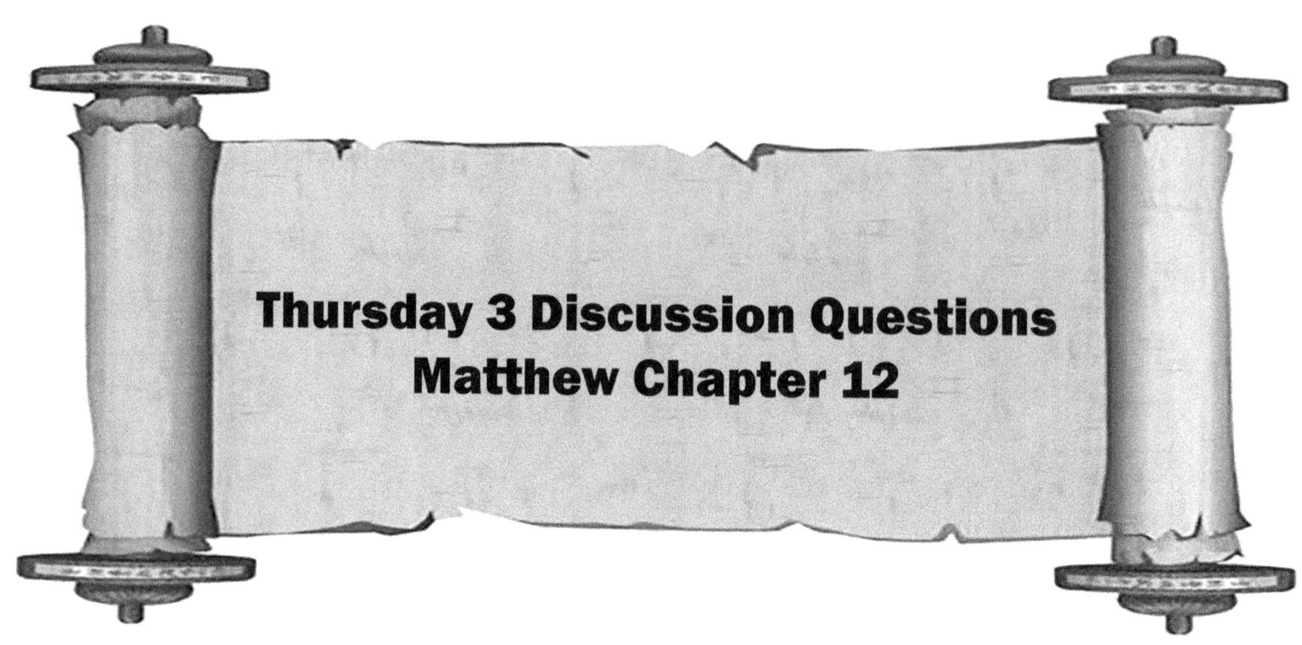

1. When Jesus and his disciples were walking on the Sabbath day, what did the disciples do? ______
2. What did the Pharisees say when they saw this? ______
3. When Jesus departed, where did he go? ______
4. What did they ask Jesus concerning the man with the withered hand, so they could accuse Jesus? ______
5. How did Jesus respond? ______
6. What did the people ask in amazement when they saw Jesus heal the man who was possessed, blind and dumb? ______
7. What did the Pharisees say when they saw Jesus heal him? ______
8. What did Jesus say about those who speak a word against the son of man? What did he say about those who speak against the Holy Spirit? ______
9. From where did Jesus say a GOOD man brings things forth? From where did Jesus say an EVIL man brings things forth? ______
10. How did Jesus say we will be justified or condemned? ______

WEEKLY REVIEW
MATTHEW CHAPTERS 9-12

NAME THAT CHAPTER

1.______ JESUS GAVE THE 12 DISCIPLES POWER TO CAUSE THE BLIND TO SEE, THE LAME TO WALK, CAST OUT UNCLEAN SPIRITS AND HEAL SICKNESSES AND DISEASES. JESUS TOLD THEM IF THEY WERE REJECTED FROM A HOUSE OR CITY, TO SHAKE THE DUST FROM THEIR FEET AND LEAVE WITH THEIR PEACE.

2.______ IN THIS CHAPTER JESUS WENT INTO HIS OWN CITY AND HEALED A MAN SICK WITH PALSY. TO SHOW THE PEOPLE HE HAD POWER ON EARTH TO FORGIVE SINS, HE TOLD THE MAN WHO WAS SICK WITH PALSY, "ARISE, TAKE UP THY BED AND GO UNTO THINE HOUSE".

3.______ THE PHARISEES QUESTION JESUS ABOUT DOING THINGS ON THE SABBATH DAY. THEY WERE ASKING QUESTIONS TO SNARE JESUS. BUT, JESUS RESPONDED TO THEIR QUESTIONS BY ASKING THEM QUESTIONS THAT WOULD MAKE THEM THINK. THIS CHAPTER ALSO WARNS US NOT TO BLASPHEME AGAINST THE HOLY SPIRIT. IT IS THE ONE SIN THAT CAN NOT BE FORGIVEN IN THIS LIFE NOR IN THE NEXT.

4.______ JOHN SENT DISCIPLES FROM THE JAIL TO SEE JESUS. THEY ASKED JESUS, ARE YOU THE ONE OR SHOULD WE LOOK FOR ANOTHER. JESUS SENT WORD BACK ABOUT THE HEALING OF THE LAME AND BLIND, ETC. JESUS TOLD THE PEOPLE ALL GOOD THINGS ABOUT JOHN THE BAPTIST AND VOUCHED FOR HIM THAT THERE WAS NOT ANY MANY LIKE HIM BORN OF A WOMAN.

TRUE OR FALSE

5. When Jesus healed the man of palsy and told him to be of good cheer and his sins were forgiven, the scribes thought, "This man blasphemeth".

____

6. Zebedee was John's brother and James' son

____

7. Jesus said, "The kingdom suffers violence and the violent take it by force"

____

FILL IN THE BLANKS

8. Behold, thy________do that which is not________to do upon the________day.
9. How much then is a________better than a________? Wherefore it is________to do well on the sabbath days.
10. For by thy________thou shalt be________, and by thy words thou shalt be ___________.

STUDENT PRAYER JOURNAL

Please use this space to record your thoughts and feelings as you travel on this spirit led journey through the word of God with us. Please know that you have brothers and sisters in this organization from all over the world praying with and for you. My prayer for you is that you will begin to see the power of God resting in each set of your footprints. As you look back and examine your past in this journal, may you realize that you were never alone and according to Hebrews 13:5, God will never leave nor forsake you. ~LADY FLORA

THE STUDY OF THE FOUR GOSPELS VOCABULARY DEFINITIONS FOR MATTHEW CHAPTERS 13-16

WORD	DEFINITIONS
1) PARABLES	
2) SOW	
3) PERCEIVE	
4) DURETH	
5) WAILING	
6) GNASHING	
7) TETRARCH	
8) VICTUALS	
9) VEXEN	
10) TRANSGRESS	

DMWW Daily Bible Reading
KJV MATTHEW CHAPTERS 13-16

CHAPTER 13

1. The same day went Jesus out of the house, and sat by the sea side.
2. And great multitudes were gathered together unto him, so that he went into a ship, and sat; and the whole multitude stood on the shore.
3. And he spake many things unto them in parables, saying, Behold, a sower went forth to sow;
4. And when he sowed, some seeds fell by the way side, and the fowls came and devoured them up:
5. Some fell upon stony places, where they had not much earth: and forthwith they sprung up, because they had no deepness of earth:
6. And when the sun was up, they were scorched; and because they had no root, they withered away.
7. And some fell among thorns; and the thorns sprung up, and choked them:
8. But other fell into good ground, and brought forth fruit, some an hundredfold, some sixtyfold, some thirtyfold.
9. Who hath ears to hear, let him hear.
10. And the disciples came, and said unto him, Why speakest thou unto them in parables?
11. He answered and said unto them, Because it is given unto you to know the mysteries of the kingdom of heaven, but to them it is not given.
12. For whosoever hath, to him shall be given, and he shall have more abundance: but whosoever hath not, from him shall be taken away even that he hath.
13. Therefore speak I to them in parables: because they seeing see not; and hearing they hear not, neither do they understand.
14. And in them is fulfilled the prophecy of Esaias, which saith, By hearing ye shall hear, and shall not understand; and seeing ye shall see, and shall not perceive:
15. For this people's heart is waxed gross, and their ears are dull of hearing, and their eyes they have closed; lest at any time they should see with their eyes and hear with their ears, and should understand with their heart, and should be converted, and I should heal them.
16. But blessed are your eyes, for they see: and your ears, for they hear.

17. For verily I say unto you, That many prophets and righteous men have desired to see those things which ye see, and have not seen them; and to hear those things which ye hear, and have not heard them.

18. Hear ye therefore the parable of the sower.

19. When any one heareth the word of the kingdom, and understandeth it not, then cometh the wicked one, and catcheth away that which was sown in his heart. This is he which received seed by the way side.

20. But he that received the seed into stony places, the same is he that heareth the word, and anon with joy receiveth it;

21. Yet hath he not root in himself, but dureth for a while: for when tribulation or persecution ariseth because of the word, by and by he is offended.

22. He also that received seed among the thorns is he that heareth the word; and the care of this world, and the deceitfulness of riches, choke the word, and he becometh unfruitful.

23. But he that received seed into the good ground is he that heareth the word, and understandeth it; which also beareth fruit, and bringeth forth, some an hundredfold, some sixty, some thirty.

24. Another parable put he forth unto them, saying, The kingdom of heaven is likened unto a man which sowed good seed in his field:

25. But while men slept, his enemy came and sowed tares among the wheat, and went his way.

26. But when the blade was sprung up, and brought forth fruit, then appeared the tares also.

27. So the servants of the householder came and said unto him, Sir, didst not thou sow good seed in thy field? from whence then hath it tares?

28. He said unto them, An enemy hath done this. The servants said unto him, Wilt thou then that we go and gather them up?

29. But he said, Nay; lest while ye gather up the tares, ye root up also the wheat with them.

30. Let both grow together until the harvest: and in the time of harvest I will say to the reapers, Gather ye together first the tares, and bind them in bundles to burn them: but gather the wheat into my barn.

31. Another parable put he forth unto them, saying, The kingdom of heaven is like to a grain of mustard seed, which a man took, and sowed in his field:

32. Which indeed is the least of all seeds: but when it is grown, it is the greatest among herbs, and becometh a tree, so that the birds of the air come and lodge in the branches thereof.

33. Another parable spake he unto them; The kingdom of heaven is like unto leaven, which a woman took, and hid in three measures of meal, till the whole was leavened.

34. All these things spake Jesus unto the multitude in parables; and without a parable spake he not unto them:

35. That it might be fulfilled which was spoken by the prophet, saying, I will open my mouth in parables; I will utter things which have been kept secret from the foundation of the world.

36. Then Jesus sent the multitude away, and went into the house: and his disciples came unto him, saying, Declare unto us the parable of the tares of the field.

37. He answered and said unto them, He that soweth the good seed is the Son of man;

38. The field is the world; the good seed are the children of the kingdom; but the tares are the children of the wicked one;

39. The enemy that sowed them is the devil; the harvest is the end of the world; and the reapers are the angels.

40. As therefore the tares are gathered and burned in the fire; so shall it be in the end of this world.

41. The Son of man shall send forth his angels, and they shall gather out of his kingdom all things that offend, and them which do iniquity;

42. And shall cast them into a furnace of fire: there shall be wailing and gnashing of teeth.

43. Then shall the righteous shine forth as the sun in the kingdom of their Father. Who hath ears to hear, let him hear.

44. Again, the kingdom of heaven is like unto treasure hid in a field; the which when a man hath found, he hideth, and for joy thereof goeth and selleth all that he hath, and buyeth that field.

45. Again, the kingdom of heaven is like unto a merchant man, seeking goodly pearls:

46. Who, when he had found one pearl of great price, went and sold all that he had, and bought it.

47. Again, the kingdom of heaven is like unto a net, that was cast into the sea, and gathered of every kind:

48. Which, when it was full, they drew to shore, and sat down, and gathered the good into vessels, but cast the bad away.

49. So shall it be at the end of the world: the angels shall come forth, and sever the wicked from among the just,

50. And shall cast them into the furnace of fire: there shall be wailing and gnashing of teeth.

51. Jesus saith unto them, Have ye understood all these things? They say unto him, Yea, Lord.

52. Then said he unto them, Therefore every scribe which is instructed unto the kingdom of heaven is like unto a man that is an householder, which bringeth forth out of his treasure things new and old.

53. And it came to pass, that when Jesus had finished these parables, he departed thence.

54. And when he was come into his own country, he taught them in their synagogue, insomuch that they were astonished, and said, Whence hath this man this wisdom, and these mighty works?

55. Is not this the carpenter's son? is not his mother called Mary? and his brethren, James, and Joses, and Simon, and Judas?

56. And his sisters, are they not all with us? Whence then hath this man all these things?

57. And they were offended in him. But Jesus said unto them, A prophet is not without honour, save in his own country, and in his own house.

58. And he did not many mighty works there because of their unbelief.

CHAPTER 14

1. At that time Herod the tetrarch heard of the fame of Jesus,

2. And said unto his servants, This is John the Baptist; he is risen from the dead; and therefore mighty works do shew forth themselves in him.

3. For Herod had laid hold on John, and bound him, and put him in prison for Herodias' sake, his brother Philip's wife.

4. For John said unto him, It is not lawful for thee to have her.

5. And when he would have put him to death, he feared the multitude, because they counted him as a prophet.

6. But when Herod's birthday was kept, the daughter of Herodias danced before them, and pleased Herod.

7. Whereupon he promised with an oath to give her whatsoever she would ask.

8. And she, being before instructed of her mother, said, Give me here John Baptist's head in a charger.

9. And the king was sorry: nevertheless for the oath's sake, and them which sat with him at meat, he commanded it to be given her.

10. And he sent, and beheaded John in the prison.

11. And his head was brought in a charger, and given to the damsel: and she brought it to her mother.

12. And his disciples came, and took up the body, and buried it, and went and told Jesus.

13. When Jesus heard of it, he departed thence by ship into a desert place apart: and when the people had heard thereof, they followed him on foot out of the cities.

14. And Jesus went forth, and saw a great multitude, and was moved with compassion toward them, and he healed their sick.

15. And when it was evening, his disciples came to him, saying, This is a desert place, and the time is now past; send the multitude away, that they may go into the villages, and buy themselves victuals.

16. But Jesus said unto them, They need not depart; give ye them to eat.

17. And they say unto him, We have here but five loaves, and two fishes.

18. He said, Bring them hither to me.

19. And he commanded the multitude to sit down on the grass, and took the five loaves, and the two fishes, and looking up to heaven, he blessed, and brake, and gave the loaves to his disciples, and the disciples to the multitude.

20. And they did all eat, and were filled: and they took up of the fragments that remained twelve baskets full.

21. And they that had eaten were about five thousand men, beside women and children.

22. And straightway Jesus constrained his disciples to get into a ship, and to go before him unto the other side, while he sent the multitudes away.

23. And when he had sent the multitudes away, he went up into a mountain apart to pray: and when the evening was come, he was there alone.

24. But the ship was now in the midst of the sea, tossed with waves: for the wind was contrary.

25. And in the fourth watch of the night Jesus went unto them, walking on the sea.

26. And when the disciples saw him walking on the sea, they were troubled, saying, It is a spirit; and they cried out for fear.

27. But straightway Jesus spake unto them, saying, Be of good cheer; it is I; be not afraid.

28. And Peter answered him and said, Lord, if it be thou, bid me come unto thee on the water.

29. And he said, Come. And when Peter was come down out of the ship, he walked on the water, to go to Jesus.

30. But when he saw the wind boisterous, he was afraid; and beginning to sink, he cried, saying, Lord, save me.

31. And immediately Jesus stretched forth his hand, and caught him, and said unto him, O thou of little faith, wherefore didst thou doubt?

32. And when they were come into the ship, the wind ceased.

33. Then they that were in the ship came and worshipped him, saying, Of a truth thou art the Son of God.

34. And when they were gone over, they came into the land of Gennesaret.

35. And when the men of that place had knowledge of him, they sent out into all that country round about, and brought unto him all that were diseased;

36. And besought him that they might only touch the hem of his garment: and as many as touched were made perfectly whole.

CHAPTER 15

1. Then came to Jesus scribes and Pharisees, which were of Jerusalem, saying,

2. Why do thy disciples transgress the tradition of the elders? for they wash not their hands when they eat bread.

3. But he answered and said unto them, Why do ye also transgress the commandment of God by your tradition?

4. For God commanded, saying, Honour thy father and mother: and, He that curseth father or mother, let him die the death.

5. But ye say, Whosoever shall say to his father or his mother, It is a gift, by whatsoever thou mightest be profited by me;

6. And honour not his father or his mother, he shall be free. Thus have ye made the commandment of God of none effect by your tradition.

7. Ye hypocrites, well did Esaias prophesy of you, saying,

8. This people draweth nigh unto me with their mouth, and honoureth me with their lips; but their heart is far from me.

9. But in vain they do worship me, teaching for doctrines the commandments of men.

10. And he called the multitude, and said unto them, Hear, and understand:

11. Not that which goeth into the mouth defileth a man; but that which cometh out of the mouth, this defileth a man.

12. Then came his disciples, and said unto him, Knowest thou that the Pharisees were offended, after they heard this saying?

13. But he answered and said, Every plant, which my heavenly Father hath not planted, shall be rooted up.

14. Let them alone: they be blind leaders of the blind. And if the blind lead the blind, both shall fall into the ditch.

15. Then answered Peter and said unto him, Declare unto us this parable.

16. And Jesus said, Are ye also yet without understanding?

17. Do not ye yet understand, that whatsoever entereth in at the mouth goeth into the belly, and is cast out into the draught?

18. But those things which proceed out of the mouth come forth from the heart; and they defile the man.

19. For out of the heart proceed evil thoughts, murders, adulteries, fornications, thefts, false witness, blasphemies:

20. These are the things which defile a man: but to eat with unwashen hands defileth not a man.

21. Then Jesus went thence, and departed into the coasts of Tyre and Sidon.

22. And, behold, a woman of Canaan came out of the same coasts, and cried unto him, saying, Have mercy on me, O Lord, thou son of David; my daughter is grievously vexed with a devil.

23. But he answered her not a word. And his disciples came and besought him, saying, Send her away; for she crieth after us.

24. But he answered and said, I am not sent but unto the lost sheep of the house of Israel.

25. Then came she and worshipped him, saying, Lord, help me.

26. But he answered and said, It is not meet to take the children's bread, and to cast it to dogs.

27. And she said, Truth, Lord: yet the dogs eat of the crumbs which fall from their masters' table.

28. Then Jesus answered and said unto her, O woman, great is thy faith: be it unto thee even as thou wilt. And her daughter was made whole from that very hour.

29. And Jesus departed from thence, and came nigh unto the sea of Galilee; and went up into a mountain, and sat down there.

30. And great multitudes came unto him, having with them those that were lame, blind, dumb, maimed, and many others, and cast them down at Jesus' feet; and he healed them:

31. Insomuch that the multitude wondered, when they saw the dumb to speak, the maimed to be whole, the lame to walk, and the blind to see: and they glorified the God of Israel.

32. Then Jesus called his disciples unto him, and said, I have compassion on the multitude, because they continue with me now three days, and have nothing to eat: and I will not send them away fasting, lest they faint in the way.

33. And his disciples say unto him, Whence should we have so much bread in the wilderness, as to fill so great a multitude?

34. And Jesus saith unto them, How many loaves have ye? And they said, Seven, and a few little fishes.

35. And he commanded the multitude to sit down on the ground.

36. And he took the seven loaves and the fishes, and gave thanks, and brake them, and gave to his disciples, and the disciples to the multitude.

37. And they did all eat, and were filled: and they took up of the broken meat that was left seven baskets full.

38. And they that did eat were four thousand men, beside women and children.

39. And he sent away the multitude, and took ship, and came into the coasts of Magdala.

CHAPTER 16

1. The Pharisees also with the Sadducees came, and tempting desired him that he would shew them a sign from heaven.

2. He answered and said unto them, When it is evening, ye say, It will be fair weather: for the sky is red.

3. And in the morning, It will be foul weather to day: for the sky is red and lowering. O ye hypocrites, ye can discern the face of the sky; but can ye not discern the signs of the times?

4. A wicked and adulterous generation seeketh after a sign; and there shall no sign be given unto it, but the sign of the prophet Jonas. And he left them, and departed.

5. And when his disciples were come to the other side, they had forgotten to take bread.

6. Then Jesus said unto them, Take heed and beware of the leaven of the Pharisees and of the Sadducees.

7. And they reasoned among themselves, saying, It is because we have taken no bread.

8. Which when Jesus perceived, he said unto them, O ye of little faith, why reason ye among yourselves, because ye have brought no bread?

9. Do ye not yet understand, neither remember the five loaves of the five thousand, and how many baskets ye took up?

10. Neither the seven loaves of the four thousand, and how many baskets ye took up?

11. How is it that ye do not understand that I spake it not to you concerning bread, that ye should beware of the leaven of the Pharisees and of the Sadducees?

12. Then understood they how that he bade them not beware of the leaven of bread, but of the doctrine of the Pharisees and of the Sadducees.

13. When Jesus came into the coasts of Caesarea Philippi, he asked his disciples, saying, Whom do men say that I the Son of man am?

14. And they said, Some say that thou art John the Baptist: some, Elias; and others, Jeremias, or one of the prophets.

15. He saith unto them, But whom say ye that I am?

16. And Simon Peter answered and said, Thou art the Christ, the Son of the living God.

17. And Jesus answered and said unto him, Blessed art thou, Simon Barjona: for flesh and blood hath not revealed it unto thee, but my Father which is in heaven.

18. And I say also unto thee, That thou art Peter, and upon this rock I will build my church; and the gates of hell shall not prevail against it.

19. And I will give unto thee the keys of the kingdom of heaven: and whatsoever thou shalt bind on earth shall be bound in heaven: and whatsoever thou shalt loose on earth shall be loosed in heaven.

20. Then charged he his disciples that they should tell no man that he was Jesus the Christ.

21. From that time forth began Jesus to shew unto his disciples, how that he must go unto Jerusalem, and suffer many things of the elders and chief priests and scribes, and be killed, and be raised again the third day.

22. Then Peter took him, and began to rebuke him, saying, Be it far from thee, Lord: this shall not be unto thee.

23. But he turned, and said unto Peter, Get thee behind me, Satan: thou art an offence unto me: for thou savourest not the things that be of God, but those that be of men.

24. Then said Jesus unto his disciples, If any man will come after me, let him deny himself, and take up his cross, and follow me.

25. For whosoever will save his life shall lose it: and whosoever will lose his life for my sake shall find it.

26. For what is a man profited, if he shall gain the whole world, and lose his own soul? or what shall a man give in exchange for his soul?

27. For the Son of man shall come in the glory of his Father with his angels; and then he shall reward every man according to his works.

28. Verily I say unto you, There be some standing here, which shall not taste of death, till they see the Son of man coming in his kingdom.

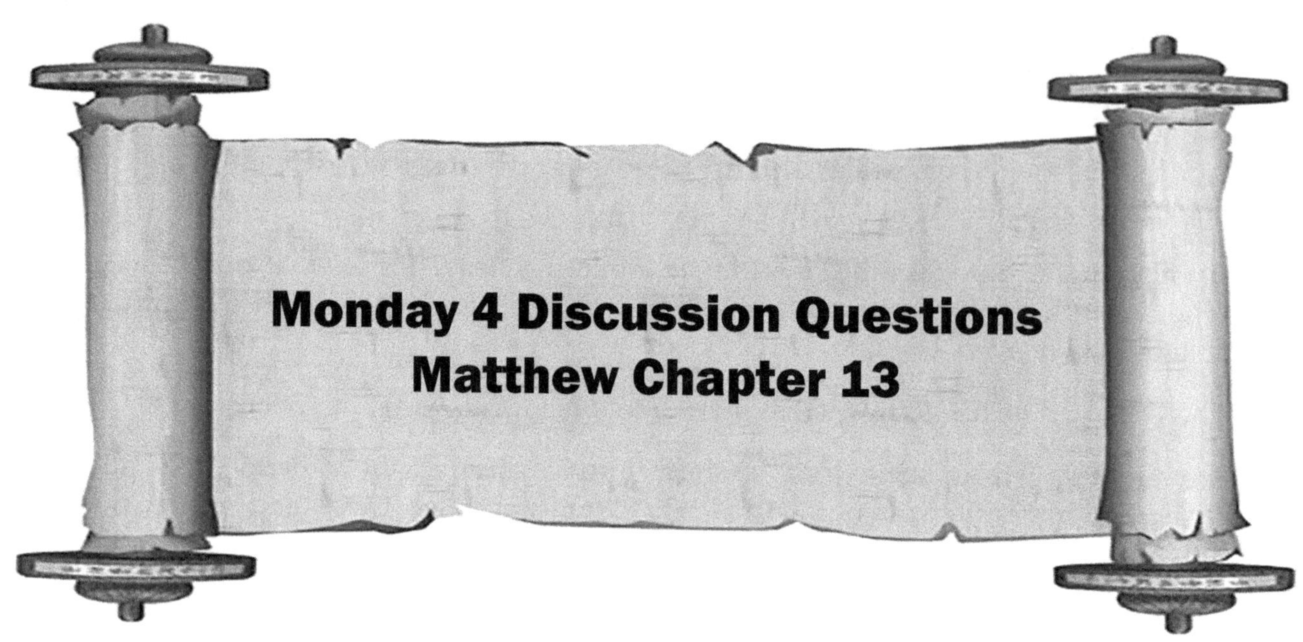

1. What happened on the same day Jesus went out of the house and sat by the sea side? ______________________________

2. Where did Jesus go from there? ______________________________

3. What did Jesus do as he sat there? ______________________________

4. In the parable when the sower went out to sow, what happened to the seeds that fell to the wayside? ______________________________

5. What happened to the seeds that fell on stony ground? ______________________________

6. What happened to the seeds that fell upon thorns? ______________________________

7. What happened to the seeds that fell on good ground? ______________________________

8. What did Jesus say happens when someone hears the word and doesn't understand it like the seeds that fell by the wayside? ______________________________

9. What did Jesus say happens when someone hears the word with joy, but he was not rooted? ______________________________

10. What did Jesus say happens to one who receives the word but with cares of the world? ______________________________

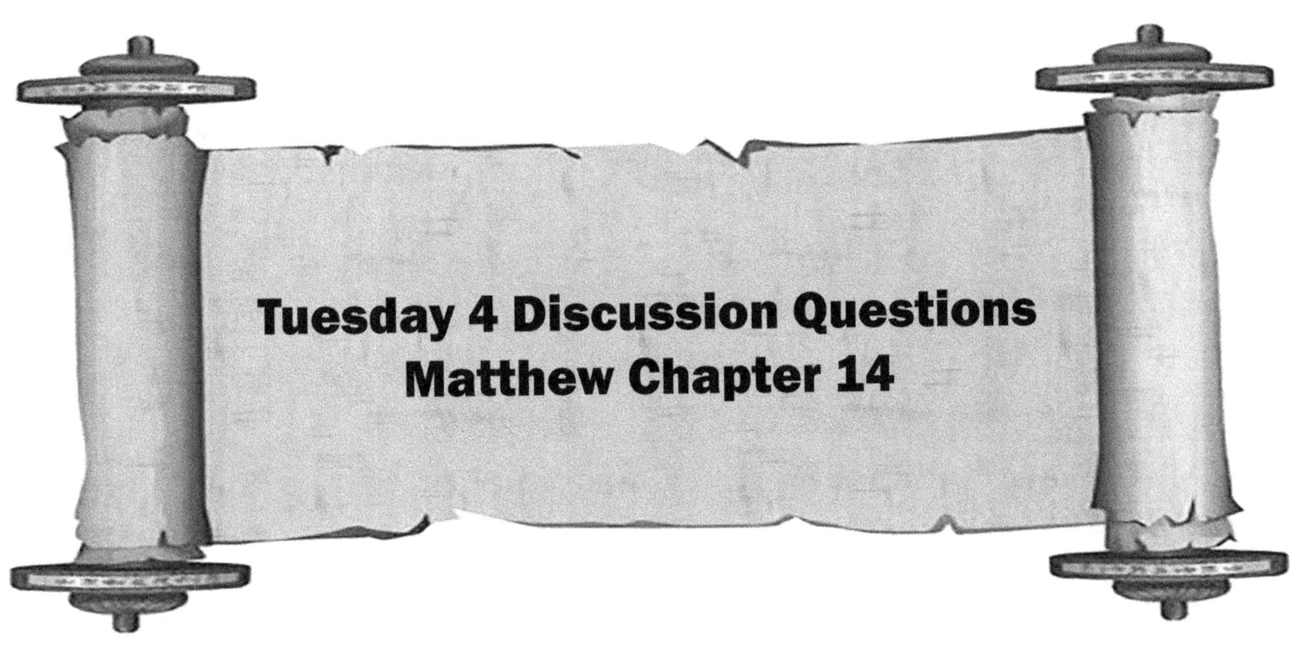

Tuesday 4 Discussion Questions
Matthew Chapter 14

1. What did Herod say to his servants when he heard of Jesus' fame? ____________________

2. Why did Herod put John in prison? ____________________

3. Why did Herod change his mind and order John's head in a charger? ____________________

4. Why did the disciples ask Jesus to send the multitude away when it was evening? ____________________

5. What did Jesus tell the disciples when they told him this? ____________________

6. What did Jesus say when they told him they only had five loaves and two fish? ____________________

7. What did Jesus do when they brought him the loaves and fish? ____________________

8. Was it enough to feed everyone after Jesus blessed it? Was there any left? How much? ____________________

9. How many men were able to eat and be filled from the 5 loves and two fish after Jesus prayed over it? ____________________

10. What did Jesus do after he fed the multitude and sent them away? ____________________

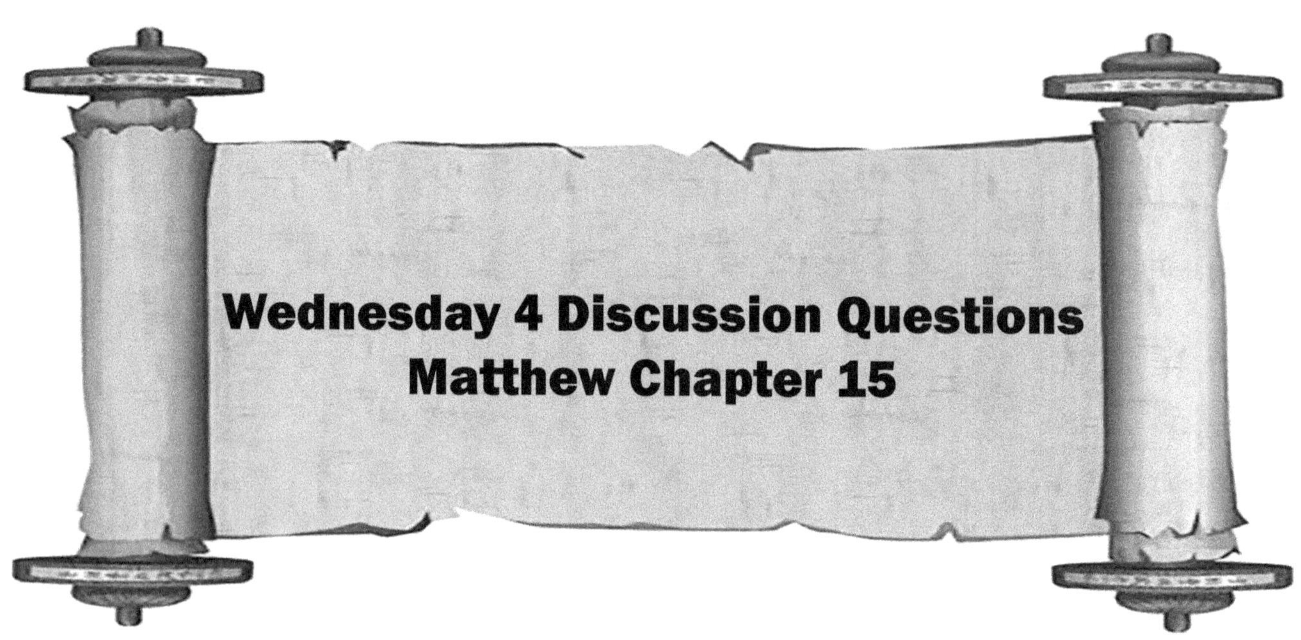

1. Where did the scribes and Pharisees that were questioning Jesus come from? ________
2. What men came to Jesus first? ________
3. What transgression of the disciples did they question Jesus about? ________
4. How did Jesus answer them? ________
5. Which commandment did Jesus say the scribes and Pharisees transgressed? ________
6. Why did Jesus say he called them hypocrites? ________
7. What did Jesus say about what goes in and out of the mouth? ________
8. Where did Jesus say things that come out of your mouth come from? What did Jesus say proceeds out from the heart? ________
9. What did Jesus say to the Canaanite woman who came and cried for him to help her daughter ? What did she answer and say to Jesus? ________
10. How many men did Jesus feed with 7 loaves and a few little fish? How many baskets were left over after they were filled? ________

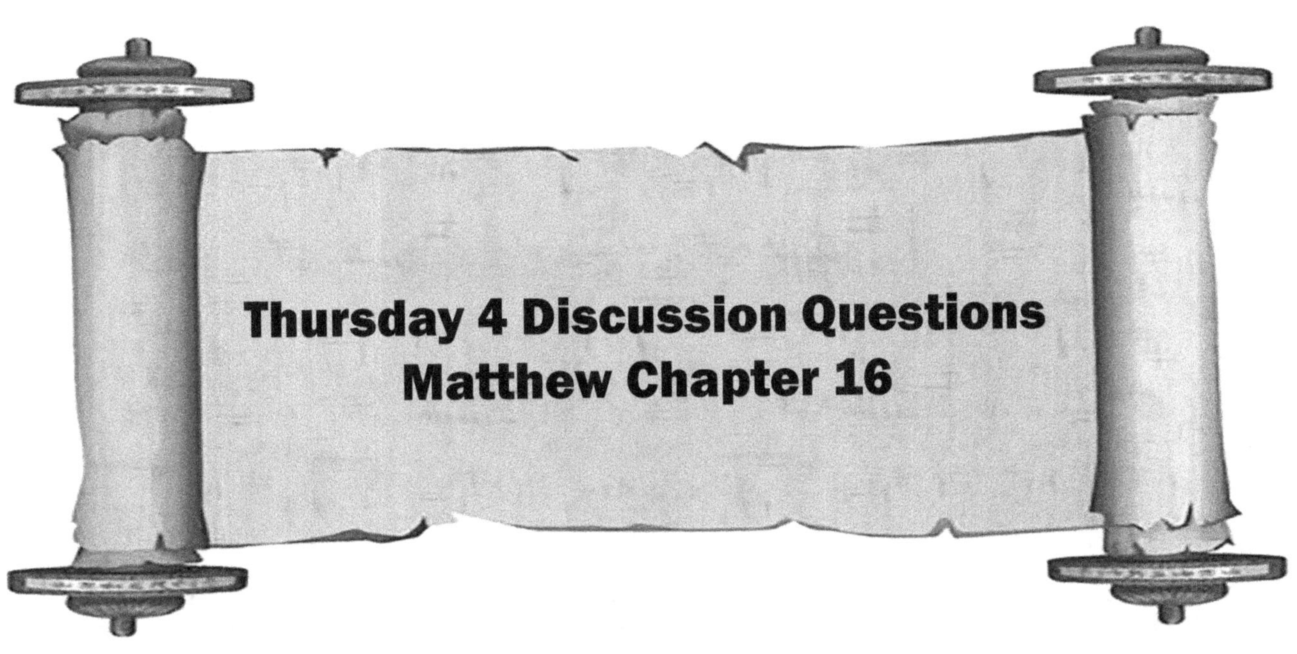

1. What did the Pharisees and Sadducees desire Jesus to show them? ______

2. What did Jesus call them? ______

3. Why did he say he called them hypocrites? ______

4. What kind of generation did Jesus say seeks after a sign? Did he give them a sign? ______

5. What did Jesus tell them to take heed and beware of? Was Jesus talking about bread? ______

6. What two instances did Jesus remind them of, to show them his concern was not with whether they brought bread or not? ______

7. How did the disciples answer when Jesus asked them who men said he was? ______

8. What was Jesus' next question to the disciples? ______

9. Which disciple answered? What did he say? ______

10. How did Jesus respond to him? ______

11. What did Jesus charge the disciples not to do when they left? ______

WEEKLY REVIEW
MATTHEW CHAPTERS 13-16

NAME THAT CHAPTER

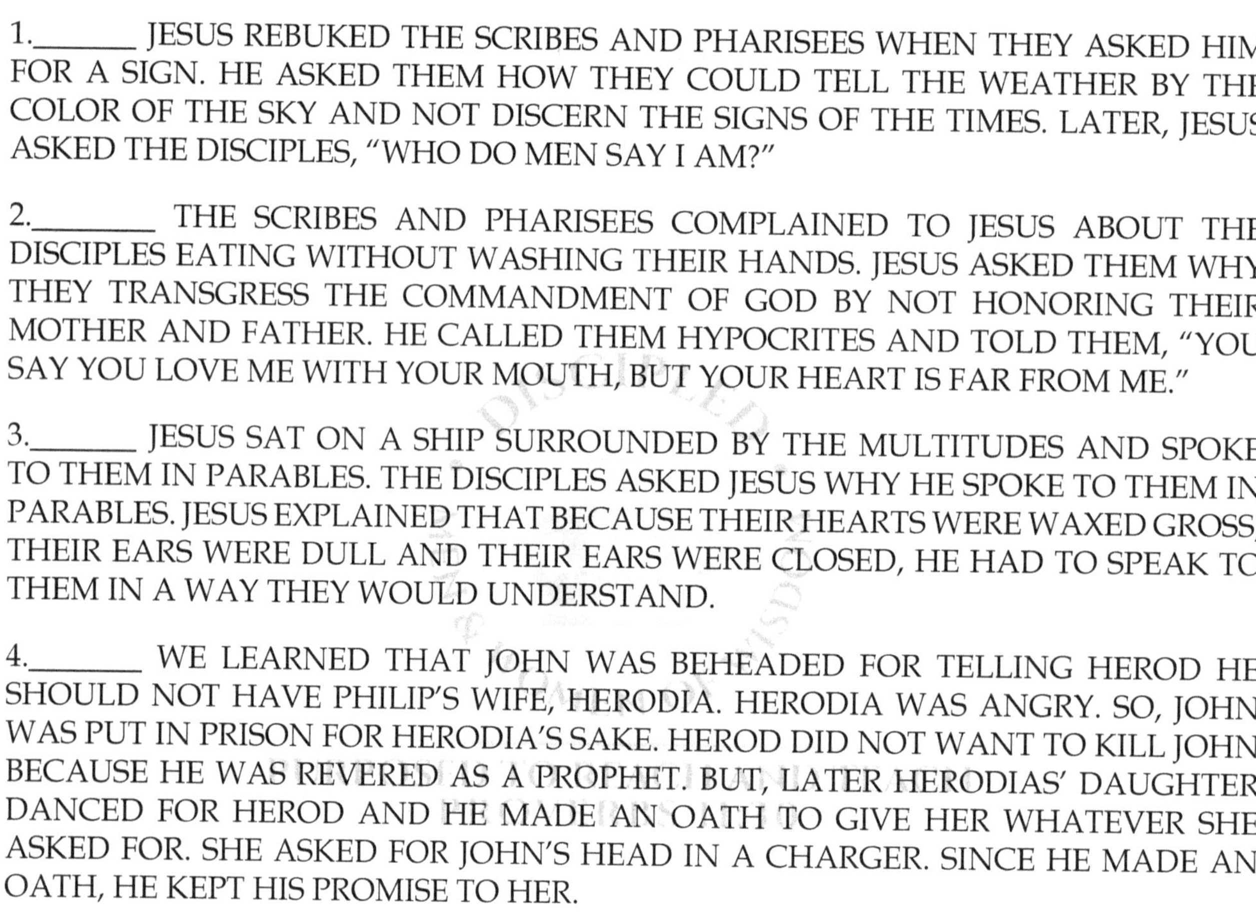

1.______ JESUS REBUKED THE SCRIBES AND PHARISEES WHEN THEY ASKED HIM FOR A SIGN. HE ASKED THEM HOW THEY COULD TELL THE WEATHER BY THE COLOR OF THE SKY AND NOT DISCERN THE SIGNS OF THE TIMES. LATER, JESUS ASKED THE DISCIPLES, "WHO DO MEN SAY I AM?"

2.______ THE SCRIBES AND PHARISEES COMPLAINED TO JESUS ABOUT THE DISCIPLES EATING WITHOUT WASHING THEIR HANDS. JESUS ASKED THEM WHY THEY TRANSGRESS THE COMMANDMENT OF GOD BY NOT HONORING THEIR MOTHER AND FATHER. HE CALLED THEM HYPOCRITES AND TOLD THEM, "YOU SAY YOU LOVE ME WITH YOUR MOUTH, BUT YOUR HEART IS FAR FROM ME."

3.______ JESUS SAT ON A SHIP SURROUNDED BY THE MULTITUDES AND SPOKE TO THEM IN PARABLES. THE DISCIPLES ASKED JESUS WHY HE SPOKE TO THEM IN PARABLES. JESUS EXPLAINED THAT BECAUSE THEIR HEARTS WERE WAXED GROSS, THEIR EARS WERE DULL AND THEIR EARS WERE CLOSED, HE HAD TO SPEAK TO THEM IN A WAY THEY WOULD UNDERSTAND.

4.______ WE LEARNED THAT JOHN WAS BEHEADED FOR TELLING HEROD HE SHOULD NOT HAVE PHILIP'S WIFE, HERODIA. HERODIA WAS ANGRY. SO, JOHN WAS PUT IN PRISON FOR HERODIA'S SAKE. HEROD DID NOT WANT TO KILL JOHN BECAUSE HE WAS REVERED AS A PROPHET. BUT, LATER HERODIAS' DAUGHTER DANCED FOR HEROD AND HE MADE AN OATH TO GIVE HER WHATEVER SHE ASKED FOR. SHE ASKED FOR JOHN'S HEAD IN A CHARGER. SINCE HE MADE AN OATH, HE KEPT HIS PROMISE TO HER.

TRUE OR FALSE

5. The seeds that fell on stony ground were devoured by the fowls.

____

Matthew 13:4-6

6. When the disciples saw Jesus walking on the sea, they cried out in fear because they thought it was a spirit.

____

Matthew 14:26

7. Before Jesus sailed to Magdala, he fed the multitude with 7 loaves of bread and a few fish.

____

Matthew 15:36-39

FILL IN THE BLANKS

8. But he answered and said, It is not_____________to take the children's_____________, and to cast it to_____________.

Matthew 15:26

9. Who hath_____________to hear,_____________him_____________.

Matthew 13:9

10. And_____________answered him and said, Lord, if it be_____________, bid me_____________unto thee on the water.

Matthew 14:28

STUDENT PRAYER JOURNAL

Please use this space to record your thoughts and feelings as you travel on this spirit led journey through the word of God with us. Please know that you have brothers and sisters in this organization from all over the world praying with and for you. My prayer for you is that you will begin to see the power of God resting in each set of your footprints. As you look back and examine your past in this journal, may you realize that you were never alone and according to Hebrews 13:5, God will never leave nor forsake you. ~LADY FLORA

THE STUDY OF THE FOUR GOSPELS VOCABULARY DEFINITIONS FOR MATTHEW CHAPTERS 17-20

WORD	DEFINITIONS
1) TRANSFIGURED	
2) PERVERSE	
3) CONVERTED	
4) MILLSTONE	
5) RECKON	
6) TALENTS	
7) TWAIN	
8) ASUNDER	
9) EUNUCHS	
10) EYE OF A NEEDLE	

DMWW Daily Bible Reading
KJV MATTHEW CHAPTERS 17-20

CHAPTER 17

1. And after six days Jesus taketh Peter, James, and John his brother, and bringeth them up into an high mountain apart,
2. And was transfigured before them: and his face did shine as the sun, and his raiment was white as the light.
3. And, behold, there appeared unto them Moses and Elias talking with him.
4. Then answered Peter, and said unto Jesus, Lord, it is good for us to be here: if thou wilt, let us make here three tabernacles; one for thee, and one for Moses, and one for Elias.
5. While he yet spake, behold, a bright cloud overshadowed them: and behold a voice out of the cloud, which said, This is my beloved Son, in whom I am well pleased; hear ye him.
6. And when the disciples heard it, they fell on their face, and were sore afraid.
7. And Jesus came and touched them, and said, Arise, and be not afraid.
8. And when they had lifted up their eyes, they saw no man, save Jesus only.
9. And as they came down from the mountain, Jesus charged them, saying, Tell the vision to no man, until the Son of man be risen again from the dead.
10. And his disciples asked him, saying, Why then say the scribes that Elias must first come?
11. And Jesus answered and said unto them, Elias truly shall first come, and restore all things.
12. But I say unto you, That Elias is come already, and they knew him not, but have done unto him whatsoever they listed. Likewise shall also the Son of man suffer of them.
13. Then the disciples understood that he spake unto them of John the Baptist.
14. And when they were come to the multitude, there came to him a certain man, kneeling down to him, and saying,
15. Lord, have mercy on my son: for he is lunatick, and sore vexed: for ofttimes he falleth into the fire, and oft into the water.
16. And I brought him to thy disciples, and they could not cure him.
17. Then Jesus answered and said, O faithless and perverse generation, how long shall I be with you? how long shall I suffer you? bring him hither to me.
18. And Jesus rebuked the devil; and he departed out of him: and the child was cured from that very hour.

19. Then came the disciples to Jesus apart, and said, Why could not we cast him out?

20. And Jesus said unto them, Because of your unbelief: for verily I say unto you, If ye have faith as a grain of mustard seed, ye shall say unto this mountain, Remove hence to yonder place; and it shall remove; and nothing shall be impossible unto you.

21. Howbeit this kind goeth not out but by prayer and fasting.

22. And while they abode in Galilee, Jesus said unto them, The Son of man shall be betrayed into the hands of men:

23. And they shall kill him, and the third day he shall be raised again. And they were exceeding sorry.

24. And when they were come to Capernaum, they that received tribute money came to Peter, and said, Doth not your master pay tribute?

25. He saith, Yes. And when he was come into the house, Jesus prevented him, saying, What thinkest thou, Simon? of whom do the kings of the earth take custom or tribute? of their own children, or of strangers?

26. Peter saith unto him, Of strangers. Jesus saith unto him, Then are the children free.

27. Notwithstanding, lest we should offend them, go thou to the sea, and cast an hook, and take up the fish that first cometh up; and when thou hast opened his mouth, thou shalt find a piece of money: that take, and give unto them for me and thee.

CHAPTER 18

1. At the same time came the disciples unto Jesus, saying, Who is the greatest in the kingdom of heaven?

2. And Jesus called a little child unto him, and set him in the midst of them,

3. And said, Verily I say unto you, Except ye be converted, and become as little children, ye shall not enter into the kingdom of heaven.

4. Whosoever therefore shall humble himself as this little child, the same is greatest in the kingdom of heaven.

5. And whoso shall receive one such little child in my name receiveth me.

6. But whoso shall offend one of these little ones which believe in me, it were better for him that a millstone were hanged about his neck, and that he were drowned in the depth of the sea.

7. Woe unto the world because of offences! for it must needs be that offences come; but woe to that man by whom the offence cometh!

8. Wherefore if thy hand or thy foot offend thee, cut them off, and cast them from thee: it is better for thee to enter into life halt or maimed, rather than having two hands or two feet to be cast into everlasting fire.

9. And if thine eye offend thee, pluck it out, and cast it from thee: it is better for thee to enter into life with one eye, rather than having two eyes to be cast into hell fire.

10. Take heed that ye despise not one of these little ones; for I say unto you, That in heaven their angels do always behold the face of my Father which is in heaven.

11. For the Son of man is come to save that which was lost.

12. How think ye? if a man have an hundred sheep, and one of them be gone astray, doth he not leave the ninety and nine, and goeth into the mountains, and seeketh that which is gone astray?

13. And if so be that he find it, verily I say unto you, he rejoiceth more of that sheep, than of the ninety and nine which went not astray.

14. Even so it is not the will of your Father which is in heaven, that one of these little ones should perish.

15. Moreover if thy brother shall trespass against thee, go and tell him his fault between thee and him alone: if he shall hear thee, thou hast gained thy brother.

16. But if he will not hear thee, then take with thee one or two more, that in the mouth of two or three witnesses every word may be established.

17. And if he shall neglect to hear them, tell it unto the church: but if he neglect to hear the church, let him be unto thee as an heathen man and a publican.

18. Verily I say unto you, Whatsoever ye shall bind on earth shall be bound in heaven: and whatsoever ye shall loose on earth shall be loosed in heaven.

19. Again I say unto you, That if two of you shall agree on earth as touching any thing that they shall ask, it shall be done for them of my Father which is in heaven.

20. For where two or three are gathered together in my name, there am I in the midst of them.

21. Then came Peter to him, and said, Lord, how oft shall my brother sin against me, and I forgive him? till seven times?

22. Jesus saith unto him, I say not unto thee, Until seven times: but, Until seventy times seven.

23. Therefore is the kingdom of heaven likened unto a certain king, which would take account of his servants.

24. And when he had begun to reckon, one was brought unto him, which owed him ten thousand talents.

25. But forasmuch as he had not to pay, his lord commanded him to be sold, and his wife, and children, and all that he had, and payment to be made.

26. The servant therefore fell down, and worshipped him, saying, Lord, have patience with me, and I will pay thee all.

27. Then the lord of that servant was moved with compassion, and loosed him, and forgave him the debt.

28. But the same servant went out, and found one of his fellowservants, which owed him an hundred pence: and he laid hands on him, and took him by the throat, saying, Pay me that thou owest.

29. And his fellowservant fell down at his feet, and besought him, saying, Have patience with me, and I will pay thee all.

30. And he would not: but went and cast him into prison, till he should pay the debt.

31. So when his fellowservants saw what was done, they were very sorry, and came and told unto their lord all that was done.

32. Then his lord, after that he had called him, said unto him, O thou wicked servant, I forgave thee all that debt, because thou desiredst me:

33. Shouldest not thou also have had compassion on thy fellowservant, even as I had pity on thee?

34. And his lord was wroth, and delivered him to the tormentors, till he should pay all that was due unto him.

35. So likewise shall my heavenly Father do also unto you, if ye from your hearts forgive not every one his brother their trespasses.

CHAPTER 19

1. And it came to pass, that when Jesus had finished these sayings, he departed from Galilee, and came into the coasts of Judaea beyond Jordan;

2. And great multitudes followed him; and he healed them there.

3. The Pharisees also came unto him, tempting him, and saying unto him, Is it lawful for a man to put away his wife for every cause?

4. And he answered and said unto them, Have ye not read, that he which made them at the beginning made them male and female,

5. And said, For this cause shall a man leave father and mother, and shall cleave to his wife: and they twain shall be one flesh?

6. Wherefore they are no more twain, but one flesh. What therefore God hath joined together, let not man put asunder.

7. They say unto him, Why did Moses then command to give a writing of divorcement, and to put her away?

8. He saith unto them, Moses because of the hardness of your hearts suffered you to put away your wives: but from the beginning it was not so.

9. And I say unto you, Whosoever shall put away his wife, except it be for fornication, and shall marry another, committeth adultery: and whoso marrieth her which is put away doth commit adultery.

10. His disciples say unto him, If the case of the man be so with his wife, it is not good to marry.

11. But he said unto them, All men cannot receive this saying, save they to whom it is given.

12. For there are some eunuchs, which were so born from their mother's womb: and there are some eunuchs, which were made eunuchs of men: and there be eunuchs, which have made themselves eunuchs for the kingdom of heaven's sake. He that is able to receive it, let him receive it.

13. Then were there brought unto him little children, that he should put his hands on them, and pray: and the disciples rebuked them.

14. But Jesus said, Suffer little children, and forbid them not, to come unto me: for of such is the kingdom of heaven.

15. And he laid his hands on them, and departed thence.

16. And, behold, one came and said unto him, Good Master, what good thing shall I do, that I may have eternal life?

17. And he said unto him, Why callest thou me good? there is none good but one, that is, God: but if thou wilt enter into life, keep the commandments.

18. He saith unto him, Which? Jesus said, Thou shalt do no murder, Thou shalt not commit adultery, Thou shalt not steal, Thou shalt not bear false witness,

19. Honour thy father and thy mother: and, Thou shalt love thy neighbour as thyself.

20. The young man saith unto him, All these things have I kept from my youth up: what lack I yet?

21. Jesus said unto him, If thou wilt be perfect, go and sell that thou hast, and give to the poor, and thou shalt have treasure in heaven: and come and follow me.

22. But when the young man heard that saying, he went away sorrowful: for he had great possessions.

23. Then said Jesus unto his disciples, Verily I say unto you, That a rich man shall hardly enter into the kingdom of heaven.

24. And again I say unto you, It is easier for a camel to go through the eye of a needle, than for a rich man to enter into the kingdom of God.

25. When his disciples heard it, they were exceedingly amazed, saying, Who then can be saved?

26. But Jesus beheld them, and said unto them, With men this is impossible; but with God all things are possible.

27. Then answered Peter and said unto him, Behold, we have forsaken all, and followed thee; what shall we have therefore?

28. And Jesus said unto them, Verily I say unto you, That ye which have followed me, in the regeneration when the Son of man shall sit in the throne of his glory, ye also shall sit upon twelve thrones, judging the twelve tribes of Israel.

29. And every one that hath forsaken houses, or brethren, or sisters, or father, or mother, or wife, or children, or lands, for my name's sake, shall receive an hundredfold, and shall inherit everlasting life.

30. But many that are first shall be last; and the last shall be first.

CHAPTER 20

1. For the kingdom of heaven is like unto a man that is an householder, which went out early in the morning to hire labourers into his vineyard.

2. And when he had agreed with the labourers for a penny a day, he sent them into his vineyard.

3. And he went out about the third hour, and saw others standing idle in the marketplace,

4. And said unto them; Go ye also into the vineyard, and whatsoever is right I will give you. And they went their way.

5. Again he went out about the sixth and ninth hour, and did likewise.

6. And about the eleventh hour he went out, and found others standing idle, and saith unto them, Why stand ye here all the day idle?

7. They say unto him, Because no man hath hired us. He saith unto them, Go ye also into the vineyard; and whatsoever is right, that shall ye receive.

8. So when even was come, the lord of the vineyard saith unto his steward, Call the labourers, and give them their hire, beginning from the last unto the first.

9. And when they came that were hired about the eleventh hour, they received every man a penny.

10. But when the first came, they supposed that they should have received more; and they likewise received every man a penny.

11. And when they had received it, they murmured against the goodman of the house,

12. Saying, These last have wrought but one hour, and thou hast made them equal unto us, which have borne the burden and heat of the day.

13. But he answered one of them, and said, Friend, I do thee no wrong: didst not thou agree with me for a penny?

14. Take that thine is, and go thy way: I will give unto this last, even as unto thee.

15. Is it not lawful for me to do what I will with mine own? Is thine eye evil, because I am good?

16. So the last shall be first, and the first last: for many be called, but few chosen.

17. And Jesus going up to Jerusalem took the twelve disciples apart in the way, and said unto them,

18. Behold, we go up to Jerusalem; and the Son of man shall be betrayed unto the chief priests and unto the scribes, and they shall condemn him to death,

19. And shall deliver him to the Gentiles to mock, and to scourge, and to crucify him: and the third day he shall rise again.

20. Then came to him the mother of Zebedees children with her sons, worshipping him, and desiring a certain thing of him.

21. And he said unto her, What wilt thou? She saith unto him, Grant that these my two sons may sit, the one on thy right hand, and the other on the left, in thy kingdom.

22. But Jesus answered and said, Ye know not what ye ask. Are ye able to drink of the cup that I shall drink of, and to be baptized with the baptism that I am baptized with? They say unto him, We are able.

23. And he saith unto them, Ye shall drink indeed of my cup, and be baptized with the baptism that I am baptized with: but to sit on my right hand, and on my left, is not mine to give, but it shall be given to them for whom it is prepared of my Father.

24. And when the ten heard it, they were moved with indignation against the two brethren.

25. But Jesus called them unto him, and said, Ye know that the princes of the Gentiles exercise dominion over them, and they that are great exercise authority upon them.

26. But it shall not be so among you: but whosoever will be great among you, let him be your minister;

27. And whosoever will be chief among you, let him be your servant:

28. Even as the Son of man came not to be ministered unto, but to minister, and to give his life a ransom for many.

29. And as they departed from Jericho, a great multitude followed him.

30. And, behold, two blind men sitting by the way side, when they heard that Jesus passed by, cried out, saying, Have mercy on us, O Lord, thou son of David.

31. And the multitude rebuked them, because they should hold their peace: but they cried the more, saying, Have mercy on us, O Lord, thou son of David.

32. And Jesus stood still, and called them, and said, What will ye that I shall do unto you?

33. They say unto him, Lord, that our eyes may be opened.

34. So Jesus had compassion on them, and touched their eyes: and immediately their eyes received sight, and they followed him.

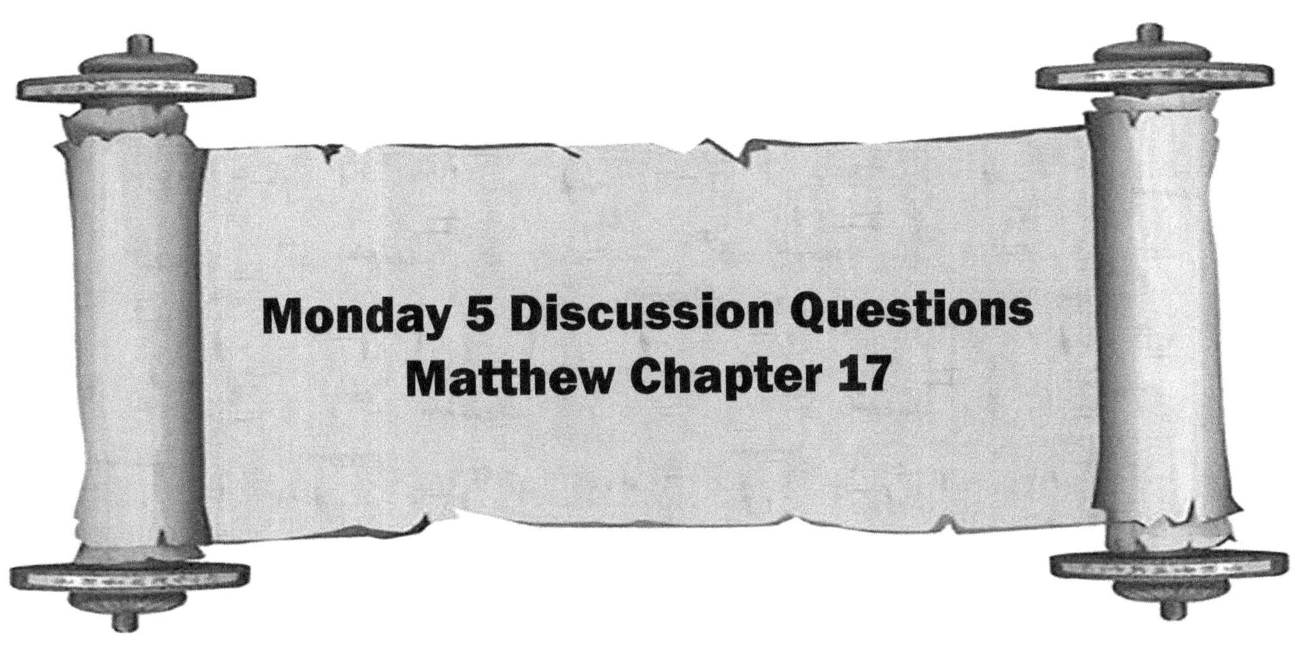

1. Who did Jesus take up to a high mountain after six days? ______

2. What did Jesus do when they got there? ______

3. How did Jesus' face and clothing look? ______

4. Who appeared before them, talking to Jesus? ______

5. What did Peter suggest to Jesus? ______

6. What did the voice from the clouds say to Peter, James and John? ______

7. What did they do when they heard the voice? ______

8. What did Jesus say to them when he touched them? What did they see when they lifted up their eyes? ______

9. What did the man tell Jesus about the disciples, when he brought his child to Jesus because he had a lunatick spirit? ______

10. What did Jesus say to the disciples' question about this kind of spirit, after he rebuked the demon out of the child? ______

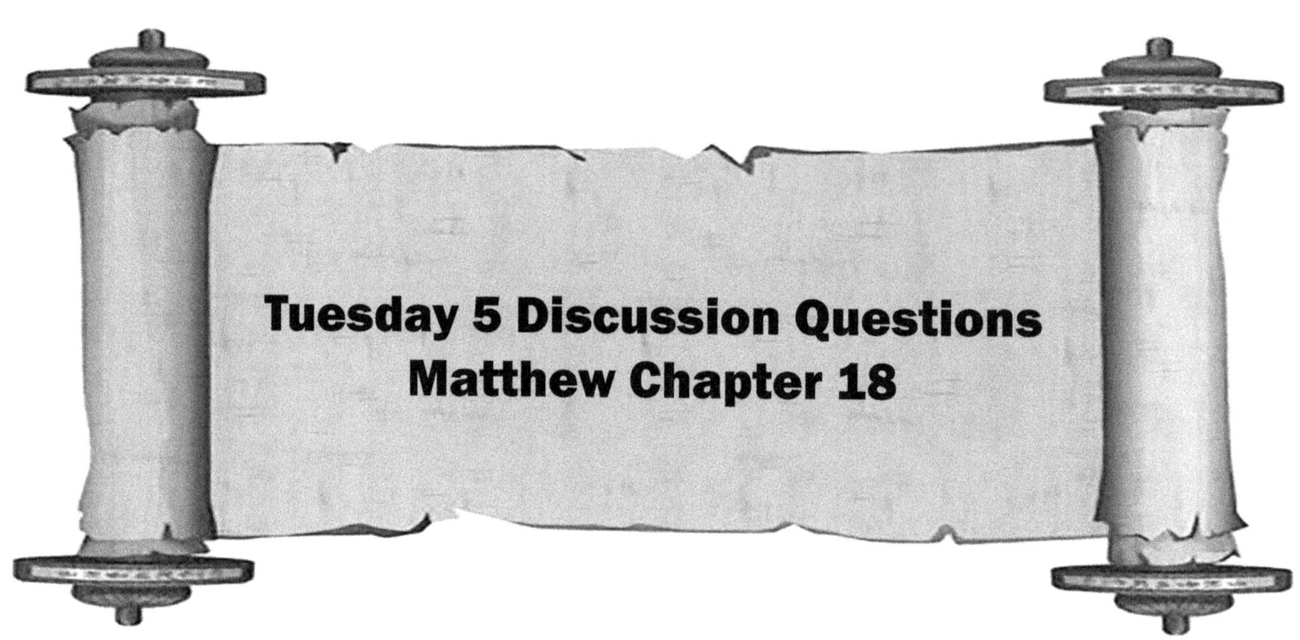

1. What question did the disciples ask Jesus? ______________________________

2. What did Jesus say about the child he set in the midst of the people? ______________________________

3. What did he tell the people they had to do to enter into the kingdom of heaven? ______________________________

4. What did Jesus say about the people who offend the little ones who believe in him? ______________________________

5. Why did he say Woe unto the world? ______________________________

6. What did he say about the people who commit the offenses that must come? ______________________________

7. What did he say to do if your hand or foot offends you? Why? ______________________________

8. What did he say to do if your eye offends you? Why? ______________________________

9. Why did he say not to despise his little ones? ______________________________

10. What did Jesus say about binding and loosing and earth and heaven? ______________________________

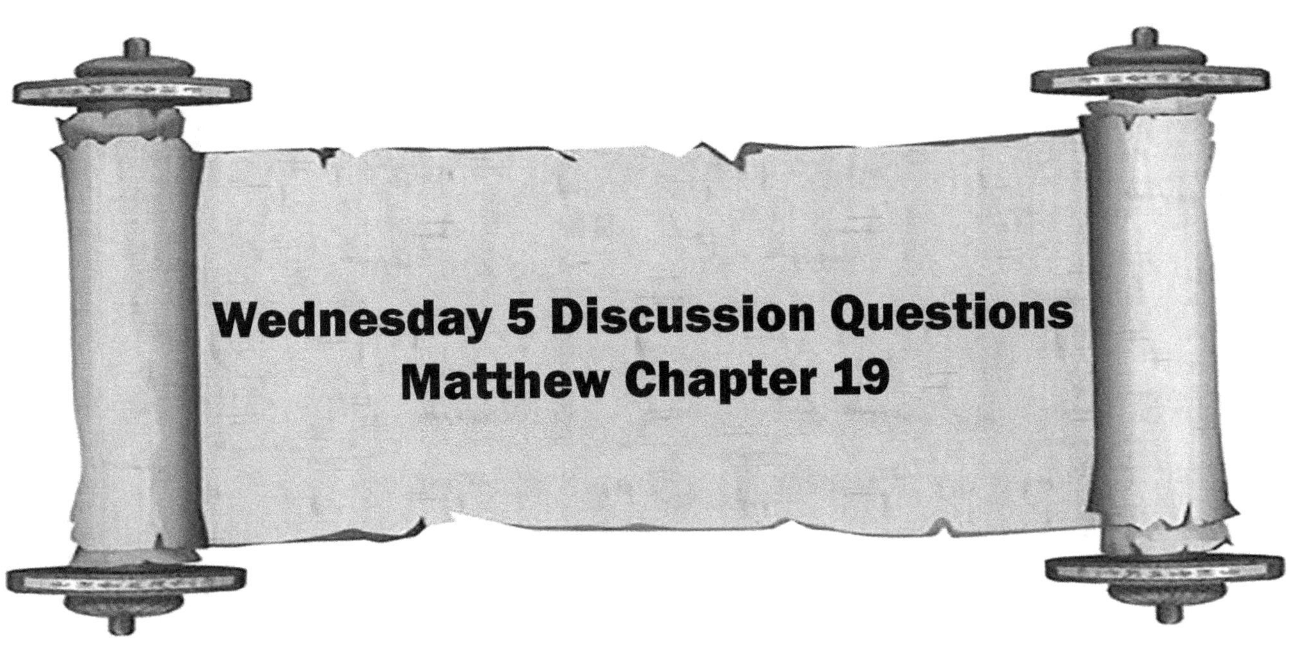

1. Where did Jesus go when he departed from Galilea? ______

2. What did the Pharisees tempt Jesus by asking? ______

3. How did Jesus respond to them? ______

4. What was Jesus' instruction concerning what God had joined together? ______

5. What was their question about what Moses said? ______

6. What did Jesus tell them? ______

7. What sin does man commit when he divorces his wife for anything other than fornication? What about the man that marries the woman that was divorced? ______

8. What did Jesus tell the disciples about the eunuchs and these sayings? ______

9. What did Jesus tell the disciples when they rebuked the children for coming to Jesus for prayer? ______

10. What did Jesus say about a rich man making it into the Kingdom of God? ______

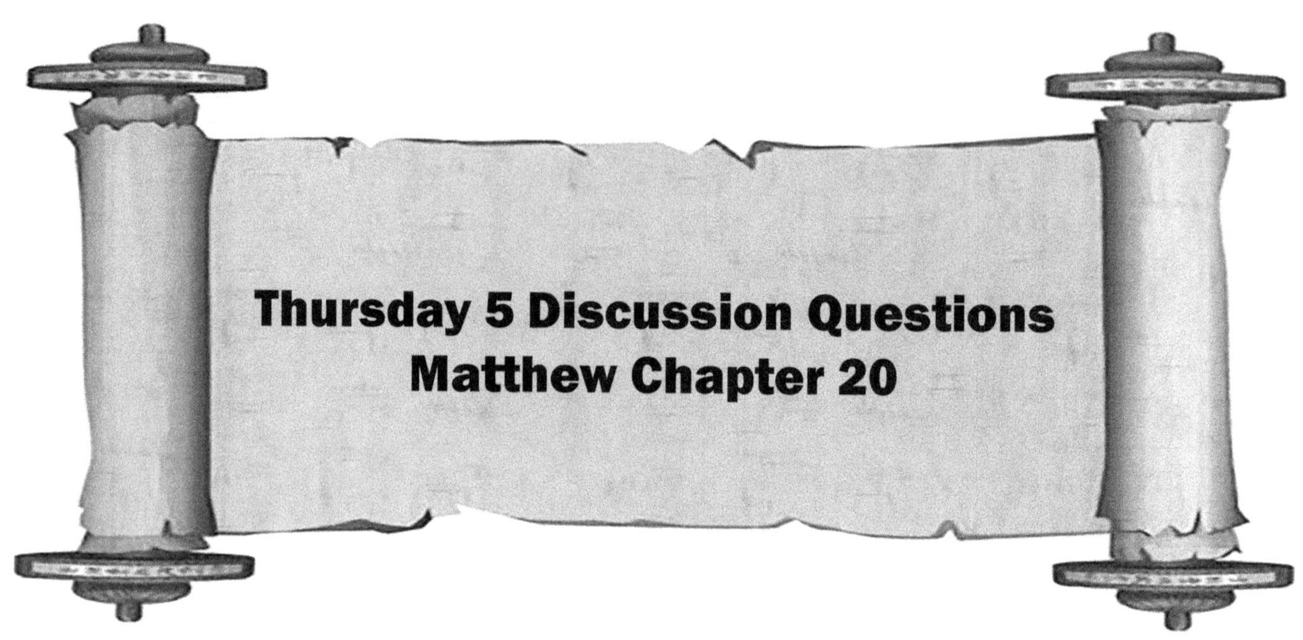

1. What did Jesus compare the kingdom of Heaven to, in this chapter? ______
2. How much did the householder agree to give the workers to labor in the vineyard? ______
3. What did the householder see in the third hour? What did he tell them to do? What did he promise them? ______
4. What did he do in the sixth and ninth hour? ______
5. What did he do in the eleventh hour? ______
6. What did he ask the men? ______
7. What was their response? ______
8. What happened that evening? ______
9. Why did the first men murmur against the goodman of the house? ______
10. How did the goodman respond to the laborers? ______

WEEKLY REVIEW
MATTHEW CHAPTERS 17-20

NAME THAT CHAPTER

1.______ JESUS TOOK PETER, JAMES AND HIS BROTHER JOHN UP INTO A HIGH MOUNTAIN AFTER SIX DAYS, AND WAS TRANSFIGURED IN FRONT OF THEM. GOD SPOKE TO THEM FROM A CLOUD AND SAID, "THIS IS MY SON IN WHOM I AM WELL PLEASED."

2.______ JESUS EXPLAINS TO THE DISCIPLES WITH A PARABLE OF A HOUSEHOLDER THAT THE KINGDOM OF HEAVEN IS LIKE THE HOUSEHOLDER HAVING THE RIGHT TO REWARD THE LABORERS THE WAY THAT HE CHOOSES. THE HOUSEHOLDER HAD PAID A PENNY A DAY TO THE PEOPLE WHO CAME ON THE FIRST CALL AS HE DID TO THOSE WHO CAME THE SIXTH, NINTH AND ELEVENTH HOUR.

3.______ WHEN JESUS TOLD THE DISCIPLES THAT IT WAS NOT LAWFUL FOR A MAN TO PUT HIS WIFE AWAY EXCEPT FOR FORNICATION, THEY QUESTIONED WHY MOSES WRITE DIVORCEMENT. JESUS EXPLAINED THAT IT WASN'T THAT WAY IN THE BEGINNING AND ONLY BECAUSE OF THE HARDNESS OF THEIR HEARTS, MOSES ALLOWED IT. HE ALSO EXPLAINS THAT IF A MAN PUTS HIS WIFE AWAY, HE COMMITS ADULTERY AND IF A MAN MARRIES HER AFTER THE DIVORCE, HE IS ALSO GUILTY OF ADULTERY.

4.______ WHEN THE DISCIPLES ASKED JESUS WHO WAS THE GREATEST IN HEAVEN, HE EXPLAINED TO THEM THAT EXCEPT THAT ONE IS CONVERTED AND COMES TO HIM AS A LITTLE CHILD, THEY WOULD NOT SEE THE KINGDOM OF HEAVEN. HE TOLD THEM THAT THE PEOPLE THAT COME AS LITTLE CHILDREN ARE THE GREATEST IN THE KINGDOM OF GOD.

TRUE OR FALSE

5. THE LABORERS WERE ALL HAPPY WITH THE WAGES THEY RECEIVED FOR WORKING IN THE VINEYARD.

____

6. Peter said, "It is good for us to be here: if thou wilt, let us make here three tabernacles; one for thee, and one for Moses, and one for Elias.

____

7. JESUS TOLD PETER THAT ONE MUST FORGIVE ANOTHER SEVENTY TIMES SEVEN.

____

FILL IN THE BLANKS

8. For where____________or __________are gathered____________in my name, there am I in the midst of them.

9. ____________this kind__________not out but by prayer and __________.

10. With ________ this is ____________; but with____________all things are possible.

STUDENT PRAYER JOURNAL

Please use this space to record your thoughts and feelings as you travel on this spirit led journey through the word of God with us. Please know that you have brothers and sisters in this organization from all over the world praying with and for you. My prayer for you is that you will begin to see the power of God resting in each set of your footprints. As you look back and examine your past in this journal, may you realize that you were never alone and according to Hebrews 13:5, God will never leave nor forsake you. ~LADY FLORA

The Study of The Four Gospels
Matthew Chapters 21-24
VOCABULARY DEFINITIONS

WORD	DEFINITIONS
1. NIGH	
2. OUGHT	
3. MONEYCHANGERS	
4. HOSANNA	
5. HUSBANDMAN	
6. SUPERSCRIPTION	
7. PHYLACTERIES	
8. ABASED	
9. PESTILENCE	
10. GOODMAN	

DMWW Daily Bible Reading
KJV MATTHEW CHAPTERS 21-24

CHAPTER 21

1. And when they drew nigh unto Jerusalem, and were come to Bethphage, unto the mount of Olives, then sent Jesus two disciples,
2. Saying unto them, Go into the village over against you, and straightway ye shall find an ass tied, and a colt with her: loose them, and bring them unto me.
3. And if any man say ought unto you, ye shall say, The Lord hath need of them; and straightway he will send them.
4. All this was done, that it might be fulfilled which was spoken by the prophet, saying,
5. Tell ye the daughter of Sion, Behold, thy King cometh unto thee, meek, and sitting upon an ass, and a colt the foal of an ass.
6. And the disciples went, and did as Jesus commanded them,
7. And brought the ass, and the colt, and put on them their clothes, and they set him thereon.
8. And a very great multitude spread their garments in the way; others cut down branches from the trees, and strawed them in the way.
9. And the multitudes that went before, and that followed, cried, saying, Hosanna to the son of David: Blessed is he that cometh in the name of the Lord; Hosanna in the highest.
10. And when he was come into Jerusalem, all the city was moved, saying, Who is this?
11. And the multitude said, This is Jesus the prophet of Nazareth of Galilee.
12. And Jesus went into the temple of God, and cast out all them that sold and bought in the temple, and overthrew the tables of the moneychangers, and the seats of them that sold doves,
13. And said unto them, It is written, My house shall be called the house of prayer; but ye have made it a den of thieves.
14. And the blind and the lame came to him in the temple; and he healed them.
15. And when the chief priests and scribes saw the wonderful things that he did, and the children crying in the temple, and saying, Hosanna to the son of David; they were sore displeased,
16. And said unto him, Hearest thou what these say? And Jesus saith unto them, Yea; have ye never read, Out of the mouth of babes and sucklings thou hast perfected praise?
17. And he left them, and went out of the city into Bethany; and he lodged there.

18. Now in the morning as he returned into the city, he hungered.

19. And when he saw a fig tree in the way, he came to it, and found nothing thereon, but leaves only, and said unto it, Let no fruit grow on thee henceforward for ever. And presently the fig tree withered away.

20. And when the disciples saw it, they marvelled, saying, How soon is the fig tree withered away!

21. Jesus answered and said unto them, Verily I say unto you, If ye have faith, and doubt not, ye shall not only do this which is done to the fig tree, but also if ye shall say unto this mountain, Be thou removed, and be thou cast into the sea; it shall be done.

22. And all things, whatsoever ye shall ask in prayer, believing, ye shall receive.

23. And when he was come into the temple, the chief priests and the elders of the people came unto him as he was teaching, and said, By what authority doest thou these things? and who gave thee this authority?

24. And Jesus answered and said unto them, I also will ask you one thing, which if ye tell me, I in like wise will tell you by what authority I do these things.

25. The baptism of John, whence was it? from heaven, or of men? And they reasoned with themselves, saying, If we shall say, From heaven; he will say unto us, Why did ye not then believe him?

26. But if we shall say, Of men; we fear the people; for all hold John as a prophet.

27. And they answered Jesus, and said, We cannot tell. And he said unto them, Neither tell I you by what authority I do these things.

28. But what think ye? A certain man had two sons; and he came to the first, and said, Son, go work to day in my vineyard.

29. He answered and said, I will not: but afterward he repented, and went.

30. And he came to the second, and said likewise. And he answered and said, I go, sir: and went not.

31. Whether of them twain did the will of his father? They say unto him, The first. Jesus saith unto them, Verily I say unto you, That the publicans and the harlots go into the kingdom of God before you.

32. For John came unto you in the way of righteousness, and ye believed him not: but the publicans and the harlots believed him: and ye, when ye had seen it, repented not afterward, that ye might believe him.

33. Hear another parable: There was a certain householder, which planted a vineyard, and hedged it round about, and digged a winepress in it, and built a tower, and let it out to husbandmen, and went into a far country:

34. And when the time of the fruit drew near, he sent his servants to the husbandmen, that they might receive the fruits of it.

35. And the husbandmen took his servants, and beat one, and killed another, and stoned another.

36. Again, he sent other servants more than the first: and they did unto them likewise.

37. But last of all he sent unto them his son, saying, They will reverence my son.

38. But when the husbandmen saw the son, they said among themselves, This is the heir; come, let us kill him, and let us seize on his inheritance.

39. And they caught him, and cast him out of the vineyard, and slew him.

40. When the lord therefore of the vineyard cometh, what will he do unto those husbandmen?

41. They say unto him, He will miserably destroy those wicked men, and will let out his vineyard unto other husbandmen, which shall render him the fruits in their seasons.

42. Jesus saith unto them, Did ye never read in the scriptures, The stone which the builders rejected, the same is become the head of the corner: this is the Lord's doing, and it is marvellous in our eyes?

43. Therefore say I unto you, The kingdom of God shall be taken from you, and given to a nation bringing forth the fruits thereof.

44. And whosoever shall fall on this stone shall be broken: but on whomsoever it shall fall, it will grind him to powder.

45. And when the chief priests and Pharisees had heard his parables, they perceived that he spake of them.

46. But when they sought to lay hands on him, they feared the multitude, because they took him for a prophet.

CHAPTER 22

1. And Jesus answered and spake unto them again by parables, and said,

2. The kingdom of heaven is like unto a certain king, which made a marriage for his son,

3. And sent forth his servants to call them that were bidden to the wedding: and they would not come.

4. Again, he sent forth other servants, saying, Tell them which are bidden, Behold, I have prepared my dinner: my oxen and my fatlings are killed, and all things are ready: come unto the marriage.

5. But they made light of it, and went their ways, one to his farm, another to his merchandise:

6. And the remnant took his servants, and entreated them spitefully, and slew them.

7. But when the king heard thereof, he was wroth: and he sent for0th his armies, and destroyed those murderers, and burned up their city.

8. Then saith he to his servants, The wedding is ready, but they which were bidden were not worthy.

9. Go ye therefore into the highways, and as many as ye shall find, bid to the marriage.

10. So those servants went out into the highways, and gathered together all as many as they found, both bad and good: and the wedding was furnished with guests.

11. And when the king came in to see the guests, he saw there a man which had not on a wedding garment:

12. And he saith unto him, Friend, how camest thou in hither not having a wedding garment? And he was speechless.

13. Then said the king to the servants, Bind him hand and foot, and take him away, and cast him into outer darkness, there shall be weeping and gnashing of teeth.

14. For many are called, but few are chosen.

15. Then went the Pharisees, and took counsel how they might entangle him in his talk.

16. And they sent out unto him their disciples with the Herodians, saying, Master, we know that thou art true, and teachest the way of God in truth, neither carest thou for any man: for thou regardest not the person of men.

17. Tell us therefore, What thinkest thou? Is it lawful to give tribute unto Caesar, or not?

18. But Jesus perceived their wickedness, and said, Why tempt ye me, ye hypocrites?

19. Shew me the tribute money. And they brought unto him a penny.

20. And he saith unto them, Whose is this image and superscription?

21. They say unto him, Caesar's. Then saith he unto them, Render therefore unto Caesar the things which are Caesar's; and unto God the things that are God's.

22. When they had heard these words, they marvelled, and left him, and went their way.

23. The same day came to him the Sadducees, which say that there is no resurrection, and asked him,

24. Saying, Master, Moses said, If a man die, having no children, his brother shall marry his wife, and raise up seed unto his brother.

25. Now there were with us seven brethren: and the first, when he had married a wife, deceased, and, having no issue, left his wife unto his brother:

26. Likewise the second also, and the third, unto the seventh.

27. And last of all the woman died also.

28. Therefore in the resurrection whose wife shall she be of the seven? for they all had her.

29. Jesus answered and said unto them, Ye do err, not knowing the scriptures, nor the power of God.

30. For in the resurrection they neither marry, nor are given in marriage, but are as the angels of God in heaven.

31. But as touching the resurrection of the dead, have ye not read that which was spoken unto you by God, saying,

32. I am the God of Abraham, and the God of Isaac, and the God of Jacob? God is not the God of the dead, but of the living.

33. And when the multitude heard this, they were astonished at his doctrine.

34. But when the Pharisees had heard that he had put the Sadducees to silence, they were gathered together.

35. Then one of them, which was a lawyer, asked him a question, tempting him, and saying,

36. Master, which is the great commandment in the law?

37. Jesus said unto him, Thou shalt love the Lord thy God with all thy heart, and with all thy soul, and with all thy mind.

38. This is the first and great commandment.

39. And the second is like unto it, Thou shalt love thy neighbour as thyself.

40. On these two commandments hang all the law and the prophets.

41. While the Pharisees were gathered together, Jesus asked them,

42. Saying, What think ye of Christ? whose son is he? They say unto him, The son of David.

43. He saith unto them, How then doth David in spirit call him Lord, saying,

44. The Lord said unto my Lord, Sit thou on my right hand, till I make thine enemies thy footstool?

45. If David then call him Lord, how is he his son?

46. And no man was able to answer him a word, neither durst any man from that day forth ask him any more questions.

CHAPTER 23

1. Then spake Jesus to the multitude, and to his disciples,

2. Saying The scribes and the Pharisees sit in Moses' seat:

3. All therefore whatsoever they bid you observe, that observe and do; but do not ye after their works: for they say, and do not.

4. For they bind heavy burdens and grievous to be borne, and lay them on men's shoulders; but they themselves will not move them with one of their fingers.

5. But all their works they do for to be seen of men: they make broad their phylacteries, and enlarge the borders of their garments,

6. And love the uppermost rooms at feasts, and the chief seats in the synagogues,

7. And greetings in the markets, and to be called of men, Rabbi, Rabbi.

8. But be not ye called Rabbi: for one is your Master, even Christ; and all ye are brethren.

9. And call no man your father upon the earth: for one is your Father, which is in heaven.

10. Neither be ye called masters: for one is your Master, even Christ.

11. But he that is greatest among you shall be your servant.

12. And whosoever shall exalt himself shall be abased; and he that shall humble himself shall be exalted.

13. But woe unto you, scribes and Pharisees, hypocrites! for ye shut up the kingdom of heaven against men: for ye neither go in yourselves, neither suffer ye them that are entering to go in.

14. Woe unto you, scribes and Pharisees, hypocrites! for ye devour widows' houses, and for a pretence make long prayer: therefore ye shall receive the greater damnation.

15. Woe unto you, scribes and Pharisees, hypocrites! for ye compass sea and land to make one proselyte, and when he is made, ye make him twofold more the child of hell than yourselves.

16. Woe unto you, ye blind guides, which say, Whosoever shall swear by the temple, it is nothing; but whosoever shall swear by the gold of the temple, he is a debtor!

17. Ye fools and blind: for whether is greater, the gold, or the temple that sanctifieth the gold?

18. And, Whosoever shall swear by the altar, it is nothing; but whosoever sweareth by the gift that is upon it, he is guilty.

19. Ye fools and blind: for whether is greater, the gift, or the altar that sanctifieth the gift?

20. Whoso therefore shall swear by the altar, sweareth by it, and by all things thereon.

21. And whoso shall swear by the temple, sweareth by it, and by him that dwelleth therein.

22. And he that shall swear by heaven, sweareth by the throne of God, and by him that sitteth thereon.

23. Woe unto you, scribes and Pharisees, hypocrites! for ye pay tithe of mint and anise and cummin, and have omitted the weightier matters of the law, judgment, mercy, and faith: these ought ye to have done, and not to leave the other undone.

24. Ye blind guides, which strain at a gnat, and swallow a camel.

25. Woe unto you, scribes and Pharisees, hypocrites! for ye make clean the outside of the cup and of the platter, but within they are full of extortion and excess.

26. Thou blind Pharisee, cleanse first that which is within the cup and platter, that the outside of them may be clean also.

27. Woe unto you, scribes and Pharisees, hypocrites! for ye are like unto whited sepulchres, which indeed appear beautiful outward, but are within full of dead men's bones, and of all uncleanness.

28. Even so ye also outwardly appear righteous unto men, but within ye are full of hypocrisy and iniquity.

29. Woe unto you, scribes and Pharisees, hypocrites! because ye build the tombs of the prophets, and garnish the sepulchres of the righteous,

30. And say, If we had been in the days of our fathers, we would not have been partakers with them in the blood of the prophets.

31. Wherefore ye be witnesses unto yourselves, that ye are the children of them which killed the prophets.

32. Fill ye up then the measure of your fathers.

33. Ye serpents, ye generation of vipers, how can ye escape the damnation of hell?

34. Wherefore, behold, I send unto you prophets, and wise men, and scribes: and some of them ye shall kill and crucify; and some of them shall ye scourge in your synagogues, and persecute them from city to city:

35. That upon you may come all the righteous blood shed upon the earth, from the blood of righteous Abel unto the blood of Zacharias son of Barachias, whom ye slew between the temple and the altar.

36. Verily I say unto you, All these things shall come upon this generation.

37. O Jerusalem, Jerusalem, thou that killest the prophets, and stonest them which are sent unto thee, how often would I have gathered thy children together, even as a hen gathereth her chickens under her wings, and ye would not!

38. Behold, your house is left unto you desolate.

39. For I say unto you, Ye shall not see me henceforth, till ye shall say, Blessed is he that cometh in the name of the Lord.

CHAPTER 24

1. And Jesus went out, and departed from the temple: and his disciples came to him for to shew him the buildings of the temple.

2. And Jesus said unto them, See ye not all these things? verily I say unto you, There shall not be left here one stone upon another, that shall not be thrown down.

3. And as he sat upon the mount of Olives, the disciples came unto him privately, saying, Tell us, when shall these things be? and what shall be the sign of thy coming, and of the end of the world?

4. And Jesus answered and said unto them, Take heed that no man deceive you.

5. For many shall come in my name, saying, I am Christ; and shall deceive many.

6. And ye shall hear of wars and rumours of wars: see that ye be not troubled: for all these things must come to pass, but the end is not yet.

7. For nation shall rise against nation, and kingdom against kingdom: and there shall be famines, and pestilences, and earthquakes, in divers places.

8. All these are the beginning of sorrows.

9. Then shall they deliver you up to be afficted, and shall kill you: and ye shall be hated of all nations for my name's sake.

10. And then shall many be offended, and shall betray one another, and shall hate one another.

11. And many false prophets shall rise, and shall deceive many.

12. And because iniquity shall abound, the love of many shall wax cold.

13. But he that shall endure unto the end, the same shall be saved.

14. And this gospel of the kingdom shall be preached in all the world for a witness unto all nations; and then shall the end come.

15. When ye therefore shall see the abomination of desolation, spoken of by Daniel the prophet, stand in the holy place, (whoso readeth, let him understand:)

16. Then let them which be in Judaea flee into the mountains:

17. Let him which is on the housetop not come down to take any thing out of his house:

18. Neither let him which is in the field return back to take his clothes.

19. And woe unto them that are with child, and to them that give suck in those days!

20. But pray ye that your flight be not in the winter, neither on the sabbath day:

21. For then shall be great tribulation, such as was not since the beginning of the world to this time, no, nor ever shall be.

22. And except those days should be shortened, there should no flesh be saved: but for the elect's sake those days shall be shortened.

23. Then if any man shall say unto you, Lo, here is Christ, or there; believe it not.

24. For there shall arise false Christs, and false prophets, and shall shew great signs and wonders; insomuch that, if it were possible, they shall deceive the very elect.

25. Behold, I have told you before.

26. Wherefore if they shall say unto you, Behold, he is in the desert; go not forth: behold, he is in the secret chambers; believe it not.

27. For as the lightning cometh out of the east, and shineth even unto the west; so shall also the coming of the Son of man be.

28. For wheresoever the carcase is, there will the eagles be gathered together.

29. Immediately after the tribulation of those days shall the sun be darkened, and the moon shall not give her light, and the stars shall fall from heaven, and the powers of the heavens shall be shaken:

30. And then shall appear the sign of the Son of man in heaven: and then shall all the tribes of the earth mourn, and they shall see the Son of man coming in the clouds of heaven with power and great glory.

31. And he shall send his angels with a great sound of a trumpet, and they shall gather together his elect from the four winds, from one end of heaven to the other.

32. Now learn a parable of the fig tree; When his branch is yet tender, and putteth forth leaves, ye know that summer is nigh:

33. So likewise ye, when ye shall see all these things, know that it is near, even at the doors.

34. Verily I say unto you, This generation shall not pass, till all these things be fulfilled.

35. Heaven and earth shall pass away, but my words shall not pass away.

36. But of that day and hour knoweth no man, no, not the angels of heaven, but my Father only.

37. But as the days of Noah were, so shall also the coming of the Son of man be.

38. For as in the days that were before the flood they were eating and drinking, marrying and giving in marriage, until the day that Noe entered into the ark,

39. And knew not until the flood came, and took them all away; so shall also the coming of the Son of man be.

40. Then shall two be in the field; the one shall be taken, and the other left.

41. Two women shall be grinding at the mill; the one shall be taken, and the other left.

42. Watch therefore: for ye know not what hour your Lord doth come.

43. But know this, that if the goodman of the house had known in what watch the thief would come, he would have watched, and would not have suffered his house to be broken up.

44. Therefore be ye also ready: for in such an hour as ye think not the Son of man cometh.

45. Who then is a faithful and wise servant, whom his lord hath made ruler over his household, to give them meat in due season?

46. Blessed is that servant, whom his lord when he cometh shall find so doing.

47. Verily I say unto you, That he shall make him ruler over all his goods.

48. But and if that evil servant shall say in his heart, My lord delayeth his coming;

49. And shall begin to smite his fellowservants, and to eat and drink with the drunken;

50. The lord of that servant shall come in a day when he looketh not for him, and in an hour that he is not aware of,

51. And shall cut him asunder, and appoint him his portion with the hypocrites: there shall be weeping and gnashing of teeth.

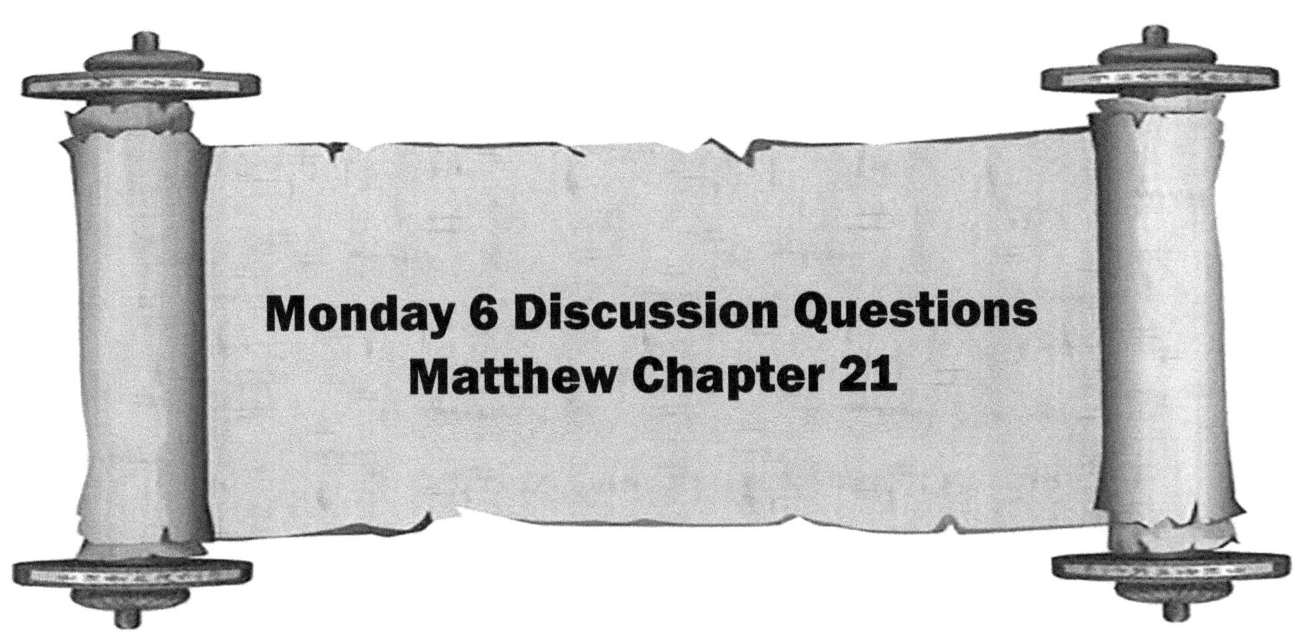

Monday 6 Discussion Questions
Matthew Chapter 21

1. What mountain did they go to when they got to Bethpage? ______

2. What did Jesus tell the two disciples they would find when he sent them to the village? ______

3. What did Jesus tell the disciples to tell Sion's daughter? ______

4. What was the multitude crying out? ______

5. Who did Jesus cast out when he went into the temple? ______

6. Jesus said his house should be called a house of prayer. What did he say they made it? ______

7. How did the scribes and Pharisees feel about the wonderful things Jesus had done? ______

8. What did Jesus do to the fig tree that did not bear fruit? ______

9. How did Jesus compare what he did to the fig tree, to what they could do to a mountain? ______

10. Why did Jesus tell the people the harlots and publicans would see heaven before they would? ______

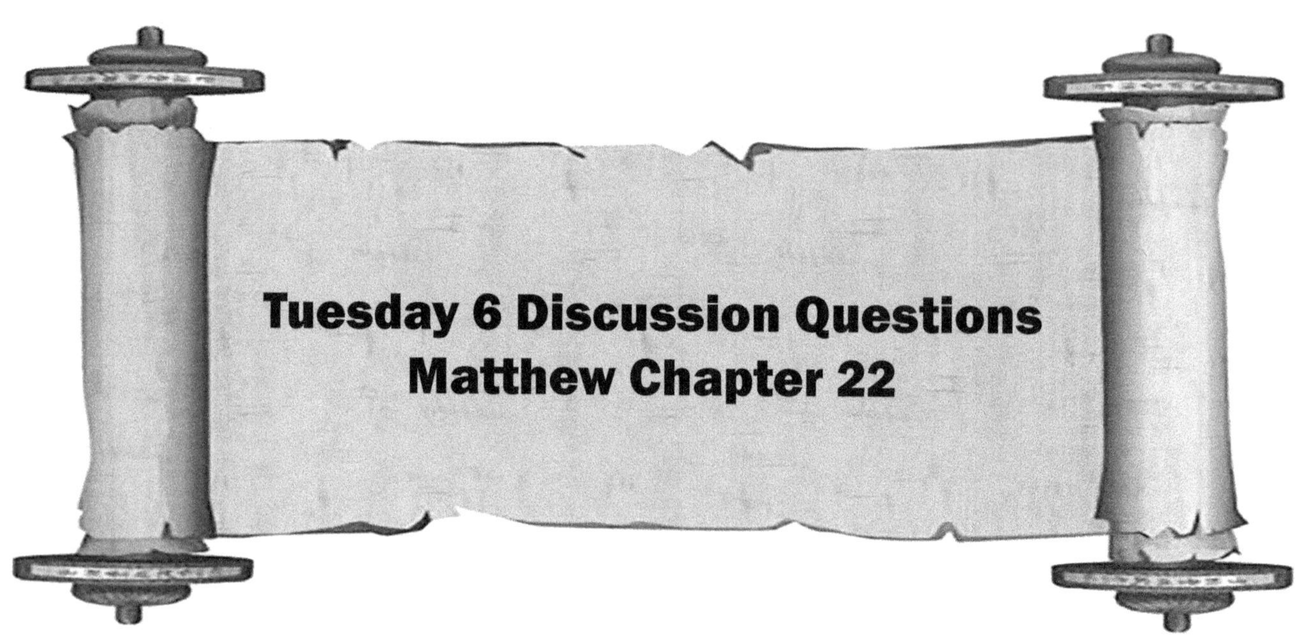

Tuesday 6 Discussion Questions
Matthew Chapter 22

1. What did Jesus tell the disciples, Heaven is like in chapter 22? ______

2. What happened when the king sent forth for the ones who had been bidden to come to the wedding? ______

3. What did they do when he sent for them to come again? ______

4. What did the king do when he heard about their response? ______

5. The wedding was ready. But there was no one worthy to come. What did the king tell the servants to do about it? ______

6. What did the servants do to furnish the wedding with guests? ______

7. What did the king see when he went in to see the guests? ______

8. What did he ask the man? *How did the man answer?* ______

9. *What did the king order the servants to do to the man?* ______

10. What did Jesus tell them about the difference between the called and the chosen? ______

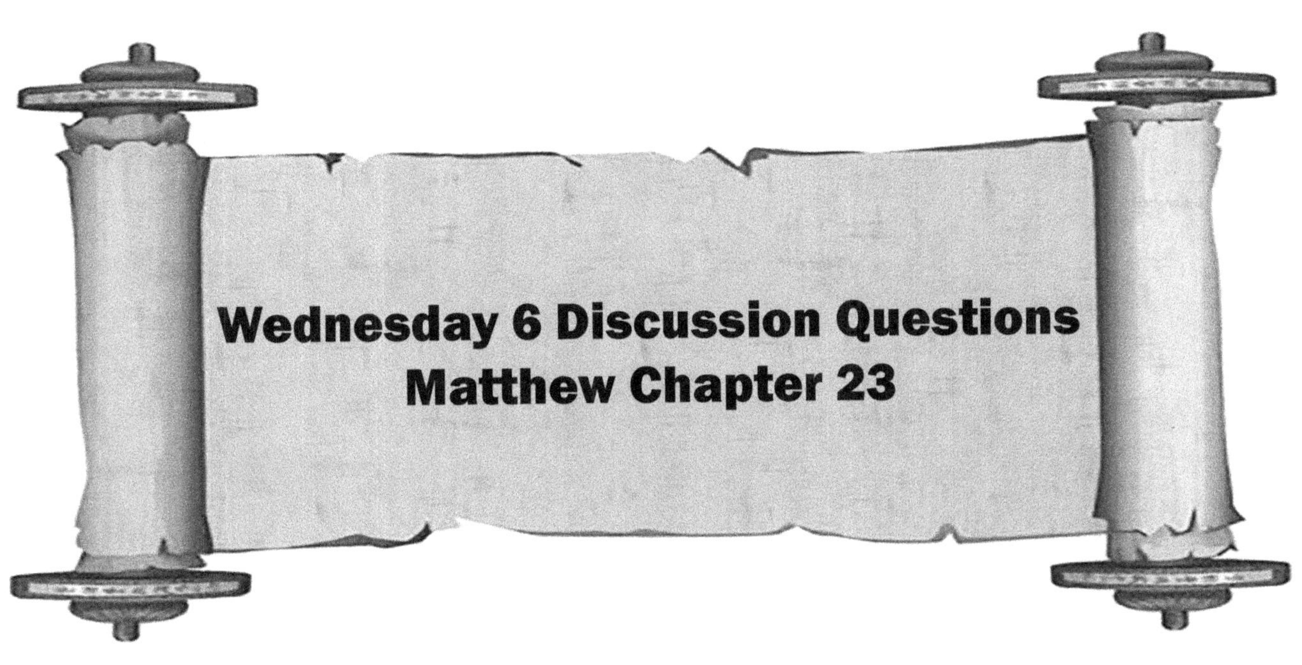

1. Who did Jesus say was sitting in Moses' seat? ______

2. What did Jesus tell the disciples to do and what did he tell them not to do? ______

3. Why did Jesus say they do their works? ______

4. What do they make broad and enlarge? ______

5. What are some other things that Jesus didn't like about their behavior? ______

6. Why did Jesus command that no man be called Rabbi, Master or Father? ______

7. How did Jesus explain the difference between those who exalt themselves and those who humble themselves? ______

8. What was Jesus talking about when he scolded the scribes and Pharisees about cleaning the outside of the cup and platter? ______

9. What did the scribes and Pharisees do to the prophets that Jesus sent? ______

10. What didJesus tell Jerusalem would happen to those who persecuted the prophets? ______

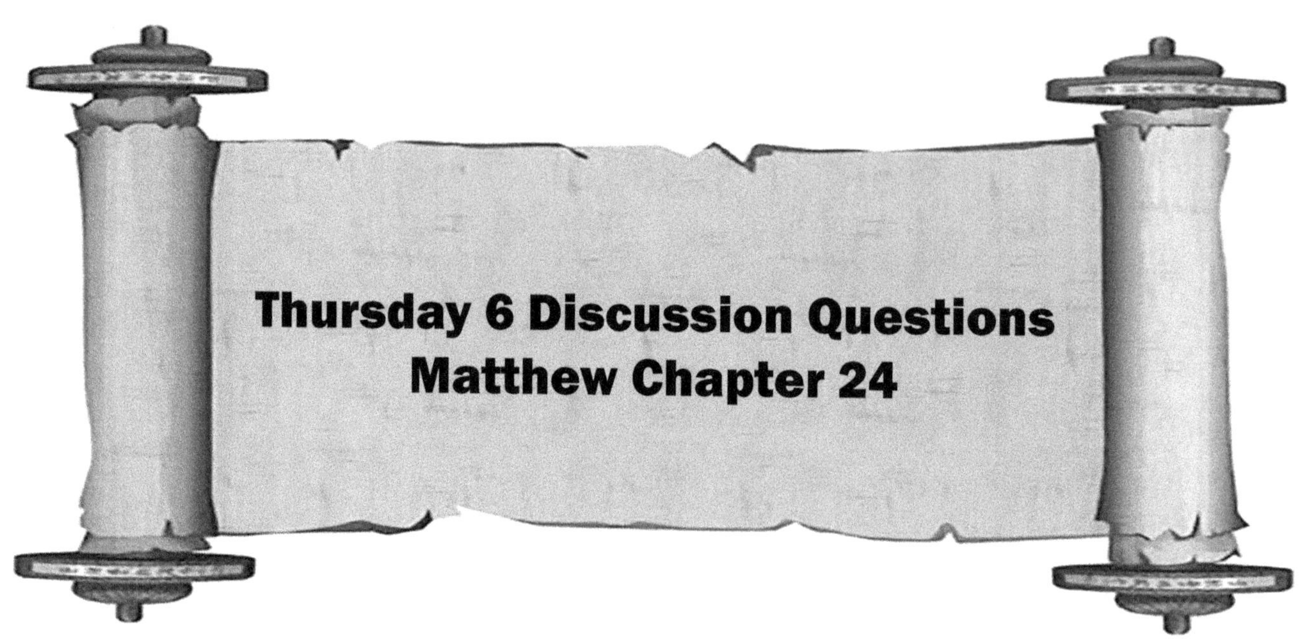

1. What did Jesus tell the disciples about all the buildings he showed them?

2. What did Jesus tell the disciples, when they asked him, "When will all the things happen?

3. List the things Jesus said will be the beginning of sorrows?

4. What did Jesus say will happen for a witness, before the end of the world?

5. What did Jesus say about those on the rooftop or those in the fields?

6. What does Jesus the false prophets will show and do?

7. What does Jesus want us to do if someone tells us he is in the desert or in the secret chambers?

8. What are all the things Jesus told the disciples will happen immediately after the tribulation?

9. Jesus said, "When his branch is yet tender, and putteth forth leaves, ye know that summer is nigh: So likewise ye, when ye shall see all these things, know that it is near, even at the doors." What did he say about things passing away and not passing away? Who did he say knows when the world will end?

10. How did Jesus compare Noah and the Flood, to the way the end of the world will be?

WEEKLY REVIEW
MATTHEW CHAPTERS 21-24

NAME THAT CHAPTER

1._______ JESUS WARNS THE DISCIPLES NOT TO DO LIKE THE PHARISEES AND SCRIBES, DOING GOOD TO BE SEEN OF MAN. HE TOLD THEM HOW THEY LOVED TO SIT IN THE CHIEF SEATS AND TO BE CALLED RABBI. JESUS SAID TO BE SURE NOT TO BE TITLED OR CALLED RABBI AND MASTER, FOR CHRIST IS OUR RABBI AND MASTER. NEITHER SHOULD WE BE CALLED FATHER. HE EXPLAINED THAT THE NAME FATHER BELONGS ONLY TO GOD OUR FATHER IN HEAVEN.

2._______ JESUS WAS ANGRY WHEN HE WENT INTO THE TEMPLE AND SAW BUYING AND SELLING AND THREW OVER THE TABLES OF THE MONEY CHANGERS. HE PROCLAIMED, THIS HOUSE SHOULD BE CALLED THE HOUSE OF PRAYER BUT YOU HAVE MADE IT A DEN OF THIEVES

3._______ JESUS TEACHES OF THE SIGNS OF THE TIMES SO WE WON'T BE FOOLED BY THE FALSE PROPHETS. HE WARNS US THAT THEY WILL DO GREAT SIGNS AND WONDERS TO FOOL THE VERY ELECT. JESUS WARN US THAT HE WILL NOT BE WHERE THEY PROPHECY IN DESERTS AND SECRET PLACES. HE SHALL APPEAR IN THE CLOUDS. HE TELLS US OF THE BEGINNING OF SORROWS. HE GIVES US SIGNS TO LOOK FOR AND TELLS US THE END WILL BE LIKE THE DAYS OF NOAH AND THE ARK, WHEN THE RAINS CAME SUDDENLY. BUT HE CAN NOT TELL US WHEN THE WORLD WILL END AND HE SAYS NO MAN CAN. NOT EVEN THE ANGELS KNOW.

4._______ JESUS GAVE THE DISCIPLES A PARABLE OF A KING SENDING FORPEOPLE TO COME TO HIS SON'S WEDDING AND PEOPLE WOULD NOT COME. WHEN HE SENT AGAIN THEY MADE LIGHT OF IT AND WENT ABOUT THEIR DAY. THE KING SENT THE SERVANTS BACK OUT TO INVITE ANYONE THEY COULD FIND TO COME; GOOD OR BAD. ONE CAME WITHOUT WEDDING GARMENTS AND WAS BOUND AND TAKEN AWAY TO BE CAST INTO OUTER DARKNESS.

TRUE OR FALSE

5. JESUS GOT HUNGRY ONE MORNING AND CURSED A TREE THAT HAD NO FRUIT, BUT ONLY HAD LEAVES ON IT.

____

Matthew 21:18, 19

6. JESUS SAID "LOVE THY NEIGHBOR AS THYSELF" IS LIKE THE FIRST AND GREAT COMMANDMENT."

____

Matthew 22:37-39

7. THE SCRIBES AND PHARISEES SAT IN MOSES' SEAT.

____

Matthew 23:2

FILL IN THE BLANKS

8. Ye blind____________, which strain at a____________, and____________a camel.

Matthew 23:24

9. And all things,____________ye shall ask in____________, believing, ye shall____________.

Matthew 21:22

10. All____________are the____________of____________.

Matthew 24:8

STUDENT PRAYER JOURNAL

Please use this space to record your thoughts and feelings as you travel on this spirit led journey through the word of God with us. Please know that you have brothers and sisters in this organization from all over the world praying with and for you. My prayer for you is that you will begin to see the power of God resting in each set of your footprints. As you look back and examine your past in this journal, may you realize that you were never alone and according to Hebrews 13:5, God will never leave nor forsake you. ~LADY FLORA

THE STUDY OF THE FOUR GOSPELS VOCABULARY DEFINITIONS FOR MATTHEW CHAPTERS 25-28

WORD	DEFINITIONS
1) LIKENED	
2) TALENTS	
3) RECKON	
4) STRAWED	
5) USURY	
6) SUBTILITY	
7) ALABASTER	
8) WROUGHT	
9) SMITE	
10)BEWRAY	

DMWW Daily Bible Reading
KJV MATTHEW CHAPTERS 25-28

CHAPTER 25

1. Then shall the kingdom of heaven be likened unto ten virgins, which took their lamps, and went forth to meet the bridegroom.
2. And five of them were wise, and five were foolish.
3. They that were foolish took their lamps, and took no oil with them:
4. But the wise took oil in their vessels with their lamps.
5. While the bridegroom tarried, they all slumbered and slept.
6. And at midnight there was a cry made, Behold, the bridegroom cometh; go ye out to meet him.
7. Then all those virgins arose, and trimmed their lamps.
8. And the foolish said unto the wise, Give us of your oil; for our lamps are gone out.
9. But the wise answered, saying, Not so; lest there be not enough for us and you: but go ye rather to them that sell, and buy for yourselves.
10. And while they went to buy, the bridegroom came; and they that were ready went in with him to the marriage: and the door was shut.
11. Afterward came also the other virgins, saying, Lord, Lord, open to us.
12. But he answered and said, Verily I say unto you, I know you not.
13. Watch therefore, for ye know neither the day nor the hour wherein the Son of man cometh.
14. For the kingdom of heaven is as a man travelling into a far country, who called his own servants, and delivered unto them his goods.
15. And unto one he gave five talents, to another two, and to another one; to every man according to his several ability; and straightway took his journey.
16. Then he that had received the five talents went and traded with the same, and made them other five talents.
17. And likewise he that had received two, he also gained other two.
18. But he that had received one went and digged in the earth, and hid his lord's money.
19. After a long time the lord of those servants cometh, and reckoneth with them.

20. And so he that had received five talents came and brought other five talents, saying, Lord, thou deliveredst unto me five talents: behold, I have gained beside them five talents more.

21. His lord said unto him, Well done, thou good and faithful servant: thou hast been faithful over a few things, I will make thee ruler over many things: enter thou into the joy of thy lord.

22. He also that had received two talents came and said, Lord, thou deliveredst unto me two talents: behold, I have gained two other talents beside them.

23. His lord said unto him, Well done, good and faithful servant; thou hast been faithful over a few things, I will make thee ruler over many things: enter thou into the joy of thy lord.

24. Then he which had received the one talent came and said, Lord, I knew thee that thou art an hard man, reaping where thou hast not sown, and gathering where thou hast not strawed:

25. And I was afraid, and went and hid thy talent in the earth: lo, there thou hast that is thine.

26. His lord answered and said unto him, Thou wicked and slothful servant, thou knewest that I reap where I sowed not, and gather where I have not strawed:

27. Thou oughtest therefore to have put my money to the exchangers, and then at my coming I should have received mine own with usury.

28. Take therefore the talent from him, and give it unto him which hath ten talents.

29. For unto every one that hath shall be given, and he shall have abundance: but from him that hath not shall be taken away even that which he hath.

30. And cast ye the unprofitable servant into outer darkness: there shall be weeping and gnashing of teeth.

31. When the Son of man shall come in his glory, and all the holy angels with him, then shall he sit upon the throne of his glory:

32. And before him shall be gathered all nations: and he shall separate them one from another, as a shepherd divideth his sheep from the goats:

33. And he shall set the sheep on his right hand, but the goats on the left.

34. Then shall the King say unto them on his right hand, Come, ye blessed of my Father, inherit the kingdom prepared for you from the foundation of the world:

35. For I was an hungred, and ye gave me meat: I was thirsty, and ye gave me drink: I was a stranger, and ye took me in:

36. Naked, and ye clothed me: I was sick, and ye visited me: I was in prison, and ye came unto me.

37. Then shall the righteous answer him, saying, Lord, when saw we thee an hungred, and fed thee? or thirsty, and gave thee drink?

38. When saw we thee a stranger, and took thee in? or naked, and clothed thee?

39. Or when saw we thee sick, or in prison, and came unto thee?

40. And the King shall answer and say unto them, Verily I say unto you, Inasmuch as ye have done it unto one of the least of these my brethren, ye have done it unto me.

41. Then shall he say also unto them on the left hand, Depart from me, ye cursed, into everlasting fire, prepared for the devil and his angels:

42. For I was an hungred, and ye gave me no meat: I was thirsty, and ye gave me no drink:

43. I was a stranger, and ye took me not in: naked, and ye clothed me not: sick, and in prison, and ye visited me not.

44. Then shall they also answer him, saying, Lord, when saw we thee an hungred, or athirst, or a stranger, or naked, or sick, or in prison, and did not minister unto thee?

45. Then shall he answer them, saying, Verily I say unto you, Inasmuch as ye did it not to one of the least of these, ye did it not to me.

46. And these shall go away into everlasting punishment: but the righteous into life eternal.

CHAPTER 26

1. And it came to pass, when Jesus had finished all these sayings, he said unto his disciples,

2. Ye know that after two days is the feast of the passover, and the Son of man is betrayed to be crucified.

3. Then assembled together the chief priests, and the scribes, and the elders of the people, unto the palace of the high priest, who was called Caiaphas,

4. And consulted that they might take Jesus by subtilty, and kill him.

5. But they said, Not on the feast day, lest there be an uproar among the people.

6. Now when Jesus was in Bethany, in the house of Simon the leper,

7. There came unto him a woman having an alabaster box of very precious ointment, and poured it on his head, as he sat at meat.

8. But when his disciples saw it, they had indignation, saying, To what purpose is this waste?

9. For this ointment might have been sold for much, and given to the poor.

10. When Jesus understood it, he said unto them, Why trouble ye the woman? for she hath wrought a good work upon me.

11. For ye have the poor always with you; but me ye have not always.

12. For in that she hath poured this ointment on my body, she did it for my burial.

13. Verily I say unto you, Wheresoever this gospel shall be preached in the whole world, there shall also this, that this woman hath done, be told for a memorial of her.

14. Then one of the twelve, called Judas Iscariot, went unto the chief priests,

15. And said unto them, What will ye give me, and I will deliver him unto you? And they covenanted with him for thirty pieces of silver.

16. And from that time he sought opportunity to betray him.

17. Now the first day of the feast of unleavened bread the disciples came to Jesus, saying unto him, Where wilt thou that we prepare for thee to eat the passover?

18. And he said, Go into the city to such a man, and say unto him, The Master saith, My time is at hand; I will keep the passover at thy house with my disciples.

19. And the disciples did as Jesus had appointed them; and they made ready the passover.

20. Now when the even was come, he sat down with the twelve.

21. And as they did eat, he said, Verily I say unto you, that one of you shall betray me.

22. And they were exceeding sorrowful, and began every one of them to say unto him, Lord, is it I?

23. And he answered and said, He that dippeth his hand with me in the dish, the same shall betray me.

24. The Son of man goeth as it is written of him: but woe unto that man by whom the Son of man is betrayed! it had been good for that man if he had not been born.

25. Then Judas, which betrayed him, answered and said, Master, is it I? He said unto him, Thou hast said.

26. And as they were eating, Jesus took bread, and blessed it, and brake it, and gave it to the disciples, and said, Take, eat; this is my body.

27. And he took the cup, and gave thanks, and gave it to them, saying, Drink ye all of it;

28. For this is my blood of the new testament, which is shed for many for the remission of sins.

29. But I say unto you, I will not drink henceforth of this fruit of the vine, until that day when I drink it new with you in my Father's kingdom.

30. And when they had sung an hymn, they went out into the mount of Olives.

31. Then saith Jesus unto them, All ye shall be offended because of me this night: for it is written, I will smite the shepherd, and the sheep of the flock shall be scattered abroad.

32. But after I am risen again, I will go before you into Galilee.

33. Peter answered and said unto him, Though all men shall be offended because of thee, yet will I never be offended.

34. Jesus said unto him, Verily I say unto thee, That this night, before the cock crow, thou shalt deny me thrice.

35. Peter said unto him, Though I should die with thee, yet will I not deny thee. Likewise also said all the disciples.

36. Then cometh Jesus with them unto a place called Gethsemane, and saith unto the disciples, Sit ye here, while I go and pray yonder.

37. And he took with him Peter and the two sons of Zebedee, and began to be sorrowful and very heavy.

38. Then saith he unto them, My soul is exceeding sorrowful, even unto death: tarry ye here, and watch with me.

39. And he went a little farther, and fell on his face, and prayed, saying, O my Father, if it be possible, let this cup pass from me: nevertheless not as I will, but as thou wilt.

40. And he cometh unto the disciples, and findeth them asleep, and saith unto Peter, What, could ye not watch with me one hour?

41. Watch and pray, that ye enter not into temptation: the spirit indeed is willing, but the flesh is weak.

42. He went away again the second time, and prayed, saying, O my Father, if this cup may not pass away from me, except I drink it, thy will be done.

43. And he came and found them asleep again: for their eyes were heavy.

44. And he left them, and went away again, and prayed the third time, saying the same words.

45. Then cometh he to his disciples, and saith unto them, Sleep on now, and take your rest: behold, the hour is at hand, and the Son of man is betrayed into the hands of sinners.

46. Rise, let us be going: behold, he is at hand that doth betray me.

47. And while he yet spake, lo, Judas, one of the twelve, came, and with him a great multitude with swords and staves, from the chief priests and elders of the people.

48. Now he that betrayed him gave them a sign, saying, Whomsoever I shall kiss, that same is he: hold him fast.

49. And forthwith he came to Jesus, and said, Hail, master; and kissed him.

50. And Jesus said unto him, Friend, wherefore art thou come? Then came they, and laid hands on Jesus and took him.

51. And, behold, one of them which were with Jesus stretched out his hand, and drew his sword, and struck a servant of the high priest's, and smote off his ear.

52. Then said Jesus unto him, Put up again thy sword into his place: for all they that take the sword shall perish with the sword.

53. Thinkest thou that I cannot now pray to my Father, and he shall presently give me more than twelve legions of angels?

54. But how then shall the scriptures be fulfilled, that thus it must be?

55. In that same hour said Jesus to the multitudes, Are ye come out as against a thief with swords and staves for to take me? I sat daily with you teaching in the temple, and ye laid no hold on me.

56. But all this was done, that the scriptures of the prophets might be fulfilled. Then all the disciples forsook him, and fled.

57. And they that had laid hold on Jesus led him away to Caiaphas the high priest, where the scribes and the elders were assembled.

58. But Peter followed him afar off unto the high priest's palace, and went in, and sat with the servants, to see the end.

59. Now the chief priests, and elders, and all the council, sought false witness against Jesus, to put him to death;

60. But found none: yea, though many false witnesses came, yet found they none. At the last came two false witnesses,

61. And said, This fellow said, I am able to destroy the temple of God, and to build it in three days.

62. And the high priest arose, and said unto him, Answerest thou nothing? what is it which these witness against thee?

63. But Jesus held his peace, And the high priest answered and said unto him, I adjure thee by the living God, that thou tell us whether thou be the Christ, the Son of God.

64. Jesus saith unto him, Thou hast said: nevertheless I say unto you, Hereafter shall ye see the Son of man sitting on the right hand of power, and coming in the clouds of heaven.

65. Then the high priest rent his clothes, saying, He hath spoken blasphemy; what further need have we of witnesses? behold, now ye have heard his blasphemy.

66. What think ye? They answered and said, He is guilty of death.

67. Then did they spit in his face, and buffeted him; and others smote him with the palms of their hands,

68. Saying, Prophesy unto us, thou Christ, Who is he that smote thee?

69. Now Peter sat without in the palace: and a damsel came unto him, saying, Thou also wast with Jesus of Galilee.

70. But he denied before them all, saying, I know not what thou sayest.

71. And when he was gone out into the porch, another maid saw him, and said unto them that were there, This fellow was also with Jesus of Nazareth.

72. And again he denied with an oath, I do not know the man.

73. And after a while came unto him they that stood by, and said to Peter, Surely thou also art one of them; for thy speech bewrayeth thee.

74. Then began he to curse and to swear, saying, I know not the man. And immediately the cock crew.

75. And Peter remembered the word of Jesus, which said unto him, Before the cock crow, thou shalt deny me thrice. And he went out, and wept bitterly.

CHAPTER 27

1. When the morning was come, all the chief priests and elders of the people took counsel against Jesus to put him to death:

2. And when they had bound him, they led him away, and delivered him to Pontius Pilate the governor.

3. Then Judas, which had betrayed him, when he saw that he was condemned, repented himself, and brought again the thirty pieces of silver to the chief priests and elders,

4. Saying, I have sinned in that I have betrayed the innocent blood. And they said, What is that to us? see thou to that.

5. And he cast down the pieces of silver in the temple, and departed, and went and hanged himself.

6. And the chief priests took the silver pieces, and said, It is not lawful for to put them into the treasury, because it is the price of blood.

7. And they took counsel, and bought with them the potter's field, to bury strangers in.

8. Wherefore that field was called, The field of blood, unto this day.

9. Then was fulfilled that which was spoken by Jeremy the prophet, saying, And they took the thirty pieces of silver, the price of him that was valued, whom they of the children of Israel did value;

10. And gave them for the potter's field, as the Lord appointed me.

11. And Jesus stood before the governor: and the governor asked him, saying, Art thou the King of the Jews? And Jesus said unto him, Thou sayest.

12. And when he was accused of the chief priests and elders, he answered nothing.

13. Then said Pilate unto him, Hearest thou not how many things they witness against thee?

14. And he answered him to never a word; insomuch that the governor marvelled greatly.

15. Now at that feast the governor was wont to release unto the people a prisoner, whom they would.

16. And they had then a notable prisoner, called Barabbas.

17. Therefore when they were gathered together, Pilate said unto them, Whom will ye that I release unto you? Barabbas, or Jesus which is called Christ?

18. For he knew that for envy they had delivered him.

19. When he was set down on the judgment seat, his wife sent unto him, saying, Have thou nothing to do with that just man: for I have suffered many things this day in a dream because of him.

20. But the chief priests and elders persuaded the multitude that they should ask Barabbas, and destroy Jesus.

21. The governor answered and said unto them, Whether of the twain will ye that I release unto you? They said, Barabbas.

22. Pilate saith unto them, What shall I do then with Jesus which is called Christ? They all say unto him, Let him be crucified.

23. And the governor said, Why, what evil hath he done? But they cried out the more, saying, Let him be crucified.

24. When Pilate saw that he could prevail nothing, but that rather a tumult was made, he took water, and washed his hands before the multitude, saying, I am innocent of the blood of this just person: see ye to it.

25. Then answered all the people, and said, His blood be on us, and on our children.

26. Then released he Barabbas unto them: and when he had scourged Jesus, he delivered him to be crucified.

27. Then the soldiers of the governor took Jesus into the common hall, and gathered unto him the whole band of soldiers.

28. And they stripped him, and put on him a scarlet robe.

29. And when they had platted a crown of thorns, they put it upon his head, and a reed in his right hand: and they bowed the knee before him, and mocked him, saying, Hail, King of the Jews!

30. And they spit upon him, and took the reed, and smote him on the head.

31. And after that they had mocked him, they took the robe off from him, and put his own raiment on him, and led him away to crucify him.

32. And as they came out, they found a man of Cyrene, Simon by name: him they compelled to bear his cross.

33. And when they were come unto a place called Golgotha, that is to say, a place of a skull,

34. They gave him vinegar to drink mingled with gall: and when he had tasted thereof, he would not drink.

35. And they crucified him, and parted his garments, casting lots: that it might be fulfilled which was spoken by the prophet, They parted my garments among them, and upon my vesture did they cast lots.

36. And sitting down they watched him there;

37. And set up over his head his accusation written, This Is Jesus The King Of The Jews.

38. Then were there two thieves crucified with him, one on the right hand, and another on the left.

39. And they that passed by reviled him, wagging their heads,

40. And saying, Thou that destroyest the temple, and buildest it in three days, save thyself. If thou be the Son of God, come down from the cross.

41. Likewise also the chief priests mocking him, with the scribes and elders, said,

42. He saved others; himself he cannot save. If he be the King of Israel, let him now come down from the cross, and we will believe him.

43. He trusted in God; let him deliver him now, if he will have him: for he said, I am the Son of God.

44. The thieves also, which were crucified with him, cast the same in his teeth.

45. Now from the sixth hour there was darkness over all the land unto the ninth hour.

46. And about the ninth hour Jesus cried with a loud voice, saying, Eli, Eli, lama sabachthani? that is to say, My God, my God, why hast thou forsaken me?

47. Some of them that stood there, when they heard that, said, This man calleth for Elias.

48. And straightway one of them ran, and took a spunge, and filled it with vinegar, and put it on a reed, and gave him to drink.

49. The rest said, Let be, let us see whether Elias will come to save him.

50. Jesus, when he had cried again with a loud voice, yielded up the ghost.

51. And, behold, the veil of the temple was rent in twain from the top to the bottom; and the earth did quake, and the rocks rent;

52. And the graves were opened; and many bodies of the saints which slept arose,

53. And came out of the graves after his resurrection, and went into the holy city, and appeared unto many.

54. Now when the centurion, and they that were with him, watching Jesus, saw the earthquake, and those things that were done, they feared greatly, saying, Truly this was the Son of God.

55. And many women were there beholding afar off, which followed Jesus from Galilee, ministering unto him:

56. Among which was Mary Magdalene, and Mary the mother of James and Joses, and the mother of Zebedees children.

57. When the even was come, there came a rich man of Arimathaea, named Joseph, who also himself was Jesus' disciple:

58. He went to Pilate, and begged the body of Jesus. Then Pilate commanded the body to be delivered.

59. And when Joseph had taken the body, he wrapped it in a clean linen cloth,

60. And laid it in his own new tomb, which he had hewn out in the rock: and he rolled a great stone to the door of the sepulchre, and departed.

61. And there was Mary Magdalene, and the other Mary, sitting over against the sepulchre.

62. Now the next day, that followed the day of the preparation, the chief priests and Pharisees came together unto Pilate,

63. Saying, Sir, we remember that that deceiver said, while he was yet alive, After three days I will rise again.

64. Command therefore that the sepulchre be made sure until the third day, lest his disciples come by night, and steal him away, and say unto the people, He is risen from the dead: so the last error shall be worse than the first.

65. Pilate said unto them, Ye have a watch: go your way, make it as sure as ye can.

66. So they went, and made the sepulchre sure, sealing the stone, and setting a watch.

CHAPTER 28

1. In the end of the sabbath, as it began to dawn toward the first day of the week, came Mary Magdalene and the other Mary to see the sepulchre.

2. And, behold, there was a great earthquake: for the angel of the Lord descended from heaven, and came and rolled back the stone from the door, and sat upon it.

3. His countenance was like lightning, and his raiment white as snow:

4. And for fear of him the keepers did shake, and became as dead men.

5. And the angel answered and said unto the women, Fear not ye: for I know that ye seek Jesus, which was crucified.

6. He is not here: for he is risen, as he said. Come, see the place where the Lord lay.

7. And go quickly, and tell his disciples that he is risen from the dead; and, behold, he goeth before you into Galilee; there shall ye see him: lo, I have told you.

8. And they departed quickly from the sepulchre with fear and great joy; and did run to bring his disciples word.

9. And as they went to tell his disciples, behold, Jesus met them, saying, All hail. And they came and held him by the feet, and worshipped him.

10. Then said Jesus unto them, Be not afraid: go tell my brethren that they go into Galilee, and there shall they see me.

11. Now when they were going, behold, some of the watch came into the city, and shewed unto the chief priests all the things that were done.

12. And when they were assembled with the elders, and had taken counsel, they gave large money unto the soldiers,

13. Saying, Say ye, His disciples came by night, and stole him away while we slept.

14. And if this come to the governor's ears, we will persuade him, and secure you.

15. So they took the money, and did as they were taught: and this saying is commonly reported among the Jews until this day.

16. Then the eleven disciples went away into Galilee, into a mountain where Jesus had appointed them.

17. And when they saw him, they worshipped him: but some doubted.

18. And Jesus came and spake unto them, saying, All power is given unto me in heaven and in earth.

19. Go ye therefore, and teach all nations, baptizing them in the name of the Father, and of the Son, and of the Holy Ghost:

20. Teaching them to observe all things whatsoever I have commanded you: and, lo, I am with you always, even unto the end of the world. Amen.

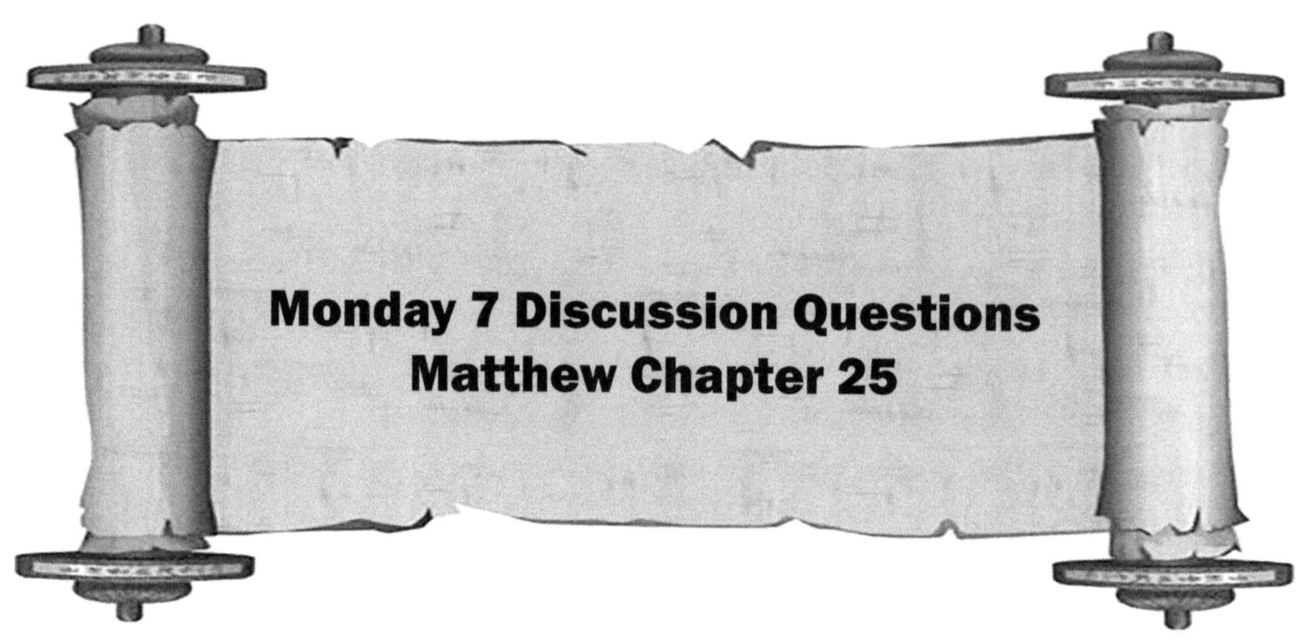

1. In this chapter, what did Jesus say the kingdom of Heaven would be likened unto? ___

2. How many virgins were wise? How many were foolish? ___

3. What did the wise virgins do that the foolish virgins did not do before coming? ___

4. What did they all do while the bridegroom tarried? ___

5. What did the foolish virgins ask the wise virgins to share? What was the wise virgins' response? ___

6. What were the foolish virgins doing when Jesus came? ___

7. When the foolish virgins came back from buying oil at the last minute and asked Jesus to let them in, what was Jesus' response? ___

8. When the man traveling into a far country gave his servants 1, 2, and 5 talents, and then returned, what had each servant done with his talents? ___

9. When Jesus gave the example of people feeding him, clothing him, visiting him in jail and while sick, the people were confused because they didn't remember doing these things to or for Jesus. Please explain what Jesus meant when he was speaking of these things. ___

10. What did Jesus tell the people that explains "the way that we treat each other, is the way we are ultimately treating him? ___

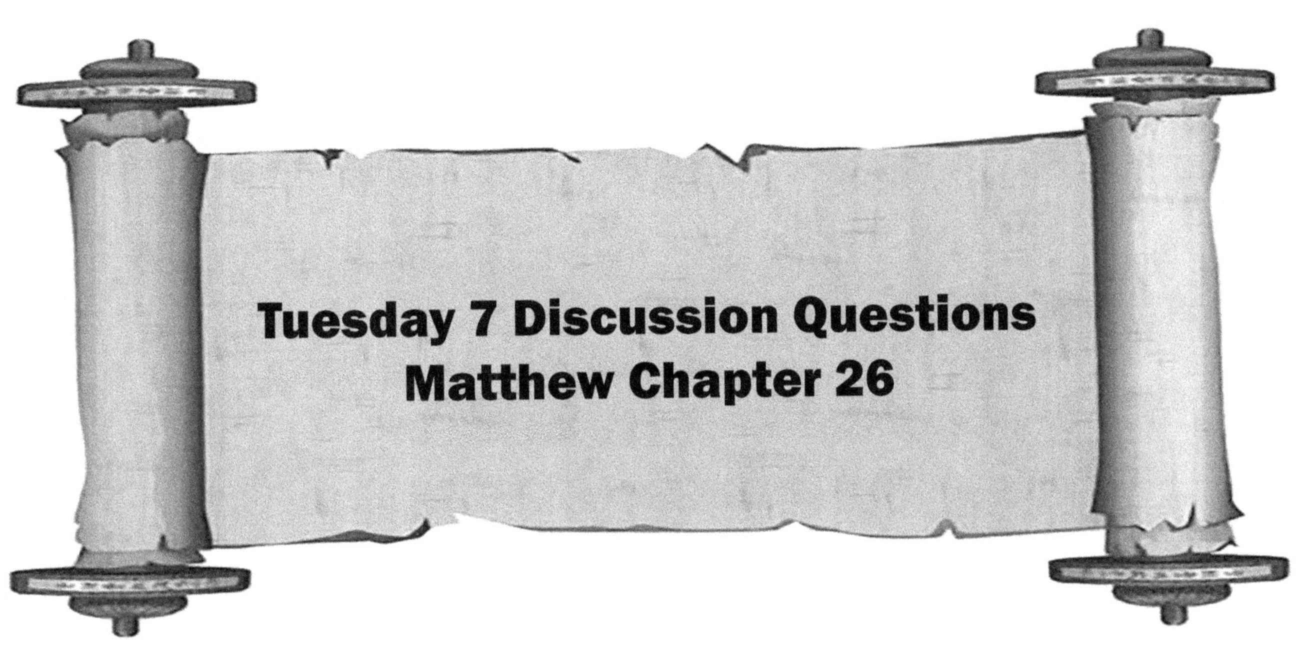

1. What did Jesus tell the disciples would happen in two days at the Passover feast? ____

2. Who all gathered together at the high priest Caiaphas' palace? ____

3. They wanted to kill Jesus but why did they decide not to do it on feast day? ____

4. What happened to Jesus while he was at Simon the leper's house? ____

5. What did the disciples say about what she had done? ____

6. How did Jesus respond to what she did? ____

7. What did Jesus say about the gospel and what the woman had done? ____

8. What did Jesus say when he took bread, and blessed it, and broke it, and gave it to the disciples? ____

9. What did Peter say after Jesus said men would be offended because of him? How did Jesus respond to what Peter said? ____

10. What did Peter and all the disciples then say to Jesus? ____

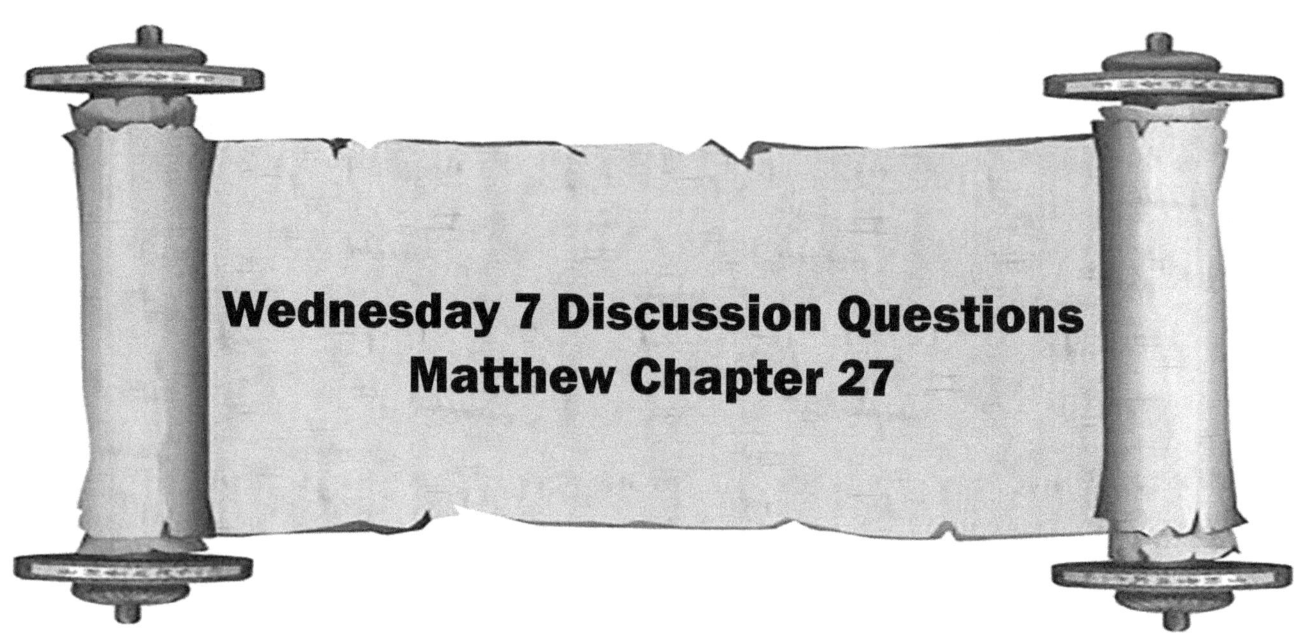

Wednesday 7 Discussion Questions
Matthew Chapter 27

1. When morning came what did all the chief priests and elders of the people do? _______
2. After they bound him and led him away, who did they deliver him to? ___________
3. After Judas Iscariot betrayed Jesus he threw down the silver in the temple and went to hang himself. What did the priests say about the silver? _______________
4. What did they do with it? ___________________________
5. What is that field called? ___________________________
6. What did Jesus say when he was accused by the chief priests? What did he say when Pilate questioned him? ___________________________
7. When Pilate had two prisoners at the feast, (Barabbas and Jesus), what did Pilate ask the people? ___________________________
8. When Pilate saw that he couldn't prevail and there was a tumult in the multitude, what did he do and say to them? ___________________________
9. When they got to Golgotha, what did they give Jesus to drink? Did Jesus drink it? _____
10. What happened from the 6th to the 9th hour? What happened in the ninth hour? ____
11. What happened when Jesus cried aloud and gave up the ghost? ___________
12. What happened to the graves after the earthquake? ______________
13. Where did they go and appear after the resurrection? ______________
14. Who ministered to Jesus as he came from Galilee? ______________
15. Name three women that were among those watching and following Jesus? ___________

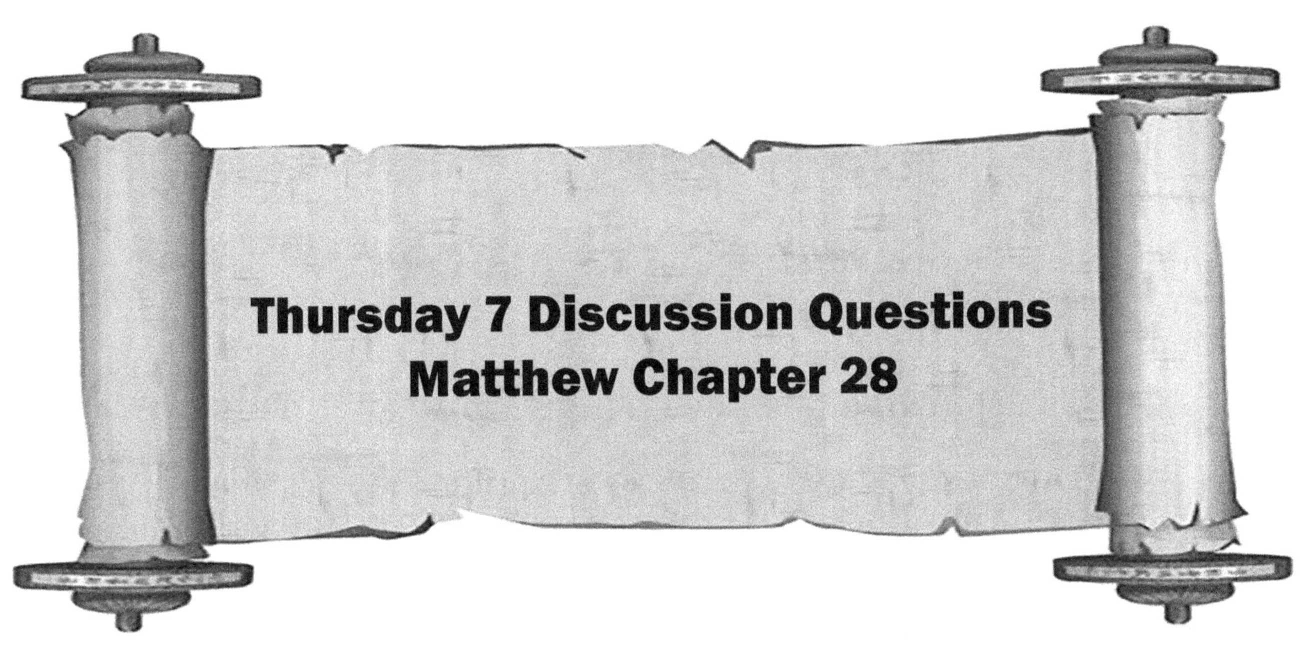

1. Who went to see the sepulcher as it began to dawn toward the first day of the week, at the end of the Sabbath? ______

2. What did the angel of the Lord do that caused the earthquake? ______

3. Describe the angel's countenance and raiment? ______

4. Why did the keepers shake and become as dead men? ______

5. What did the angel tell Mary and Mary Magdalene to do? ______

6. What did they do when Jesus met them on their way to tell the disciples? ______

7. What did the elders assemble and take counsel to pay large money to the soldiers to say? ______

8. Did the soldiers take the bribe money and commit the act? ______

9. Did the people believe the soldiers? What do some people believe about the soldier's lie to this day? What did the elders tell the soldiers they would do if the governor heard about their scheme? ______

10. What was Jesus' last instruction to the disciples in the book of Matthew? ______

WEEKLY REVIEW
MATTHEW CHAPTERS 25-28

NAME THAT CHAPTER

1.______ IN THIS CHAPTER, WE SAW CHIEF ELDERS AND PRIESTS PLANNING TO KILL JESUS. AFTER JUDAS HAD BETRAYED JESUS HE THREW THE MONEY DOWN IN THE TEMPLE AND RAN OUT TO HANG HIMSELF. THE CHIEF ELDERS DECIDED THAT SINCE THE MONEY WAS CONSIDERED BLOOD MONEY, THEY WOULD BUY A FIELD TO BURY STRANGERS. THE PLACE IS CALLED THE FIELD OF BLOOD.

2.______ THIS CHAPTER GIVES A PARABLE OF TEN VIRGINS WHO WENT TO MEET THE BRIDEGROOM. 5 WERE WISE FIVE WERE FOOLISH. THE 5 FOOLISH DID NOT BRING OIL FOR THEIR LAMPS. WHILE THEY WERE GONE TRYING TO GET OIL, JESUS CAME AND TOOK THE 5 WISE VIRGINS AWAY.

3.______JESUS TOLD HIS DISCIPLES THAT HE WOULD BE BETRAYED TO BE CRUCIFIED AT THE PASSOVER FEAST. MEANWHILE THE CHIEF PRIESTS, ELDERS AND SCRIBES GATHERED AT CAIAPHAS' PALACE AND PLANNED TO KILL JESUS. WHEN JESUS WENT TO SIMON THE LEPER'S HOUSE A WOMAN CAME TO POUR PRECIOUS OINTMENT FROM HER ALABASTER BOX UPON JESUS' HEAD. THE DISCIPLES WERE UPSET BECAUSE THEY FELT LIKE SHE WASTED THE OIL. JESUS TOLD THEM TO LEAVE HER ALONE BECAUSE SHE HAD DONE A GOOD THING. HE SAID WHEREVER THE GOSPEL IS PREACHED, WHAT SHE DID WOULD BE TOLD AS A MEMORIAL FOR HER.

4.______THIS CHAPTER GAVE US INSIGHT INTO THE TIME WHEN THE ANGEL CAME AND ROLLED THE STONE AWAY TO REVEAL JESUS' EMPTY TOMB TO MARY AND MARY MAGDALENE. THERE WAS AN EARTHQUAKE WHEN HE DID THIS AND IT CAUSED THE KEEPERS TO BE AS DEAD MEN FROM FEAR. THE ANGEL SENT THE MARYS TO TELL THE DISCIPLES WHAT THEY SAW. THE SOLDIERS WERE BRIBED BY THE ELDERS TO TELL EVERYONE THAT SOMEONE STOLE JESUS WHILE THEY SLEPT, SO NO ONE WOULD BELIEVE HE ROSE FROM THE DEAD.

TRUE OR FALSE

5. JESUS LAST INSTRUCTION TO US WAS TO GO AND TEACH ALL NATIONS, BAPTIZING THEM IN THE NAME OF THE FATHER THE SON AND THE HOLY GHOST. TEACHING THEM TO OBSERVED THE COMMANDMENTS.

____

6. THERE WAS A TRAVELING MAN WHO LEFT 3 OF HIS SERVANTS WITH TALENTS. ONE WITH 1 TALENT, ONE WITH 2 TALENTS AND ONE WITH 5 TALENTS

____

7. JESUS TOOK BREAD AND BROKE IT. THEN HE HAD EACH DISCIPLE TO DO THE SAME AND OFFER IT TO HIM AS THEIR LAST OFFERING.

____

FILL IN THE BLANKS

8. FOR THIS IS MY_____________OF THE NEW_____________, WHICH I_____________ FOR THE REMISSION OF SIN

9. HIS_____________WAS LIKE_____________AND HIS RAIMENT WAS_____________ AS SNOW.

10. _____________ THEREFORE, FOR YE KNOW_____________THE DAY NOR THE_____________WHEREIN THE SON OF MAN COMETH

THE BOOK OF MATTHEW
FINAL PART 1
Word Comprehension

Use the following 30 words from our study of MATTHEW in a sentence to show your understanding of the vocabulary word given. This assignment is worth 500 points when completed. DUE ON MONDAY, SEPTEMBER 6, 2021.

WORD		PERSONAL SENTENCE
1) LAMENTATION		
2) PUBLICANS		
3) BEELZEBUB		
4) FARTHING		
5) DURETH		
6) TETRARCH		
7) VICTUALS		
8) TWAIN		
9) TRANSFIGURED		
10) EUNUCHS		
11) USURY		
12) SUBTILITY		
13) STAVES		
14) ADJURE		
15) TUMULT		
16) INDIGNATION		
17) PARABLES		
18) WAILING		
19) PURGE		
20) GARNER		
21) PINNACLE		
22) PALSY		

23) LUNATICK		
24) PRIVILY		
25) LEATHERN		
26) BEGAT		
27) DILIGENT		
28) ESPOUSED		
29) BLASPHEMY		
30) BRIDECHAMBER		

NAME______________________________

DATE COMPLETED______________________________

TIME COMPLETED______________________________

THE BOOK OF MATTHEW
FINAL PART 2 - SECTION 1: The Generations

SUMMARIZING CHAPTER 1

Matthew chapter 1 gives us information about who parented whom in the generation lineage. There are three sets of 14 generations. These generations include the time of 1) Abraham to David 2) David to the carrying away into Babylon and 3) The carrying away of Babylon to Christ.

Please list the people in the 3 sets of generations below:

GENERATION SET 1

1.	8.
2.	9.
3.	10.
4.	11.
5.	12.
6.	13.
7.	14.

GENERATION SET 2

1.	8.
2.	9.
3.	10.
4.	11.
5.	12.
6.	13.
7.	14.

GENERATION SET 3

1.	8.

2.	9.
3.	10.
4.	11.
5.	12.
6.	13.
7.	14.

THE BOOK OF MATTHEW
FINAL PART 3 - The 13th Disciple
Assignment Due by Friday

Your assignment will be to go on a journey with Jesus through the book of Matthew, as one of his disciples. Beginning with chapter four, you will make an account of each of your stops on the journey. You will record the visits, teachings, healings and things that happened. Please include any parables Jesus used and their meanings.

Each chapter from Matthew Chapter 4 to Matthew Chapter 28 should have a synopsis paragraph included.

The closing for this informative/persuasive essay will be a call to action. You will need to persuade your reader to consider the information you have given in the synopses and accept Christ as their personal savior.

Blessed Learning be unto you.

REFLECTIONS PAGE

This page is to keep a diary of how you felt when studying this book and what you learned or discovered in this class that helped you relate the Bible situations to situations in today's world. Jot down notes of spiritual revelations you received while studying that you may want to use in future messages you may preach.

The Study of
THE BOOK OF MARK

Begin Date________________________

Course End Date____________________________

Study Guide Prepared and Distributed by
The Discipled Men & Women of Wisdom, International

INTRODUCTION TO THE BOOK OF MARK

Welcome to the study of the book of Mark. This is the second book in the set of books, commonly known as "The Four Gospels" in the King James Version of The Holy Bible. As we study the book of Mark, it will feel like you are reading something you have already read. This is because Mark will be giving his version of the things that happened on the journey he traveled with Matthew, which we just read. There will be some similar accounts. But, the words and points of view may show some differences in what you read.

This is one of the reasons I teach you not to debate scripture. Especially when you have not read the whole Bible in context. You will find people debating whether or not specific words were used in a situation spoken of in the Bible. Once you have read a few books in context, you will see that both people debating are right. They just read from two different books of the Bible that were two men using two different perspectives and alternate words to describe the same situation.

As we read our daily chapters, take note of any things you read about for the first time in the book of Mark which were not written about in the book of Matthew. You will be asked to tell the differences in the books in your Final Test.

MY PRAYER JOURNAL

Please use this space to record your thoughts and feelings as you travel on this spirit led journey through the word of God with us. Please know that you have brothers and sisters in this organization from all over the world praying with and for you. My prayer for you is that you will begin to see the power of God resting in each set of your footprints. As you look back and examine your past in this journal, may you realize that you were never alone and according to Hebrews 13:5, God will never leave nor forsake you. ~LADY FLORA

I THESSALONIANS 5:17

THE STUDY OF THE FOUR GOSPELS VOCABULARY DEFINITIONS FOR MARK CHAPTERS 1-4

Define the following words. This assignment is worth 200 points when completed ***WITH THE CLASS*** during FB LIVE Weekly Class Discussion for participation grade.

WORD	DEFINITIONS
1) REMISSION	
2) GIRDLE	
3) ASTONISHED	
4) BESEECH	
5) LEPROSY	
6) RENT	
7) MAR	
8) SHEWBREAD	
9) SYNAGOGUE	
10) PARABLES	

DMWW DAILY BIBLE READING
MARK CHAPTERS 1-4 KJV

CHAPTER 1

1. The beginning of the gospel of Jesus Christ, the Son of God;
2. As it is written in the prophets, Behold, I send my messenger before thy face, which shall prepare thy way before thee.
3. The voice of one crying in the wilderness, Prepare ye the way of the Lord, make his paths straight.
4. John did baptize in the wilderness, and preach the baptism of repentance for the remission of sins.
5. And there went out unto him all the land of Judaea, and they of Jerusalem, and were all baptized of him in the river of Jordan, confessing their sins.
6. And John was clothed with camel's hair, and with a girdle of a skin about his loins; and he did eat locusts and wild honey;
7. And preached, saying, There cometh one mightier than I after me, the latchet of whose shoes I am not worthy to stoop down and unloose.
8. I indeed have baptized you with water: but he shall baptize you with the Holy Ghost.
9. And it came to pass in those days, that Jesus came from Nazareth of Galilee, and was baptized of John in Jordan.
10. And straightway coming up out of the water, he saw the heavens opened, and the Spirit like a dove descending upon him:
11. And there came a voice from heaven, saying, Thou art my beloved Son, in whom I am well pleased.
12. And immediately the spirit driveth him into the wilderness.
13. And he was there in the wilderness forty days, tempted of Satan; and was with the wild beasts; and the angels ministered unto him.
14. Now after that John was put in prison, Jesus came into Galilee, preaching the gospel of the kingdom of God,
15. And saying, The time is fulfilled, and the kingdom of God is at hand: repent ye, and believe the gospel.
16. Now as he walked by the sea of Galilee, he saw Simon and Andrew his brother casting a net into the sea: for they were fishers.

17. And Jesus said unto them, Come ye after me, and I will make you to become fishers of men.

18. And straightway they forsook their nets, and followed him.

19. And when he had gone a little farther thence, he saw James the son of Zebedee, and John his brother, who also were in the ship mending their nets.

20. And straightway he called them: and they left their father Zebedee in the ship with the hired servants, and went after him.

21. And they went into Capernaum; and straightway on the sabbath day he entered into the synagogue, and taught.

22. And they were astonished at his doctrine: for he taught them as one that had authority, and not as the scribes.

23. And there was in their synagogue a man with an unclean spirit; and he cried out,

24. Saying, Let us alone; what have we to do with thee, thou Jesus of Nazareth? art thou come to destroy us? I know thee who thou art, the Holy One of God.

25. And Jesus rebuked him, saying, Hold thy peace, and come out of him.

26. And when the unclean spirit had torn him, and cried with a loud voice, he came out of him.

27. And they were all amazed, insomuch that they questioned among themselves, saying, What thing is this? what new doctrine is this? for with authority commandeth he even the unclean spirits, and they do obey him.

28. And immediately his fame spread abroad throughout all the region round about Galilee.

29. And forthwith, when they were come out of the synagogue, they entered into the house of Simon and Andrew, with James and John.

30. But Simon's wife's mother lay sick of a fever, and anon they tell him of her.

31. And he came and took her by the hand, and lifted her up; and immediately the fever left her, and she ministered unto them.

32. And at even, when the sun did set, they brought unto him all that were diseased, and them that were possessed with devils.

33. And all the city was gathered together at the door.

34. And he healed many that were sick of divers diseases, and cast out many devils; and suffered not the devils to speak, because they knew him.

35. And in the morning, rising up a great while before day, he went out, and departed into a solitary place, and there prayed.

36. And Simon and they that were with him followed after him.

37. And when they had found him, they said unto him, All men seek for thee.

38. And he said unto them, Let us go into the next towns, that I may preach there also: for therefore came I forth.

39. And he preached in their synagogues throughout all Galilee, and cast out devils.

40. And there came a leper to him, beseeching him, and kneeling down to him, and saying unto him, If thou wilt, thou canst make me clean.

41. And Jesus, moved with compassion, put forth his hand, and touched him, and saith unto him, I will; be thou clean.

42. And as soon as he had spoken, immediately the leprosy departed from him, and he was cleansed.

43. And he straitly charged him, and forthwith sent him away;

44. And saith unto him, See thou say nothing to any man: but go thy way, shew thyself to the priest, and offer for thy cleansing those things which Moses commanded, for a testimony unto them.

45. But he went out, and began to publish it much, and to blaze abroad the matter, insomuch that Jesus could no more openly enter into the city, but was without in desert places: and they came to him from every quarter.

CHAPTER 2

1. And again he entered into Capernaum after some days; and it was noised that he was in the house.

2. And straightway many were gathered together, insomuch that there was no room to receive them, no, not so much as about the door: and he preached the word unto them.

3. And they come unto him, bringing one sick of the palsy, which was borne of four.

4. And when they could not come nigh unto him for the press, they uncovered the roof where he was: and when they had broken it up, they let down the bed wherein the sick of the palsy lay.

5. When Jesus saw their faith, he said unto the sick of the palsy, Son, thy sins be forgiven thee.

6. But there was certain of the scribes sitting there, and reasoning in their hearts,

7. Why doth this man thus speak blasphemies? who can forgive sins but God only?

8. And immediately when Jesus perceived in his spirit that they so reasoned within themselves, he said unto them, Why reason ye these things in your hearts?

9. Whether is it easier to say to the sick of the palsy, Thy sins be forgiven thee; or to say, Arise, and take up thy bed, and walk?

10. But that ye may know that the Son of man hath power on earth to forgive sins, (he saith to the sick of the palsy,)

11. I say unto thee, Arise, and take up thy bed, and go thy way into thine house.

12. And immediately he arose, took up the bed, and went forth before them all; insomuch that they were all amazed, and glorified God, saying, We never saw it on this fashion.

13. And he went forth again by the sea side; and all the multitude resorted unto him, and he taught them.

14. And as he passed by, he saw Levi the son of Alphaeus sitting at the receipt of custom, and said unto him, Follow me. And he arose and followed him.

15. And it came to pass, that, as Jesus sat at meat in his house, many publicans and sinners sat also together with Jesus and his disciples: for there were many, and they followed him.

16. And when the scribes and Pharisees saw him eat with publicans and sinners, they said unto his disciples, How is it that he eateth and drinketh with publicans and sinners?

17. When Jesus heard it, he saith unto them, They that are whole have no need of the physician, but they that are sick: I came not to call the righteous, but sinners to repentance.

18. And the disciples of John and of the Pharisees used to fast: and they come and say unto him, Why do the disciples of John and of the Pharisees fast, but thy disciples fast not?

19. And Jesus said unto them, Can the children of the bridechamber fast, while the bridegroom is with them? as long as they have the bridegroom with them, they cannot fast.

20. But the days will come, when the bridegroom shall be taken away from them, and then shall they fast in those days.

21. No man also seweth a piece of new cloth on an old garment: else the new piece that filled it up taketh away from the old, and the rent is made worse.

22. And no man putteth new wine into old bottles: else the new wine doth burst the bottles, and the wine is spilled, and the bottles will be marred: but new wine must be put into new bottles.

23. And it came to pass, that he went through the corn fields on the sabbath day; and his disciples began, as they went, to pluck the ears of corn.

24. And the Pharisees said unto him, Behold, why do they on the sabbath day that which is not lawful?

25. And he said unto them, Have ye never read what David did, when he had need, and was an hungred, he, and they that were with him?

26. How he went into the house of God in the days of Abiathar the high priest, and did eat the shewbread, which is not lawful to eat but for the priests, and gave also to them which were with him?

27. And he said unto them, The sabbath was made for man, and not man for the sabbath:

28. Therefore the Son of man is Lord also of the sabbath.

CHAPTER 3

1. And he entered again into the synagogue; and there was a man there which had a withered hand.

2. And they watched him, whether he would heal him on the sabbath day; that they might accuse him.

3. And he saith unto the man which had the withered hand, Stand forth.

4. And he saith unto them, Is it lawful to do good on the sabbath days, or to do evil? to save life, or to kill? But they held their peace.

5. And when he had looked round about on them with anger, being grieved for the hardness of their hearts, he saith unto the man, Stretch forth thine hand. And he stretched it out: and his hand was restored whole as the other.

6. And the Pharisees went forth, and straightway took counsel with the Herodians against him, how they might destroy him.

7. But Jesus withdrew himself with his disciples to the sea: and a great multitude from Galilee followed him, and from Judaea,

8. And from Jerusalem, and from Idumaea, and from beyond Jordan; and they about Tyre and Sidon, a great multitude, when they had heard what great things he did, came unto him.

9. And he spake to his disciples, that a small ship should wait on him because of the multitude, lest they should throng him.

10. For he had healed many; insomuch that they pressed upon him for to touch him, as many as had plagues.

11. And unclean spirits, when they saw him, fell down before him, and cried, saying, Thou art the Son of God.

12. And he straitly charged them that they should not make him known.

13. And he goeth up into a mountain, and calleth unto him whom he would: and they came unto him.

14. And he ordained twelve, that they should be with him, and that he might send them forth to preach,

15. And to have power to heal sicknesses, and to cast out devils:

16. And Simon he surnamed Peter;

17. And James the son of Zebedee, and John the brother of James; and he surnamed them Boanerges, which is, The sons of thunder:

18. And Andrew, and Philip, and Bartholomew, and Matthew, and Thomas, and James the son of Alphaeus, and Thaddaeus, and Simon the Canaanite,

19. And Judas Iscariot, which also betrayed him: and they went into an house.

20. And the multitude cometh together again, so that they could not so much as eat bread.

21. And when his friends heard of it, they went out to lay hold on him: for they said, He is beside himself.

22. And the scribes which came down from Jerusalem said, He hath Beelzebub, and by the prince of the devils casteth he out devils.

23. And he called them unto him, and said unto them in parables, How can Satan cast out Satan?

24. And if a kingdom be divided against itself, that kingdom cannot stand.

25. And if a house be divided against itself, that house cannot stand.

26. And if Satan rise up against himself, and be divided, he cannot stand, but hath an end.

27. No man can enter into a strong man's house, and spoil his goods, except he will first bind the strong man; and then he will spoil his house.

28. Verily I say unto you, All sins shall be forgiven unto the sons of men, and blasphemies wherewith soever they shall blaspheme:

29. But he that shall blaspheme against the Holy Ghost hath never forgiveness, but is in danger of eternal damnation.

30. Because they said, He hath an unclean spirit.

31. There came then his brethren and his mother, and, standing without, sent unto him, calling him.

32. And the multitude sat about him, and they said unto him, Behold, thy mother and thy brethren without seek for thee.

33. And he answered them, saying, Who is my mother, or my brethren?

34. And he looked round about on them which sat about him, and said, Behold my mother and my brethren!

35. For whosoever shall do the will of God, the same is my brother, and my sister, and mother.

CHAPTER 4

1. And he began again to teach by the sea side: and there was gathered unto him a great multitude, so that he entered into a ship, and sat in the sea; and the whole multitude was by the sea on the land.

2. And he taught them many things by parables, and said unto them in his doctrine,

3. Hearken; Behold, there went out a sower to sow:

4. And it came to pass, as he sowed, some fell by the way side, and the fowls of the air came and devoured it up.

5. And some fell on stony ground, where it had not much earth; and immediately it sprang up, because it had no depth of earth:

6. But when the sun was up, it was scorched; and because it had no root, it withered away.

7. And some fell among thorns, and the thorns grew up, and choked it, and it yielded no fruit.

8. And other fell on good ground, and did yield fruit that sprang up and increased; and brought forth, some thirty, and some sixty, and some an hundred.

9. And he said unto them, He that hath ears to hear, let him hear.

10. And when he was alone, they that were about him with the twelve asked of him the parable.

11. And he said unto them, Unto you it is given to know the mystery of the kingdom of God: but unto them that are without, all these things are done in parables:

12. That seeing they may see, and not perceive; and hearing they may hear, and not understand; lest at any time they should be converted, and their sins should be forgiven them.

13. And he said unto them, Know ye not this parable? and how then will ye know all parables?

14. The sower soweth the word.

15. And these are they by the way side, where the word is sown; but when they have heard, Satan cometh immediately, and taketh away the word that was sown in their hearts.

16. And these are they likewise which are sown on stony ground; who, when they have heard the word, immediately receive it with gladness;

17. And have no root in themselves, and so endure but for a time: afterward, when affliction or persecution ariseth for the word's sake, immediately they are offended.

18. And these are they which are sown among thorns; such as hear the word,

19. And the cares of this world, and the deceitfulness of riches, and the lusts of other things entering in, choke the word, and it becometh unfruitful.

20. And these are they which are sown on good ground; such as hear the word, and receive it, and bring forth fruit, some thirtyfold, some sixty, and some an hundred.

21. And he said unto them, Is a candle brought to be put under a bushel, or under a bed? and not to be set on a candlestick?

22. For there is nothing hid, which shall not be manifested; neither was any thing kept secret, but that it should come abroad.

23. If any man have ears to hear, let him hear.

24. And he said unto them, Take heed what ye hear: with what measure ye mete, it shall be measured to you: and unto you that hear shall more be given.

25. For he that hath, to him shall be given: and he that hath not, from him shall be taken even that which he hath.

26. And he said, So is the kingdom of God, as if a man should cast seed into the ground;

27. And should sleep, and rise night and day, and the seed should spring and grow up, he knoweth not how.

28. For the earth bringeth forth fruit of herself; first the blade, then the ear, after that the full corn in the ear.

29. But when the fruit is brought forth, immediately he putteth in the sickle, because the harvest is come.

30. And he said, Whereunto shall we liken the kingdom of God? or with what comparison shall we compare it?

31. It is like a grain of mustard seed, which, when it is sown in the earth, is less than all the seeds that be in the earth:

32. But when it is sown, it groweth up, and becometh greater than all herbs, and shooteth out great branches; so that the fowls of the air may lodge under the shadow of it.

33. And with many such parables spake he the word unto them, as they were able to hear it.

34. But without a parable spake he not unto them: and when they were alone, he expounded all things to his disciples.

35. And the same day, when the even was come, he saith unto them, Let us pass over unto the other side.

36. And when they had sent away the multitude, they took him even as he was in the ship. And there were also with him other little ships.

37. And there arose a great storm of wind, and the waves beat into the ship, so that it was now full.

38. And he was in the hinder part of the ship, asleep on a pillow: and they awake him, and say unto him, Master, carest thou not that we perish?

39. And he arose, and rebuked the wind, and said unto the sea, Peace, be still. And the wind ceased, and there was a great calm.

40. And he said unto them, Why are ye so fearful? how is it that ye have no faith?

41. And they feared exceedingly, and said one to another, What manner of man is this, that even the wind and the sea obey him?

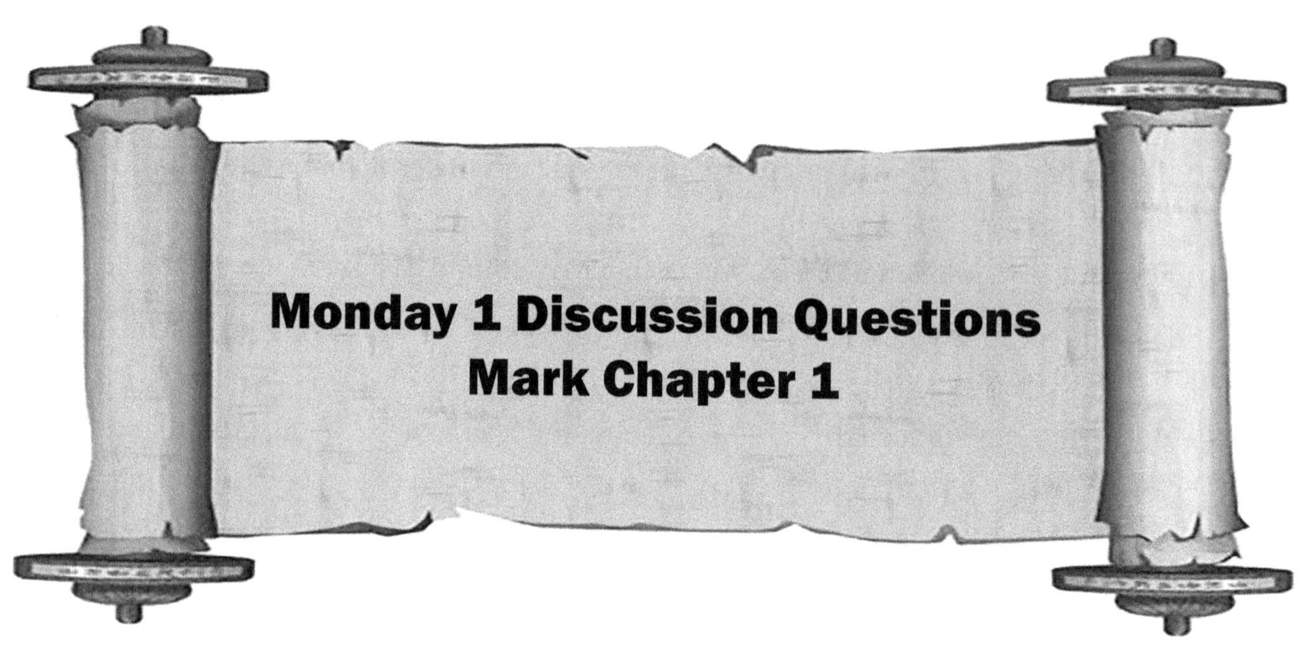

1. How does Mark describe John's voice?
2. What is the voice saying?
3. Describe John's clothes. What did he eat?
4. Who baptized Jesus when he came from Nazareth of Galilee? Where?
5. What did Jesus see when he came up from the water?
6. How long did Jesus stay in the wilderness when the spirit drove him there?
7. What did Jesus say when the disciples told him that all men were seeking for him?
8. What did Jesus tell the leper not to do after he healed him? Did the leper obey Jesus?
9. What did the leper do?
10. How did the leper's disobedience affect Jesus?

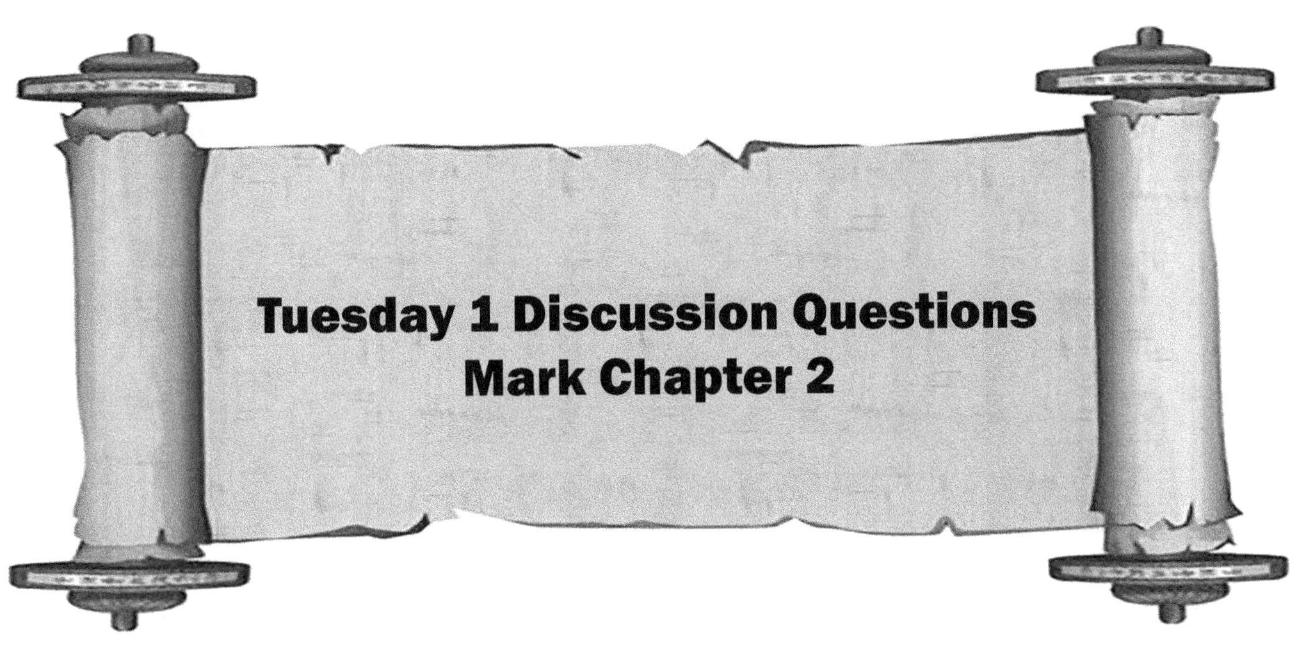

1. What happened when Jesus entered Capernaum and after a few days, people heard Jesus was in the house? ____________________

2. When people came to bring a man with palsy to Jesus and couldn't get through the door what did they do? ____________________

3. What did Jesus do? ____________________

4. Offenses will come. But what did Jesus say about the people who do the offending? ____________________

5. What was the command if a person's hand or foot offends them? Why? ____________________

6. What did he say to do if their eye offended them? Why? ____________________

7. Why did he say take heed not to despise the little ones? ____________________

8. Who did Jesus say the shepherd rejoices over more, the sheep that did not go astray or the one that returned home after going astray? ____________________

9. What did Jesus tell them to do if their brother trespassed against them? ____________________

10. What did Jesus say to do if he neglects to hear the three witnesses? ____________________

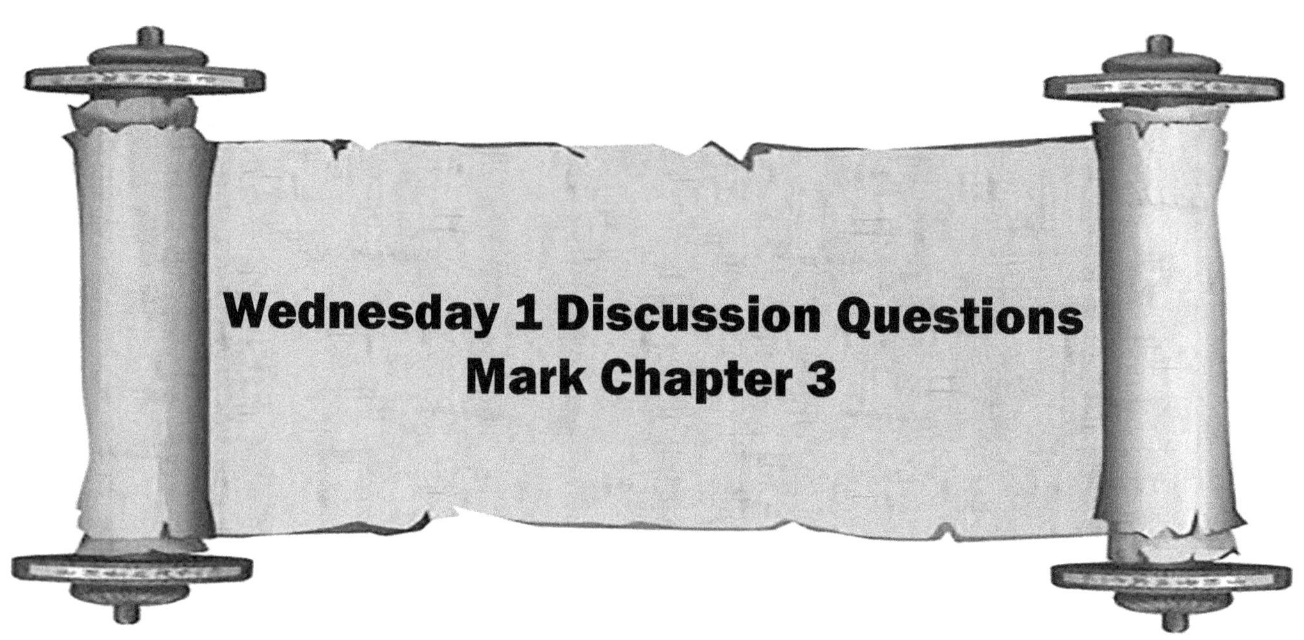

1. What were the people in the synagogue waiting to accuse Jesus of? ______________________________

2. After Jesus asked the man with the withered hand to stand, what question did he ask all the people there? ______________________________

3. Did the people answer Jesus' question? ______________________________

4. What happened when Jesus asked the man to stretch forth his hand? ______________________________

5. What are the names of the 12 men ordained to go forth and preach? ______________________________

6. List the places the multitudes came from? ______________________________

7. Why did Jesus instruct the disciples to have a ship waiting on him? ______________________________

8. What did the unclean spirits do when they saw Jesus? ______________________________

9. What did Jesus surname James the son of Zebedee and John the brother of James? ______________________________

10. What did this surname mean? ______________________________

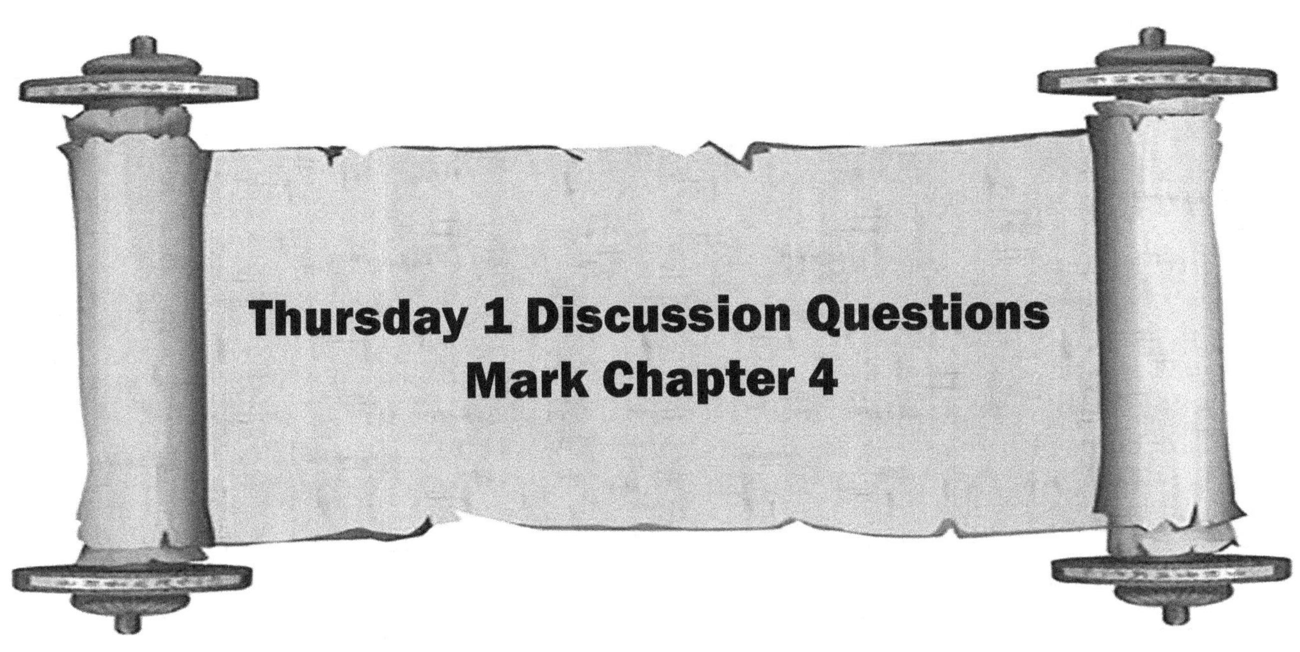

1. After the people in the multitude left, what did Jesus ask the disciples?

2. In Jesus' parable, what does the sower sow?

3. What did Jesus ask about the candlestick?

4. What did Jesus say about hidden things and secrest?

5. Why did Jesus say, "Take heed what ye hear"?

6. What did Jesus say about those who have, and those who have not?

7. How did Jesus liken the kingdom of Heaven to a seed cast on the ground?

8. How did Jesus liken the kingdom of Heaven to a mustard seed?

9. Jesus spoke many parables. When he was alone with his disciples what did he do without a parable?

10. What did Jesus say when the evening came?

WEEKLY REVIEW
MARK CHAPTERS 1-4

NAME THAT CHAPTER

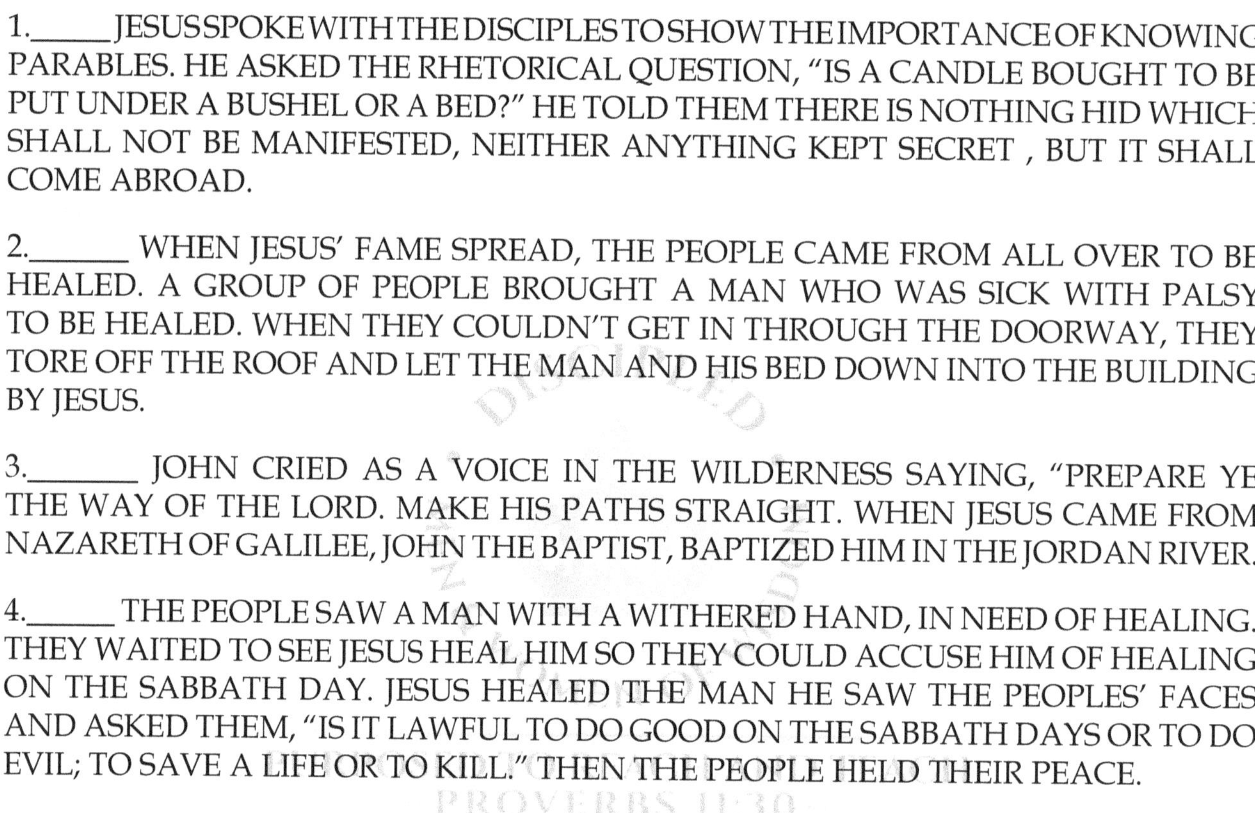

1._____ JESUS SPOKE WITH THE DISCIPLES TO SHOW THE IMPORTANCE OF KNOWING PARABLES. HE ASKED THE RHETORICAL QUESTION, "IS A CANDLE BOUGHT TO BE PUT UNDER A BUSHEL OR A BED?" HE TOLD THEM THERE IS NOTHING HID WHICH SHALL NOT BE MANIFESTED, NEITHER ANYTHING KEPT SECRET , BUT IT SHALL COME ABROAD.

2.______ WHEN JESUS' FAME SPREAD, THE PEOPLE CAME FROM ALL OVER TO BE HEALED. A GROUP OF PEOPLE BROUGHT A MAN WHO WAS SICK WITH PALSY TO BE HEALED. WHEN THEY COULDN'T GET IN THROUGH THE DOORWAY, THEY TORE OFF THE ROOF AND LET THE MAN AND HIS BED DOWN INTO THE BUILDING BY JESUS.

3._______ JOHN CRIED AS A VOICE IN THE WILDERNESS SAYING, "PREPARE YE THE WAY OF THE LORD. MAKE HIS PATHS STRAIGHT. WHEN JESUS CAME FROM NAZARETH OF GALILEE, JOHN THE BAPTIST, BAPTIZED HIM IN THE JORDAN RIVER.

4.______ THE PEOPLE SAW A MAN WITH A WITHERED HAND, IN NEED OF HEALING. THEY WAITED TO SEE JESUS HEAL HIM SO THEY COULD ACCUSE HIM OF HEALING ON THE SABBATH DAY. JESUS HEALED THE MAN HE SAW THE PEOPLES' FACES AND ASKED THEM, "IS IT LAWFUL TO DO GOOD ON THE SABBATH DAYS OR TO DO EVIL; TO SAVE A LIFE OR TO KILL." THEN THE PEOPLE HELD THEIR PEACE.

TRUE OR FALSE

5. ALL THE LAND OF JUDEA AND JERUSALEM WERE BAPTIZED BY JOHN IN THE RIVER OF JORDAN..

____

6. THE SCRIBES AND PHARISEES RIDICULED JESUS FOR EATING WITH THE PUBLICANS AND SINNERS.

____

7. WHEN JESUS WITHDREW HIMSELF WITH THE DISCIPLES TO THE SEA, THE GREAT MULTITUDE LEFT AND WENT BACK HOME TO GALILEE AND JUDEA

____

FILL IN THE BLANKS

8. And to have______________to heal______________and to______________out devils.
9. And he said to them,______________ye not this______________? And how______________ will ye know all the parables?
10. The________ __________the________________.

MY PRAYER JOURNAL

Please use this space to record your thoughts and feelings as you travel on this spirit led journey through the word of God with us. Please know that you have brothers and sisters in this organization from all over the world praying with and for you. My prayer for you is that you will begin to see the power of God resting in each set of your footprints. As you look back and examine your past in this journal, may you realize that you were never alone and according to Hebrews 13:5, God will never leave nor forsake you. ~LADY FLORA

I THESSALONIANS 5:17

THE STUDY OF THE FOUR GOSPELS VOCABULARY DEFINITIONS FOR MARK CHAPTERS 5-8

WORD	DEFINITIONS
1) GADARENE	
2) FETTERS	
3) LEGION	
4) VIRTUE	
5) ADO	
6) DAMSEL	
7) TALITHA	
8) CUMI	
9) SHOD	
10)LASCIVIOUS	

DMWW DAILY BIBLE READING
MARK CHAPTERS 5-8 KJV

CHAPTER 5

1. And they came over unto the other side of the sea, into the country of the Gadarenes.
2. And when he was come out of the ship, immediately there met him out of the tombs a man with an unclean spirit,
3. Who had his dwelling among the tombs; and no man could bind him, no, not with chains:
4. Because that he had been often bound with fetters and chains, and the chains had been plucked asunder by him, and the fetters broken in pieces: neither could any man tame him.
5. And always, night and day, he was in the mountains, and in the tombs, crying, and cutting himself with stones.
6. But when he saw Jesus afar off, he ran and worshipped him,
7. And cried with a loud voice, and said, What have I to do with thee, Jesus, thou Son of the most high God? I adjure thee by God, that thou torment me not.
8. For he said unto him, Come out of the man, thou unclean spirit.
9. And he asked him, What is thy name? And he answered, saying, My name is Legion: for we are many.
10. And he besought him much that he would not send them away out of the country.
11. Now there was there nigh unto the mountains a great herd of swine feeding.
12. And all the devils besought him, saying, Send us into the swine, that we may enter into them.
13. And forthwith Jesus gave them leave. And the unclean spirits went out, and entered into the swine: and the herd ran violently down a steep place into the sea, (they were about two thousand;) and were choked in the sea.
14. And they that fed the swine fled, and told it in the city, and in the country. And they went out to see what it was that was done.
15. And they come to Jesus, and see him that was possessed with the devil, and had the legion, sitting, and clothed, and in his right mind: and they were afraid.
16. And they that saw it told them how it befell to him that was possessed with the devil, and also concerning the swine.
17. And they began to pray him to depart out of their coasts.

18. And when he was come into the ship, he that had been possessed with the devil prayed him that he might be with him.

19. Howbeit Jesus suffered him not, but saith unto him, Go home to thy friends, and tell them how great things the Lord hath done for thee, and hath had compassion on thee.

20. And he departed, and began to publish in Decapolis how great things Jesus had done for him: and all men did marvel.

21. And when Jesus was passed over again by ship unto the other side, much people gathered unto him: and he was nigh unto the sea.

22. And, behold, there cometh one of the rulers of the synagogue, Jairus by name; and when he saw him, he fell at his feet,

23. And besought him greatly, saying, My little daughter lieth at the point of death: I pray thee, come and lay thy hands on her, that she may be healed; and she shall live.

24. And Jesus went with him; and much people followed him, and thronged him.

25. And a certain woman, which had an issue of blood twelve years,

26. And had suffered many things of many physicians, and had spent all that she had, and was nothing bettered, but rather grew worse,

27. When she had heard of Jesus, came in the press behind, and touched his garment.

28. For she said, If I may touch but his clothes, I shall be whole.

29. And straightway the fountain of her blood was dried up; and she felt in her body that she was healed of that plague.

30. And Jesus, immediately knowing in himself that virtue had gone out of him, turned him about in the press, and said, Who touched my clothes?

31. And his disciples said unto him, Thou seest the multitude thronging thee, and sayest thou, Who touched me?

32. And he looked round about to see her that had done this thing.

33. But the woman fearing and trembling, knowing what was done in her, came and fell down before him, and told him all the truth.

34. And he said unto her, Daughter, thy faith hath made thee whole; go in peace, and be whole of thy plague.

35. While he yet spake, there came from the ruler of the synagogue's house certain which said, Thy daughter is dead: why troublest thou the Master any further?

36. As soon as Jesus heard the word that was spoken, he saith unto the ruler of the synagogue, Be not afraid, only believe.

37. And he suffered no man to follow him, save Peter, and James, and John the brother of James.

38. And he cometh to the house of the ruler of the synagogue, and seeth the tumult, and them that wept and wailed greatly.

39. And when he was come in, he saith unto them, Why make ye this ado, and weep? the damsel is not dead, but sleepeth.

40. And they laughed him to scorn. But when he had put them all out, he taketh the father and the mother of the damsel, and them that were with him, and entereth in where the damsel was lying.

41. And he took the damsel by the hand, and said unto her, Talitha cumi; which is, being interpreted, Damsel, I say unto thee, arise.

42. And straightway the damsel arose, and walked; for she was of the age of twelve years. And they were astonished with a great astonishment.

43. And he charged them straitly that no man should know it; and commanded that something should be given her to eat.

CHAPTER 6

1. And he went out from thence, and came into his own country; and his disciples follow him.

2. And when the sabbath day was come, he began to teach in the synagogue: and many hearing him were astonished, saying, From whence hath this man these things? and what wisdom is this which is given unto him, that even such mighty works are wrought by his hands?

3. Is not this the carpenter, the son of Mary, the brother of James, and Joses, and of Juda, and Simon? and are not his sisters here with us? And they were offended at him.

4. But Jesus, said unto them, A prophet is not without honour, but in his own country, and among his own kin, and in his own house.

5. And he could there do no mighty work, save that he laid his hands upon a few sick folk, and healed them.

6. And he marvelled because of their unbelief. And he went round about the villages, teaching.

7. And he called unto him the twelve, and began to send them forth by two and two; and gave them power over unclean spirits;

8. And commanded them that they should take nothing for their journey, save a staff only; no scrip, no bread, no money in their purse:

9. But be shod with sandals; and not put on two coats.

10. And he said unto them, In what place soever ye enter into an house, there abide till ye depart from that place.

11. And whosoever shall not receive you, nor hear you, when ye depart thence, shake off the dust under your feet for a testimony against them. Verily I say unto you, It shall be more tolerable for Sodom and Gomorrha in the day of judgment, than for that city.

12. And they went out, and preached that men should repent.

13. And they cast out many devils, and anointed with oil many that were sick, and healed them.

14. And king Herod heard of him; (for his name was spread abroad:) and he said, That John the Baptist was risen from the dead, and therefore mighty works do shew forth themselves in him.

15. Others said, That it is Elias. And others said, That it is a prophet, or as one of the prophets.

16. But when Herod heard thereof, he said, It is John, whom I beheaded: he is risen from the dead.

17. For Herod himself had sent forth and laid hold upon John, and bound him in prison for Herodias' sake, his brother Philip's wife: for he had married her.

18. For John had said unto Herod, It is not lawful for thee to have thy brother's wife.

19. Therefore Herodias had a quarrel against him, and would have killed him; but she could not:

20. For Herod feared John, knowing that he was a just man and an holy, and observed him; and when he heard him, he did many things, and heard him gladly.

21. And when a convenient day was come, that Herod on his birthday made a supper to his lords, high captains, and chief estates of Galilee;

22. And when the daughter of the said Herodias came in, and danced, and pleased Herod and them that sat with him, the king said unto the damsel, Ask of me whatsoever thou wilt, and I will give it thee.

23. And he sware unto her, Whatsoever thou shalt ask of me, I will give it thee, unto the half of my kingdom.

24. And she went forth, and said unto her mother, What shall I ask? And she said, The head of John the Baptist.

25. And she came in straightway with haste unto the king, and asked, saying, I will that thou give me by and by in a charger the head of John the Baptist.

26. And the king was exceeding sorry; yet for his oath's sake, and for their sakes which sat with him, he would not reject her.

27. And immediately the king sent an executioner, and commanded his head to be brought: and he went and beheaded him in the prison,

28. And brought his head in a charger, and gave it to the damsel: and the damsel gave it to her mother.

29. And when his disciples heard of it, they came and took up his corpse, and laid it in a tomb.

30. And the apostles gathered themselves together unto Jesus, and told him all things, both what they had done, and what they had taught.

31. And he said unto them, Come ye yourselves apart into a desert place, and rest a while: for there were many coming and going, and they had no leisure so much as to eat.

32. And they departed into a desert place by ship privately.

33. And the people saw them departing, and many knew him, and ran afoot thither out of all cities, and outwent them, and came together unto him.

34. And Jesus, when he came out, saw much people, and was moved with compassion toward them, because they were as sheep not having a shepherd: and he began to teach them many things.

35. And when the day was now far spent, his disciples came unto him, and said, This is a desert place, and now the time is far passed:

36. Send them away, that they may go into the country round about, and into the villages, and buy themselves bread: for they have nothing to eat.

37. He answered and said unto them, Give ye them to eat. And they say unto him, Shall we go and buy two hundred pennyworth of bread, and give them to eat?

38. He saith unto them, How many loaves have ye? go and see. And when they knew, they say, Five, and two fishes.

39. And he commanded them to make all sit down by companies upon the green grass.

40. And they sat down in ranks, by hundreds, and by fifties.

41. And when he had taken the five loaves and the two fishes, he looked up to heaven, and blessed, and brake the loaves, and gave them to his disciples to set before them; and the two fishes divided he among them all.

42. And they did all eat, and were filled.

43. And they took up twelve baskets full of the fragments, and of the fishes.

44. And they that did eat of the loaves were about five thousand men.

45. And straightway he constrained his disciples to get into the ship, and to go to the other side before unto Bethsaida, while he sent away the people.

46. And when he had sent them away, he departed into a mountain to pray.

47. And when even was come, the ship was in the midst of the sea, and he alone on the land.

48. And he saw them toiling in rowing; for the wind was contrary unto them: and about the fourth watch of the night he cometh unto them, walking upon the sea, and would have passed by them.

49. But when they saw him walking upon the sea, they supposed it had been a spirit, and cried out:

50. For they all saw him, and were troubled. And immediately he talked with them, and saith unto them, Be of good cheer: it is I; be not afraid.

51. And he went up unto them into the ship; and the wind ceased: and they were sore amazed in themselves beyond measure, and wondered.

52. For they considered not the miracle of the loaves: for their heart was hardened.

53. And when they had passed over, they came into the land of Gennesaret, and drew to the shore.

54. And when they were come out of the ship, straightway they knew him,

55. And ran through that whole region round about, and began to carry about in beds those that were sick, where they heard he was.

56. And whithersoever he entered, into villages, or cities, or country, they laid the sick in the streets, and besought him that they might touch if it were but the border of his garment: and as many as touched him were made whole.

CHAPTER 7

1. Then came together unto him the Pharisees, and certain of the scribes, which came from Jerusalem.

2. And when they saw some of his disciples eat bread with defiled, that is to say, with unwashen, hands, they found fault.

3. For the Pharisees, and all the Jews, except they wash their hands oft, eat not, holding the tradition of the elders.

4. And when they come from the market, except they wash, they eat not. And many other things there be, which they have received to hold, as the washing of cups, and pots, brasen vessels, and of tables.

5. Then the Pharisees and scribes asked him, Why walk not thy disciples according to the tradition of the elders, but eat bread with unwashen hands?

6. He answered and said unto them, Well hath Esaias prophesied of you hypocrites, as it is written, This people honoureth me with their lips, but their heart is far from me.

7. Howbeit in vain do they worship me, teaching for doctrines the commandments of men.

8. For laying aside the commandment of God, ye hold the tradition of men, as the washing of pots and cups: and many other such like things ye do.

9. And he said unto them, Full well ye reject the commandment of God, that ye may keep your own tradition.

10. For Moses said, Honour thy father and thy mother; and, Whoso curseth father or mother, let him die the death:

11. But ye say, If a man shall say to his father or mother, It is Corban, that is to say, a gift, by whatsoever thou mightest be profited by me; he shall be free.

12. And ye suffer him no more to do ought for his father or his mother;

13. Making the word of God of none effect through your tradition, which ye have delivered: and many such like things do ye.

14. And when he had called all the people unto him, he said unto them, Hearken unto me every one of you, and understand:

15. There is nothing from without a man, that entering into him can defile him: but the things which come out of him, those are they that defile the man.

16. If any man have ears to hear, let him hear.

17. And when he was entered into the house from the people, his disciples asked him concerning the parable.

18. And he saith unto them, Are ye so without understanding also? Do ye not perceive, that whatsoever thing from without entereth into the man, it cannot defile him;

19. Because it entereth not into his heart, but into the belly, and goeth out into the draught, purging all meats?

20. And he said, That which cometh out of the man, that defileth the man.

21. For from within, out of the heart of men, proceed evil thoughts, adulteries, fornications, murders,

22. Thefts, covetousness, wickedness, deceit, lasciviousness, an evil eye, blasphemy, pride, foolishness:

23. All these evil things come from within, and defile the man.

24. And from thence he arose, and went into the borders of Tyre and Sidon, and entered into an house, and would have no man know it: but he could not be hid.

25. For a certain woman, whose young daughter had an unclean spirit, heard of him, and came and fell at his feet:

26. The woman was a Greek, a Syrophenician by nation; and she besought him that he would cast forth the devil out of her daughter.

27. But Jesus said unto her, Let the children first be filled: for it is not meet to take the children's bread, and to cast it unto the dogs.

28. And she answered and said unto him, Yes, Lord: yet the dogs under the table eat of the children's crumbs.

29. And he said unto her, For this saying go thy way; the devil is gone out of thy daughter.

30. And when she was come to her house, she found the devil gone out, and her daughter laid upon the bed.

31. And again, departing from the coasts of Tyre and Sidon, he came unto the sea of Galilee, through the midst of the coasts of Decapolis.

32. And they bring unto him one that was deaf, and had an impediment in his speech; and they beseech him to put his hand upon him.

33. And he took him aside from the multitude, and put his fingers into his ears, and he spit, and touched his tongue;

34. And looking up to heaven, he sighed, and saith unto him, Ephphatha, that is, Be opened.

35. And straightway his ears were opened, and the string of his tongue was loosed, and he spake plain.

36. And he charged them that they should tell no man: but the more he charged them, so much the more a great deal they published it;

37. And were beyond measure astonished, saying, He hath done all things well: he maketh both the deaf to hear, and the dumb to speak.

CHAPTER 8

1. In those days the multitude being very great, and having nothing to eat, Jesus called his disciples unto him, and saith unto them,

2. I have compassion on the multitude, because they have now been with me three days, and have nothing to eat:

3. And if I send them away fasting to their own houses, they will faint by the way: for divers of them came from far.

4. And his disciples answered him, From whence can a man satisfy these men with bread here in the wilderness?

5. And he asked them, How many loaves have ye? And they said, Seven.

6. And he commanded the people to sit down on the ground: and he took the seven loaves, and gave thanks, and brake, and gave to his disciples to set before them; and they did set them before the people.

7. And they had a few small fishes: and he blessed, and commanded to set them also before them.

8. So they did eat, and were filled: and they took up of the broken meat that was left seven baskets.

9. And they that had eaten were about four thousand: and he sent them away.

10. And straightway he entered into a ship with his disciples, and came into the parts of Dalmanutha.

11. And the Pharisees came forth, and began to question with him, seeking of him a sign from heaven, tempting him.

12. And he sighed deeply in his spirit, and saith, Why doth this generation seek after a sign? verily I say unto you, There shall no sign be given unto this generation.

13. And he left them, and entering into the ship again departed to the other side.

14. Now the disciples had forgotten to take bread, neither had they in the ship with them more than one loaf.

15. And he charged them, saying, Take heed, beware of the leaven of the Pharisees, and of the leaven of Herod.

16. And they reasoned among themselves, saying, It is because we have no bread.

17. And when Jesus knew it, he saith unto them, Why reason ye, because ye have no bread? perceive ye not yet, neither understand? have ye your heart yet hardened?

18. Having eyes, see ye not? and having ears, hear ye not? and do ye not remember?

19. When I brake the five loaves among five thousand, how many baskets full of fragments took ye up? They say unto him, Twelve.

20. And when the seven among four thousand, how many baskets full of fragments took ye up? And they said, Seven.

21. And he said unto them, How is it that ye do not understand?

22. And he cometh to Bethsaida; and they bring a blind man unto him, and besought him to touch him.

23. And he took the blind man by the hand, and led him out of the town; and when he had spit on his eyes, and put his hands upon him, he asked him if he saw ought.

24. And he looked up, and said, I see men as trees, walking.

25. After that he put his hands again upon his eyes, and made him look up: and he was restored, and saw every man clearly.

26. And he sent him away to his house, saying, Neither go into the town, nor tell it to any in the town.

27. And Jesus went out, and his disciples, into the towns of Caesarea Philippi: and by the way he asked his disciples, saying unto them, Whom do men say that I am?

28. And they answered, John the Baptist; but some say, Elias; and others, One of the prophets.

29. And he saith unto them, But whom say ye that I am? And Peter answereth and saith unto him, Thou art the Christ.

30. And he charged them that they should tell no man of him.

31. And he began to teach them, that the Son of man must suffer many things, and be rejected of the elders, and of the chief priests, and scribes, and be killed, and after three days rise again.

32. And he spake that saying openly. And Peter took him, and began to rebuke him.

33. But when he had turned about and looked on his disciples, he rebuked Peter, saying, Get thee behind me, Satan: for thou savourest not the things that be of God, but the things that be of men.

34. And when he had called the people unto him with his disciples also, he said unto them, Whosoever will come after me, let him deny himself, and take up his cross, and follow me.

35. For whosoever will save his life shall lose it; but whosoever shall lose his life for my sake and the gospel's, the same shall save it.

36. For what shall it profit a man, if he shall gain the whole world, and lose his own soul?

37. Or what shall a man give in exchange for his soul?

38. Whosoever therefore shall be ashamed of me and of my words in this adulterous and sinful generation; of him also shall the Son of man be ashamed, when he cometh in the glory of his Father with the holy angels.

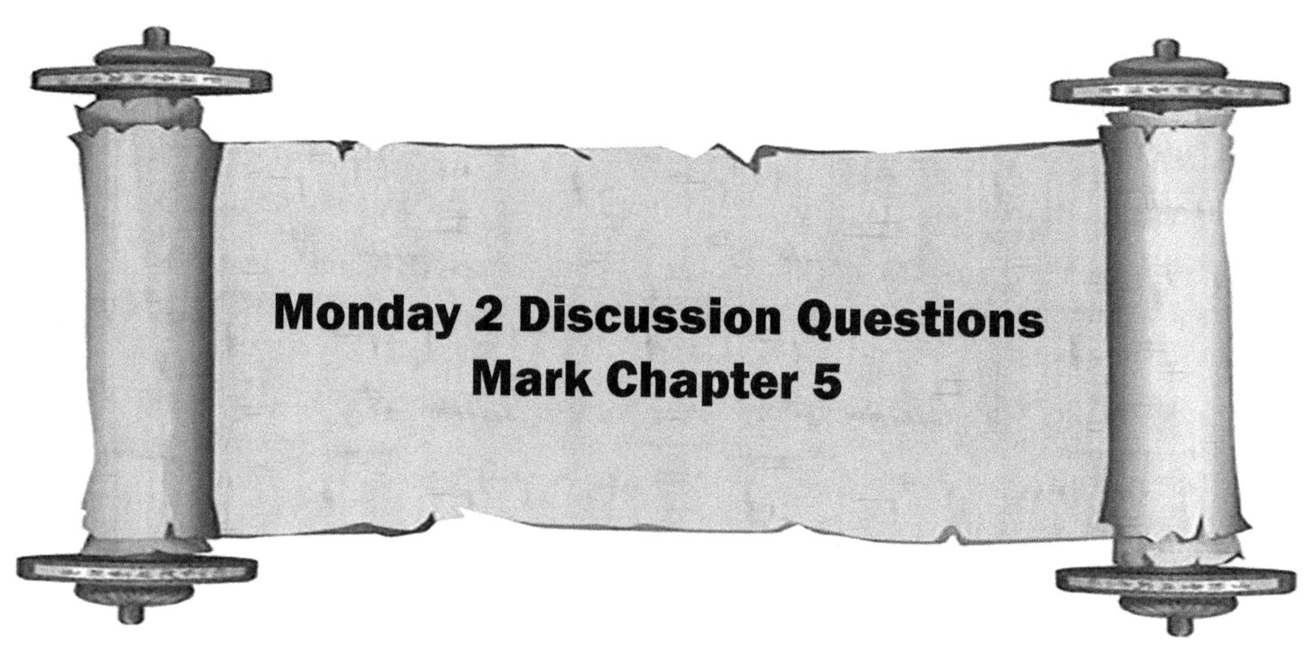

1. Who immediately met Jesus when he was coming out of the ship?
2. Where did the man come from?
3. What did the man do when he was bound in in fetters and chains?
4. What did Jairus do when he saw Jesus?
5. Who did Jesus see on his way to pray for Jairus' daughter?
6. What did the woman do that g0t Jesus' attention? Why?
7. What happened to her when she touched his clothes?
8. Who did Jesus allow to continue on his journey with him?
9. What happened when Jesus went in and told the people the damsel was not dead, but only sleeping?
10. What did he say to her when he took her hand? What does that mean?

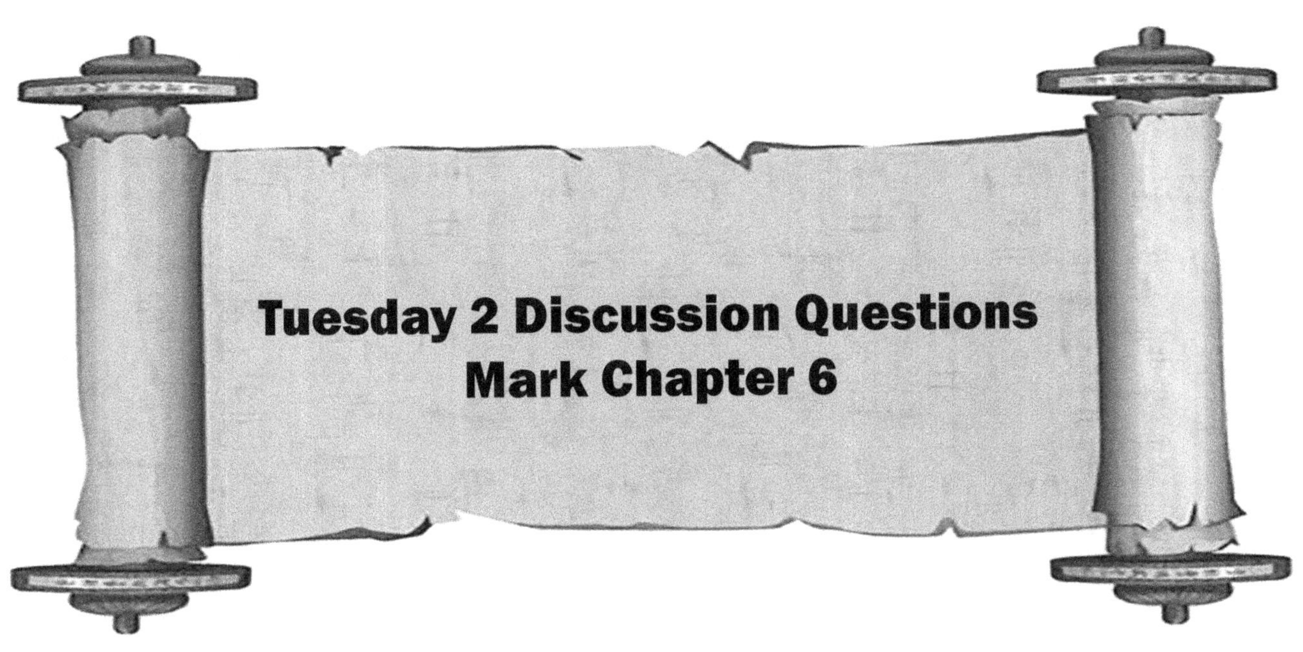

1. The people heard Jesus' teachings and were astonished. What were their questions about him? ____
____

2. What did Jesus say to those who were offended by him being a carpenter? __________
____
____

3. When Jesus called the 12 disciples to go two by two, what did he command them to take and not to take on their journey? ______________________________
____
____

4. What did Jesus say would be a testimony against those who would not receive the disciples in their home? ______________________________
____
____

5. What was the order of seating when the disciples fed the multitude? __________
____
____

6. After feeding the people, where did the disciples get on the ship? __________
____
____

7. Where did Jesus go after he sent the people away? ______________________
____
____

8. What did Jesus see at the fourth watch of the night? ______________________
____
____

9. What did Jesus tell them when he saw that they were troubled? __________
____
____

10. Did the people in Gennesaret know Jesus when the shop drew up to the shore? What happened? ____
____

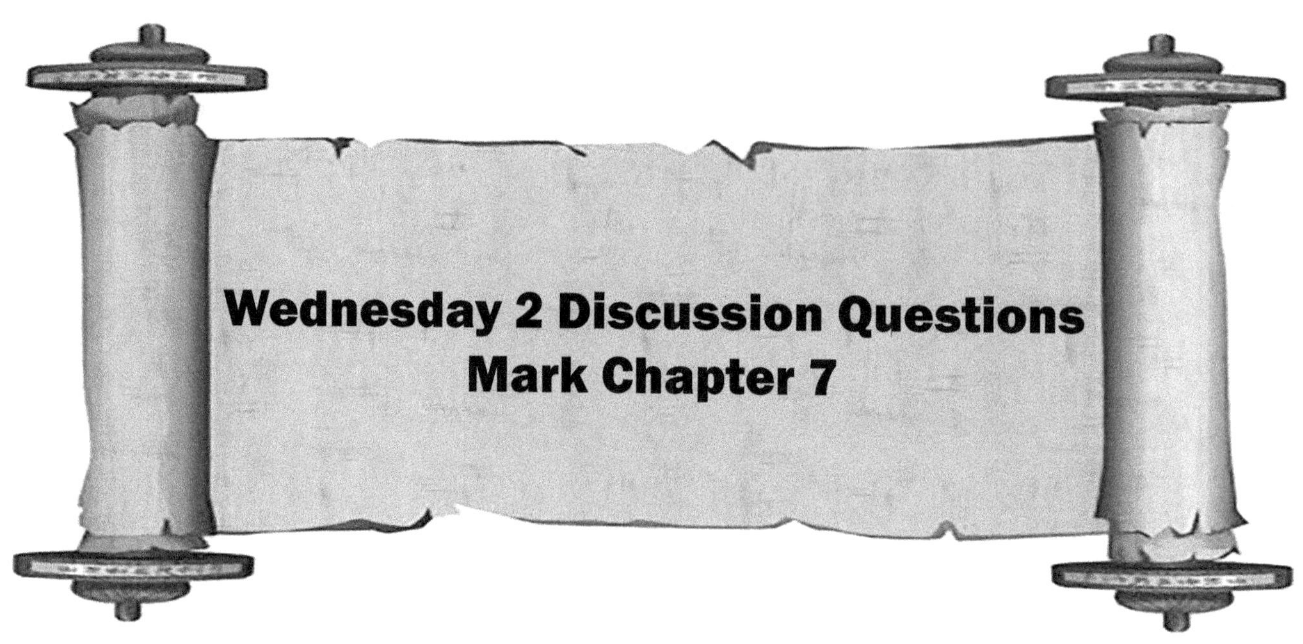

1. List some of the traditions of the Jews and Pharisees? ______

2. What did Jesus say some men lay aside to hold to the tradition of men? ______

3. Which commandment does Jesus use to illustrate his point? ______

4. What did God tell them they did to make the word of God of none effect? ______

5. When Jesus called the people unto him, what did he tell them to do? ______

6. What did Jesus say defiles the man? ______

7. Why does Jesus say these things defile the man? ______

8. What did Jesus tell them DOES NOT defile man? ______

9. Why did he tell them it doesn't? ______

10. So, did Jesus say it was a sin to eat meat? ______

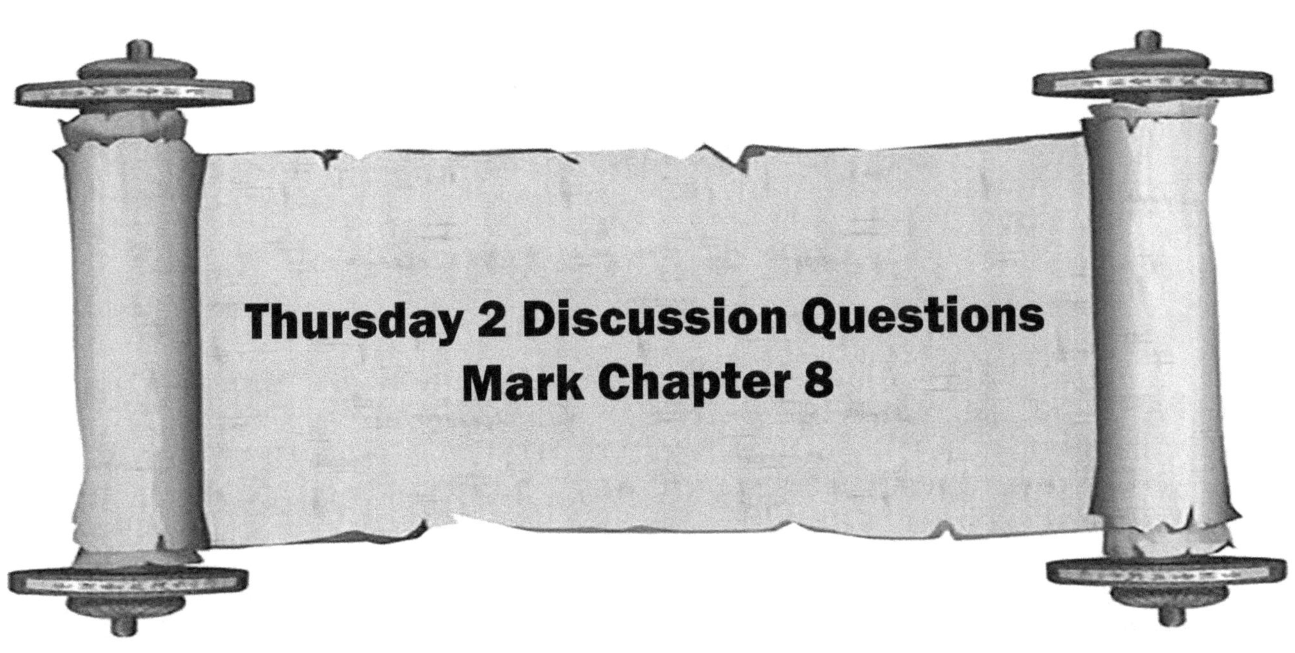

Thursday 2 Discussion Questions
Mark Chapter 8

1. The disciples worried about not having bread. What did Jesus ask them about their eyes and ears when he reminded them of times past when he had provided bread for multitudes of people?

2. What did Jesus do when they brought the blind man to him and besought him to touch him?

3. What did Jesus ask the man?

4. What was the man's answer?

5. What did Jesus do when the man told him that?

6. What happened this time?

7. Why did Peter rebuke Jesus?

8. Why did Jesus rebuke Peter? What did he say to Peter?

9. What did Jesus say those whoever would come after him must do?

10. What did Jesus say about what would happen to those who save their life and those who shall lose their life?

WEEKLY REVIEW
MARK CHAPTERS 5-8

NAME THAT CHAPTER

1.______ WHEN JESUS CAME OFF THE SHIP, HE WAS MET BY A MAN WITH AN UNCLEAN SPIRIT. HE WAS POSSESSED BY A LEGION OF DEMONS, JESUS CAST OUT THE DEMONS OUT OF THE MAN AND INTO 2,000 SWINE. THEY DEMONS CAUSED THE SWINE TO RUN WILDLY AND VIOLENTLY INTO THE SEA AND THEY WERE CHOKED AND DIED.

2.______ THE PEOPLE TOOK ISSUE WITH THE FACT THAT THE DISCIPLES WERE NOT WASHING THEIR HANDS BEFORE EATING. JESUS TOLD THEM HE WAS MORE CONCERNED WITH THEM NOT FOLLOWING GOD'S COMMANDMENT TO HONOR THEIR MOTHER AND FATHER. JESUS CALLED THEM HYPOCRITES AND SAID THEIR HONORING MAN MADE TRADITIONS OVER GOD'S LAW MADE THE WORD OF NON-EFFECT.

3.______ JESUS SENT THE DISCIPLES OUT TWO BY TWO TO SPREAD HIS WORD. HE TOLD THEM WHEN THEY WENT NOT TO TAKE ANYTHING BUT A STAFF.NO SCRIP, NO BREAD AND NO MONEY IN THEIR PURSE. JESUS TOLD THEM TO BE SHOD WITH SANDALS AND NOT TO TAKE TWO COATS. THEY MET A WOMAN WITH AN ISSUE OF BLOOD WHO WAS HEALED OF HER DISEASE WHEN SHE TOUCHED THE HEM OF JESUS' GARMENT, HER FAITH MADE HER WHOLE.

4.______ A BLIND MAN WAS BROUGHT TO JESUS TO BE HEALED. JESUS LED HIM OUT OF THE TOWN, SPIT ON HIS EYES AND PUT HIS HANDS ON HIM. THEN JESUS ASKED HIM WHAT HE SAW. THE MAN SAID HE SAW MEN AS TREES WALKING. JESUS PUT HIS HANDS ON HIM AGAIN AND COMMANDED HIM TO LOOK UP. THE MAN DID AND HE WAS RESTORED AND SAW EVERY MAN CLEARLY.

TRUE OR FALSE

5. WHEN THE MAN WITH THE UNCLEAN SPIRIT WAS BOUND WITH CHAINS AND FETTERS, HE WOULD JUST PLUCK THE CHAINS OFF.

____

6. JESUS COMMANDED THE DISCIPLES TO STAY IN WHATEVER HOUSE THEY ENTERED UNTIL THEY DEPARTED FROM THAT PLACE.

____

7. JESUS TOLD THE DISCIPLES HE HAD COMPASSION FOR THE MULTITUDE BECAUSE THEY HAD BEEN WITH HIM AND THEY HAD NOT EATEN FOR FIVE DAYS.

____

FILL IN THE BLANKS

8. BUT WHEN HE SAW_____________AFAR______________HE RAN AND ______________ HIM.

____
____
____

9. AND THEY WENT_____________AND_____________THAT MEN SHOULD _____________.

____
____
____

10. ALL THESE_____________THINGS COME FROM_____________AND_____________ THE MAN.

____
____
____

MY PRAYER JOURNAL

Please use this space to record your thoughts and feelings as you travel on this spirit led journey through the word of God with us. Please know that you have brothers and sisters in this organization from all over the world praying with and for you. My prayer for you is that you will begin to see the power of God resting in each set of your footprints. As you look back and examine your past in this journal, may you realize that you were never alone and according to Hebrews 13:5, God will never leave nor forsake you. ~LADY FLORA

I THESSALONIANS 5:17

THE STUDY OF THE FOUR GOSPELS VOCABULARY DEFINITIONS FOR MARK CHAPTERS 9-12

WORD	DEFINITIONS
1) WINEFAT	
2) HAPLY	
3) EVENTIDE	
4) PINE	
5) WONT	
6) PRECEPT	
7) SALUTE	
8) NOUGHT	
9) VERILY	
10)ERR	

DMWW DAILY BIBLE READING
MARK CHAPTERS 9-12 KJV

CHAPTER 9

1. And he said unto them, Verily I say unto you, That there be some of them that stand here, which shall not taste of death, till they have seen the kingdom of God come with power.
2. And after six days Jesus taketh with him Peter, and James, and John, and leadeth them up into an high mountain apart by themselves: and he was transfigured before them.
3. And his raiment became shining, exceeding white as snow; so as no fuller on earth can white them.
4. And there appeared unto them Elias with Moses: and they were talking with Jesus.
5. And Peter answered and said to Jesus, Master, it is good for us to be here: and let us make three tabernacles; one for thee, and one for Moses, and one for Elias.
6. For he wist not what to say; for they were sore afraid.
7. And there was a cloud that overshadowed them: and a voice came out of the cloud, saying, This is my beloved Son: hear him.
8. And suddenly, when they had looked round about, they saw no man any more, save Jesus only with themselves.
9. And as they came down from the mountain, he charged them that they should tell no man what things they had seen, till the Son of man were risen from the dead.
10. And they kept that saying with themselves, questioning one with another what the rising from the dead should mean.
11. And they asked him, saying, Why say the scribes that Elias must first come?
12. And he answered and told them, Elias verily cometh first, and restoreth all things; and how it is written of the Son of man, that he must suffer many things, and be set at nought.
13. But I say unto you, That Elias is indeed come, and they have done unto him whatsoever they listed, as it is written of him.
14. And when he came to his disciples, he saw a great multitude about them, and the scribes questioning with them.
15. And straightway all the people, when they beheld him, were greatly amazed, and running to him saluted him.
16. And he asked the scribes, What question ye with them?

17. And one of the multitude answered and said, Master, I have brought unto thee my son, which hath a dumb spirit;

18. And wheresoever he taketh him, he teareth him: and he foameth, and gnasheth with his teeth, and pineth away: and I spake to thy disciples that they should cast him out; and they could not.

19. He answereth him, and saith, O faithless generation, how long shall I be with you? how long shall I suffer you? bring him unto me.

20. And they brought him unto him: and when he saw him, straightway the spirit tare him; and he fell on the ground, and wallowed foaming.

21. And he asked his father, How long is it ago since this came unto him? And he said, Of a child.

22. And ofttimes it hath cast him into the fire, and into the waters, to destroy him: but if thou canst do any thing, have compassion on us, and help us.

23. Jesus said unto him, If thou canst believe, all things are possible to him that believeth.

24. And straightway the father of the child cried out, and said with tears, Lord, I believe; help thou mine unbelief.

25. When Jesus saw that the people came running together, he rebuked the foul spirit, saying unto him, Thou dumb and deaf spirit, I charge thee, come out of him, and enter no more into him.

26. And the spirit cried, and rent him sore, and came out of him: and he was as one dead; insomuch that many said, He is dead.

27. But Jesus took him by the hand, and lifted him up; and he arose.

28. And when he was come into the house, his disciples asked him privately, Why could not we cast him out?

29. And he said unto them, This kind can come forth by nothing, but by prayer and fasting.

30. And they departed thence, and passed through Galilee; and he would not that any man should know it.

31. For he taught his disciples, and said unto them, The Son of man is delivered into the hands of men, and they shall kill him; and after that he is killed, he shall rise the third day.

32. But they understood not that saying, and were afraid to ask him.

33. And he came to Capernaum: and being in the house he asked them, What was it that ye disputed among yourselves by the way?

34. But they held their peace: for by the way they had disputed among themselves, who should be the greatest.

35. And he sat down, and called the twelve, and saith unto them, If any man desire to be first, the same shall be last of all, and servant of all.

36. And he took a child, and set him in the midst of them: and when he had taken him in his arms, he said unto them,

37. Whosoever shall receive one of such children in my name, receiveth me: and whosoever shall receive me, receiveth not me, but him that sent me.

38. And John answered him, saying, Master, we saw one casting out devils in thy name, and he followeth not us: and we forbad him, because he followeth not us.

39. But Jesus said, Forbid him not: for there is no man which shall do a miracle in my name, that can lightly speak evil of me.

40. For he that is not against us is on our part.

41. For whosoever shall give you a cup of water to drink in my name, because ye belong to Christ, verily I say unto you, he shall not lose his reward.

42. And whosoever shall offend one of these little ones that believe in me, it is better for him that a millstone were hanged about his neck, and he were cast into the sea.

43. And if thy hand offend thee, cut it off: it is better for thee to enter into life maimed, than having two hands to go into hell, into the fire that never shall be quenched:

44. Where their worm dieth not, and the fire is not quenched.

45. And if thy foot offend thee, cut it off: it is better for thee to enter halt into life, than having two feet to be cast into hell, into the fire that never shall be quenched:

46. Where their worm dieth not, and the fire is not quenched.

47. And if thine eye offend thee, pluck it out: it is better for thee to enter into the kingdom of God with one eye, than having two eyes to be cast into hell fire:

48. Where their worm dieth not, and the fire is not quenched.

49. For every one shall be salted with fire, and every sacrifice shall be salted with salt.

50. Salt is good: but if the salt have lost his saltness, wherewith will ye season it? Have salt in yourselves, and have peace one with another.

CHAPTER 10

1. And he arose from thence, and cometh into the coasts of Judaea by the farther side of Jordan: and the people resort unto him again; and, as he was wont, he taught them again.

2. And the Pharisees came to him, and asked him, Is it lawful for a man to put away his wife? tempting him.

3. And he answered and said unto them, What did Moses command you?

4. And they said, Moses suffered to write a bill of divorcement, and to put her away.

5. And Jesus answered and said unto them, For the hardness of your heart he wrote you this precept.

6. But from the beginning of the creation God made them male and female.

7. For this cause shall a man leave his father and mother, and cleave to his wife;

8. And they twain shall be one flesh: so then they are no more twain, but one flesh.

9. What therefore God hath joined together, let not man put asunder.

10. And in the house his disciples asked him again of the same matter.

11. And he saith unto them, Whosoever shall put away his wife, and marry another, committeth adultery against her.

12. And if a woman shall put away her husband, and be married to another, she committeth adultery.

13. And they brought young children to him, that he should touch them: and his disciples rebuked those that brought them.

14. But when Jesus saw it, he was much displeased, and said unto them, Suffer the little children to come unto me, and forbid them not: for of such is the kingdom of God.

15. Verily I say unto you, Whosoever shall not receive the kingdom of God as a little child, he shall not enter therein.

16. And he took them up in his arms, put his hands upon them, and blessed them.

17. And when he was gone forth into the way, there came one running, and kneeled to him, and asked him, Good Master, what shall I do that I may inherit eternal life?

18. And Jesus said unto him, Why callest thou me good? there is none good but one, that is, God.

19. Thou knowest the commandments, Do not commit adultery, Do not kill, Do not steal, Do not bear false witness, Defraud not, Honour thy father and mother.

20. And he answered and said unto him, Master, all these have I observed from my youth.

21. Then Jesus beholding him loved him, and said unto him, One thing thou lackest: go thy way, sell whatsoever thou hast, and give to the poor, and thou shalt have treasure in heaven: and come, take up the cross, and follow me.

22. And he was sad at that saying, and went away grieved: for he had great possessions.

23. And Jesus looked round about, and saith unto his disciples, How hardly shall they that have riches enter into the kingdom of God!

24. And the disciples were astonished at his words. But Jesus answereth again, and saith unto them, Children, how hard is it for them that trust in riches to enter into the kingdom of God!

25. It is easier for a camel to go through the eye of a needle, than for a rich man to enter into the kingdom of God.

26. And they were astonished out of measure, saying among themselves, Who then can be saved?

27. And Jesus looking upon them saith, With men it is impossible, but not with God: for with God all things are possible.

28. Then Peter began to say unto him, Lo, we have left all, and have followed thee.

29. And Jesus answered and said, Verily I say unto you, There is no man that hath left house, or brethren, or sisters, or father, or mother, or wife, or children, or lands, for my sake, and the gospel's,

30. But he shall receive an hundredfold now in this time, houses, and brethren, and sisters, and mothers, and children, and lands, with persecutions; and in the world to come eternal life.

31. But many that are first shall be last; and the last first.

32. And they were in the way going up to Jerusalem; and Jesus went before them: and they were amazed; and as they followed, they were afraid. And he took again the twelve, and began to tell them what things should happen unto him,

33. Saying, Behold, we go up to Jerusalem; and the Son of man shall be delivered unto the chief priests, and unto the scribes; and they shall condemn him to death, and shall deliver him to the Gentiles:

34. And they shall mock him, and shall scourge him, and shall spit upon him, and shall kill him: and the third day he shall rise again.

35. And James and John, the sons of Zebedee, come unto him, saying, Master, we would that thou shouldest do for us whatsoever we shall desire.

36. And he said unto them, What would ye that I should do for you?

37. They said unto him, Grant unto us that we may sit, one on thy right hand, and the other on thy left hand, in thy glory.

38. But Jesus said unto them, Ye know not what ye ask: can ye drink of the cup that I drink of? and be baptized with the baptism that I am baptized with?

39. And they said unto him, We can. And Jesus said unto them, Ye shall indeed drink of the cup that I drink of; and with the baptism that I am baptized withal shall ye be baptized:

40. But to sit on my right hand and on my left hand is not mine to give; but it shall be given to them for whom it is prepared.

41. And when the ten heard it, they began to be much displeased with James and John.

42. But Jesus called them to him, and saith unto them, Ye know that they which are accounted to rule over the Gentiles exercise lordship over them; and their great ones exercise authority upon them.

43. But so shall it not be among you: but whosoever will be great among you, shall be your minister:

44. And whosoever of you will be the chiefest, shall be servant of all.

45. For even the Son of man came not to be ministered unto, but to minister, and to give his life a ransom for many.

46. And they came to Jericho: and as he went out of Jericho with his disciples and a great number of people, blind Bartimaeus, the son of Timaeus, sat by the highway side begging.

47. And when he heard that it was Jesus of Nazareth, he began to cry out, and say, Jesus, thou son of David, have mercy on me.

48. And many charged him that he should hold his peace: but he cried the more a great deal, Thou son of David, have mercy on me.

49. And Jesus stood still, and commanded him to be called. And they call the blind man, saying unto him, Be of good comfort, rise; he calleth thee.

50. And he, casting away his garment, rose, and came to Jesus.

51. And Jesus answered and said unto him, What wilt thou that I should do unto thee? The blind man said unto him, Lord, that I might receive my sight.

52. And Jesus said unto him, Go thy way; thy faith hath made thee whole. And immediately he received his sight, and followed Jesus in the way.

CHAPTER 11

1. And when they came nigh to Jerusalem, unto Bethphage and Bethany, at the mount of Olives, he sendeth forth two of his disciples,

2. And saith unto them, Go your way into the village over against you: and as soon as ye be entered into it, ye shall find a colt tied, whereon never man sat; loose him, and bring him.

3. And if any man say unto you, Why do ye this? say ye that the Lord hath need of him; and straightway he will send him hither.

4. And they went their way, and found the colt tied by the door without in a place where two ways met; and they loose him.

5. And certain of them that stood there said unto them, What do ye, loosing the colt?

6. And they said unto them even as Jesus had commanded: and they let them go.

7. And they brought the colt to Jesus, and cast their garments on him; and he sat upon him.

8. And many spread their garments in the way: and others cut down branches off the trees, and strawed them in the way.

9. And they that went before, and they that followed, cried, saying, Hosanna; Blessed is he that cometh in the name of the Lord:

10. Blessed be the kingdom of our father David, that cometh in the name of the Lord: Hosanna in the highest.

11. And Jesus entered into Jerusalem, and into the temple: and when he had looked round about upon all things, and now the eventide was come, he went out unto Bethany with the twelve.

12. And on the morrow, when they were come from Bethany, he was hungry:

13. And seeing a fig tree afar off having leaves, he came, if haply he might find any thing thereon: and when he came to it, he found nothing but leaves; for the time of figs was not yet.

14. And Jesus answered and said unto it, No man eat fruit of thee hereafter for ever. And his disciples heard it.

15. And they come to Jerusalem: and Jesus went into the temple, and began to cast out them that sold and bought in the temple, and overthrew the tables of the moneychangers, and the seats of them that sold doves;

16. And would not suffer that any man should carry any vessel through the temple.

17. And he taught, saying unto them, Is it not written, My house shall be called of all nations the house of prayer? but ye have made it a den of thieves.

18. And the scribes and chief priests heard it, and sought how they might destroy him: for they feared him, because all the people was astonished at his doctrine.

19. And when even was come, he went out of the city.

20. And in the morning, as they passed by, they saw the fig tree dried up from the roots.

21. And Peter calling to remembrance saith unto him, Master, behold, the fig tree which thou cursedst is withered away.

22. And Jesus answering saith unto them, Have faith in God.

23. For verily I say unto you, That whosoever shall say unto this mountain, Be thou removed, and be thou cast into the sea; and shall not doubt in his heart, but shall believe that those things which he saith shall come to pass; he shall have whatsoever he saith.

24. Therefore I say unto you, What things soever ye desire, when ye pray, believe that ye receive them, and ye shall have them.

25. And when ye stand praying, forgive, if ye have ought against any: that your Father also which is in heaven may forgive you your trespasses.

26. But if ye do not forgive, neither will your Father which is in heaven forgive your trespasses.

27. And they come again to Jerusalem: and as he was walking in the temple, there come to him the chief priests, and the scribes, and the elders,

28. And say unto him, By what authority doest thou these things? and who gave thee this authority to do these things?

29. And Jesus answered and said unto them, I will also ask of you one question, and answer me, and I will tell you by what authority I do these things.

30. The baptism of John, was it from heaven, or of men? answer me.

31. And they reasoned with themselves, saying, If we shall say, From heaven; he will say, Why then did ye not believe him?

32. But if we shall say, Of men; they feared the people: for all men counted John, that he was a prophet indeed.

33. And they answered and said unto Jesus, We cannot tell. And Jesus answering saith unto them, Neither do I tell you by what authority I do these things.

CHAPTER 12

1. And he began to speak unto them by parables. A certain man planted a vineyard, and set an hedge about it, and digged a place for the winefat, and built a tower, and let it out to husbandmen, and went into a far country.

2. And at the season he sent to the husbandmen a servant, that he might receive from the husbandmen of the fruit of the vineyard.

3. And they caught him, and beat him, and sent him away empty.

4. And again he sent unto them another servant; and at him they cast stones, and wounded him in the head, and sent him away shamefully handled.

5. And again he sent another; and him they killed, and many others; beating some, and killing some.

6. Having yet therefore one son, his wellbeloved, he sent him also last unto them, saying, They will reverence my son.

7. But those husbandmen said among themselves, This is the heir; come, let us kill him, and the inheritance shall be ours.'

8. And they took him, and killed him, and cast him out of the vineyard.

9. What shall therefore the lord of the vineyard do? he will come and destroy the husbandmen, and will give the vineyard unto others.

10. And have ye not read this scripture; The stone which the builders rejected is become the head of the corner:

11. This was the Lord's doing, and it is marvellous in our eyes?

12. And they sought to lay hold on him, but feared the people: for they knew that he had spoken the parable against them: and they left him, and went their way.

13. And they send unto him certain of the Pharisees and of the Herodians, to catch him in his words.

14. And when they were come, they say unto him, Master, we know that thou art true, and carest for no man: for thou regardest not the person of men, but teachest the way of God in truth: Is it lawful to give tribute to Caesar, or not?

15. Shall we give, or shall we not give? But he, knowing their hypocrisy, said unto them, Why tempt ye me? bring me a penny, that I may see it.

16. And they brought it. And he saith unto them, Whose is this image and superscription? And they said unto him, Caesar's.

17. And Jesus answering said unto them, Render to Caesar the things that are Caesar's, and to God the things that are God's. And they marvelled at him.

18. Then come unto him the Sadducees, which say there is no resurrection; and they asked him, saying,

19. Master, Moses wrote unto us, If a man's brother die, and leave his wife behind him, and leave no children, that his brother should take his wife, and raise up seed unto his brother.

20. Now there were seven brethren: and the first took a wife, and dying left no seed.

21. And the second took her, and died, neither left he any seed: and the third likewise.

22. And the seven had her, and left no seed: last of all the woman died also.

23. In the resurrection therefore, when they shall rise, whose wife shall she be of them? for the seven had her to wife.

24. And Jesus answering said unto them, Do ye not therefore err, because ye know not the scriptures, neither the power of God?

25. For when they shall rise from the dead, they neither marry, nor are given in marriage; but are as the angels which are in heaven.

26. And as touching the dead, that they rise: have ye not read in the book of Moses, how in the bush God spake unto him, saying, I am the God of Abraham, and the God of Isaac, and the God of Jacob?

27. He is not the God of the dead, but the God of the living: ye therefore do greatly err.

28. And one of the scribes came, and having heard them reasoning together, and perceiving that he had answered them well, asked him, Which is the first commandment of all?

29. And Jesus answered him, The first of all the commandments is, Hear, O Israel; The Lord our God is one Lord:

30. And thou shalt love the Lord thy God with all thy heart, and with all thy soul, and with all thy mind, and with all thy strength: this is the first commandment.

31. And the second is like, namely this, Thou shalt love thy neighbour as thyself. There is none other commandment greater than these.

32. And the scribe said unto him, Well, Master, thou hast said the truth: for there is one God; and there is none other but he:

33. And to love him with all the heart, and with all the understanding, and with all the soul, and with all the strength, and to love his neighbour as himself, is more than all whole burnt offerings and sacrifices.

34. And when Jesus saw that he answered discreetly, he said unto him, Thou art not far from the kingdom of God. And no man after that durst ask him any question.

35. And Jesus answered and said, while he taught in the temple, How say the scribes that Christ is the son of David?

36. For David himself said by the Holy Ghost, The Lord said to my Lord, Sit thou on my right hand, till I make thine enemies thy footstool.

37. David therefore himself calleth him Lord; and whence is he then his son? And the common people heard him gladly.

38. And he said unto them in his doctrine, Beware of the scribes, which love to go in long clothing, and love salutations in the marketplaces,

39. And the chief seats in the synagogues, and the uppermost rooms at feasts:

40. Which devour widows' houses, and for a pretence make long prayers: these shall receive greater damnation.

41. And Jesus sat over against the treasury, and beheld how the people cast money into the treasury: and many that were rich cast in much.

42. And there came a certain poor widow, and she threw in two mites, which make a farthing.

43. And he called unto him his disciples, and saith unto them, Verily I say unto you, That this poor widow hath cast more in, than all they which have cast into the treasury:

44. For all they did cast in of their abundance; but she of her want did cast in all that she had, even all her living.

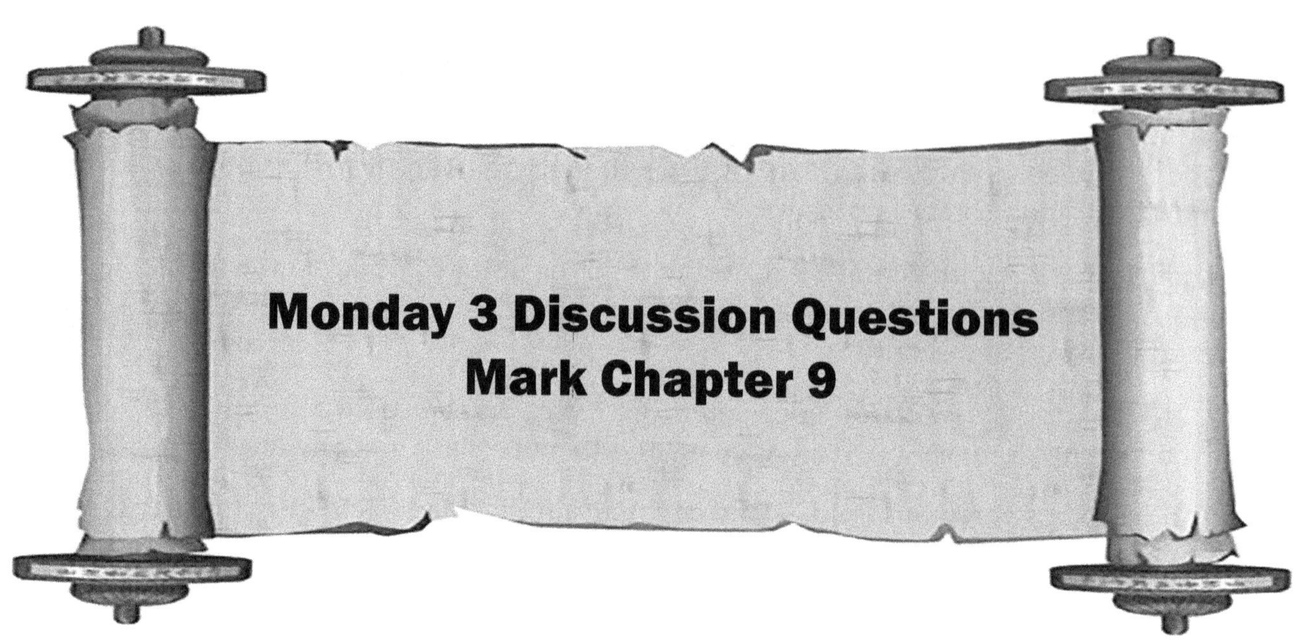

1. Jesus declared that some people would not taste death until what happened? ________

2. After six days who did Jesus take with him? ________

3. Where did Jesus lead them? ________

4. What did Jesus do when they got there? ________

5. What did John do when he saw someone who was not with them, casting out devils? ________

6. What did Jesus say about John forbidding the man? ________

7. What did Jesus say about anyone who brings you a cup of water in Jesus' name, because you belong to Christ? ________

8. If someone offends someone who believes in Jesus, he said it would be better for them if what happened? ________

9. What were they commanded to do if their hand offended them? If their foot offended them? If their eye offended them? ________

10. What did Jesus say to have in ourselves and with one another? ________

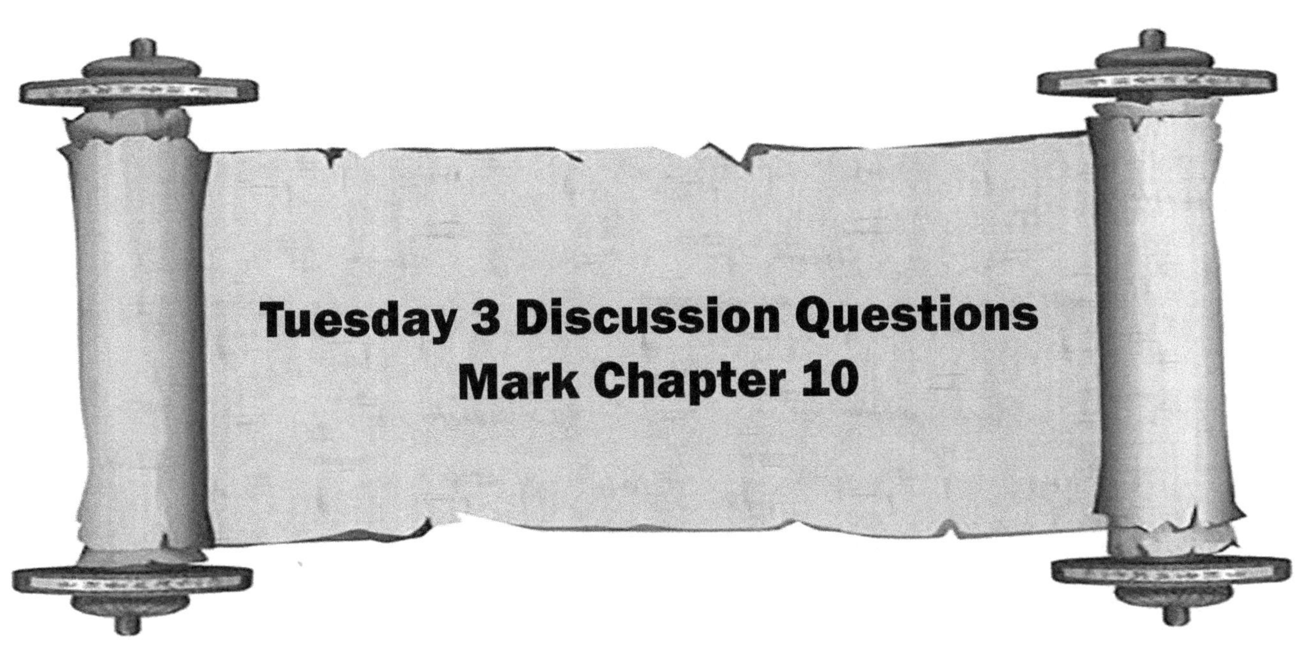

1. What did Jesus say when the Pharisees asked him if it was lawful for a man to put away his wife? ______________________________

2. What was their answer? ______________________________

3. How did Jesus respond to them? ______________________________

4. What did he say God made from the beginning of the creation? ______________________________

5. Jesus said a man should leave who and cleave to whom? ______________________________

6. If a male and female marry and are no longer twain, what do they become? ______________________________

7. When Jesus had gone forth into the way, what did the man who came running kneel and ask him? ______________________________

8. Jesus told him there is none good but whom? ______________________________

9. What did Jesus say to the man who told him that he had observed all his commandments from his youth? ______________________________

10. What did he tell him would happen if he obeyed? ______________________________

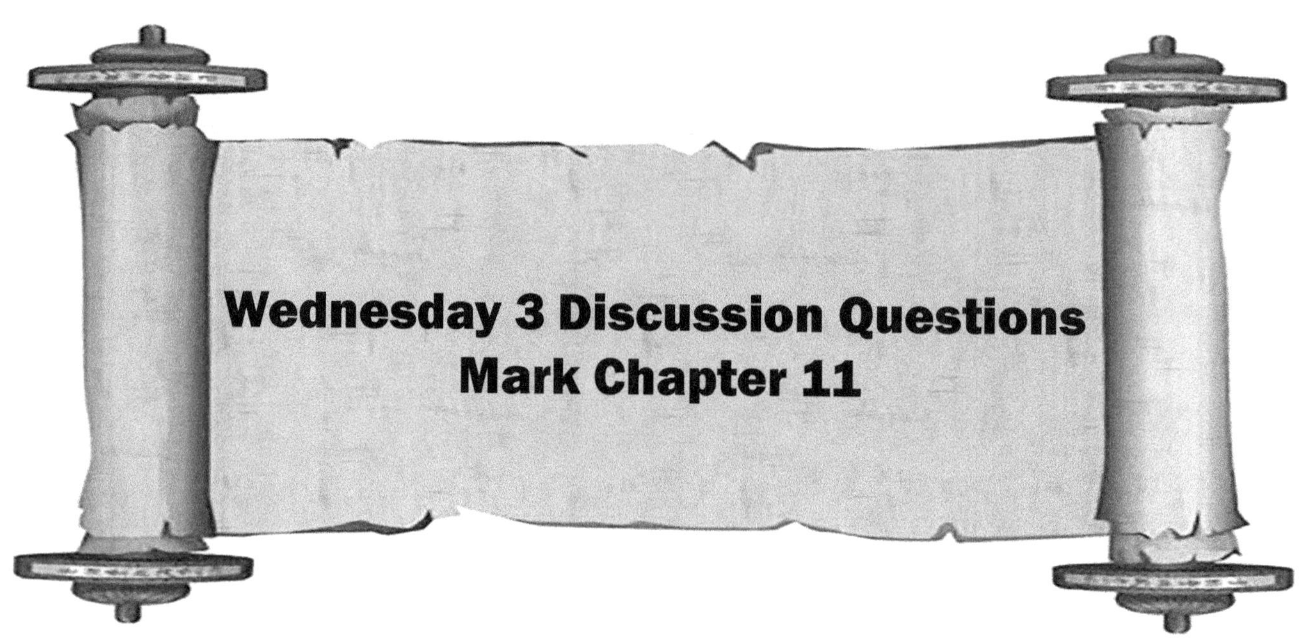

1. How many disciples did Jesus send forth when they got to the mount of Olives? ____
2. What did he send them to the village to do? ____
3. What did Jesus tell them to do to the colt? ____
4. What did they cast on the colt for Jesus to sit on? ____
5. What did Jesus say would happen if you pray for forgiveness but have an ought against your brother? ____
6. Who did Jesus cast out of the temple? What did Jesus do to the tables and the seats? ____
7. What did Jesus not suffer any man to do after this? ____
8. What did Jesus say all nations should call his house? What did he say they had made it? ____
9. When the chief priests, scribes, and elders asked Jesus by what authority he did things, what did he say? What was their answer? ____
10. What was Jesus' response to their answer? ____

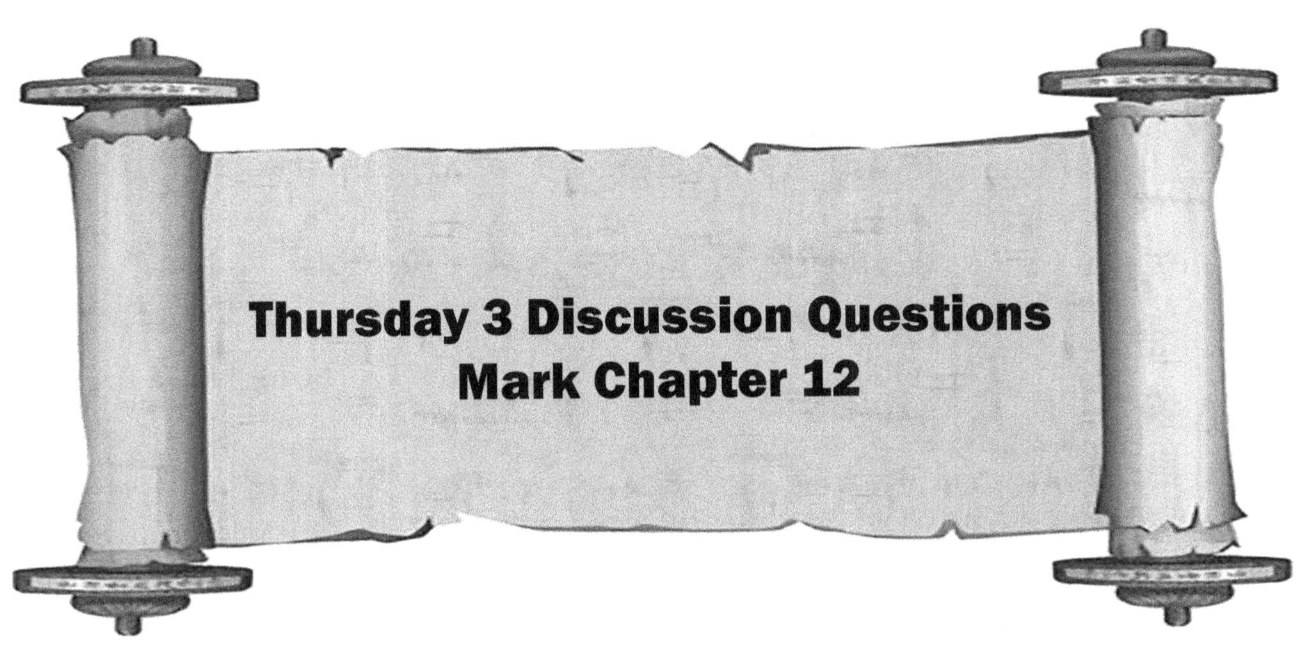

1. In the parable when a man planted a vineyard, what did he set around it? ________

2. What did he dig a place for? ________

3. What did he build? ________

4. What happened to the stone that the builders rejected? ________

5. Why was it marvelous in their sight? ________

6. What were the Sadducees asking concerning a brother's wife? ________

7. How did Jesus answer them? ________

8. Jesus explained that God is not the God of who, but of whom? ________

9. What did Jesus say is the first commandment? ________

10. What did he say the second commandment is? ________

WEEKLY REVIEW
MARK CHAPTERS 9-12

NAME THAT CHAPTER

1.______ THERE IS A PARABLE THAT SAYS THE STONE THAT THE BUILDERS REJECTED BECAME THE HEAD CORNERSTONE. THE PEOPLE TRIED TO TRICK JESUS INTO SAYING THE WRONG WORDS IN THIS CHAPTER. THEY ASKED IF IT WAS LAWFUL TO GIVE TRIBUTE TO CESAR OR NOT. JESUS SAID. "RENDER TO CESAR WHAT IS CESAR'S AND GIVE TO GOD THE THINGS THAT ARE GOD'S

2.______ THE PHARISEES ASKED JESUS IF IT WAS LAWFUL FOR A MAN TO PUT AWAY HIS WIFE. GOD ASKED THEM WHAT MOSES SAID. THEY SAID MOSES WROTE A BILL OF DIVORCE. JESUS SAID MOSES DID THAT BECAUSE OF THE HARDNESS OF THEIR HEART. BUT, THAT GOD MADE MALE TO LEAVE HIS MOTHER AND FATHER AND CLEAVE TO HIS WIFE..

3.______ AFTER 6 DAYS JESUS TOOK PETER, JAMES AND JOHN UP INTO A HIGH MOUNTAIN BY THEMSELVES AND WAS TRANSFIGURED BEFORE THEIR EYES. HIS CLOTHES BEGAN TO SHINE WHITE AS SNOW. THEN MOSES AND ELIAS APPEARED TALKING TO JESUS. SOMEONE FROM THE MULTITUDE BROUGHT HIS SON WITH A DEAF AND DUMB SPIRIT TO THE DISCIPLES TO BE HEALED.BUT THEY COULDN'T HEALL HIM. JESUS TAUGHT THEM SOME DEMONS COME OUT ONLY BY FASTING AND PRAYER.

4.______ WHEN JESUS ENTERED INTO JERUSALEM, HE WENT IN THE TEMPLE AND EVENING CAME. HE WENT TO BETHANY WITH THE 12 DISCIPLES. THE NEXT DAY WHEN THEY CAME BACK, JESUS WAS HUNGRY AND WENT TO A TREE FULL OF LEAVES, BUT HAD NO FRUIT ON IT. HE CURSED THE TREE.

TRUE OR FALSE

5. THE SADDUCEES BELIEVED IN THE RESURRECTION OF JESUS CHRIST.

____

MARK __________

6. JESUS SAID, ALL THINGS ARE POSSIBLE TO THEM THAT BELIEVE.

____

MARK __________

7. AFTER JESUS CAST OUT THE PEOPLE WHO BOUGHT AND SOLD IN THE TEMPLE, HE WOULD NOT LET ANY MAN CARRY ANY VESSELS GO THROUGH THE TEMPLE.

____

MARK __________

FILL IN THE BLANKS

8. WHAT____________GOD HATH____________TOGETHER, LET NO MAN PUT____________.

____

____

____

Mark____________

9. THIS WAS THE____________DOING AND IT IS____________IN OUR____________

____

____

____

Mark____________

10. FOR HE THAT IS__________ __________US IS ON OUR____________.

____

____

____

Mark____________

MY PRAYER JOURNAL

Please use this space to record your thoughts and feelings as you travel on this spirit led journey through the word of God with us. Please know that you have brothers and sisters in this organization from all over the world praying with and for you. My prayer for you is that you will begin to see the power of God resting in each set of your footprints. As you look back and examine your past in this journal, may you realize that you were never alone and according to Hebrews 13:5, God will never leave nor forsake you. ~LADY FLORA

I THESSALONIANS 5:17

THE STUDY OF THE MINOR PROPHETS VOCABULARY DEFINITIONS FOR MARK CHAPTERS 13-16

WORD	DEFINITIONS
1) GOODMAN	
2) SPIKENARD	
3) DESOLATION	
4) ABOMINATION	
5) PORTER	
6) UTTERMOST	
7) UNLEAVENED	
8) GUESTCHAMBER	
9) STAVES	
10) BLASPHEMY	

DMWW DAILY BIBLE READING
MARK CHAPTERS 13-16 KJV

CHAPTER 13

1. And as he went out of the temple, one of his disciples saith unto him, Master, see what manner of stones and what buildings are here!
2. And Jesus answering said unto him, Seest thou these great buildings? there shall not be left one stone upon another, that shall not be thrown down.
3. And as he sat upon the mount of Olives over against the temple, Peter and James and John and Andrew asked him privately,
4. Tell us, when shall these things be? and what shall be the sign when all these things shall be fulfilled?
5. And Jesus answering them began to say, Take heed lest any man deceive you:
6. For many shall come in my name, saying, I am Christ; and shall deceive many.
7. And when ye shall hear of wars and rumours of wars, be ye not troubled: for such things must needs be; but the end shall not be yet.
8. For nation shall rise against nation, and kingdom against kingdom: and there shall be earthquakes in divers places, and there shall be famines and troubles: these are the beginnings of sorrows.
9. But take heed to yourselves: for they shall deliver you up to councils; and in the synagogues ye shall be beaten: and ye shall be brought before rulers and kings for my sake, for a testimony against them.
10. And the gospel must first be published among all nations.
11. But when they shall lead you, and deliver you up, take no thought beforehand what ye shall speak, neither do ye premeditate: but whatsoever shall be given you in that hour, that speak ye: for it is not ye that speak, but the Holy Ghost.
12. Now the brother shall betray the brother to death, and the father the son; and children shall rise up against their parents, and shall cause them to be put to death.
13. And ye shall be hated of all men for my name's sake: but he that shall endure unto the end, the same shall be saved.
14. But when ye shall see the abomination of desolation, spoken of by Daniel the prophet, standing where it ought not, (let him that readeth understand,) then let them that be in Judaea flee to the mountains:
15. And let him that is on the housetop not go down into the house, neither enter therein, to take any thing out of his house:

16. And let him that is in the field not turn back again for to take up his garment.

17. But woe to them that are with child, and to them that give suck in those days!

18. And pray ye that your flight be not in the winter.

19. For in those days shall be affliction, such as was not from the beginning of the creation which God created unto this time, neither shall be.

20. And except that the Lord had shortened those days, no flesh should be saved: but for the elect's sake, whom he hath chosen, he hath shortened the days.

21. And then if any man shall say to you, Lo, here is Christ; or, lo, he is there; believe him not:

22. For false Christs and false prophets shall rise, and shall shew signs and wonders, to seduce, if it were possible, even the elect.

23. But take ye heed: behold, I have foretold you all things.

24. But in those days, after that tribulation, the sun shall be darkened, and the moon shall not give her light,

25. And the stars of heaven shall fall, and the powers that are in heaven shall be shaken.

26. And then shall they see the Son of man coming in the clouds with great power and glory.

27. And then shall he send his angels, and shall gather together his elect from the four winds, from the uttermost part of the earth to the uttermost part of heaven.

28. Now learn a parable of the fig tree; When her branch is yet tender, and putteth forth leaves, ye know that summer is near:

29. So ye in like manner, when ye shall see these things come to pass, know that it is nigh, even at the doors.

30. Verily I say unto you, that this generation shall not pass, till all these things be done.

31. Heaven and earth shall pass away: but my words shall not pass away.

32. But of that day and that hour knoweth no man, no, not the angels which are in heaven, neither the Son, but the Father.

33. Take ye heed, watch and pray: for ye know not when the time is.

34. For the Son of Man is as a man taking a far journey, who left his house, and gave authority to his servants, and to every man his work, and commanded the porter to watch.

35. Watch ye therefore: for ye know not when the master of the house cometh, at even, or at midnight, or at the cockcrowing, or in the morning:

36. Lest coming suddenly he find you sleeping.

37. And what I say unto you I say unto all, Watch.

CHAPTER 14

1. After two days was the feast of the passover, and of unleavened bread: and the chief priests and the scribes sought how they might take him by craft, and put him to death.

2. But they said, Not on the feast day, lest there be an uproar of the people.

3. And being in Bethany in the house of Simon the leper, as he sat at meat, there came a woman having an alabaster box of ointment of spikenard very precious; and she brake the box, and poured it on his head.

4. And there were some that had indignation within themselves, and said, Why was this waste of the ointment made?

5. For it might have been sold for more than three hundred pence, and have been given to the poor. And they murmured against her.

6. And Jesus said, Let her alone; why trouble ye her? she hath wrought a good work on me.

7. For ye have the poor with you always, and whensoever ye will ye may do them good: but me ye have not always.

8. She hath done what she could: she is come aforehand to anoint my body to the burying.

9. Verily I say unto you, Wheresoever this gospel shall be preached throughout the whole world, this also that she hath done shall be spoken of for a memorial of her.

10. And Judas Iscariot, one of the twelve, went unto the chief priests, to betray him unto them.

11. And when they heard it, they were glad, and promised to give him money. And he sought how he might conveniently betray him.

12. And the first day of unleavened bread, when they killed the passover, his disciples said unto him, Where wilt thou that we go and prepare that thou mayest eat the passover?

13. And he sendeth forth two of his disciples, and saith unto them, Go ye into the city, and there shall meet you a man bearing a pitcher of water: follow him.

14. And wheresoever he shall go in, say ye to the goodman of the house, The Master saith, Where is the guestchamber, where I shall eat the passover with my disciples?

15. And he will shew you a large upper room furnished and prepared: there make ready for us.

16. And his disciples went forth, and came into the city, and found as he had said unto them: and they made ready the passover.

17. And in the evening he cometh with the twelve.

18. And as they sat and did eat, Jesus said, Verily I say unto you, One of you which eateth with me shall betray me.

19. And they began to be sorrowful, and to say unto him one by one, Is it I? and another said, Is it I?

20. And he answered and said unto them, It is one of the twelve, that dippeth with me in the dish.

21. The Son of man indeed goeth, as it is written of him: but woe to that man by whom the Son of man is betrayed! good were it for that man if he had never been born.

22. And as they did eat, Jesus took bread, and blessed, and brake it, and gave to them, and said, Take, eat: this is my body.

23. And he took the cup, and when he had given thanks, he gave it to them: and they all drank of it.

24. And he said unto them, This is my blood of the new testament, which is shed for many.

25. Verily I say unto you, I will drink no more of the fruit of the vine, until that day that I drink it new in the kingdom of God.

26. And when they had sung an hymn, they went out into the mount of Olives.

27. And Jesus saith unto them, All ye shall be offended because of me this night: for it is written, I will smite the shepherd, and the sheep shall be scattered.

28. But after that I am risen, I will go before you into Galilee.

29. But Peter said unto him, Although all shall be offended, yet will not I.

30. And Jesus saith unto him, Verily I say unto thee, That this day, even in this night, before the cock crow twice, thou shalt deny me thrice.

31. But he spake the more vehemently, If I should die with thee, I will not deny thee in any wise. Likewise also said they all.

32. And they came to a place which was named Gethsemane: and he saith to his disciples, Sit ye here, while I shall pray.

33. And he taketh with him Peter and James and John, and began to be sore amazed, and to be very heavy;

34. And saith unto them, My soul is exceeding sorrowful unto death: tarry ye here, and watch.

35. And he went forward a little, and fell on the ground, and prayed that, if it were possible, the hour might pass from him.

36. And he said, Abba, Father, all things are possible unto thee; take away this cup from me: nevertheless not what I will, but what thou wilt.

37. And he cometh, and findeth them sleeping, and saith unto Peter, Simon, sleepest thou? couldest not thou watch one hour?

38. Watch ye and pray, lest ye enter into temptation. The spirit truly is ready, but the flesh is weak.

39. And again he went away, and prayed, and spake the same words.

40. And when he returned, he found them asleep again, (for their eyes were heavy,) neither wist they what to answer him.

41. And he cometh the third time, and saith unto them, Sleep on now, and take your rest: it is enough, the hour is come; behold, the Son of man is betrayed into the hands of sinners.

42. Rise up, let us go; lo, he that betrayeth me is at hand.

43. And immediately, while he yet spake, cometh Judas, one of the twelve, and with him a great multitude with swords and staves, from the chief priests and the scribes and the elders.

44. And he that betrayed him had given them a token, saying, Whomsoever I shall kiss, that same is he; take him, and lead him away safely.

45. And as soon as he was come, he goeth straightway to him, and saith, Master, master; and kissed him.

46. And they laid their hands on him, and took him.

47. And one of them that stood by drew a sword, and smote a servant of the high priest, and cut off his ear.

48. And Jesus answered and said unto them, Are ye come out, as against a thief, with swords and with staves to take me?

49. I was daily with you in the temple teaching, and ye took me not: but the scriptures must be fulfilled.

50. And they all forsook him, and fled.

51. And there followed him a certain young man, having a linen cloth cast about his naked body; and the young men laid hold on him:

52. And he left the linen cloth, and fled from them naked.

53. And they led Jesus away to the high priest: and with him were assembled all the chief priests and the elders and the scribes.

54. And Peter followed him afar off, even into the palace of the high priest: and he sat with the servants, and warmed himself at the fire.

55. And the chief priests and all the council sought for witness against Jesus to put him to death; and found none.

56. For many bare false witness against him, but their witness agreed not together.

57. And there arose certain, and bare false witness against him, saying,

58. We heard him say, I will destroy this temple that is made with hands, and within three days I will build another made without hands.

59. But neither so did their witness agree together.

60. And the high priest stood up in the midst, and asked Jesus, saying, Answerest thou nothing? what is it which these witness against thee?

61. But he held his peace, and answered nothing. Again the high priest asked him, and said unto him, Art thou the Christ, the Son of the Blessed?

62. And Jesus said, I am: and ye shall see the Son of man sitting on the right hand of power, and coming in the clouds of heaven.

63. Then the high priest rent his clothes, and saith, What need we any further witnesses?

64. Ye have heard the blasphemy: what think ye? And they all condemned him to be guilty of death.

65. And some began to spit on him, and to cover his face, and to buffet him, and to say unto him, Prophesy: and the servants did strike him with the palms of their hands.

66. And as Peter was beneath in the palace, there cometh one of the maids of the high priest:

67. And when she saw Peter warming himself, she looked upon him, and said, And thou also wast with Jesus of Nazareth.

68. But he denied, saying, I know not, neither understand I what thou sayest. And he went out into the porch; and the cock crew.

69. And a maid saw him again, and began to say to them that stood by, This is one of them.

70. And he denied it again. And a little after, they that stood by said again to Peter, Surely thou art one of them: for thou art a Galilaean, and thy speech agreeth thereto.

71. But he began to curse and to swear, saying, I know not this man of whom ye speak.

72. And the second time the cock crew. And Peter called to mind the word that Jesus said unto him, Before the cock crow twice, thou shalt deny me thrice. And when he thought thereon, he wept.

CHAPTER 15

1. And straightway in the morning the chief priests held a consultation with the elders and scribes and the whole council, and bound Jesus, and carried him away, and delivered him to Pilate.

2. And Pilate asked him, Art thou the King of the Jews? And he answering said unto them, Thou sayest it.

3. And the chief priests accused him of many things: but he answered nothing.

4. And Pilate asked him again, saying, Answerest thou nothing? behold how many things they witness against thee.

5. But Jesus yet answered nothing; so that Pilate marvelled.

6. Now at that feast he released unto them one prisoner, whomsoever they desired.

7. And there was one named Barabbas, which lay bound with them that had made insurrection with him, who had committed murder in the insurrection.

8. And the multitude crying aloud began to desire him to do as he had ever done unto them.

9. But Pilate answered them, saying, Will ye that I release unto you the King of the Jews?

10. For he knew that the chief priests had delivered him for envy.

11. But the chief priests moved the people, that he should rather release Barabbas unto them.

12. And Pilate answered and said again unto them, What will ye then that I shall do unto him whom ye call the King of the Jews?

13. And they cried out again, Crucify him.

14. Then Pilate said unto them, Why, what evil hath he done? And they cried out the more exceedingly, Crucify him.

15. And so Pilate, willing to content the people, released Barabbas unto them, and delivered Jesus, when he had scourged him, to be crucified.

16. And the soldiers led him away into the hall, called Praetorium; and they call together the whole band.

17. And they clothed him with purple, and platted a crown of thorns, and put it about his head,

18. And began to salute him, Hail, King of the Jews!

19. And they smote him on the head with a reed, and did spit upon him, and bowing their knees worshipped him.

20. And when they had mocked him, they took off the purple from him, and put his own clothes on him, and led him out to crucify him.

21. And they compel one Simon a Cyrenian, who passed by, coming out of the country, the father of Alexander and Rufus, to bear his cross.

22. And they bring him unto the place Golgotha, which is, being interpreted, The place of a skull.

23. And they gave him to drink wine mingled with myrrh: but he received it not.

24. And when they had crucified him, they parted his garments, casting lots upon them, what every man should take.

25. And it was the third hour, and they crucified him.

26. And the superscription of his accusation was written over, The King Of The Jews.

27. And with him they crucify two thieves; the one on his right hand, and the other on his left.

28. And the scripture was fulfilled, which saith, And he was numbered with the transgressors.

29. And they that passed by railed on him, wagging their heads, and saying, Ah, thou that destroyest the temple, and buildest it in three days,

30. Save thyself, and come down from the cross.

31. Likewise also the chief priests mocking said among themselves with the scribes, He saved others; himself he cannot save.

32. Let Christ the King of Israel descend now from the cross, that we may see and believe. And they that were crucified with him reviled him.

33. And when the sixth hour was come, there was darkness over the whole land until the ninth hour.

34. And at the ninth hour Jesus cried with a loud voice, saying, Eloi, Eloi, lama sabachthani? which is, being interpreted, My God, my God, why hast thou forsaken me?

35. And some of them that stood by, when they heard it, said, Behold, he calleth Elias.

36. And one ran and filled a spunge full of vinegar, and put it on a reed, and gave him to drink, saying, Let alone; let us see whether Elias will come to take him down.

37. And Jesus cried with a loud voice, and gave up the ghost.

38. And the veil of the temple was rent in twain from the top to the bottom.

39. And when the centurion, which stood over against him, saw that he so cried out, and gave up the ghost, he said, Truly this man was the Son of God.

40. There were also women looking on afar off: among whom was Mary Magdalene, and Mary the mother of James the less and of Joses, and Salome;

41. (Who also, when he was in Galilee, followed him, and ministered unto him;) and many other women which came up with him unto Jerusalem.

42. And now when the even was come, because it was the preparation, that is, the day before the sabbath,

43. Joseph of Arimathaea, an honourable counsellor, which also waited for the kingdom of God, came, and went in boldly unto Pilate, and craved the body of Jesus.

44. And Pilate marvelled if he were already dead: and calling unto him the centurion, he asked him whether he had been any while dead.

45. And when he knew it of the centurion, he gave the body to Joseph.

46. And he bought fine linen, and took him down, and wrapped him in the linen, and laid him in a sepulchre which was hewn out of a rock, and rolled a stone unto the door of the sepulchre.

47. And Mary Magdalene and Mary the mother of Joses beheld where he was laid.

CHAPTER 16

1. And when the sabbath was past, Mary Magdalene, and Mary the mother of James, and Salome, had bought sweet spices, that they might come and anoint him.
2. And very early in the morning the first day of the week, they came unto the sepulchre at the rising of the sun.
3. And they said among themselves, Who shall roll us away the stone from the door of the sepulchre?
4. And when they looked, they saw that the stone was rolled away: for it was very great.
5. And entering into the sepulchre, they saw a young man sitting on the right side, clothed in a long white garment; and they were affrighted.
6. And he saith unto them, Be not affrighted: Ye seek Jesus of Nazareth, which was crucified: he is risen; he is not here: behold the place where they laid him.
7. But go your way, tell his disciples and Peter that he goeth before you into Galilee: there shall ye see him, as he said unto you.
8. And they went out quickly, and fled from the sepulchre; for they trembled and were amazed: neither said they any thing to any man; for they were afraid.
9. Now when Jesus was risen early the first day of the week, he appeared first to Mary Magdalene, out of whom he had cast seven devils.
10. And she went and told them that had been with him, as they mourned and wept.
11. And they, when they had heard that he was alive, and had been seen of her, believed not.
12. After that he appeared in another form unto two of them, as they walked, and went into the country.
13. And they went and told it unto the residue: neither believed they them.
14. Afterward he appeared unto the eleven as they sat at meat, and upbraided them with their unbelief and hardness of heart, because they believed not them which had seen him after he was risen.
15. And he said unto them, Go ye into all the world, and preach the gospel to every creature.
16. He that believeth and is baptized shall be saved; but he that believeth not shall be damned.
17. And these signs shall follow them that believe; In my name shall they cast out devils; they shall speak with new tongues;
18. They shall take up serpents; and if they drink any deadly thing, it shall not hurt them; they shall lay hands on the sick, and they shall recover.

19. So then after the Lord had spoken unto them, he was received up into heaven, and sat on the right hand of God.

20. And they went forth, and preached every where, the Lord working with them, and confirming the word with signs following. Amen.

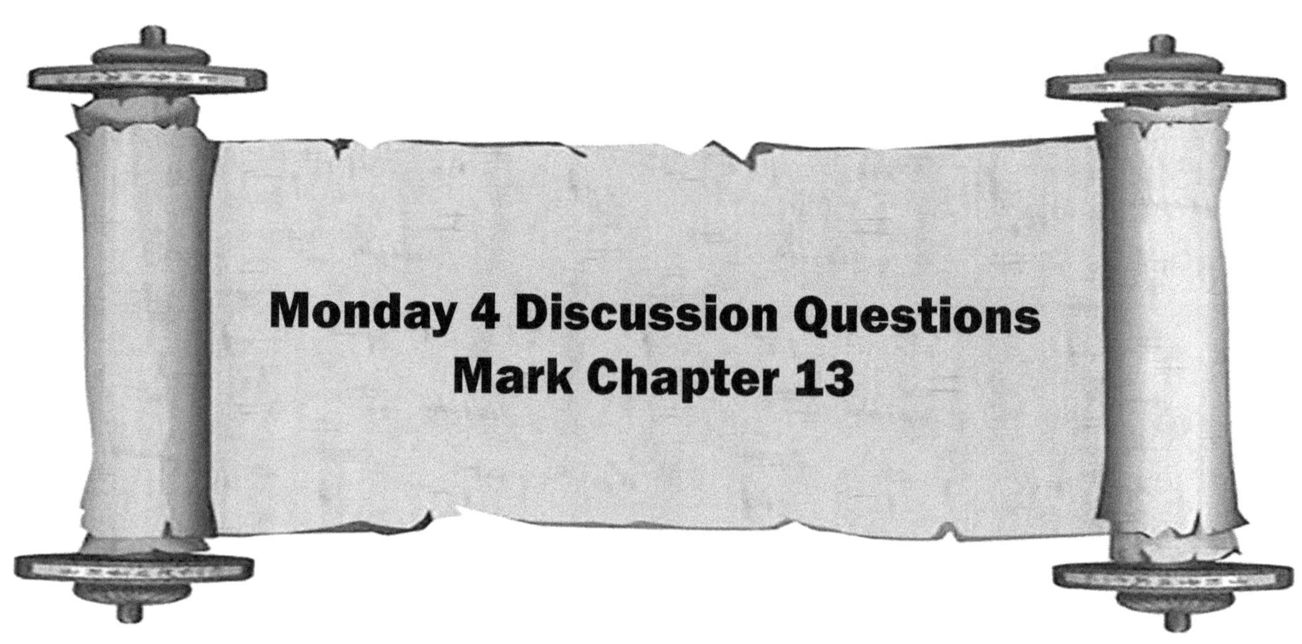

Monday 4 Discussion Questions
Mark Chapter 13

1. What did the disciple say to Jesus as he went out of the temple? ______________________
____
____

2. What was Jesus' answer to the disciple? ______________________
____
____

3. What are the names of the disciples that had a private conversation with Jesus? ______
____
____

4. What were they asking Jesus about in this conversation? ______________________
____
____

5. What is the first thing Jesus told them to do? ______________________
____
____

6. Why did he tell them this? ______________________
____
____

7. What things did Jesus say we would hear, but the end is not yet? ______________________
____
____

8. List the things Jesus said would be the beginning of sorrows? ______________________
____
____

9. What did Jesus say you should do when people deliver you up? ______________________
____
____

10. What should you say? ______________________
____
____

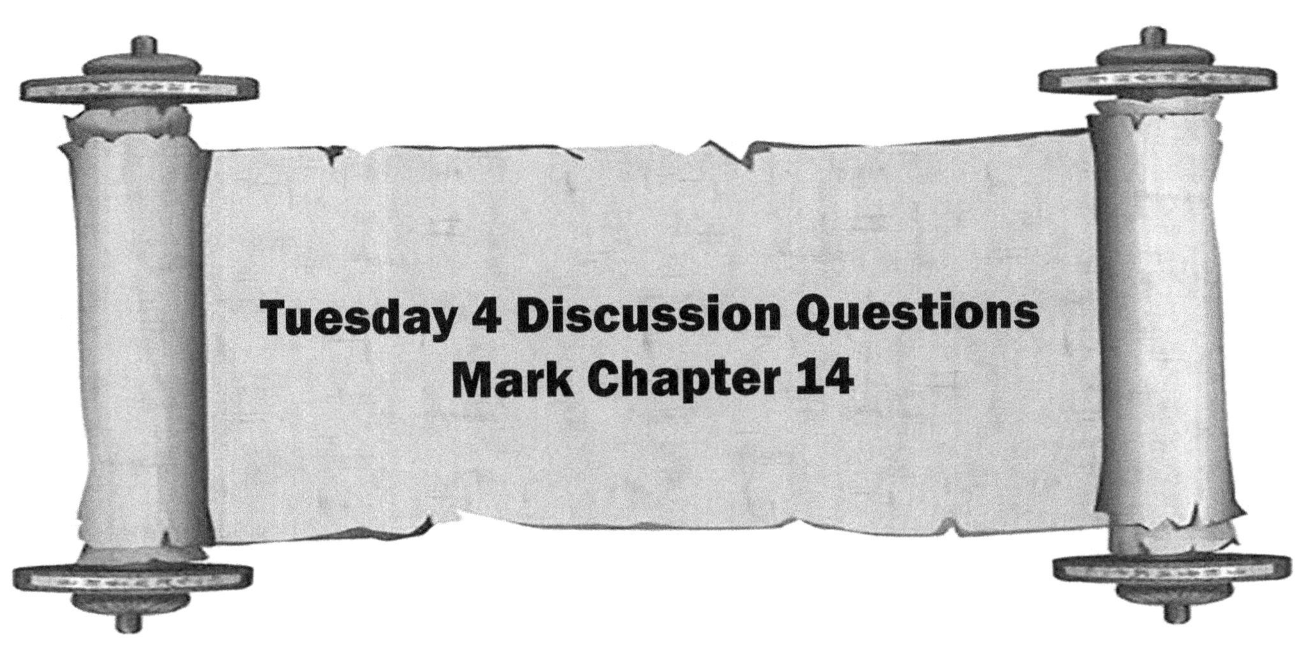

1. What were the chief priests and scribes doing at the feast of the passover? ______

2. Why did they decide not to do it on the feast day? ______

3. What did the disciples ask Jesus on the first day of unleavened bread, when they killed the passover? ______

4. What did Jesustell two of the disciples to do? ______

5. Did they find a place to prepare for the passover? ______

6. What did Jesus say when they asked who would betray him? ______

7. When Jesus took the bread, blessed it, broke it, and gave it to them, what did he say it was?. ______

8. What did he say about the cup after he blessed it and gave it to them? ______

9. When did the Lord say he would drink of the fruit of the vine again? ______

10. What did they do after they sang a hymn? ______

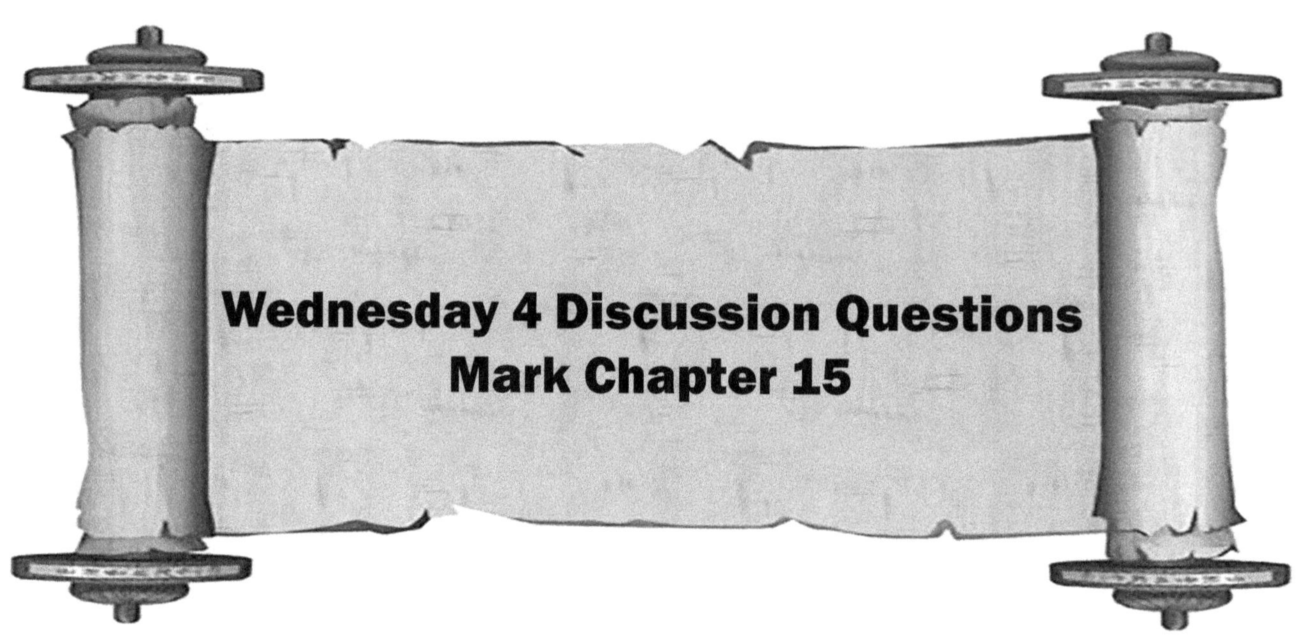

1. What did the elders, scribes, and council hold that morning? ______________________

2. What did they do next? ______________________

3. What was the name of the hall where the souldiers led him away? ______________________

4. What did the people take off Jesus after they had mocked him? ______________________

5. What does Golgotha mean? ______________________

6. What did they give Jesus to drink? Did he take it? ______________________

7. What hour was it when they crucified the lord? ______________________

8. What happened when the sixth hour came? ______________________

9. What happened at the ninth hour? ______________________

10. What did the centurion say when he heard him cry out and saw him give up the ghost? ______________________

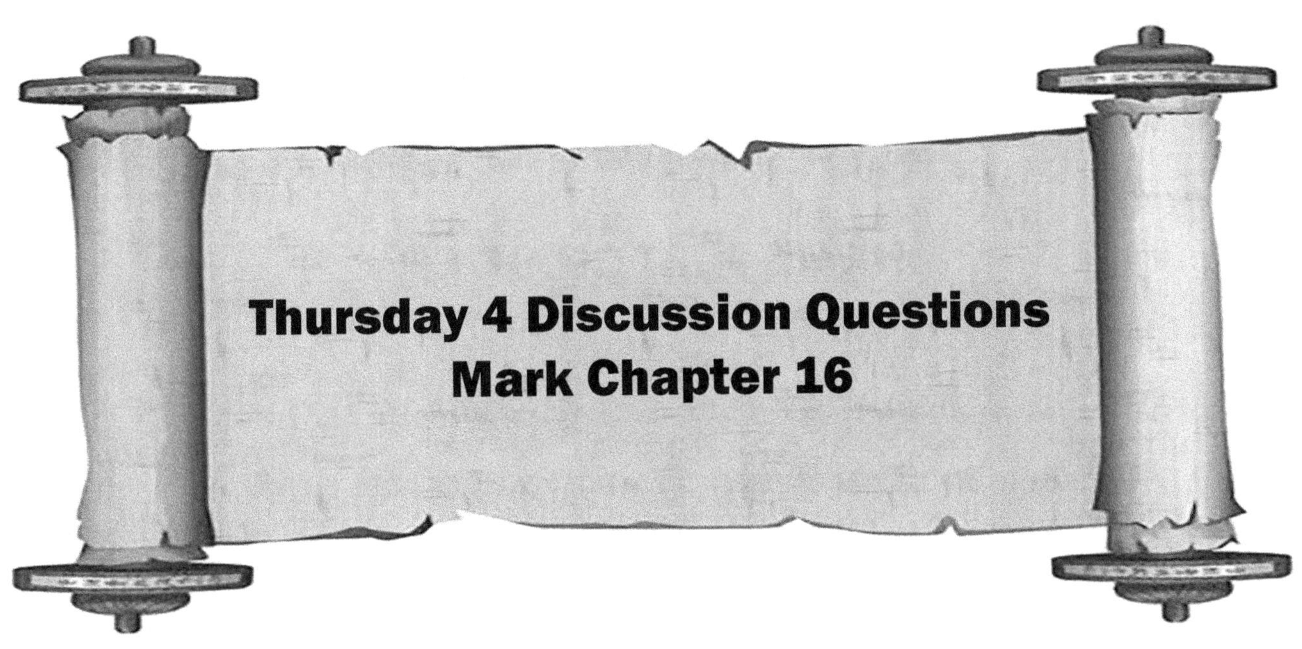

1. Who was carrying sweet spices after the Sabbath had passed? ______

2. What were they going to do with it? ______

3. What were they asking themselves on the way to the tomb? ______

4. What did they see when they arrived? ______

5. What did they see when they walked inside? ______

6. What did the angel tell them to do? ______

7. Who did Jesus appear to first on the first day of the week? ______

8. Who did he say would be saved and who would be damned? ______

9. What signs did he say would follow those who believe? ______

10. What did Jesus say to have in ourselves and with one another? ______

WEEKLY REVIEW
MARK CHAPTERS 13-16

NAME THAT CHAPTER

1._______ WHEN THE SABBATH HAD PASSED, MARY MAGDALENE AND MARY, THE MOTHER OF JAMES AND SALOME, BOUGHT SPICES TO ANOINT JESUS' BODY. AS THEY WERE WALKING ALONG THE WAY THEY BEGAN TO WONDER WHO WOULD HELP THEM ROLL THE STONE AWAY FROM THE SEPULCHER. WHEN THEY ARRIVED THE STONE HAD ALREADY BEEN ROLLED AWAY AND AN ANGEL MET THEM THERE. HE TOLD THEM NOT TO FEAR. JESUS WAS RISEN.

2._______ PETER, JAMES, JOHN, AND ANDREW HAD A PRIVATE CONVERSATION WITH JESUS. THEY ASKED HIM WHEN THE END OF THE WORLD WOULD COME AND WHAT SIGNS THERE WOULD BE TO TELL THEM THAT ALL THINGS WERE FULFILLED. JESUS WARNED THEM NOT TO BE DECEIVED BY THE MANY THAT WOULD COME AND CALL THEMSELVES JESUS. HE SAID THERE WILL BE WARS AND RUMORS OF WARS. NATIONS WILL RISE AGAINST NATIONS AND KINGDOMS AGAINST KINGDOMS.THERE WILL BE EARTHQUAKES IN DIVERS PLACES, FAMINES AND TROUBLES. JESUS PROCLAIMED THAT THE GOSPEL WILL BE PREACHED IN ALL THE WORLD AS A WITNESS TO EVERY NATION BEFORE HE RETURNS.

3._______ A WOMAN CAME AND POURED SPIKENARD OIL FROM HER ALABASTER BOX ONTO JESUS' HEAD. THE PEOPLE WHO SAW IT WERE UPSET BECAUSE THEY FELT THAT THE OINTMENT WAS WASTED AND COULD HAVE BEEN SOLD TO HELP THE POOR. JESUS TOLD THEM TO LEAVE HER ALONE. HE TOLD THEM THAT SHE HAD DONE A GOOD THING AND THAT SHE SHOULD BE REMEMBERED WHEREVER THE GOSPEL SHALL BE PREACHED AS A MEMORIAL OF HER.

4._______ THE CHIEF PRIESTS BOUND JESUS AND CARRIED HIM AWAY TO PILATE. PILATE ASKED JESUS IF HE WAS THE KING OF THE JEWS. BUT, JESUS DID NOT ANSWER.PILATE ASKED HIM IF HE HAD ANYTHING TO SAY ABOUT ALL THE WITNESSES AGAINST HIM. HE STILL SAID NOTHING. PILATE MARVELLED. THEN HE ASKED THE PEOPLE IF THEY WANTED JESUS OR BARABBAS. THEY ALL CRIED OUT "CRUCIFY HIM" AND SO JESUS WAS CRUCIFIED AND BARABBAS WAS RELEASED

TRUE OR FALSE

5. THEY SCRIBED "THE KING OF THE JEWS ABOVE JESUS ON THE CROSS WHEN HE WAS CRUCIFIED

____

MARK _________

6. JESUS TOLD THE DISCIPLES THE SIGNS THAT SHALL FOLLOW THOSE WHO BELIEVE. IN JESUS' NAME THEY SHALL CAST OUT DEVILS, THEY SHALL SPEAK WITH NEW TONGUES, THEY SHALL TAKE UP SERPENTS; AND IF THEY DRINK ANY DEADLY THING, IT SHALL NOT HURT THEM; THEY SHALL LAY HANDS ON THE SICK AND THEY ____________

MARK _________

7. THE CHIEF PRIESTS DECIDED TO CRUCIFY JESUS ON THE DAY OF THE FEAST REGARDLESS OF THE UPROAR OF THE PEOPLE.

____

MARK _________

FILL IN THE BLANKS

8. AND THE ________ MUST FIRST BE________AMONG ALL__________'

Mark____________

____

____

____

9. AND_________YE THAT YOUR________ BE NOT IN THE __________.

MARK _________

____

____

____

10. HE THAT BELIEVETH AND IS_________SHALL BE SAVED; BUT HE THAT_________ NOT SHALL BE_________.

____

____

____

Mark____________

MARK FINAL TEST
PART 1-COMPREHENSION

THERE ARE SEVERAL NEW VOCABULARY DEFINITIONS THAT WE ENCOUNTERED IN THE BOOK OF MARK. YOUR INSTRUCTOR WILL CHOOSE 30 WORDS FROM THE LESSON FOR YOU TO USE FOR THIS ASSIGNMENT:

To determine your comprehension of the VOCABULARY DEFINITIONS that we have studied in this book, please use the following words in a complete sentence of your own. Then tell what scripture the word occurs in.
Please use the King James Version.

1)	16)
2)	17)
3)	18)
4)	19)
5)	20)
6)	21)
7)	22)
8)	23)
9)	24)
10)	25)
11)	26)
12)	27)
13)	28)
14)	29)
15)	30)

HOW TO WRITE A STANDARD SHORT ESSAY FOR DMWW INTERNATIONAL

Discipled Men and Women of Wisdom International practices formal essay writing to develop the art of informed persuasion, by combining two types of essay writings. They are the informative essay and the persuasive essay.

Our goal is to minister to others in a way that persuades them to walk in the truth as we know it, with fact based information from the Holy Bible and our personal experiences which relate to this information. You may also include outside sources that are credible as long as you cite anything you reference.

The element of persuasion according to Romans 8:38,39 ***"For I am persuaded that neither death, nor life, nor angels, nor principalities, nor powers,nor things present nor things to come, nor height, nor depth, nor any other creature shall be able to separate us from theLove of God, which is in Christ Jesus our Lord."*** is what takes place in the mind when one makes a conscious decision to follow Christ.

MARK Essay

(Due by Midnight)

Write a three page essay that summarizes the book of MARK. Make sure you check off each thing on the rubric list below, before turning it in, to ensure the best grade possible. This assignment is worth **300 points.**

Essay includes a thesis statement and introduction paragraph	/ 50 pts
The student conveys full comprehension of the vocabulary definitions, by using at least 20 of the words correctly in this essay.	/ 50 pts
Student shows understanding and use of weekly discussion question information	/ 50 pts
Student Understands and demonstrates the purpose of the detailed instructions given to the Children of Israel in this book.	/ 50 pts
The student used information from the book of Exodus to show God's undying love for his people.	/ 50 pts
Student's closing includes call to action (salvation or repentance),	/ 50 pts

The following three blank pages are to be used to write your essay.

Name: ______________________________
Time: ______________________________
Date Due:____________________________

Essay Page 1

Essay Page 2

Essay Page 3

REFLECTIONS OF MARK

This page is to keep a diary of how you felt when studying this book and what you learned or discovered in this class that helped you relate the Bible situations to situations in today's world. Jot down notes of spiritual revelations you received while studying that you may want to use in future messages you may preach.

The Study of
THE BOOK OF LUKE

Begin Date______________________

Course End Date______________________

Study Guide Prepared and Distributed by
The Discipled Men & Women of Wisdom, International

INTRODUCTION TO THE BOOK OF LUKE

Welcome to the study of the book of Luke, the third book in the volume we call "The Four Gospels". This book has 24 chapters and this class will last 6 weeks. You will find that this book is similar to both Matthew and Mark. Because Luke was traveling on the same journey with Jesus as he went from town to town and city to city. There will be a few unique experiences we will see in Luke that are not in the accounts of Mark or Matthew. The stories and parables that are the same will even have some differences.

This is because it is told from their own words, from their own perspesctives. This book will begin with Luke explaining why he is writing to Theophilus, having perfect understanding of all things from the very first.

As you continue to study with us, as we travel on this amazing journey through the word of God, you will experience different emotions, have multiple questions, and you may even have responded to certain situations on the travels with the disciples, in your mind. Feel free to examine those thoughts and share them with your class. You will start by using a bible dictionary to complete the vocabulary page. Then you will read one chapter per day Monday through Thursday and answer the corresponding questions.

On Fridays, you will complete the weekly review and be prepared to meet with your instructor and classmates online for class participation on Saturday. Ready? Let's Get Started!

MY PRAYER JOURNAL

Please use this space to record your thoughts and feelings as you travel on this spirit led journey through the word of God with us. Please know that you have brothers and sisters in this organization from all over the world praying with and for you. My prayer for you is that you will begin to see the power of God resting in each set of your footprints. As you look back and examine your past in this journal, may you realize that you were never alone and according to Hebrews 13:5, God will never leave nor forsake you. ~LADY FLORA

I THESSALONIANS 5:17

THE STUDY OF THE FOUR GOSPELS VOCABULARY DEFINITIONS FOR LUKE CHAPTERS 1-4

WORD	DEFINITIONS
1) VEHEMENTLY	
2) BECKON	
3) TOILED	
4) COMMUNE	
5) CONSOLE	
6) PARABLE	
7) CONDEMN	
8) PERCEIVE	
9) MOTE	
10) GLUTTONOUS	

DMWW DAILY BIBLE READING
LUKE CHAPTERS 1-4

CHAPTER 1

1. Forasmuch as many have taken in hand to set forth in order a declaration of those things which are most surely believed among us,
2. Even as they delivered them unto us, which from the beginning were eyewitnesses, and ministers of the word;
3. It seemed good to me also, having had perfect understanding of all things from the very first, to write unto thee in order, most excellent Theophilus,
4. That thou mightest know the certainty of those things, wherein thou hast been instructed.
5. There was in the days of Herod, the king of Judaea, a certain priest named Zacharias, of the course of Abia: and his wife was of the daughters of Aaron, and her name was Elisabeth.
6. And they were both righteous before God, walking in all the commandments and ordinances of the Lord blameless.
7. And they had no child, because that Elisabeth was barren, and they both were now well stricken in years.
8. And it came to pass, that while he executed the priest's office before God in the order of his course,
9. According to the custom of the priest's office, his lot was to burn incense when he went into the temple of the Lord.
10. And the whole multitude of the people were praying without at the time of incense.
11. And there appeared unto him an angel of the Lord standing on the right side of the altar of incense.
12. And when Zacharias saw him, he was troubled, and fear fell upon him.
13. But the angel said unto him, Fear not, Zacharias: for thy prayer is heard; and thy wife Elisabeth shall bear thee a son, and thou shalt call his name John.
14. And thou shalt have joy and gladness; and many shall rejoice at his birth.
15. For he shall be great in the sight of the Lord, and shall drink neither wine nor strong drink; and he shall be filled with the Holy Ghost, even from his mother's womb.
16. And many of the children of Israel shall he turn to the Lord their God.
17. And he shall go before him in the spirit and power of Elias, to turn the hearts of the fathers to the children, and the disobedient to the wisdom of the just; to make ready a people prepared for the Lord.

18. And Zacharias said unto the angel, Whereby shall I know this? for I am an old man, and my wife well stricken in years.

19. And the angel answering said unto him, I am Gabriel, that stand in the presence of God; and am sent to speak unto thee, and to shew thee these glad tidings.

20. And, behold, thou shalt be dumb, and not able to speak, until the day that these things shall be performed, because thou believest not my words, which shall be fulfilled in their season.

21. And the people waited for Zacharias, and marvelled that he tarried so long in the temple.

22. And when he came out, he could not speak unto them: and they perceived that he had seen a vision in the temple: for he beckoned unto them, and remained speechless.

23. And it came to pass, that, as soon as the days of his ministration were accomplished, he departed to his own house.

24. And after those days his wife Elisabeth conceived, and hid herself five months, saying,

25. Thus hath the Lord dealt with me in the days wherein he looked on me, to take away my reproach among men.

26. And in the sixth month the angel Gabriel was sent from God unto a city of Galilee, named Nazareth,

27. To a virgin espoused to a man whose name was Joseph, of the house of David; and the virgin's name was Mary.

28. And the angel came in unto her, and said, Hail, thou that art highly favoured, the Lord is with thee: blessed art thou among women.

29. And when she saw him, she was troubled at his saying, and cast in her mind what manner of salutation this should be.

30. And the angel said unto her, Fear not, Mary: for thou hast found favour with God.

31. And, behold, thou shalt conceive in thy womb, and bring forth a son, and shalt call his name Jesus.

32. He shall be great, and shall be called the Son of the Highest: and the Lord God shall give unto him the throne of his father David:

33. And he shall reign over the house of Jacob for ever; and of his kingdom there shall be no end.

34. Then said Mary unto the angel, How shall this be, seeing I know not a man?

35. And the angel answered and said unto her, The Holy Ghost shall come upon thee, and the power of the Highest shall overshadow thee: therefore also that holy thing which shall be born of thee shall be called the Son of God.

36. And, behold, thy cousin Elisabeth, she hath also conceived a son in her old age: and this is the sixth month with her, who was called barren.

37. For with God nothing shall be impossible.

38. And Mary said, Behold the handmaid of the Lord; be it unto me according to thy word. And the angel departed from her.

39. And Mary arose in those days, and went into the hill country with haste, into a city of Juda;

40. And entered into the house of Zacharias, and saluted Elisabeth.

41. And it came to pass, that, when Elisabeth heard the salutation of Mary, the babe leaped in her womb; and Elisabeth was filled with the Holy Ghost:

42. And she spake out with a loud voice, and said, Blessed art thou among women, and blessed is the fruit of thy womb.

43. And whence is this to me, that the mother of my Lord should come to me?

44. For, lo, as soon as the voice of thy salutation sounded in mine ears, the babe leaped in my womb for joy.

45. And blessed is she that believed: for there shall be a performance of those things which were told her from the Lord.

46. And Mary said, My soul doth magnify the Lord,

47. And my spirit hath rejoiced in God my Saviour.

48. For he hath regarded the low estate of his handmaiden: for, behold, from henceforth all generations shall call me blessed.

49. For he that is mighty hath done to me great things; and holy is his name.

50. And his mercy is on them that fear him from generation to generation.

51. He hath shewed strength with his arm; he hath scattered the proud in the imagination of their hearts.

52. He hath put down the mighty from their seats, and exalted them of low degree.

53. He hath filled the hungry with good things; and the rich he hath sent empty away.

54. He hath helped his servant Israel, in remembrance of his mercy;

55. As he spake to our fathers, to Abraham, and to his seed for ever.

56. And Mary abode with her about three months, and returned to her own house.

57. Now Elisabeth's full time came that she should be delivered; and she brought forth a son.

58. And her neighbours and her cousins heard how the Lord had shewed great mercy upon her; and they rejoiced with her.

59. And it came to pass, that on the eighth day they came to circumcise the child; and they called him Zacharias, after the name of his father.

60. And his mother answered and said, Not so; but he shall be called John.

61. And they said unto her, There is none of thy kindred that is called by this name.

62. And they made signs to his father, how he would have him called.

63. And he asked for a writing table, and wrote, saying, His name is John. And they marvelled all.

64. And his mouth was opened immediately, and his tongue loosed, and he spake, and praised God.

65. And fear came on all that dwelt round about them: and all these sayings were noised abroad throughout all the hill country of Judaea.

66. And all they that heard them laid them up in their hearts, saying, What manner of child shall this be! And the hand of the Lord was with him.

67. And his father Zacharias was filled with the Holy Ghost, and prophesied, saying,

68. Blessed be the Lord God of Israel; for he hath visited and redeemed his people,

69. And hath raised up an horn of salvation for us in the house of his servant David;

70. As he spake by the mouth of his holy prophets, which have been since the world began:

71. That we should be saved from our enemies, and from the hand of all that hate us;

72. To perform the mercy promised to our fathers, and to remember his holy covenant;

73. The oath which he sware to our father Abraham,

74. That he would grant unto us, that we being delivered out of the hand of our enemies might serve him without fear,

75. In holiness and righteousness before him, all the days of our life.

76. And thou, child, shalt be called the prophet of the Highest: for thou shalt go before the face of the Lord to prepare his ways;

77. To give knowledge of salvation unto his people by the remission of their sins,

78. Through the tender mercy of our God; whereby the dayspring from on high hath visited us,

79. To give light to them that sit in darkness and in the shadow of death, to guide our feet into the way of peace.

80. And the child grew, and waxed strong in spirit, and was in the deserts till the day of his shewing unto Israel.

CHAPTER 2

1. And it came to pass in those days, that there went out a decree from Caesar Augustus that all the world should be taxed.

2. (And this taxing was first made when Cyrenius was governor of Syria.)

3. And all went to be taxed, every one into his own city.

4. And Joseph also went up from Galilee, out of the city of Nazareth, into Judaea, unto the city of David, which is called Bethlehem; (because he was of the house and lineage of David:)

5. To be taxed with Mary his espoused wife, being great with child.

6. And so it was, that, while they were there, the days were accomplished that she should be delivered.

7. And she brought forth her firstborn son, and wrapped him in swaddling clothes, and laid him in a manger; because there was no room for them in the inn.

8. And there were in the same country shepherds abiding in the field, keeping watch over their flock by night.

9. And, lo, the angel of the Lord came upon them, and the glory of the Lord shone round about them: and they were sore afraid.

10. And the angel said unto them, Fear not: for, behold, I bring you good tidings of great joy, which shall be to all people.

11. For unto you is born this day in the city of David a Saviour, which is Christ the Lord.

12. And this shall be a sign unto you; Ye shall find the babe wrapped in swaddling clothes, lying in a manger.

13. And suddenly there was with the angel a multitude of the heavenly host praising God, and saying,

14. Glory to God in the highest, and on earth peace, good will toward men.

15. And it came to pass, as the angels were gone away from them into heaven, the shepherds said one to another, Let us now go even unto Bethlehem, and see this thing which is come to pass, which the Lord hath made known unto us.

16. And they came with haste, and found Mary, and Joseph, and the babe lying in a manger.

17. And when they had seen it, they made known abroad the saying which was told them concerning this child.

18. And all they that heard it wondered at those things which were told them by the shepherds.

19. But Mary kept all these things, and pondered them in her heart.

20. And the shepherds returned, glorifying and praising God for all the things that they had heard and seen, as it was told unto them.

21. And when eight days were accomplished for the circumcising of the child, his name was called Jesus, which was so named of the angel before he was conceived in the womb.

22. And when the days of her purification according to the law of Moses were accomplished, they brought him to Jerusalem, to present him to the Lord;

23. (As it is written in the law of the Lord, Every male that openeth the womb shall be called holy to the Lord;)

24. And to offer a sacrifice according to that which is said in the law of the Lord, A pair of turtledoves, or two young pigeons.

25. And, behold, there was a man in Jerusalem, whose name was Simeon; and the same man was just and devout, waiting for the consolation of Israel: and the Holy Ghost was upon him.

26. And it was revealed unto him by the Holy Ghost, that he should not see death, before he had seen the Lord's Christ.

27. And he came by the Spirit into the temple: and when the parents brought in the child Jesus, to do for him after the custom of the law,

28. Then took he him up in his arms, and blessed God, and said,

29. Lord, now lettest thou thy servant depart in peace, according to thy word:

30. For mine eyes have seen thy salvation,

31. Which thou hast prepared before the face of all people;

32. A light to lighten the Gentiles, and the glory of thy people Israel.

33. And Joseph and his mother marvelled at those things which were spoken of him.

34. And Simeon blessed them, and said unto Mary his mother, Behold, this child is set for the fall and rising again of many in Israel; and for a sign which shall be spoken against;

35. (Yea, a sword shall pierce through thy own soul also,) that the thoughts of many hearts may be revealed.

36. And there was one Anna, a prophetess, the daughter of Phanuel, of the tribe of Aser: she was of a great age, and had lived with an husband seven years from her virginity;

37. And she was a widow of about fourscore and four years, which departed not from the temple, but served God with fastings and prayers night and day.

38. And she coming in that instant gave thanks likewise unto the Lord, and spake of him to all them that looked for redemption in Jerusalem.

39. And when they had performed all things according to the law of the Lord, they returned into Galilee, to their own city Nazareth.

40. And the child grew, and waxed strong in spirit, filled with wisdom: and the grace of God was upon him.

41. Now his parents went to Jerusalem every year at the feast of the passover.

42. And when he was twelve years old, they went up to Jerusalem after the custom of the feast.

43. And when they had fulfilled the days, as they returned, the child Jesus tarried behind in Jerusalem; and Joseph and his mother knew not of it.

44. But they, supposing him to have been in the company, went a day's journey; and they sought him among their kinsfolk and acquaintance.

45. And when they found him not, they turned back again to Jerusalem, seeking him.

46. And it came to pass, that after three days they found him in the temple, sitting in the midst of the doctors, both hearing them, and asking them questions.

47. And all that heard him were astonished at his understanding and answers.

48. And when they saw him, they were amazed: and his mother said unto him, Son, why hast thou thus dealt with us? behold, thy father and I have sought thee sorrowing.

49. And he said unto them, How is it that ye sought me? wist ye not that I must be about my Father's business?

50. And they understood not the saying which he spake unto them.

51. And he went down with them, and came to Nazareth, and was subject unto them: but his mother kept all these sayings in her heart.

52. And Jesus increased in wisdom and stature, and in favor with God and man.

CHAPTER 3

1. Now in the fifteenth year of the reign of Tiberius Caesar, Pontius Pilate being governor of Judaea, and Herod being tetrarch of Galilee, and his brother Philip tetrarch of Ituraea and of the region of Trachonitis, and Lysanias the tetrarch of Abilene,

2. Annas and Caiaphas being the high priests, the word of God came unto John the son of Zacharias in the wilderness.

3. And he came into all the country about Jordan, preaching the baptism of repentance for the remission of sins;

4. As it is written in the book of the words of Esaias the prophet, saying, The voice of one crying in the wilderness, Prepare ye the way of the Lord, make his paths straight.

5. Every valley shall be filled, and every mountain and hill shall be brought low; and the crooked shall be made straight, and the rough ways shall be made smooth;

6. And all flesh shall see the salvation of God.

7. Then said he to the multitude that came forth to be baptized of him, O generation of vipers, who hath warned you to flee from the wrath to come?

8. Bring forth therefore fruits worthy of repentance, and begin not to say within yourselves, We have Abraham to our father: for I say unto you, That God is able of these stones to raise up children unto Abraham.

9. And now also the axe is laid unto the root of the trees: every tree therefore which bringeth not forth good fruit is hewn down, and cast into the fire.

10. And the people asked him, saying, What shall we do then?

11. He answereth and saith unto them, He that hath two coats, let him impart to him that hath none; and he that hath meat, let him do likewise.

12. Then came also publicans to be baptized, and said unto him, Master, what shall we do?

13. And he said unto them, Exact no more than that which is appointed you.

14. And the soldiers likewise demanded of him, saying, And what shall we do? And he said unto them, Do violence to no man, neither accuse any falsely; and be content with your wages.

15. And as the people were in expectation, and all men mused in their hearts of John, whether he were the Christ, or not;

16. John answered, saying unto them all, I indeed baptize you with water; but one mightier than I cometh, the latchet of whose shoes I am not worthy to unloose: he shall baptize you with the Holy Ghost and with fire:

17. Whose fan is in his hand, and he will throughly purge his floor, and will gather the wheat into his garner; but the chaff he will burn with fire unquenchable.

18. And many other things in his exhortation preached he unto the people.

19. But Herod the tetrarch, being reproved by him for Herodias his brother Philip's wife, and for all the evils which Herod had done,

20. Added yet this above all, that he shut up John in prison.

21. Now when all the people were baptized, it came to pass, that Jesus also being baptized, and praying, the heaven was opened,

22. And the Holy Ghost descended in a bodily shape like a dove upon him, and a voice came from heaven, which said, Thou art my beloved Son; in thee I am well pleased.

23. And Jesus himself began to be about thirty years of age, being (as was supposed) the son of Joseph, which was the son of Heli,

24. Which was the son of Matthat, which was the son of Levi, which was the son of Melchi, which was the son of Janna, which was the son of Joseph,

25. Which was the son of Mattathias, which was the son of Amos, which was the son of Naum, which was the son of Esli, which was the son of Nagge,

26. Which was the son of Maath, which was the son of Mattathias, which was the son of Semei, which was the son of Joseph, which was the son of Juda,

27. Which was the son of Joanna, which was the son of Rhesa, which was the son of Zorobabel, which was the son of Salathiel, which was the son of Neri,

28. Which was the son of Melchi, which was the son of Addi, which was the son of Cosam, which was the son of Elmodam, which was the son of Er,

29. Which was the son of Jose, which was the son of Eliezer, which was the son of Jorim, which was the son of Matthat, which was the son of Levi,

30. Which was the son of Simeon, which was the son of Juda, which was the son of Joseph, which was the son of Jonan, which was the son of Eliakim,

31. Which was the son of Melea, which was the son of Menan, which was the son of Mattatha, which was the son of Nathan, which was the son of David,

32. Which was the son of Jesse, which was the son of Obed, which was the son of Booz, which was the son of Salmon, which was the son of Naasson,

33. Which was the son of Aminadab, which was the son of Aram, which was the son of Esrom, which was the son of Phares, which was the son of Juda,

34. Which was the son of Jacob, which was the son of Isaac, which was the son of Abraham, which was the son of Thara, which was the son of Nachor,

35. Which was the son of Saruch, which was the son of Ragau, which was the son of Phalec, which was the son of Heber, which was the son of Sala,

36. Which was the son of Cainan, which was the son of Arphaxad, which was the son of Sem, which was the son of Noe, which was the son of Lamech,

37. Which was the son of Mathusala, which was the son of Enoch, which was the son of Jared, which was the son of Maleleel, which was the son of Cainan,

38. Which was the son of Enos, which was the son of Seth, which was the son of Adam, which was the son of God.

CHAPTER 4

1. And Jesus being full of the Holy Ghost returned from Jordan, and was led by the Spirit into the wilderness,

2. Being forty days tempted of the devil. And in those days he did eat nothing: and when they were ended, he afterward hungered.

3. And the devil said unto him, If thou be the Son of God, command this stone that it be made bread.

4. And Jesus answered him, saying, It is written, That man shall not live by bread alone, but by every word of God.

5. And the devil, taking him up into an high mountain, shewed unto him all the kingdoms of the world in a moment of time.

6. And the devil said unto him, All this power will I give thee, and the glory of them: for that is delivered unto me; and to whomsoever I will I give it.

7. If thou therefore wilt worship me, all shall be thine.

8. And Jesus answered and said unto him, Get thee behind me, Satan: for it is written, Thou shalt worship the Lord thy God, and him only shalt thou serve.

9. And he brought him to Jerusalem, and set him on a pinnacle of the temple, and said unto him, If thou be the Son of God, cast thyself down from hence:

10. For it is written, He shall give his angels charge over thee, to keep thee:

11. And in their hands they shall bear thee up, lest at any time thou dash thy foot against a stone.

12. And Jesus answering said unto him, It is said, Thou shalt not tempt the Lord thy God.

13. And when the devil had ended all the temptation, he departed from him for a season.

14. And Jesus returned in the power of the Spirit into Galilee: and there went out a fame of him through all the region round about.

15. And he taught in their synagogues, being glorified of all.

16. And he came to Nazareth, where he had been brought up: and, as his custom was, he went into the synagogue on the sabbath day, and stood up for to read.

17. And there was delivered unto him the book of the prophet Esaias. And when he had opened the book, he found the place where it was written,

18. The Spirit of the Lord is upon me, because he hath anointed me to preach the gospel to the poor; he hath sent me to heal the brokenhearted, to preach deliverance to the captives, and recovering of sight to the blind, to set at liberty them that are bruised,

19. To preach the acceptable year of the Lord.

20. And he closed the book, and he gave it again to the minister, and sat down. And the eyes of all them that were in the synagogue were fastened on him.

21. And he began to say unto them, This day is this scripture fulfilled in your ears.

22. And all bare him witness, and wondered at the gracious words which proceeded out of his mouth. And they said, Is not this Joseph's son?

23. And he said unto them, Ye will surely say unto me this proverb, Physician, heal thyself: whatsoever we have heard done in Capernaum, do also here in thy country.

24. And he said, Verily I say unto you, No prophet is accepted in his own country.

25. But I tell you of a truth, many widows were in Israel in the days of Elias, when the heaven was shut up three years and six months, when great famine was throughout all the land;

26. But unto none of them was Elias sent, save unto Sarepta, a city of Sidon, unto a woman that was a widow.

27. And many lepers were in Israel in the time of Eliseus the prophet; and none of them was cleansed, saving Naaman the Syrian.

28. And all they in the synagogue, when they heard these things, were filled with wrath,

29. And rose up, and thrust him out of the city, and led him unto the brow of the hill whereon their city was built, that they might cast him down headlong.

30. But he passing through the midst of them went his way,

31. And came down to Capernaum, a city of Galilee, and taught them on the sabbath days.

32. And they were astonished at his doctrine: for his word was with power.

33. And in the synagogue there was a man, which had a spirit of an unclean devil, and cried out with a loud voice,

34. Saying, Let us alone; what have we to do with thee, thou Jesus of Nazareth? art thou come to destroy us? I know thee who thou art; the Holy One of God.

35. And Jesus rebuked him, saying, Hold thy peace, and come out of him. And when the devil had thrown him in the midst, he came out of him, and hurt him not.

36. And they were all amazed, and spake among themselves, saying, What a word is this! for with authority and power he commandeth the unclean spirits, and they come out.

37. And the fame of him went out into every place of the country round about.

38. And he arose out of the synagogue, and entered into Simon's house. And Simon's wife's mother was taken with a great fever; and they besought him for her.

39. And he stood over her, and rebuked the fever; and it left her: and immediately she arose and ministered unto them.

40. Now when the sun was setting, all they that had any sick with divers diseases brought them unto him; and he laid his hands on every one of them, and healed them.

41. And devils also came out of many, crying out, and saying, Thou art Christ the Son of God. And he rebuking them suffered them not to speak: for they knew that he was Christ.

42. And when it was day, he departed and went into a desert place: and the people sought him, and came unto him, and stayed him, that he should not depart from them.

43. And he said unto them, I must preach the kingdom of God to other cities also: for therefore am I sent.

44. And he preached in the synagogues of Galilee.

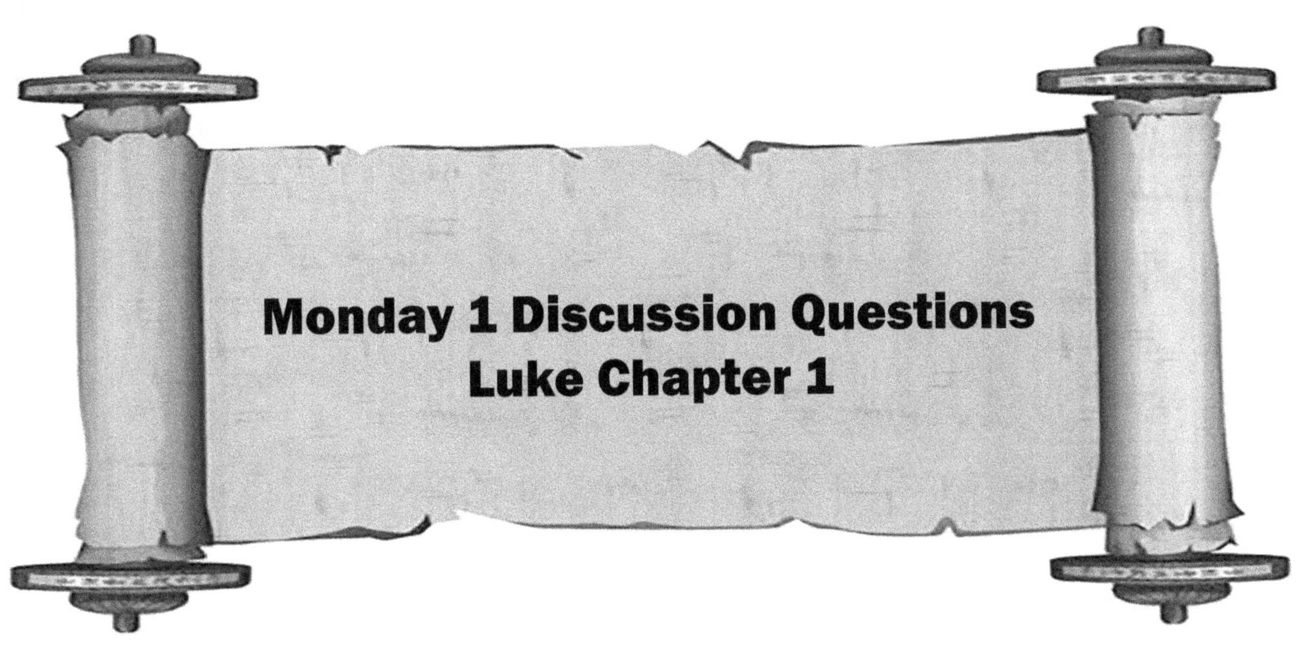

1. Why is Luke writing this book? ______

2. Who is he writing to? ______

3. What was the name of the king of Judea? ______

4. What was the name of the priest who was a member of the priestly order of Abia? ______

5. What was his wife's name? Who was her father? ______

6. What was Zacharias's job to do when he went into the temple? ______

7. What month was Gabriel sent to Galilee? ______

8. Why did the angel say to Mary when he saw she was troubled? ______

9. What did the angel tell Mary about her cousin? ______

10. What happened when Elisabeth heard the salutation of Mary? ______

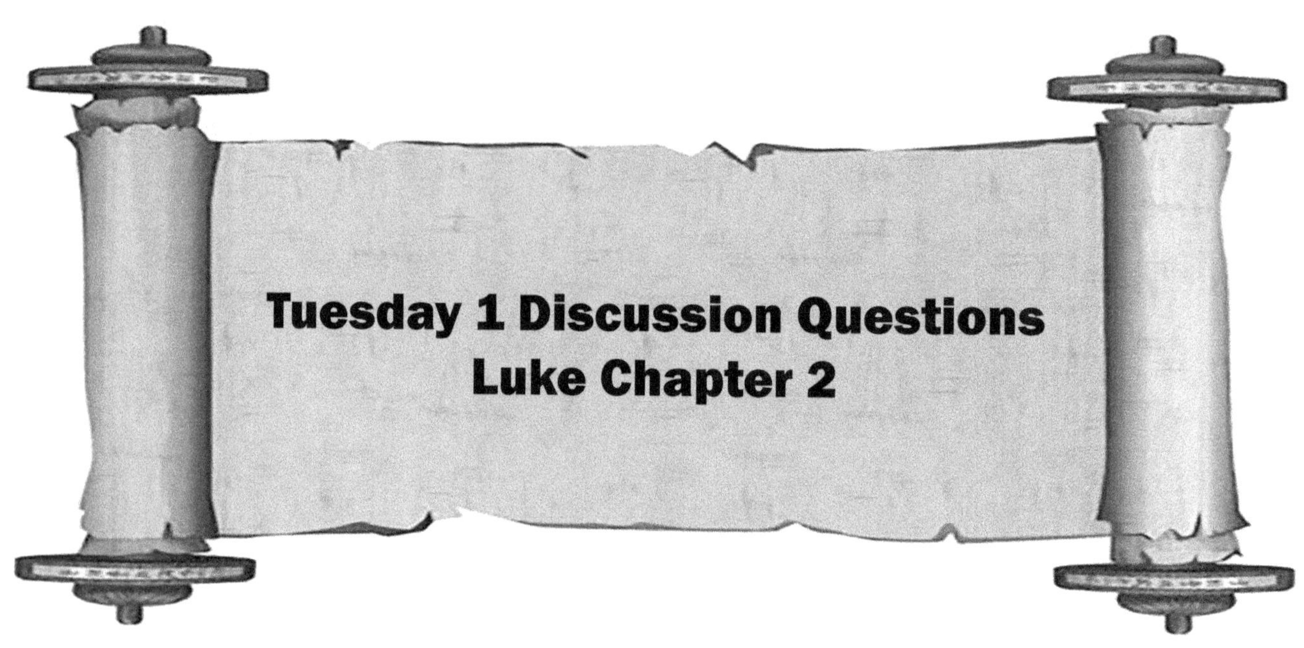

1. What is the decree that went out from Caesar? ______________________

2. When was this taxing first made? ______________________

3. Where did Joseph go to be taxed? ______________________

4. Who was with him? What were they going to do while they were there? ______________________

5. What did Mary dress the baby in and lay him down to sleep in? Why? ______________________

6. What did the angels say to each other when the angel left? ______________________

7. What happened 8 days after the baby was born? ______________________

8. What did they do with the baby after Mary's days of purification were accomplished? ______________________

9. What is written in the law about every male that opens the womb? ______________________

10. What was the sacrifice they were supposed to offer? ______________________

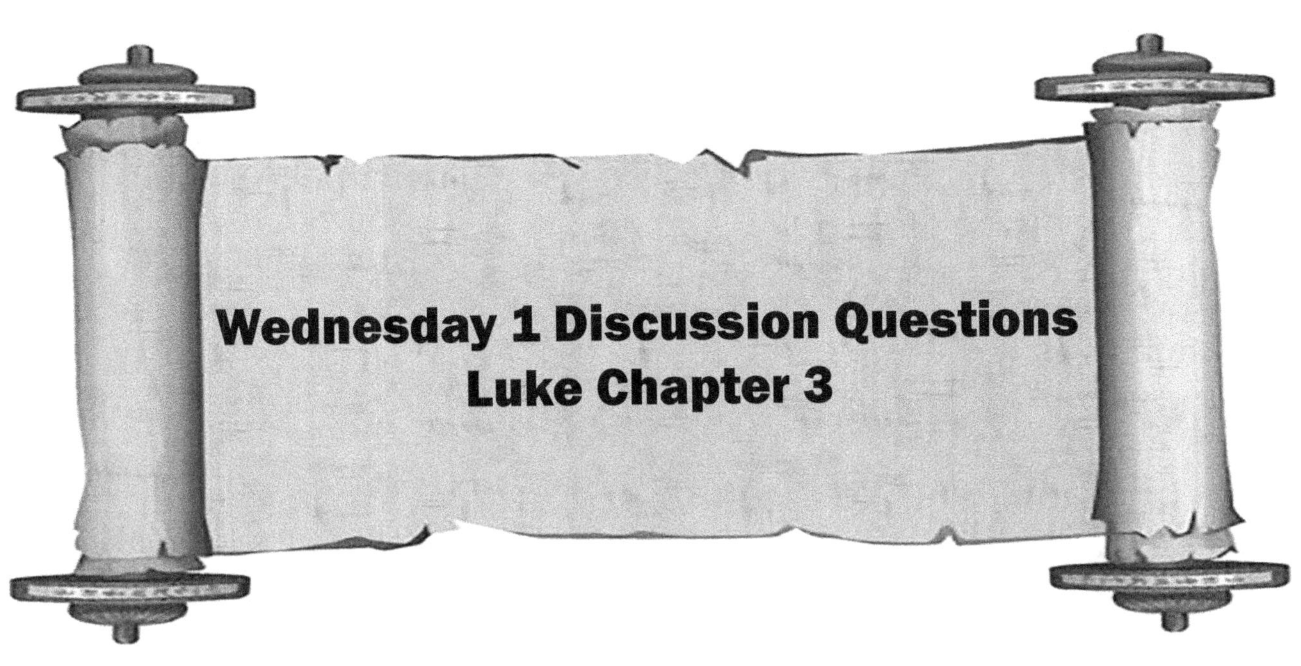

1. Who was in their 15th year of reign in this chapter? ______________________________

2. Who was the governor of Judea? ______________________________

3. Who was the tetrarch of Galilee? Who was the tetrarch of Iturea? Who was the tetrarch of Abilene? ______________________________

4. Who were the high priests? ______________________________

5. Who did God speak to in the wilderness? ______________________________

6. What was he crying in the wilderness? ______________________________

7. What was he preaching about the valleys,mountains, crooked andrough ways? ______________________________

8. What did he say to the multitudes who came forth to be baptized? ______________________________

9. When the people wondered if John was Jesus or not, what did John say? ______________________________

10. What happened after Jesus was baptized and prayed? ______________________________

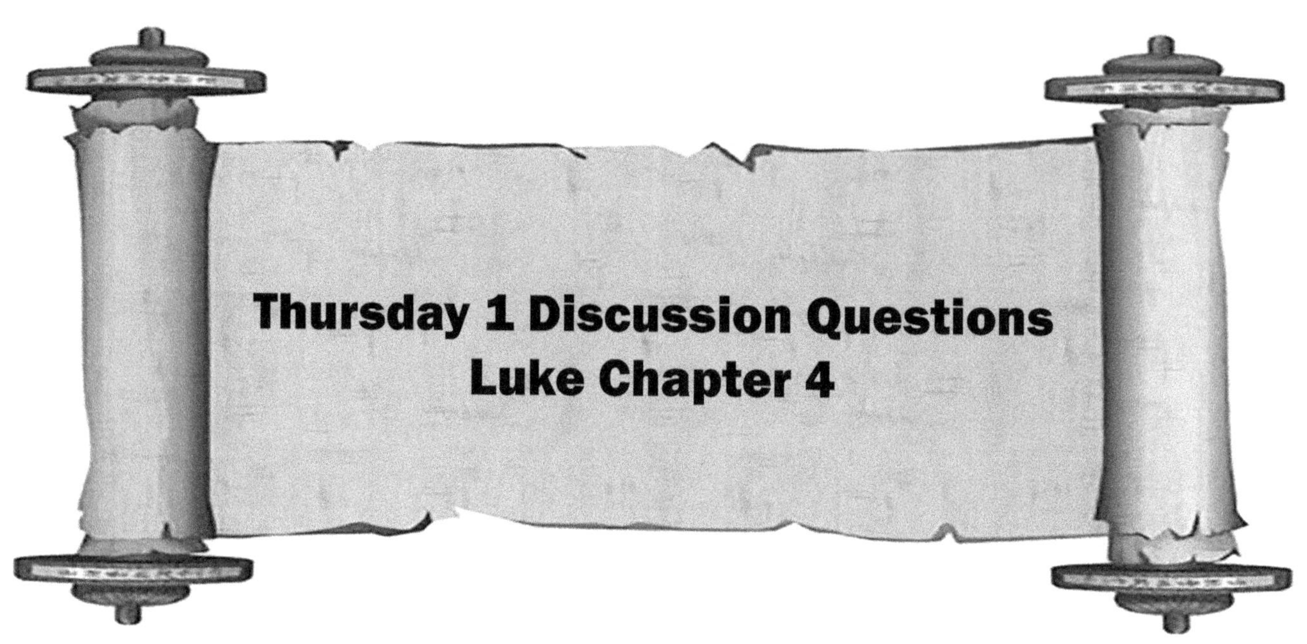

Thursday 1 Discussion Questions
Luke Chapter 4

1. What happened when Jesus returned from Jordan full of the Holy Ghost? ____________

2. How many days was Jesus tempted by the devil? What did he eat during that time? ____________

3. What did the devil say to Jesus and how did Jesus respond? ____________

4. What did the devil do next? ____________

5. What did the devil promise to give Jesus? What did he tell Jesus to do to get it? ____________

6. What did Jesus answer him saying? ____________

7. What did the devil tell Jesus to do when he set him on a pinnacle of the temple? How did Jesus reply to Satan? ____________

8. What did the devil do after he had ended all the temptation? ____________

9. When the book of Esias was delivered to Jesus, where did the book open? ____________

10. What did he do with the book when he had finished? ____________

WEEKLY REVIEW
LUKE CHAPTERS 1-4

NAME THAT CHAPTER

1.______ AFTER JESUS HAD FASTED 40 DAYS, HE WAS HUNGRY. THE DEVIL CAME TO TEMPT HIM BY TELLING HIM TO COMMAND THE STONE TO BE TURNED TO BREAD. JESUS RESISTED SATAN'S TEMPTATION AND SAID MAN SHALL NOT LIVE BY BREAD ALONE BUT BY EVERY WORD OF GOD.

2._______ JOHN WENT ABOUT PREACHING REPENTANCE AND BAPTIZING THE PEOPLE. THEY BEGAN TO WONDER IF JOHN WAS JESUS CHRIST. JOHN QUICKLY CORRECTED THEM AND TOLD THEM, "I INDEED BAPTIZE YOU WITH WATER. BUT ONE MIGHTIER THAN I COMETH THE LATCHET OF WHOSE SHOES I AM NOT WORTHY TO UNLOOSE. HE SHALL BAPTIZE YOU WITH THE HOLY GHOST AND WITH FIRE".

3.______ JOSEPH HAD TRAVELED WITH HIS ESPOUSED WIFE MARY TO BETHLEHEM TO BE TAXED. WHILE THEY WERE THERE SHE GAVE BIRTH TO HER FIRSTBORN SON AND WRAPPED HIM IN SWADDLING CLOTHES AND LAID HIM IN A MANGER BECAUSE THERE WAS NO ROOM FOR THEM IN THE INN.

4.______ WHEN AN ANGEL OF THE LORD APPEARED ON THE RIGHT SIDE OF THE ALTAR OF INCENSE, IT SCARED ZACHARIAS. BUT, THE ANGEL TOLD HIM NOT TO FEAR AND THAT HIS PRAYER HAD BEEN HEARD. HE ANNOUNCED TO HIM THAT HIS WIFE ELISABETH, WOULD BEAR HIM A SON NAMED JOHN.

TRUE OR FALSE

5. THE ANGEL TOLD ZACHARIAS THAT HIS SON, JOHN WOULD NOT DRINK WINE NOR STRONG DRINK.

____

LUKE 1:15

6. AFTER JESUS WAS BORN, THEY BROUGHT HIM TO JERUSALEM TO OFFER A PAIR OF TURTLE DOVES AND TWO YOUNG PIGEONS AS A SACRIFICE.

____

LUKE 2:22-24

7. PONTIUS PILATE WAS THE GOVERNOR OF JUDEA DURING TIBERIUS CAESAR'S 10TH YEAR REIGN

____

LUKE 3:1

FILL IN THE BLANKS

8. AND ALL____________SHALL____________THE____________OF GOD

9. ____________TO GOD IN THE____________AND ON____________PEACE, GOOD WILL TOWARD MEN

10. ____________, I SAY UNTO YOU, NO____________IS ACCEPTED IN HIS OWN____________.

MY PRAYER JOURNAL

Please use this space to record your thoughts and feelings as you travel on this spirit led journey through the word of God with us. Please know that you have brothers and sisters in this organization from all over the world praying with and for you. My prayer for you is that you will begin to see the power of God resting in each set of your footprints. As you look back and examine your past in this journal, may you realize that you were never alone and according to Hebrews 13:5, God will never leave nor forsake you. ~LADY FLORA

I THESSALONIANS 5:17

THE STUDY OF THE FOUR GOSPELS VOCABULARY DEFINITIONS FOR LUKE CHAPTERS 5-8

WORD	DEFINITIONS
1) MURMUR	
2) DRAUGHT	
3) BLASPHEMIES	
4) PUBLICAN	
5) BRIDECHAMBER	
6) COMMUNE	
7) VEX	
8) REPROACH	
9) VIRTUE	
10) BRAMBLE	

DMWW DAILY BIBLE READING
LUKE CHAPTERS 5-8 KJV

CHAPTER 5

1. And it came to pass, that, as the people pressed upon him to hear the word of God, he stood by the lake of Gennesaret,
2. And saw two ships standing by the lake: but the fishermen were gone out of them, and were washing their nets.
3. And he entered into one of the ships, which was Simon's, and prayed him that he would thrust out a little from the land. And he sat down, and taught the people out of the ship.
4. Now when he had left speaking, he said unto Simon, Launch out into the deep, and let down your nets for a draught.
5. And Simon answering said unto him, Master, we have toiled all the night, and have taken nothing: nevertheless at thy word I will let down the net.
6. And when they had this done, they inclosed a great multitude of fishes: and their net brake.
7. And they beckoned unto their partners, which were in the other ship, that they should come and help them. And they came, and filled both the ships, so that they began to sink.
8. When Simon Peter saw it, he fell down at Jesus' knees, saying, Depart from me; for I am a sinful man, O Lord.
9. For he was astonished, and all that were with him, at the draught of the fishes which they had taken:
10. And so was also James, and John, the sons of Zebedee, which were partners with Simon. And Jesus said unto Simon, Fear not; from henceforth thou shalt catch men.
11. And when they had brought their ships to land, they forsook all, and followed him.
12. And it came to pass, when he was in a certain city, behold a man full of leprosy: who seeing Jesus fell on his face, and besought him, saying, Lord, if thou wilt, thou canst make me clean.
13. And he put forth his hand, and touched him, saying, I will: be thou clean. And immediately the leprosy departed from him.
14. And he charged him to tell no man: but go, and shew thyself to the priest, and offer for thy cleansing, according as Moses commanded, for a testimony unto them.
15. But so much the more went there a fame abroad of him: and great multitudes came together to hear, and to be healed by him of their infirmities.

16. And he withdrew himself into the wilderness, and prayed.

17. And it came to pass on a certain day, as he was teaching, that there were Pharisees and doctors of the law sitting by, which were come out of every town of Galilee, and Judaea, and Jerusalem: and the power of the Lord was present to heal them.

18. And, behold, men brought in a bed a man which was taken with a palsy: and they sought means to bring him in, and to lay him before him.

19. And when they could not find by what way they might bring him in because of the multitude, they went upon the housetop, and let him down through the tiling with his couch into the midst before Jesus.

20. And when he saw their faith, he said unto him, Man, thy sins are forgiven thee.

21. And the scribes and the Pharisees began to reason, saying, Who is this which speaketh blasphemies? Who can forgive sins, but God alone?

22. But when Jesus perceived their thoughts, he answering said unto them, What reason ye in your hearts?

23. Whether is easier, to say, Thy sins be forgiven thee; or to say, Rise up and walk?

24. But that ye may know that the Son of man hath power upon earth to forgive sins, (he said unto the sick of the palsy,) I say unto thee, Arise, and take up thy couch, and go into thine house.

25. And immediately he rose up before them, and took up that whereon he lay, and departed to his own house, glorifying God.

26. And they were all amazed, and they glorified God, and were filled with fear, saying, We have seen strange things to day.

27. And after these things he went forth, and saw a publican, named Levi, sitting at the receipt of custom: and he said unto him, Follow me.

28. And he left all, rose up, and followed him.

29. And Levi made him a great feast in his own house: and there was a great company of publicans and of others that sat down with them.

30. But their scribes and Pharisees murmured against his disciples, saying, Why do ye eat and drink with publicans and sinners?

31. And Jesus answering said unto them, They that are whole need not a physician; but they that are sick.

32. I came not to call the righteous, but sinners to repentance.

33. And they said unto him, Why do the disciples of John fast often, and make prayers, and likewise the disciples of the Pharisees; but thine eat and drink?

34. And he said unto them, Can ye make the children of the bridechamber fast, while the bridegroom is with them?

35. But the days will come, when the bridegroom shall be taken away from them, and then shall they fast in those days.

36. And he spake also a parable unto them; No man putteth a piece of a new garment upon an old; if otherwise, then both the new maketh a rent, and the piece that was taken out of the new agreeth not with the old.

37. And no man putteth new wine into old bottles; else the new wine will burst the bottles, and be spilled, and the bottles shall perish.

38. But new wine must be put into new bottles; and both are preserved.

39. No man also having drunk old wine straightway desireth new: for he saith, The old is better.

CHAPTER 6

1. And it came to pass on the second sabbath after the first, that he went through the corn fields; and his disciples plucked the ears of corn, and did eat, rubbing them in their hands.

2. And certain of the Pharisees said unto them, Why do ye that which is not lawful to do on the sabbath days?

3. And Jesus answering them said, Have ye not read so much as this, what David did, when himself was an hungred, and they which were with him;

4. How he went into the house of God, and did take and eat the shewbread, and gave also to them that were with him; which it is not lawful to eat but for the priests alone?

5. And he said unto them, That the Son of man is Lord also of the sabbath.

6. And it came to pass also on another sabbath, that he entered into the synagogue and taught: and there was a man whose right hand was withered.

7. And the scribes and Pharisees watched him, whether he would heal on the sabbath day; that they might find an accusation against him.

8. But he knew their thoughts, and said to the man which had the withered hand, Rise up, and stand forth in the midst. And he arose and stood forth.

9. Then said Jesus unto them, I will ask you one thing; Is it lawful on the sabbath days to do good, or to do evil? to save life, or to destroy it?

10. And looking round about upon them all, he said unto the man, Stretch forth thy hand. And he did so: and his hand was restored whole as the other.

11. And they were filled with madness; and communed one with another what they might do to Jesus.

12. And it came to pass in those days, that he went out into a mountain to pray, and continued all night in prayer to God.

13. And when it was day, he called unto him his disciples: and of them he chose twelve, whom also he named apostles;

14. Simon, (whom he also named Peter,) and Andrew his brother, James and John, Philip and Bartholomew,

15. Matthew and Thomas, James the son of Alphaeus, and Simon called Zelotes,

16. And Judas the brother of James, and Judas Iscariot, which also was the traitor.

17. And he came down with them, and stood in the plain, and the company of his disciples, and a great multitude of people out of all Judaea and Jerusalem, and from the sea coast of Tyre and Sidon, which came to hear him, and to be healed of their diseases;

18. And they that were vexed with unclean spirits: and they were healed.

19. And the whole multitude sought to touch him: for there went virtue out of him, and healed them all.

20. And he lifted up his eyes on his disciples, and said, Blessed be ye poor: for yours is the kingdom of God.

21. Blessed are ye that hunger now: for ye shall be filled. Blessed are ye that weep now: for ye shall laugh.

22. Blessed are ye, when men shall hate you, and when they shall separate you from their company, and shall reproach you, and cast out your name as evil, for the Son of man's sake.

23. Rejoice ye in that day, and leap for joy: for, behold, your reward is great in heaven: for in the like manner did their fathers unto the prophets.

24. But woe unto you that are rich! for ye have received your consolation.

25. Woe unto you that are full! for ye shall hunger. Woe unto you that laugh now! for ye shall mourn and weep.

26. Woe unto you, when all men shall speak well of you! for so did their fathers to the false prophets.

27. But I say unto you which hear, Love your enemies, do good to them which hate you,

28. Bless them that curse you, and pray for them which despitefully use you.

29. And unto him that smiteth thee on the one cheek offer also the other; and him that taketh away thy cloak forbid not to take thy coat also.

30. Give to every man that asketh of thee; and of him that taketh away thy goods ask them not again.

31. And as ye would that men should do to you, do ye also to them likewise.

32. For if ye love them which love you, what thank have ye? for sinners also love those that love them.

33. And if ye do good to them which do good to you, what thank have ye? for sinners also do even the same.

34. And if ye lend to them of whom ye hope to receive, what thank have ye? for sinners also lend to sinners, to receive as much again.

35. But love ye your enemies, and do good, and lend, hoping for nothing again; and your reward shall be great, and ye shall be the children of the Highest: for he is kind unto the unthankful and to the evil.

36. Be ye therefore merciful, as your Father also is merciful.

37. Judge not, and ye shall not be judged: condemn not, and ye shall not be condemned: forgive, and ye shall be forgiven:

38. Give, and it shall be given unto you; good measure, pressed down, and shaken together, and running over, shall men give into your bosom. For with the same measure that ye mete withal it shall be measured to you again.

39. And he spake a parable unto them, Can the blind lead the blind? shall they not both fall into the ditch?

40. The disciple is not above his master: but every one that is perfect shall be as his master.

41. And why beholdest thou the mote that is in thy brother's eye, but perceivest not the beam that is in thine own eye?

42. Either how canst thou say to thy brother, Brother, let me pull out the mote that is in thine eye, when thou thyself beholdest not the beam that is in thine own eye? Thou hypocrite, cast out first the beam out of thine own eye, and then shalt thou see clearly to pull out the mote that is in thy brother's eye.

43. For a good tree bringeth not forth corrupt fruit; neither doth a corrupt tree bring forth good fruit.

44. For every tree is known by his own fruit. For of thorns men do not gather figs, nor of a bramble bush gather they grapes.

45. A good man out of the good treasure of his heart bringeth forth that which is good; and an evil man out of the evil treasure of his heart bringeth forth that which is evil: for of the abundance of the heart his mouth speaketh.

46. And why call ye me, Lord, Lord, and do not the things which I say?

47. Whosoever cometh to me, and heareth my sayings, and doeth them, I will shew you to whom he is like:

48. He is like a man which built an house, and digged deep, and laid the foundation on a rock: and when the flood arose, the stream beat vehemently upon that house, and could not shake it: for it was founded upon a rock.

49. But he that heareth, and doeth not, is like a man that without a foundation built an house upon the earth; against which the stream did beat vehemently, and immediately it fell; and the ruin of that house was great.

CHAPTER 7

1. Now when he had ended all his sayings in the audience of the people, he entered into Capernaum.

2. And a certain centurion's servant, who was dear unto him, was sick, and ready to die.

3. And when he heard of Jesus, he sent unto him the elders of the Jews, beseeching him that he would come and heal his servant.

4. And when they came to Jesus, they besought him instantly, saying, That he was worthy for whom he should do this:

5. For he loveth our nation, and he hath built us a synagogue.

6. Then Jesus went with them. And when he was now not far from the house, the centurion sent friends to him, saying unto him, Lord, trouble not thyself: for I am not worthy that thou shouldest enter under my roof:

7. Wherefore neither thought I myself worthy to come unto thee: but say in a word, and my servant shall be healed.

8. For I also am a man set under authority, having under me soldiers, and I say unto one, Go, and he goeth; and to another, Come, and he cometh; and to my servant, Do this, and he doeth it.

9. When Jesus heard these things, he marvelled at him, and turned him about, and said unto the people that followed him, I say unto you, I have not found so great faith, no, not in Israel.

10. And they that were sent, returning to the house, found the servant whole that had been sick.

11. And it came to pass the day after, that he went into a city called Nain; and many of his disciples went with him, and much people.

12. Now when he came nigh to the gate of the city, behold, there was a dead man carried out, the only son of his mother, and she was a widow: and much people of the city was with her.

13. And when the Lord saw her, he had compassion on her, and said unto her, Weep not.

14. And he came and touched the bier: and they that bare him stood still. And he said, Young man, I say unto thee, Arise.

15. And he that was dead sat up, and began to speak. And he delivered him to his mother.

16. And there came a fear on all: and they glorified God, saying, That a great prophet is risen up among us; and, That God hath visited his people.

17. And this rumour of him went forth throughout all Judaea, and throughout all the region round about.

18. And the disciples of John shewed him of all these things.

19. And John calling unto him two of his disciples sent them to Jesus, saying, Art thou he that should come? or look we for another?

20. When the men were come unto him, they said, John Baptist hath sent us unto thee, saying, Art thou he that should come? or look we for another?

21. And in that same hour he cured many of their infirmities and plagues, and of evil spirits; and unto many that were blind he gave sight.

22. Then Jesus answering said unto them, Go your way, and tell John what things ye have seen and heard; how that the blind see, the lame walk, the lepers are cleansed, the deaf hear, the dead are raised, to the poor the gospel is preached.

23. And blessed is he, whosoever shall not be offended in me.

24. And when the messengers of John were departed, he began to speak unto the people concerning John, What went ye out into the wilderness for to see? A reed shaken with the wind?

25. But what went ye out for to see? A man clothed in soft raiment? Behold, they which are gorgeously apparelled, and live delicately, are in kings' courts.

26. But what went ye out for to see? A prophet? Yea, I say unto you, and much more than a prophet.

27. This is he, of whom it is written, Behold, I send my messenger before thy face, which shall prepare thy way before thee.

28. For I say unto you, Among those that are born of women there is not a greater prophet than John the Baptist: but he that is least in the kingdom of God is greater than he.

29. And all the people that heard him, and the publicans, justified God, being baptized with the baptism of John.

30. But the Pharisees and lawyers rejected the counsel of God against themselves, being not baptized of him.

31. And the Lord said, Whereunto then shall I liken the men of this generation? and to what are they like?

32. They are like unto children sitting in the marketplace, and calling one to another, and saying, We have piped unto you, and ye have not danced; we have mourned to you, and ye have not wept.

33. For John the Baptist came neither eating bread nor drinking wine; and ye say, He hath a devil.

34. The Son of man is come eating and drinking; and ye say, Behold a gluttonous man, and a winebibber, a friend of publicans and sinners!

35. But wisdom is justified of all her children.

36. And one of the Pharisees desired him that he would eat with him. And he went into the Pharisee's house, and sat down to meat.

37. And, behold, a woman in the city, which was a sinner, when she knew that Jesus sat at meat in the Pharisee's house, brought an alabaster box of ointment,

38. And stood at his feet behind him weeping, and began to wash his feet with tears, and did wipe them with the hairs of her head, and kissed his feet, and anointed them with the ointment.

39. Now when the Pharisee which had bidden him saw it, he spake within himself, saying, This man, if he were a prophet, would have known who and what manner of woman this is that toucheth him: for she is a sinner.

40. And Jesus answering said unto him, Simon, I have somewhat to say unto thee. And he saith, Master, say on.

41. There was a certain creditor which had two debtors: the one owed five hundred pence, and the other fifty.

42. And when they had nothing to pay, he frankly forgave them both. Tell me therefore, which of them will love him most?

43. Simon answered and said, I suppose that he, to whom he forgave most. And he said unto him, Thou hast rightly judged.

44. And he turned to the woman, and said unto Simon, Seest thou this woman? I entered into thine house, thou gavest me no water for my feet: but she hath washed my feet with tears, and wiped them with the hairs of her head.

45. Thou gavest me no kiss: but this woman since the time I came in hath not ceased to kiss my feet.

46. My head with oil thou didst not anoint: but this woman hath anointed my feet with ointment.

47. Wherefore I say unto thee, Her sins, which are many, are forgiven; for she loved much: but to whom little is forgiven, the same loveth little.

48. And he said unto her, Thy sins are forgiven.

49. And they that sat at meat with him began to say within themselves, Who is this that forgiveth sins also?

50. And he said to the woman, Thy faith hath saved thee; go in peace.

CHAPTER 8

1. And it came to pass afterward, that he went throughout every city and village, preaching and shewing the glad tidings of the kingdom of God: and the twelve were with him,

2. And certain women, which had been healed of evil spirits and infirmities, Mary called Magdalene, out of whom went seven devils,

3. And Joanna the wife of Chuza Herod's steward, and Susanna, and many others, which ministered unto him of their substance.

4. And when much people were gathered together, and were come to him out of every city, he spake by a parable:

5. A sower went out to sow his seed: and as he sowed, some fell by the way side; and it was trodden down, and the fowls of the air devoured it.

6. And some fell upon a rock; and as soon as it was sprung up, it withered away, because it lacked moisture.

7. And some fell among thorns; and the thorns sprang up with it, and choked it.

8. And other fell on good ground, and sprang up, and bare fruit an hundredfold. And when he had said these things, he cried, He that hath ears to hear, let him hear.

9. And his disciples asked him, saying, What might this parable be?

10. And he said, Unto you it is given to know the mysteries of the kingdom of God: but to others in parables; that seeing they might not see, and hearing they might not understand.

11. Now the parable is this: The seed is the word of God.

12. Those by the way side are they that hear; then cometh the devil, and taketh away the word out of their hearts, lest they should believe and be saved.

13. They on the rock are they, which, when they hear, receive the word with joy; and these have no root, which for a while believe, and in time of temptation fall away.

14. And that which fell among thorns are they, which, when they have heard, go forth, and are choked with cares and riches and pleasures of this life, and bring no fruit to perfection.

15. But that on the good ground are they, which in an honest and good heart, having heard the word, keep it, and bring forth fruit with patience.

16. No man, when he hath lighted a candle, covereth it with a vessel, or putteth it under a bed; but setteth it on a candlestick, that they which enter in may see the light.

17. For nothing is secret, that shall not be made manifest; neither any thing hid, that shall not be known and come abroad.

18. Take heed therefore how ye hear: for whosoever hath, to him shall be given; and whosoever hath not, from him shall be taken even that which he seemeth to have.

19. Then came to him his mother and his brethren, and could not come at him for the press.

20. And it was told him by certain which said, Thy mother and thy brethren stand without, desiring to see thee.

21. And he answered and said unto them, My mother and my brethren are these which hear the word of God, and do it.

22. Now it came to pass on a certain day, that he went into a ship with his disciples: and he said unto them, Let us go over unto the other side of the lake. And they launched forth.

23. But as they sailed he fell asleep: and there came down a storm of wind on the lake; and they were filled with water, and were in jeopardy.

24. And they came to him, and awoke him, saying, Master, master, we perish. Then he arose, and rebuked the wind and the raging of the water: and they ceased, and there was a calm.

25. And he said unto them, Where is your faith? And they being afraid wondered, saying one to another, What manner of man is this! for he commandeth even the winds and water, and they obey him.

26. And they arrived at the country of the Gadarenes, which is over against Galilee.

27. And when he went forth to land, there met him out of the city a certain man, which had devils long time, and ware no clothes, neither abode in any house, but in the tombs.

28. When he saw Jesus, he cried out, and fell down before him, and with a loud voice said, What have I to do with thee, Jesus, thou Son of God most high? I beseech thee, torment me not.

29. (For he had commanded the unclean spirit to come out of the man. For oftentimes it had caught him: and he was kept bound with chains and in fetters; and he brake the bands, and was driven of the devil into the wilderness.)

30. And Jesus asked him, saying, What is thy name? And he said, Legion: because many devils were entered into him.

31. And they besought him that he would not command them to go out into the deep.

32. And there was there an herd of many swine feeding on the mountain: and they besought him that he would suffer them to enter into them. And he suffered them.

33. Then went the devils out of the man, and entered into the swine: and the herd ran violently down a steep place into the lake, and were choked.

34. When they that fed them saw what was done, they fled, and went and told it in the city and in the country.

35. Then they went out to see what was done; and came to Jesus, and found the man, out of whom the devils were departed, sitting at the feet of Jesus, clothed, and in his right mind: and they were afraid.

36. They also which saw it told them by what means he that was possessed of the devils was healed.

37. Then the whole multitude of the country of the Gadarenes round about besought him to depart from them; for they were taken with great fear: and he went up into the ship, and returned back again.

38. Now the man out of whom the devils were departed besought him that he might be with him: but Jesus sent him away, saying,

39. Return to thine own house, and shew how great things God hath done unto thee. And he went his way, and published throughout the whole city how great things Jesus had done unto him.

40. And it came to pass, that, when Jesus was returned, the people gladly received him: for they were all waiting for him.

41. And, behold, there came a man named Jairus, and he was a ruler of the synagogue: and he fell down at Jesus' feet, and besought him that he would come into his house:

42. For he had one only daughter, about twelve years of age, and she lay a dying. But as he went the people thronged him.

43. And a woman having an issue of blood twelve years, which had spent all her living upon physicians, neither could be healed of any,

44. Came behind him, and touched the border of his garment: and immediately her issue of blood stanched.

45. And Jesus said, Who touched me? When all denied, Peter and they that were with him said, Master, the multitude throng thee and press thee, and sayest thou, Who touched me?

46. And Jesus said, Somebody hath touched me: for I perceive that virtue is gone out of me.

47. And when the woman saw that she was not hid, she came trembling, and falling down before him, she declared unto him before all the people for what cause she had touched him, and how she was healed immediately.

48. And he said unto her, Daughter, be of good comfort: thy faith hath made thee whole; go in peace.

49. While he yet spake, there cometh one from the ruler of the synagogue's house, saying to him, Thy daughter is dead; trouble not the Master.

50. But when Jesus heard it, he answered him, saying, Fear not: believe only, and she shall be made whole.

51. And when he came into the house, he suffered no man to go in, save Peter, and James, and John, and the father and the mother of the maiden.

52. And all wept, and bewailed her: but he said, Weep not; she is not dead, but sleepeth.

53. And they laughed him to scorn, knowing that she was dead.

54. And he put them all out, and took her by the hand, and called, saying, Maid, arise.

55. And her spirit came again, and she arose straightway: and he commanded to give her meat.

56. And her parents were astonished: but he charged them that they should tell no man what was done.

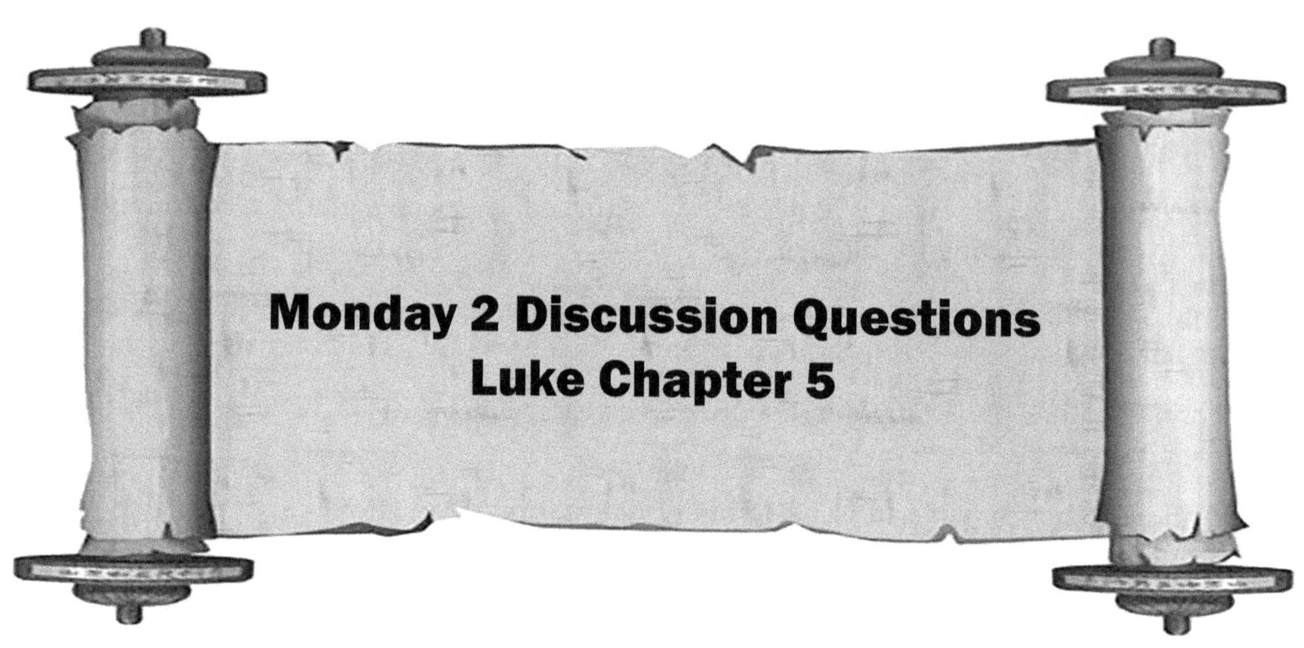

1. Where was Jesus standing while people were pressing on him to hear his teaching? ______

2. Where were the fishermen who owned the two ships Jesus saw? ______

3. What did Jesus ask Simon to do before he sat down to teach the people? ______

4. When Jesus finished teaching what did he tell Simon to do with the nets? ______

5. What did Simon say and do? ______

6. What happened when they obeyed? ______

7. What did they ask their partners on the other ship to do? What happened when the partners did this? ______

8. What did Simon Peter say when he fell down at Jesus' knees? ______

9. What did Jesus tell Simon not to do? Why? ______

10. What did the angel tell Mary about her cousin? ______

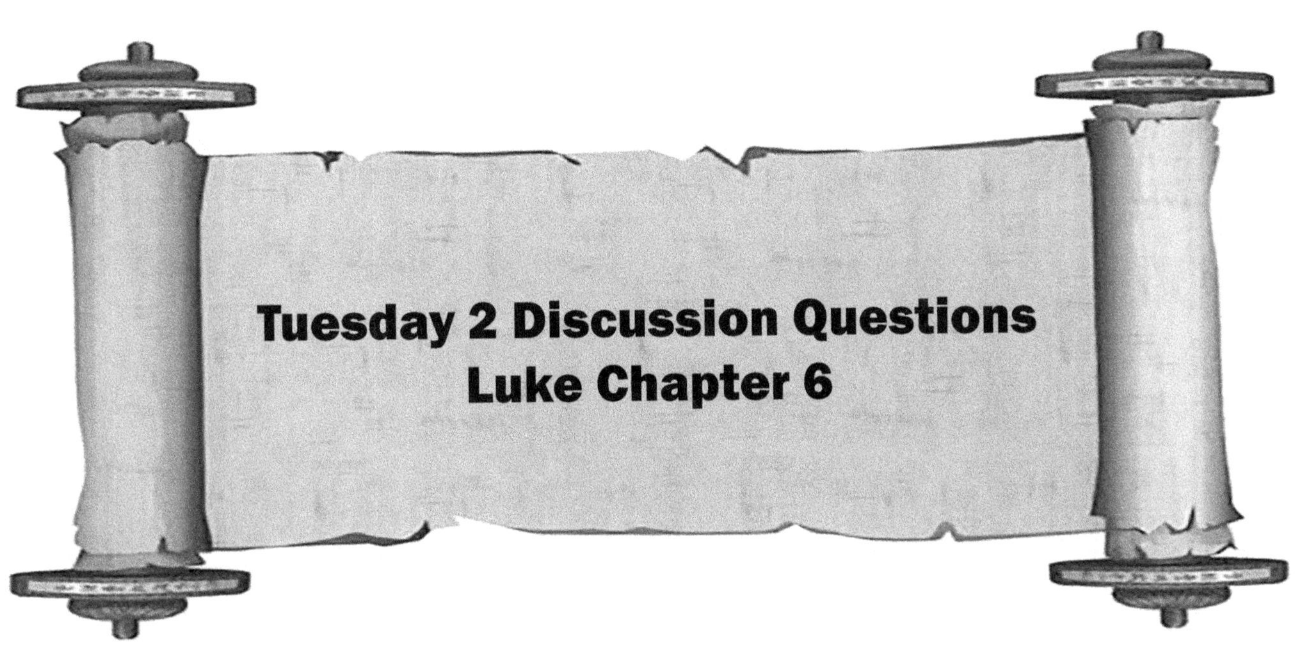

1. Where was Jesus walking on the second sabbath after the first? ______
2. What did the disciples do with the corn? ______
3. What did the Pharisees ask the disciples? ______
4. What did Jesus remind them that David did in the house of the Lord when he was hungry? ______
5. What did Jesus say on the Sabbath day, to the man with the withered hand? What did the man do? ______
6. What did Jesus ask the Pharisees after the man stood? ______
7. What did the man do when the Lord told him to stretch forth his hand? ______
8. Were the people happy and excited to see a man healed by Jesus? How did they feel? What did they do? ______
9. After Jesus had prayed all night, who did he call unto himself? How many of them did he choose? What did he name them? ______
10. What did Jesus say when he looked upon his disciples to bless them? ______

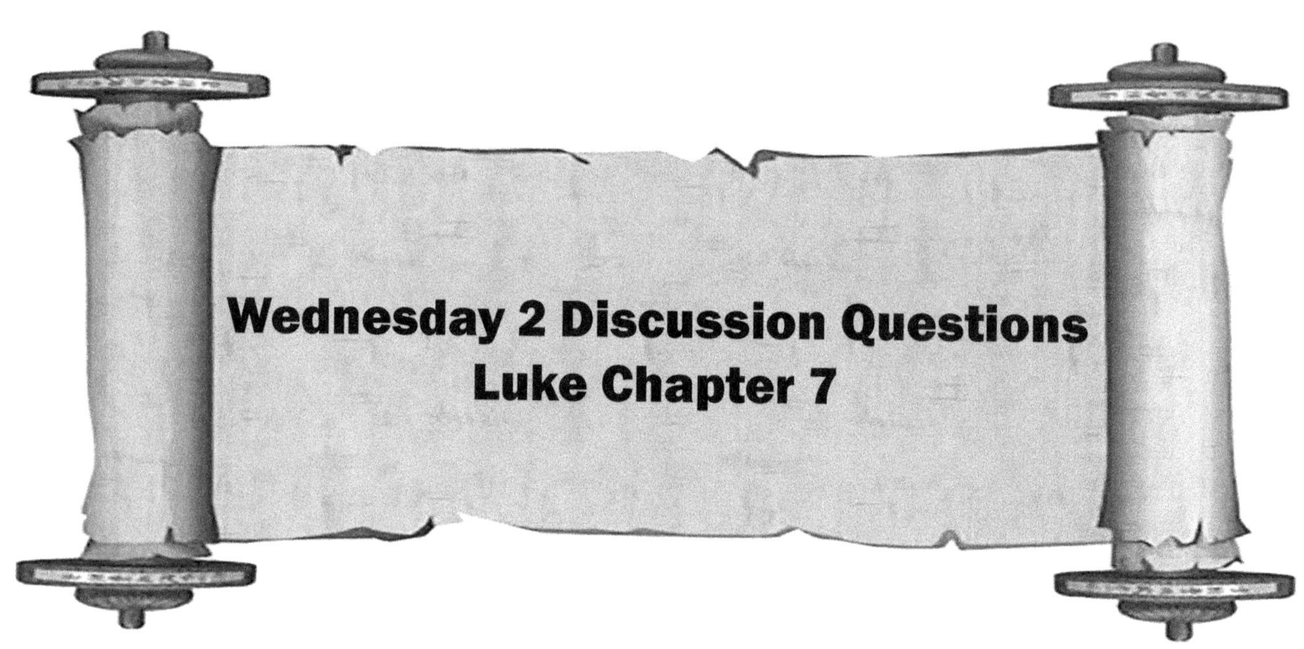

1. Where did Jesus go when he had finished talking with the people? ______________________

2. Who sent the elders to Jesus to beseech him to come and heal the centurion man? ______________________

3. What were they trying to convince Jesus about the man? ______________________

4. What did they say about this man? ______________________

5. What message did the man send to the Lord when he came close to his house? ______________________

6. What did Jesus say when he heard what the centurion man had said? ______________________

7. What did the two disciples John sent to Jesus say to him? ______________________

8. What did Jesus do in that same hour? ______________________

9. What did Jesu tell the men to do? ______________________

10. What did Jesus say about those who would not be offended by him? ______________________

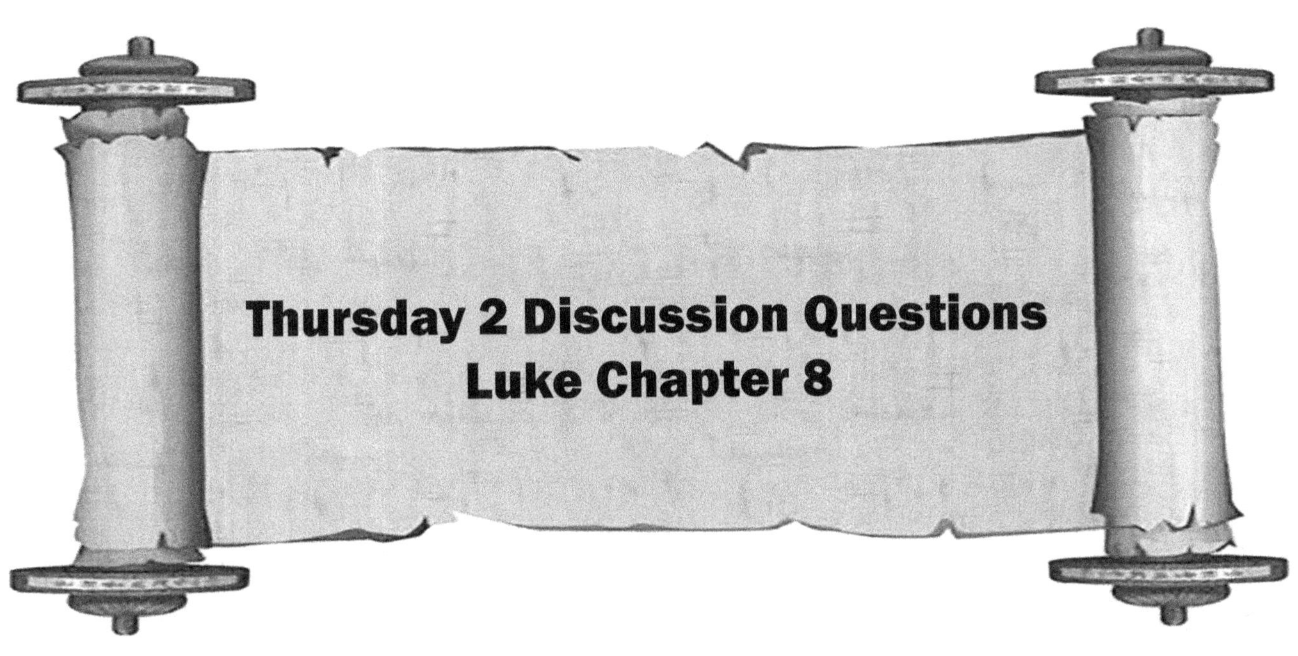

1. Who was with Jesus when he went throughout the cities and villages preaching? ____

2. There were many women traveling with him as he ministered. Who were they? ____

3. What is the parable he began speaking about? ____

4. What happened to the seed that fell by the wayside? ____

5. What happened to the seed that fell on the rocks? ____

6. What happened to the seed that fell among the thorns? ____

7. What happened to the seed that fell on good ground? They sprang up, and bare fruit a hundredfold ____

8. Why did Jesus say when the disciples asked what the parable was about? ____

9. What did he say the seed in the parable meant? ____

10. How did Jesus explain the seed and the good ground? ____

WEEKLY REVIEW
LUKE CHAPTERS 5-8

NAME THAT CHAPTER

1.______ ALONG WITH THE 12 DISCIPLES THAT FOLLOWED JESUS WERE CERTAIN WOMEN WHO HAD BEEN HEALED OF EVIL SPIRITS AND CERTAIN DISEASES. THESE WOMEN INCLUDED MARY MAGDALENE, JOANA THE WIFE OF CHUZA, WHO WAS HEROD'S STEWARD, SUSANA AND MANY OTHERS. THESE WOMEN MINISTERED TO JESUS OF THEIR SUBSTANCE ALONG HIS JOURNEY. IN THIS CHAPTER, JESUS SPOKE A PARABLE ABOUT SEED AND THE SOWER. HE EXPLAINED TO THE PEOPLE THAT THE SEED WAS THE WORD OF GOD.

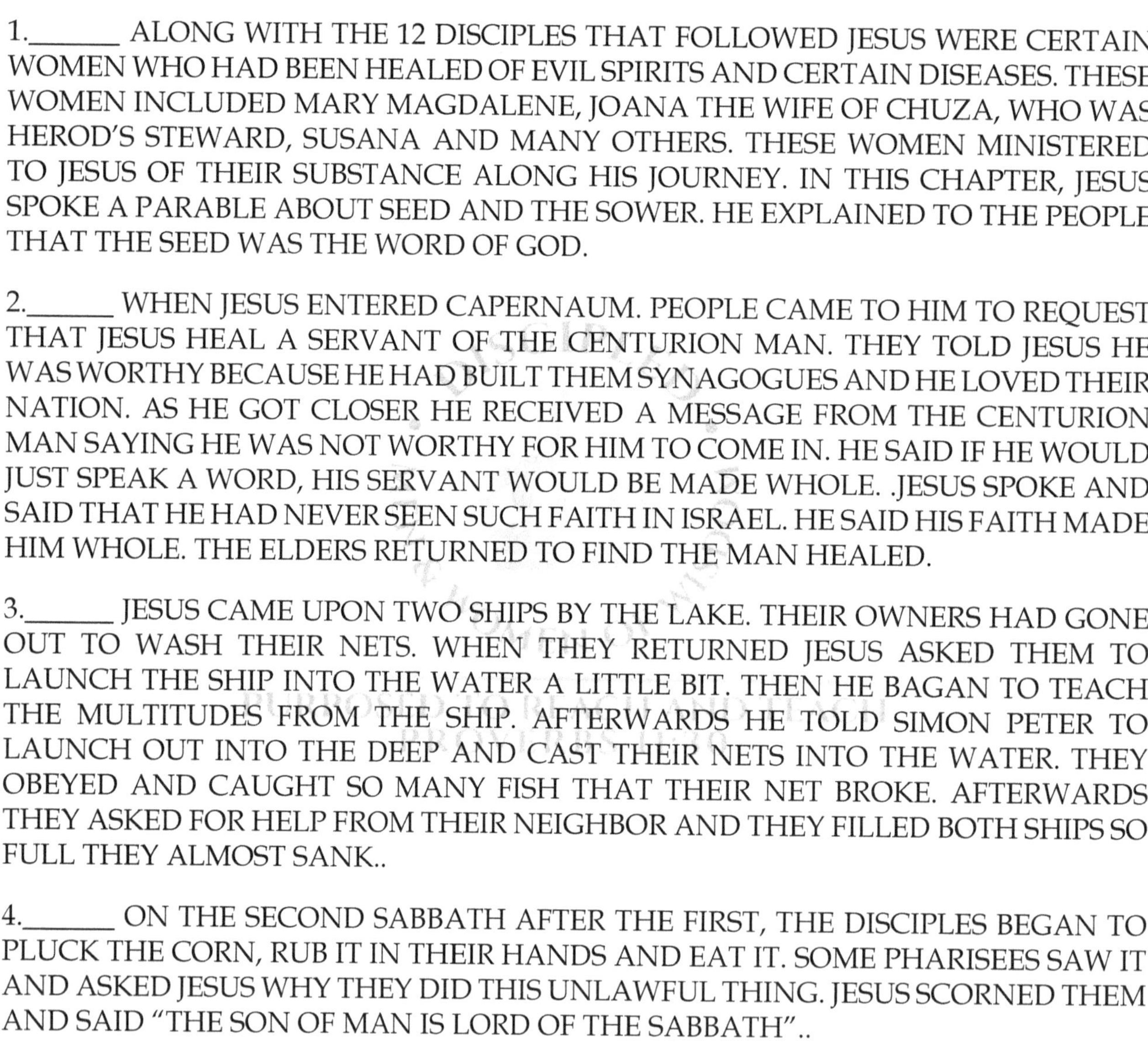

2.______ WHEN JESUS ENTERED CAPERNAUM. PEOPLE CAME TO HIM TO REQUEST THAT JESUS HEAL A SERVANT OF THE CENTURION MAN. THEY TOLD JESUS HE WAS WORTHY BECAUSE HE HAD BUILT THEM SYNAGOGUES AND HE LOVED THEIR NATION. AS HE GOT CLOSER HE RECEIVED A MESSAGE FROM THE CENTURION MAN SAYING HE WAS NOT WORTHY FOR HIM TO COME IN. HE SAID IF HE WOULD JUST SPEAK A WORD, HIS SERVANT WOULD BE MADE WHOLE. .JESUS SPOKE AND SAID THAT HE HAD NEVER SEEN SUCH FAITH IN ISRAEL. HE SAID HIS FAITH MADE HIM WHOLE. THE ELDERS RETURNED TO FIND THE MAN HEALED.

3.______ JESUS CAME UPON TWO SHIPS BY THE LAKE. THEIR OWNERS HAD GONE OUT TO WASH THEIR NETS. WHEN THEY RETURNED JESUS ASKED THEM TO LAUNCH THE SHIP INTO THE WATER A LITTLE BIT. THEN HE BAGAN TO TEACH THE MULTITUDES FROM THE SHIP. AFTERWARDS HE TOLD SIMON PETER TO LAUNCH OUT INTO THE DEEP AND CAST THEIR NETS INTO THE WATER. THEY OBEYED AND CAUGHT SO MANY FISH THAT THEIR NET BROKE. AFTERWARDS THEY ASKED FOR HELP FROM THEIR NEIGHBOR AND THEY FILLED BOTH SHIPS SO FULL THEY ALMOST SANK..

4.______ ON THE SECOND SABBATH AFTER THE FIRST, THE DISCIPLES BEGAN TO PLUCK THE CORN, RUB IT IN THEIR HANDS AND EAT IT. SOME PHARISEES SAW IT AND ASKED JESUS WHY THEY DID THIS UNLAWFUL THING. JESUS SCORNED THEM AND SAID "THE SON OF MAN IS LORD OF THE SABBATH"..

TRUE OR FALSE

5. IN THE PARABLE JESUS GAVE SOWER WENT OUT TO SOW HIS SEED AND AS HE SOWED, SOME FELL BY THE WAYSIDE, AND IT WAS TRODDEN DOWN, AND THE FOWLS OF THE AIR DEVOURED IT.

____

LUKE 8:5

6. WHEN JESUS HEALED THE MAN OF LEPROSY, HE TOLD HIM TO GO AND NOT TO TELL ANYONE.

____

LUKE 5:14

7. JESUS SAID IF SOMEONE STEALS FROM YOU, DON'T ASK FOR IT BACK

____

LUKE 6:30

FILL IN THE BLANKS

8. BUT______________IS______________OF ALL HER______________.
9. AND HE______________HIMSELF INTO THE______________AND ______________
10. BUT______________UNTO YE THAT ARE______________! FOR YE HAVE RECEIVED YOUR______________.

MY PRAYER JOURNAL

Please use this space to record your thoughts and feelings as you travel on this spirit led journey through the word of God with us. Please know that you have brothers and sisters in this organization from all over the world praying with and for you. My prayer for you is that you will begin to see the power of God resting in each set of your footprints. As you look back and examine your past in this journal, may you realize that you were never alone and according to Hebrews 13:5, God will never leave nor forsake you. ~LADY FLORA

I THESSALONIANS 5:17

THE STUDY OF THE FOUR GOSPELS VOCABULARY DEFINITIONS FOR LUKE CHAPTERS 9-12

WORD	DEFINITIONS
1) PERPLEXED	
2) TETRARCH	
3) VICTUALS	
4) COUNTENANCE	
5) GLISTERING	
6) PRUDENT	
7) CUMBERED	
8) HALLOWED	
9) PAPS	
10) RAVENING	

DMWW DAILY BIBLE READING
LUKE CHAPTERS 9-12 KJV

CHAPTER 9

1. Then he called his twelve disciples together, and gave them power and authority over all devils, and to cure diseases.
2. And he sent them to preach the kingdom of God, and to heal the sick.
3. And he said unto them, Take nothing for your journey, neither staves, nor scrip, neither bread, neither money; neither have two coats apiece.
4. And whatsoever house ye enter into, there abide, and thence depart.
5. And whosoever will not receive you, when ye go out of that city, shake off the very dust from your feet for a testimony against them.
6. And they departed, and went through the towns, preaching the gospel, and healing every where.
7. Now Herod the tetrarch heard of all that was done by him: and he was perplexed, because that it was said of some, that John was risen from the dead;
8. And of some, that Elias had appeared; and of others, that one of the old prophets was risen again.
9. And Herod said, John have I beheaded: but who is this, of whom I hear such things? And he desired to see him.
10. And the apostles, when they were returned, told him all that they had done. And he took them, and went aside privately into a desert place belonging to the city called Bethsaida.
11. And the people, when they knew it, followed him: and he received them, and spake unto them of the kingdom of God, and healed them that had need of healing.
12. And when the day began to wear away, then came the twelve, and said unto him, Send the multitude away, that they may go into the towns and country round about, and lodge, and get victuals: for we are here in a desert place.
13. But he said unto them, Give ye them to eat. And they said, We have no more but five loaves and two fishes; except we should go and buy meat for all this people.
14. For they were about five thousand men. And he said to his disciples, Make them sit down by fifties in a company.
15. And they did so, and made them all sit down.
16. Then he took the five loaves and the two fishes, and looking up to heaven, he blessed them, and brake, and gave to the disciples to set before the multitude.

17. And they did eat, and were all filled: and there was taken up of fragments that remained to them twelve baskets.

18. And it came to pass, as he was alone praying, his disciples were with him: and he asked them, saying, Whom say the people that I am?

19. They answering said, John the Baptist; but some say, Elias; and others say, that one of the old prophets is risen again.

20. He said unto them, But whom say ye that I am? Peter answering said, The Christ of God.

21. And he straitly charged them, and commanded them to tell no man that thing;

22. Saying, The Son of man must suffer many things, and be rejected of the elders and chief priests and scribes, and be slain, and be raised the third day.

23. And he said to them all, If any man will come after me, let him deny himself, and take up his cross daily, and follow me.

24. For whosoever will save his life shall lose it: but whosoever will lose his life for my sake, the same shall save it.

25. For what is a man advantaged, if he gain the whole world, and lose himself, or be cast away?

26. For whosoever shall be ashamed of me and of my words, of him shall the Son of man be ashamed, when he shall come in his own glory, and in his Father's, and of the holy angels.

27. But I tell you of a truth, there be some standing here, which shall not taste of death, till they see the kingdom of God.

28. And it came to pass about an eight days after these sayings, he took Peter and John and James, and went up into a mountain to pray.

29. And as he prayed, the fashion of his countenance was altered, and his raiment was white and glistering.

30. And, behold, there talked with him two men, which were Moses and Elias:

31. Who appeared in glory, and spake of his decease which he should accomplish at Jerusalem.

32. But Peter and they that were with him were heavy with sleep: and when they were awake, they saw his glory, and the two men that stood with him.

33. And it came to pass, as they departed from him, Peter said unto Jesus, Master, it is good for us to be here: and let us make three tabernacles; one for thee, and one for Moses, and one for Elias: not knowing what he said.

34. While he thus spake, there came a cloud, and overshadowed them: and they feared as they entered into the cloud.

35. And there came a voice out of the cloud, saying, This is my beloved Son: hear him.

36. And when the voice was past, Jesus was found alone. And they kept it close, and told no man in those days any of those things which they had seen.

37. And it came to pass, that on the next day, when they were come down from the hill, much people met him.

38. And, behold, a man of the company cried out, saying, Master, I beseech thee, look upon my son: for he is mine only child.

39. And, lo, a spirit taketh him, and he suddenly crieth out; and it teareth him that he foameth again, and bruising him hardly departeth from him.

40. And I besought thy disciples to cast him out; and they could not.

41. And Jesus answering said, O faithless and perverse generation, how long shall I be with you, and suffer you? Bring thy son hither.

42. And as he was yet a coming, the devil threw him down, and tare him. And Jesus rebuked the unclean spirit, and healed the child, and delivered him again to his father.

43. And they were all amazed at the mighty power of God. But while they wondered every one at all things which Jesus did, he said unto his disciples,

44. Let these sayings sink down into your ears: for the Son of man shall be delivered into the hands of men.

45. But they understood not this saying, and it was hid from them, that they perceived it not: and they feared to ask him of that saying.

46. Then there arose a reasoning among them, which of them should be greatest.

47. And Jesus, perceiving the thought of their heart, took a child, and set him by him,

48. And said unto them, Whosoever shall receive this child in my name receiveth me: and whosoever shall receive me receiveth him that sent me: for he that is least among you all, the same shall be great.

49. And John answered and said, Master, we saw one casting out devils in thy name; and we forbad him, because he followeth not with us.

50. And Jesus said unto him, Forbid him not: for he that is not against us is for us.

51. And it came to pass, when the time was come that he should be received up, he stedfastly set his face to go to Jerusalem,

52. And sent messengers before his face: and they went, and entered into a village of the Samaritans, to make ready for him.

53. And they did not receive him, because his face was as though he would go to Jerusalem.

54. And when his disciples James and John saw this, they said, Lord, wilt thou that we command fire to come down from heaven, and consume them, even as Elias did?

55. But he turned, and rebuked them, and said, Ye know not what manner of spirit ye are of.

56. For the Son of man is not come to destroy men's lives, but to save them. And they went to another village.

57. And it came to pass, that, as they went in the way, a certain man said unto him, Lord, I will follow thee whithersoever thou goest.

58. And Jesus said unto him, Foxes have holes, and birds of the air have nests; but the Son of man hath not where to lay his head.

59. And he said unto another, Follow me. But he said, Lord, suffer me first to go and bury my father.

60. Jesus said unto him, Let the dead bury their dead: but go thou and preach the kingdom of God.

61. And another also said, Lord, I will follow thee; but let me first go bid them farewell, which are at home at my house.

62. And Jesus said unto him, No man, having put his hand to the plough, and looking back, is fit for the kingdom of God.

CHAPTER 10

1. After these things the Lord appointed other seventy also, and sent them two and two before his face into every city and place, whither he himself would come.

2. Therefore said he unto them, The harvest truly is great, but the labourers are few: pray ye therefore the Lord of the harvest, that he would send forth labourers into his harvest.

3. Go your ways: behold, I send you forth as lambs among wolves.

4. Carry neither purse, nor scrip, nor shoes: and salute no man by the way.

5. And into whatsoever house ye enter, first say, Peace be to this house.

6. And if the son of peace be there, your peace shall rest upon it: if not, it shall turn to you again.

7. And in the same house remain, eating and drinking such things as they give: for the labourer is worthy of his hire. Go not from house to house.

8. And into whatsoever city ye enter, and they receive you, eat such things as are set before you:

9. And heal the sick that are therein, and say unto them, The kingdom of God is come nigh unto you.

10. But into whatsoever city ye enter, and they receive you not, go your ways out into the streets of the same, and say,

11. Even the very dust of your city, which cleaveth on us, we do wipe off against you: notwithstanding be ye sure of this, that the kingdom of God is come nigh unto you.

12. But I say unto you, that it shall be more tolerable in that day for Sodom, than for that city.

13. Woe unto thee, Chorazin! woe unto thee, Bethsaida! for if the mighty works had been done in Tyre and Sidon, which have been done in you, they had a great while ago repented, sitting in sackcloth and ashes.

14. But it shall be more tolerable for Tyre and Sidon at the judgment, than for you.

15. And thou, Capernaum, which art exalted to heaven, shalt be thrust down to hell.

16. He that heareth you heareth me; and he that despiseth you despiseth me; and he that despiseth me despiseth him that sent me.

17. And the seventy returned again with joy, saying, Lord, even the devils are subject unto us through thy name.

18. And he said unto them, I beheld Satan as lightning fall from heaven.

19. Behold, I give unto you power to tread on serpents and scorpions, and over all the power of the enemy: and nothing shall by any means hurt you.

20. Notwithstanding in this rejoice not, that the spirits are subject unto you; but rather rejoice, because your names are written in heaven.

21. In that hour Jesus rejoiced in spirit, and said, I thank thee, O Father, Lord of heaven and earth, that thou hast hid these things from the wise and prudent, and hast revealed them unto babes: even so, Father; for so it seemed good in thy sight.

22. All things are delivered to me of my Father: and no man knoweth who the Son is, but the Father; and who the Father is, but the Son, and he to whom the Son will reveal him.

23. And he turned him unto his disciples, and said privately, Blessed are the eyes which see the things that ye see:

24. For I tell you, that many prophets and kings have desired to see those things which ye see, and have not seen them; and to hear those things which ye hear, and have not heard them.

25. And, behold, a certain lawyer stood up, and tempted him, saying, Master, what shall I do to inherit eternal life?

26. He said unto him, What is written in the law? how readest thou?

27. And he answering said, Thou shalt love the Lord thy God with all thy heart, and with all thy soul, and with all thy strength, and with all thy mind; and thy neighbour as thyself.

28. And he said unto him, Thou hast answered right: this do, and thou shalt live.

29. But he, willing to justify himself, said unto Jesus, And who is my neighbour?

30. And Jesus answering said, A certain man went down from Jerusalem to Jericho, and fell among thieves, which stripped him of his raiment, and wounded him, and departed, leaving him half dead.

31. And by chance there came down a certain priest that way: and when he saw him, he passed by on the other side.

32. And likewise a Levite, when he was at the place, came and looked on him, and passed by on the other side.

33. But a certain Samaritan, as he journeyed, came where he was: and when he saw him, he had compassion on him,

34. And went to him, and bound up his wounds, pouring in oil and wine, and set him on his own beast, and brought him to an inn, and took care of him.

35. And on the morrow when he departed, he took out two pence, and gave them to the host, and said unto him, Take care of him; and whatsoever thou spendest more, when I come again, I will repay thee.

36. Which now of these three, thinkest thou, was neighbour unto him that fell among the thieves?

37. And he said, He that shewed mercy on him. Then said Jesus unto him, Go, and do thou likewise.

38. Now it came to pass, as they went, that he entered into a certain village: and a certain woman named Martha received him into her house.

39. And she had a sister called Mary, which also sat at Jesus' feet, and heard his word.

40. But Martha was cumbered about much serving, and came to him, and said, Lord, dost thou not care that my sister hath left me to serve alone? bid her therefore that she help me.

41. And Jesus answered and said unto her, Martha, Martha, thou art careful and troubled about many things:

42. But one thing is needful: and Mary hath chosen that good part, which shall not be taken away from her.

CHAPTER 11

1. And it came to pass, that, as he was praying in a certain place, when he ceased, one of his disciples said unto him, Lord, teach us to pray, as John also taught his disciples.

2. And he said unto them, When ye pray, say, Our Father which art in heaven, Hallowed be thy name. Thy kingdom come. Thy will be done, as in heaven, so in earth.

3. Give us day by day our daily bread.

4. And forgive us our sins; for we also forgive every one that is indebted to us. And lead us not into temptation; but deliver us from evil.

5. And he said unto them, Which of you shall have a friend, and shall go unto him at midnight, and say unto him, Friend, lend me three loaves;

6. For a friend of mine in his journey is come to me, and I have nothing to set before him?

7. And he from within shall answer and say, Trouble me not: the door is now shut, and my children are with me in bed; I cannot rise and give thee.

8. I say unto you, Though he will not rise and give him, because he is his friend, yet because of his importunity he will rise and give him as many as he needeth.

9. And I say unto you, Ask, and it shall be given you; seek, and ye shall find; knock, and it shall be opened unto you.

10. For every one that asketh receiveth; and he that seeketh findeth; and to him that knocketh it shall be opened.

11. If a son shall ask bread of any of you that is a father, will he give him a stone? or if he ask a fish, will he for a fish give him a serpent?

12. Or if he shall ask an egg, will he offer him a scorpion?

13. If ye then, being evil, know how to give good gifts unto your children: how much more shall your heavenly Father give the Holy Spirit to them that ask him?

14. And he was casting out a devil, and it was dumb. And it came to pass, when the devil was gone out, the dumb spake; and the people wondered.

15. But some of them said, He casteth out devils through Beelzebub the chief of the devils.

16. And others, tempting him, sought of him a sign from heaven.

17. But he, knowing their thoughts, said unto them, Every kingdom divided against itself is brought to desolation; and a house divided against a house falleth.

18. If Satan also be divided against himself, how shall his kingdom stand? because ye say that I cast out devils through Beelzebub.

19. And if I by Beelzebub cast out devils, by whom do your sons cast them out? therefore shall they be your judges.

20. But if I with the finger of God cast out devils, no doubt the kingdom of God is come upon you.

21. When a strong man armed keepeth his palace, his goods are in peace:

22. But when a stronger than he shall come upon him, and overcome him, he taketh from him all his armour wherein he trusted, and divideth his spoils.

23. He that is not with me is against me: and he that gathereth not with me scattereth.

24. When the unclean spirit is gone out of a man, he walketh through dry places, seeking rest; and finding none, he saith, I will return unto my house whence I came out.

25. And when he cometh, he findeth it swept and garnished.

26. Then goeth he, and taketh to him seven other spirits more wicked than himself; and they enter in, and dwell there: and the last state of that man is worse than the first.

27. And it came to pass, as he spake these things, a certain woman of the company lifted up her voice, and said unto him, Blessed is the womb that bare thee, and the paps which thou hast sucked.

28. But he said, Yea rather, blessed are they that hear the word of God, and keep it.

29. And when the people were gathered thick together, he began to say, This is an evil generation: they seek a sign; and there shall no sign be given it, but the sign of Jonas the prophet.

30. For as Jonas was a sign unto the Ninevites, so shall also the Son of man be to this generation.

31. The queen of the south shall rise up in the judgment with the men of this generation, and condemn them: for she came from the utmost parts of the earth to hear the wisdom of Solomon; and, behold, a greater than Solomon is here.

32. The men of Nineve shall rise up in the judgment with this generation, and shall condemn it: for they repented at the preaching of Jonas; and, behold, a greater than Jonas is here.

33. No man, when he hath lighted a candle, putteth it in a secret place, neither under a bushel, but on a candlestick, that they which come in may see the light.

34. The light of the body is the eye: therefore when thine eye is single, thy whole body also is full of light; but when thine eye is evil, thy body also is full of darkness.

35. Take heed therefore that the light which is in thee be not darkness.

36. If thy whole body therefore be full of light, having no part dark, the whole shall be full of light, as when the bright shining of a candle doth give thee light.

37. And as he spake, a certain Pharisee besought him to dine with him: and he went in, and sat down to meat.

38. And when the Pharisee saw it, he marvelled that he had not first washed before dinner.

39. And the Lord said unto him, Now do ye Pharisees make clean the outside of the cup and the platter; but your inward part is full of ravening and wickedness.

40. Ye fools, did not he that made that which is without make that which is within also?

41. But rather give alms of such things as ye have; and, behold, all things are clean unto you.

42. But woe unto you, Pharisees! for ye tithe mint and rue and all manner of herbs, and pass over judgment and the love of God: these ought ye to have done, and not to leave the other undone.

43. Woe unto you, Pharisees! for ye love the uppermost seats in the synagogues, and greetings in the markets.

44. Woe unto you, scribes and Pharisees, hypocrites! for ye are as graves which appear not, and the men that walk over them are not aware of them.

45. Then answered one of the lawyers, and said unto him, Master, thus saying thou reproachest us also.

46. And he said, Woe unto you also, ye lawyers! for ye lade men with burdens grievous to be borne, and ye yourselves touch not the burdens with one of your fingers.

47. Woe unto you! for ye build the sepulchres of the prophets, and your fathers killed them.

48. Truly ye bear witness that ye allow the deeds of your fathers: for they indeed killed them, and ye build their sepulchres.

49. Therefore also said the wisdom of God, I will send them prophets and apostles, and some of them they shall slay and persecute:

50. That the blood of all the prophets, which was shed from the foundation of the world, may be required of this generation;

51. From the blood of Abel unto the blood of Zacharias which perished between the altar and the temple: verily I say unto you, It shall be required of this generation.

52. Woe unto you, lawyers! for ye have taken away the key of knowledge: ye entered not in yourselves, and them that were entering in ye hindered.

53. And as he said these things unto them, the scribes and the Pharisees began to urge him vehemently, and to provoke him to speak of many things:

54. Laying wait for him, and seeking to catch something out of his mouth, that they might accuse him.

CHAPTER 12

1. In the mean time, when there were gathered together an innumerable multitude of people, insomuch that they trode one upon another, he began to say unto his disciples first of all, Beware ye of the leaven of the Pharisees, which is hypocrisy.

2. For there is nothing covered, that shall not be revealed; neither hid, that shall not be known.

3. Therefore whatsoever ye have spoken in darkness shall be heard in the light; and that which ye have spoken in the ear in closets shall be proclaimed upon the housetops.

4. And I say unto you my friends, Be not afraid of them that kill the body, and after that have no more that they can do.

5. But I will forewarn you whom ye shall fear: Fear him, which after he hath killed hath power to cast into hell; yea, I say unto you, Fear him.

6. Are not five sparrows sold for two farthings, and not one of them is forgotten before God?

7. But even the very hairs of your head are all numbered. Fear not therefore: ye are of more value than many sparrows.

8. Also I say unto you, Whosoever shall confess me before men, him shall the Son of man also confess before the angels of God:

9. But he that denieth me before men shall be denied before the angels of God.

10. And whosoever shall speak a word against the Son of man, it shall be forgiven him: but unto him that blasphemeth against the Holy Ghost it shall not be forgiven.

11. And when they bring you unto the synagogues, and unto magistrates, and powers, take ye no thought how or what thing ye shall answer, or what ye shall say:

12. For the Holy Ghost shall teach you in the same hour what ye ought to say.

13. And one of the company said unto him, Master, speak to my brother, that he divide the inheritance with me.

14. And he said unto him, Man, who made me a judge or a divider over you?

15. And he said unto them, Take heed, and beware of covetousness: for a man's life consisteth not in the abundance of the things which he possesseth.

16. And he spake a parable unto them, saying, The ground of a certain rich man brought forth plentifully:

17. And he thought within himself, saying, What shall I do, because I have no room where to bestow my fruits?

18. And he said, This will I do: I will pull down my barns, and build greater; and there will I bestow all my fruits and my goods.

19. And I will say to my soul, Soul, thou hast much goods laid up for many years; take thine ease, eat, drink, and be merry.

20. But God said unto him, Thou fool, this night thy soul shall be required of thee: then whose shall those things be, which thou hast provided?

21. So is he that layeth up treasure for himself, and is not rich toward God.

22. And he said unto his disciples, Therefore I say unto you, Take no thought for your life, what ye shall eat; neither for the body, what ye shall put on.

23. The life is more than meat, and the body is more than raiment.

24. Consider the ravens: for they neither sow nor reap; which neither have storehouse nor barn; and God feedeth them: how much more are ye better than the fowls?

25. And which of you with taking thought can add to his stature one cubit?

26. If ye then be not able to do that thing which is least, why take ye thought for the rest?

27. Consider the lilies how they grow: they toil not, they spin not; and yet I say unto you, that Solomon in all his glory was not arrayed like one of these.

28. If then God so clothe the grass, which is to day in the field, and to morrow is cast into the oven; how much more will he clothe you, O ye of little faith?

29. And seek not ye what ye shall eat, or what ye shall drink, neither be ye of doubtful mind.

30. For all these things do the nations of the world seek after: and your Father knoweth that ye have need of these things.

31. But rather seek ye the kingdom of God; and all these things shall be added unto you.

32. Fear not, little flock; for it is your Father's good pleasure to give you the kingdom.

33. Sell that ye have, and give alms; provide yourselves bags which wax not old, a treasure in the heavens that faileth not, where no thief approacheth, neither moth corrupteth.

34. For where your treasure is, there will your heart be also.

35. Let your loins be girded about, and your lights burning;

36. And ye yourselves like unto men that wait for their lord, when he will return from the wedding; that when he cometh and knocketh, they may open unto him immediately.

37. Blessed are those servants, whom the lord when he cometh shall find watching: verily I say unto you, that he shall gird himself, and make them to sit down to meat, and will come forth and serve them.

38. And if he shall come in the second watch, or come in the third watch, and find them so, blessed are those servants.

39. And this know, that if the goodman of the house had known what hour the thief would come, he would have watched, and not have suffered his house to be broken through.

40. Be ye therefore ready also: for the Son of man cometh at an hour when ye think not.

41. Then Peter said unto him, Lord, speakest thou this parable unto us, or even to all?

42. And the Lord said, Who then is that faithful and wise steward, whom his lord shall make ruler over his household, to give them their portion of meat in due season?

43. Blessed is that servant, whom his lord when he cometh shall find so doing.

44. Of a truth I say unto you, that he will make him ruler over all that he hath.

45. But and if that servant say in his heart, My lord delayeth his coming; and shall begin to beat the menservants and maidens, and to eat and drink, and to be drunken;

46. The lord of that servant will come in a day when he looketh not for him, and at an hour when he is not aware, and will cut him in sunder, and will appoint him his portion with the unbelievers.

47. And that servant, which knew his lord's will, and prepared not himself, neither did according to his will, shall be beaten with many stripes.

48. But he that knew not, and did commit things worthy of stripes, shall be beaten with few stripes. For unto whomsoever much is given, of him shall be much required: and to whom men have committed much, of him they will ask the more.

49. I am come to send fire on the earth; and what will I, if it be already kindled?

50. But I have a baptism to be baptized with; and how am I straitened till it be accomplished!

51. Suppose ye that I am come to give peace on earth? I tell you, Nay; but rather division:

52. For from henceforth there shall be five in one house divided, three against two, and two against three.

53. The father shall be divided against the son, and the son against the father; the mother against the daughter, and the daughter against the mother; the mother in law against her daughter in law, and the daughter in law against her mother in law.

54. And he said also to the people, When ye see a cloud rise out of the west, straightway ye say, There cometh a shower; and so it is.

55. And when ye see the south wind blow, ye say, There will be heat; and it cometh to pass.

56. Ye hypocrites, ye can discern the face of the sky and of the earth; but how is it that ye do not discern this time?

57. Yea, and why even of yourselves judge ye not what is right?

58. When thou goest with thine adversary to the magistrate, as thou art in the way, give diligence that thou mayest be delivered from him; lest he hale thee to the judge, and the judge deliver thee to the officer, and the officer cast thee into prison.

59. I tell thee, thou shalt not depart thence, till thou hast paid the very last mite.

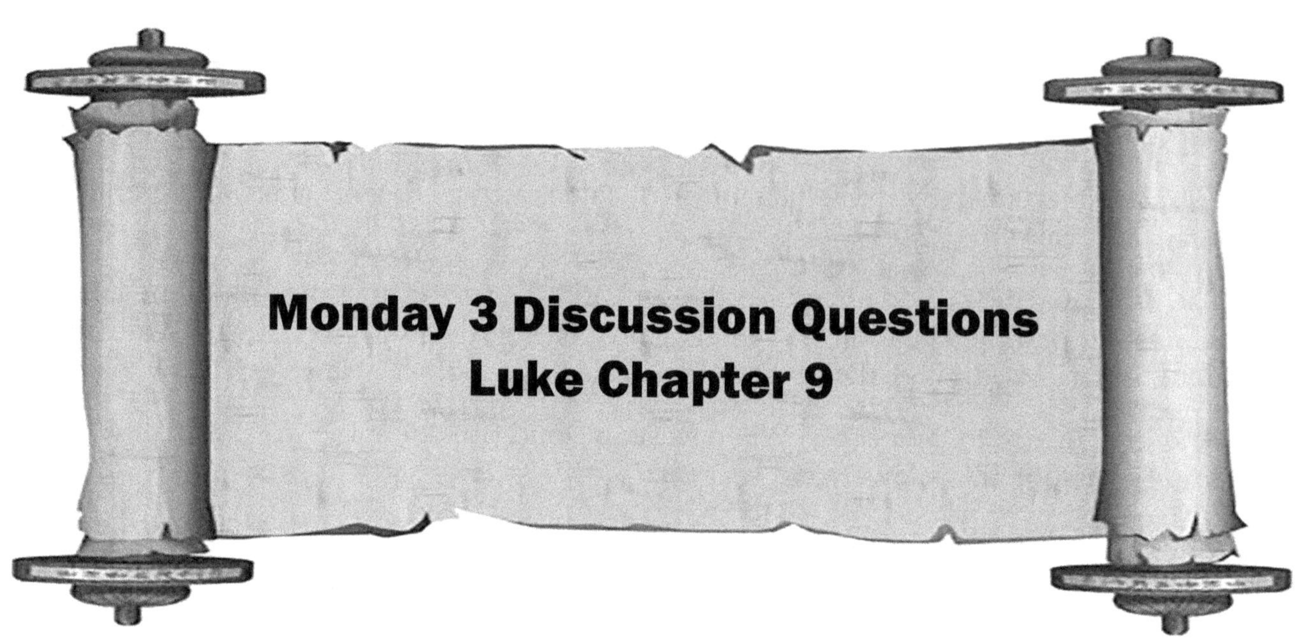

1. When Jesus called his twelve disciples together, what did he give them power and authority to do? __________

2. What did he send them to do? __________

3. What did Jesus tell them to take for their journey? __________

4. What instructions did he give them about where they should stay? __________

5. What did he tell them to do when they were not received in a city? __________

6. Why was Herod perplexed? __________

7. What did Herod desire to see him? __________

8. Where did he take the apostles after they returned and told them all they had done? __________

9. What did the apostles want Jesus to tell the multitude when it started getting late? __________

10. What did Jesus tell the disciples to do? __________

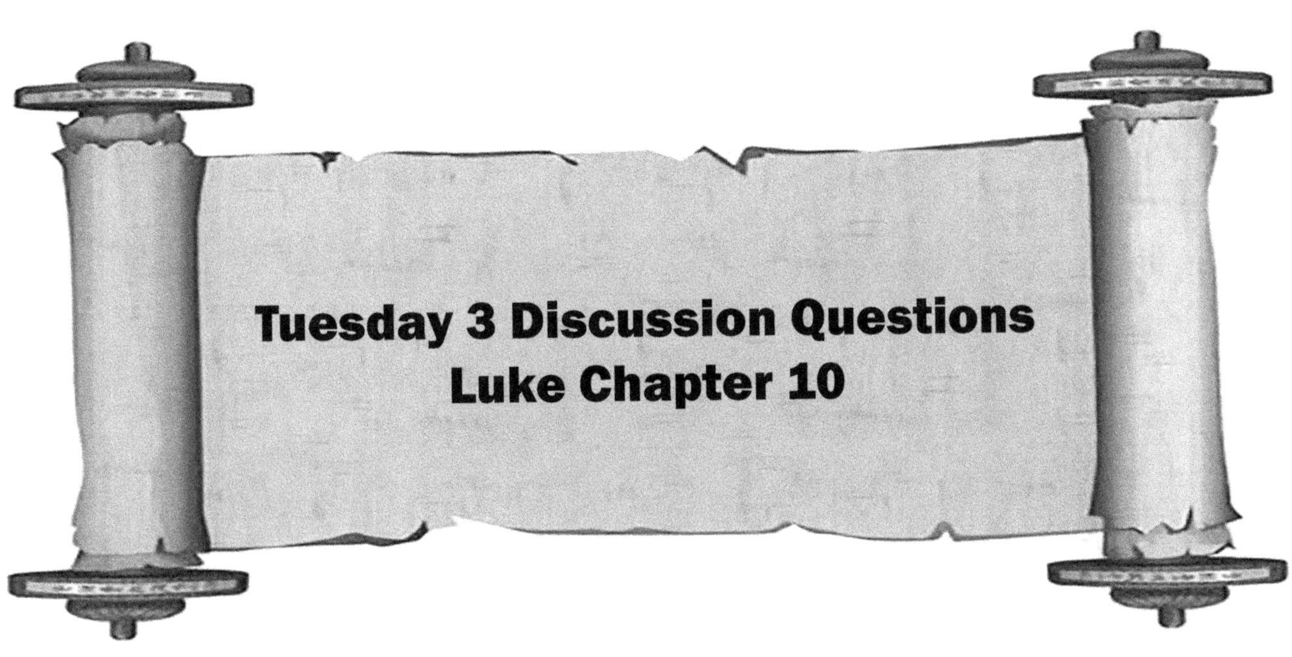

1. How many more people did the Lord appoint to go into the cities?

2. What order did he send them in?

3. What did he tell them about the harvest and laborers?

4. What were they told not to carry or do?

5. Whose house were they told to stay in? What would happen to that house?

6. What did they say to the people in the cities that did not receive them?

7. What did the seventy return to Jesus and say?

8. Who is the only one who knows who the father is? Who is the only one who knows who the son is?

9. What did the lawyer stand up and tempt the Lord saying? What was the Lord's response to him? What was the lawyer's response?

10. What did the Lord say about the lawyer's answer?

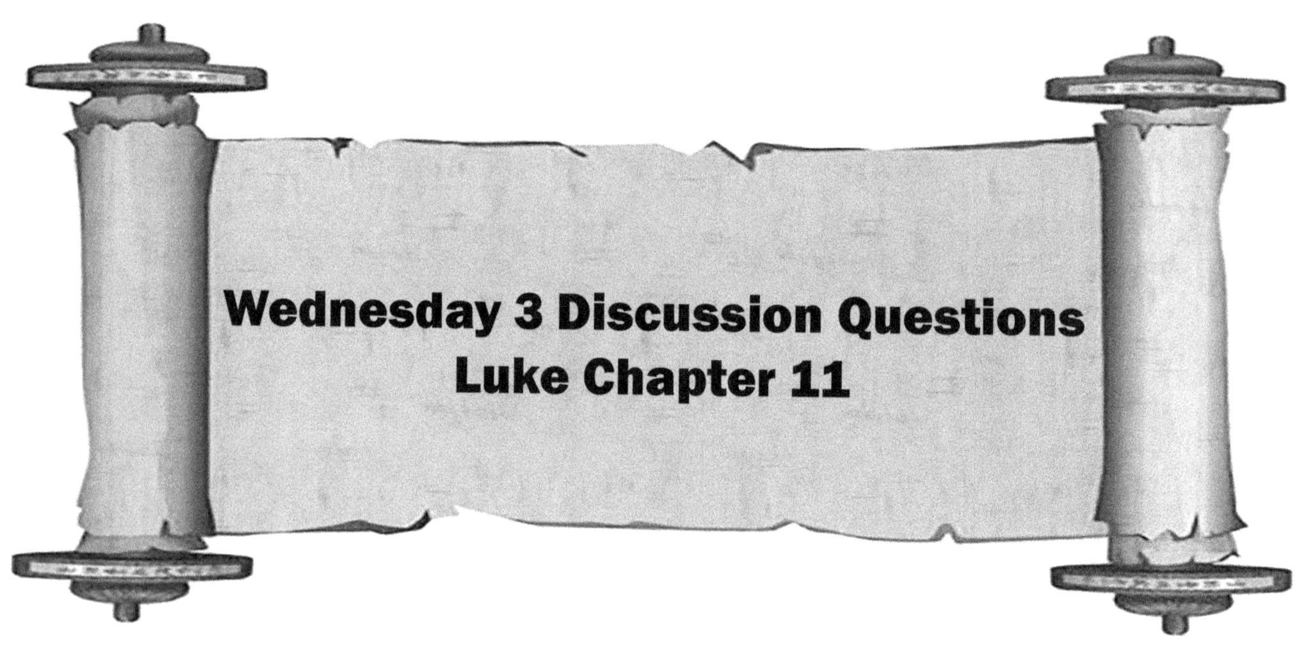

1. What did the disciple ask the Lord to teach them?
2. What did the Lord teach the disciples about asking, seeking, and knocking?
3. What happens to a kingdom divided against itself and a house divided against a house?
4. What does an unclean spirit do when he goes out from a man?
5. Why does the Lord say this is an evil generation?
6. Where should a man put a candle after he lights it? Why?
7. What did the Lord say to the Pharisee who complained about the disciples not washing their hands before eating?
8. Why did the Lord say woe unto them concerning their tithes?
9. Why did the Lord give woe unto the lawyers?
10. Why did the Pharisees keep provoking the Lord to speak of many things?

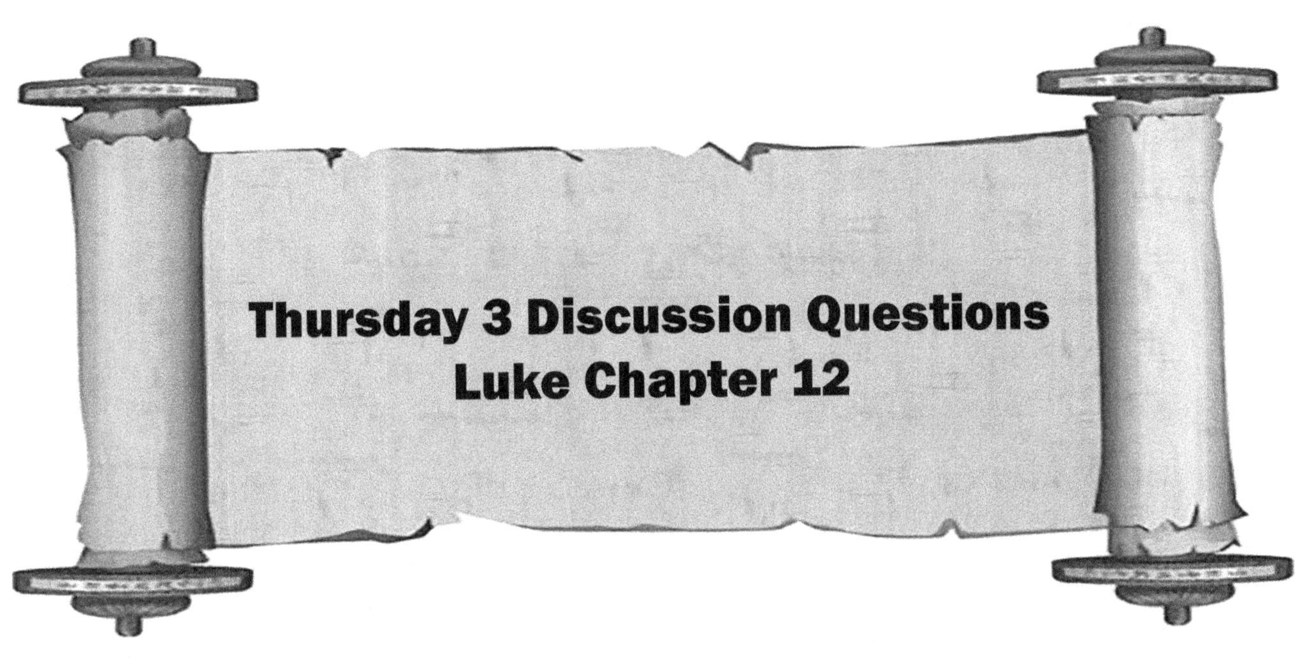

1. What did the Lord tell the disciples to beware of ? Why? ______________________

2. What did the Lord say about things that are covered and hidden? ______________

3. Why did the Lord say not to fear people who can kill your body? Who did he say we should fear? ______________________

4. What will happen to the ones who confess Jesus before men?What will happen to those who deny him. ______________________

5. What happens if someone blasphemes against the Holy Ghost? ______________

6. What did the Lord say to the brother's who were fighting over an inheritance? ______

7. Why did the Lord say to take no thought for your life, what ye shall eat; neither for the body, what ye shall put on? ______________________

8. Why did the Lord say seek not what you shall eat, or what you shall drink, neither be doubtful? ______________________

9. What should we seek? What will happen when we do? ______________________

10. What did the Lord say about a man's treasure and his heart? ______________

WEEKLY REVIEW
LUKE CHAPTERS 9-12

NAME THAT CHAPTER

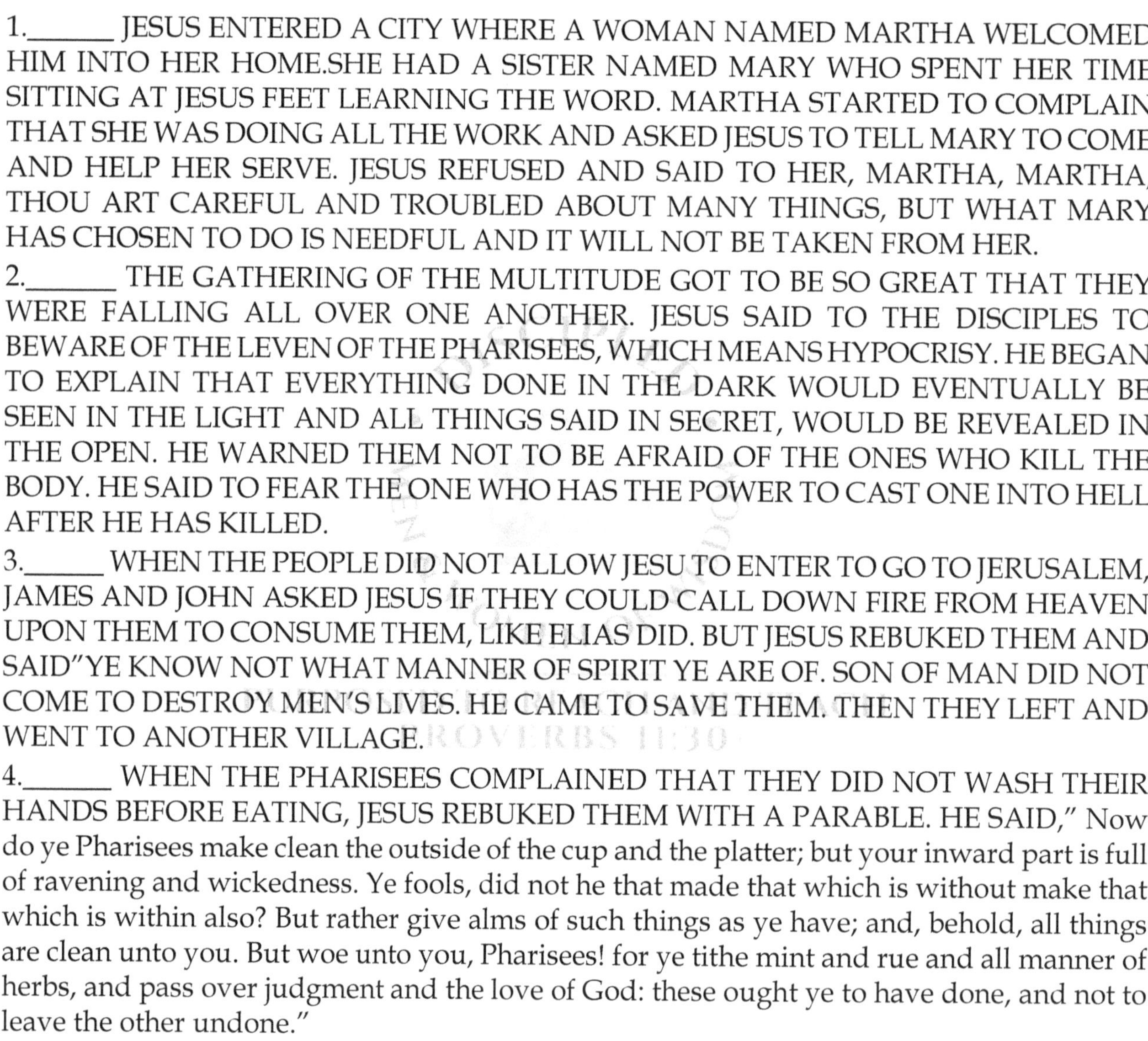

1.______ JESUS ENTERED A CITY WHERE A WOMAN NAMED MARTHA WELCOMED HIM INTO HER HOME.SHE HAD A SISTER NAMED MARY WHO SPENT HER TIME SITTING AT JESUS FEET LEARNING THE WORD. MARTHA STARTED TO COMPLAIN THAT SHE WAS DOING ALL THE WORK AND ASKED JESUS TO TELL MARY TO COME AND HELP HER SERVE. JESUS REFUSED AND SAID TO HER, MARTHA, MARTHA, THOU ART CAREFUL AND TROUBLED ABOUT MANY THINGS, BUT WHAT MARY HAS CHOSEN TO DO IS NEEDFUL AND IT WILL NOT BE TAKEN FROM HER.

2.______ THE GATHERING OF THE MULTITUDE GOT TO BE SO GREAT THAT THEY WERE FALLING ALL OVER ONE ANOTHER. JESUS SAID TO THE DISCIPLES TO BEWARE OF THE LEVEN OF THE PHARISEES, WHICH MEANS HYPOCRISY. HE BEGAN TO EXPLAIN THAT EVERYTHING DONE IN THE DARK WOULD EVENTUALLY BE SEEN IN THE LIGHT AND ALL THINGS SAID IN SECRET, WOULD BE REVEALED IN THE OPEN. HE WARNED THEM NOT TO BE AFRAID OF THE ONES WHO KILL THE BODY. HE SAID TO FEAR THE ONE WHO HAS THE POWER TO CAST ONE INTO HELL AFTER HE HAS KILLED.

3.______ WHEN THE PEOPLE DID NOT ALLOW JESU TO ENTER TO GO TO JERUSALEM, JAMES AND JOHN ASKED JESUS IF THEY COULD CALL DOWN FIRE FROM HEAVEN UPON THEM TO CONSUME THEM, LIKE ELIAS DID. BUT JESUS REBUKED THEM AND SAID"YE KNOW NOT WHAT MANNER OF SPIRIT YE ARE OF. SON OF MAN DID NOT COME TO DESTROY MEN'S LIVES. HE CAME TO SAVE THEM. THEN THEY LEFT AND WENT TO ANOTHER VILLAGE.

4.______ WHEN THE PHARISEES COMPLAINED THAT THEY DID NOT WASH THEIR HANDS BEFORE EATING, JESUS REBUKED THEM WITH A PARABLE. HE SAID," Now do ye Pharisees make clean the outside of the cup and the platter; but your inward part is full of ravening and wickedness. Ye fools, did not he that made that which is without make that which is within also? But rather give alms of such things as ye have; and, behold, all things are clean unto you. But woe unto you, Pharisees! for ye tithe mint and rue and all manner of herbs, and pass over judgment and the love of God: these ought ye to have done, and not to leave the other undone."

TRUE OR FALSE

5. JESUS TOLD THE LAWYERS, "Woe unto you also, ye lawyers! for ye lade men with burdens grievous to be borne, and ye yourselves touch not the burdens with one of your fingers".

____

6. HEROD HAD NO DESIRE TO SEE THE MAN THEY WERE TELLING HIM ABOUT BECAUSE HE KNEW HE HAD BEHEADED JOHN

____

7. Jesus Said, "Are not two sparrows sold for five farthings, and not one of them is forgotten before God?

____

FILL IN THE BLANKS

8. Woe unto you,____________! for ye love the____________seats in the____________, and greetings in the markets.
9. And he sent them to____________the____________of God, and to____________ I the sick.
10. But he that____________me before____________shall be denied before the____________ of God.

MY PRAYER JOURNAL

Please use this space to record your thoughts and feelings as you travel on this spirit led journey through the word of God with us. Please know that you have brothers and sisters in this organization from all over the world praying with and for you. My prayer for you is that you will begin to see the power of God resting in each set of your footprints. As you look back and examine your past in this journal, may you realize that you were never alone and according to Hebrews 13:5, God will never leave nor forsake you. ~LADY FLORA

I THESSALONIANS 5:17

THE STUDY OF THE FOUR GOSPELS VOCABULARY DEFINITIONS FOR LUKE CHAPTERS 13-16

Define the following words. This assignment is worth 200 points when completed ***WITH THE CLASS*** during FB LIVE Weekly Class Discussion for participation grade.

WORD	DEFINITIONS
1) SILOAM	
2) DUNG	
3) ADVERSARIES	
4) STRAIT GATE	
5) CURES	
6) BROOD	
7) ABASE	
8) RECOMPENSE	
9) AMBASSAGE	
10)MAMMON	

DMWW DAILY BIBLE READING
LUKE CHAPTERS 13-16

CHAPTER 13

1. There were present at that season some that told him of the Galilaeans, whose blood Pilate had mingled with their sacrifices.
2. And Jesus answering said unto them, Suppose ye that these Galilaeans were sinners above all the Galilaeans, because they suffered such things?
3. I tell you, Nay: but, except ye repent, ye shall all likewise perish.
4. Or those eighteen, upon whom the tower in Siloam fell, and slew them, think ye that they were sinners above all men that dwelt in Jerusalem?
5. I tell you, Nay: but, except ye repent, ye shall all likewise perish.
6. He spake also this parable; A certain man had a fig tree planted in his vineyard; and he came and sought fruit thereon, and found none.
7. Then said he unto the dresser of his vineyard, Behold, these three years I come seeking fruit on this fig tree, and find none: cut it down; why cumbereth it the ground?
8. And he answering said unto him, Lord, let it alone this year also, till I shall dig about it, and dung it:
9. And if it bear fruit, well: and if not, then after that thou shalt cut it down. 10 And he was teaching in one of the synagogues on the sabbath.
10. And, behold, there was a woman which had a spirit of infirmity eighteen years, and was bowed together, and could in no wise lift up herself.
11. And when Jesus saw her, he called her to him, and said unto her, Woman, thou art loosed from thine infirmity.
12. And he laid his hands on her: and immediately she was made straight, and glorified God.
13. And the ruler of the synagogue answered with indignation, because that Jesus had healed on the sabbath day, and said unto the people, There are six days in which men ought to work: in them therefore come and be healed, and not on the sabbath day.
14. The Lord then answered him, and said, Thou hypocrite, doth not each one of you on the sabbath loose his ox or his ass from the stall, and lead him away to watering?
15. And ought not this woman, being a daughter of Abraham, whom Satan hath bound, lo, these eighteen years, be loosed from this bond on the sabbath day?

16. And when he had said these things, all his adversaries were ashamed: and all the people rejoiced for all the glorious things that were done by him.

17. Then said he, Unto what is the kingdom of God like? and whereunto shall I resemble it?

18. It is like a grain of mustard seed, which a man took, and cast into his garden; and it grew, and waxed a great tree; and the fowls of the air lodged in the branches of it.

19. And again he said, Whereunto shall I liken the kingdom of God?

20. It is like leaven, which a woman took and hid in three measures of meal, till the whole was leavened.

21. And he went through the cities and villages, teaching, and journeying toward Jerusalem.

22. Then said one unto him, Lord, are there few that be saved? And he said unto them, 24
Strive to enter in at the strait gate: for many, I say unto you, will seek to enter in, and shall not be able.

23. When once the master of the house is risen up, and hath shut to the door, and ye begin to stand without, and to knock at the door, saying, Lord, Lord, open unto us; and he shall answer and say unto you, I know you not whence ye are:

24. Then shall ye begin to say, We have eaten and drunk in thy presence, and thou hast taught in our streets.

25. But he shall say, I tell you, I know you not whence ye are; depart from me, all ye workers of iniquity.

26. There shall be weeping and gnashing of teeth, when ye shall see Abraham, and Isaac, and Jacob, and all the prophets, in the kingdom of God, and you yourselves thrust out.

27. And they shall come from the east, and from the west, and from the north, and from the south, and shall sit down in the kingdom of God.

28. And, behold, there are last which shall be first, and there are first which shall be last. 31
The same day there came certain of the Pharisees, saying unto him, Get thee out, and depart hence: for Herod will kill thee.

29. And he said unto them, Go ye, and tell that fox, Behold, I cast out devils, and I do cures to day and to morrow, and the third day I shall be perfected.

30. Nevertheless I must walk to day, and to morrow, and the day following: for it cannot be that a prophet perish out of Jerusalem.

31. O Jerusalem, Jerusalem, which killest the prophets, and stonest them that are sent unto thee; how often would I have gathered thy children together, as a hen doth gather her brood under her wings, and ye would not!

32. Behold, your house is left unto you desolate: and verily I say unto you, Ye shall not see me, until the time come when ye shall say, Blessed is he that cometh in the name of the Lord.

CHAPTER 14

1. And it came to pass, as he went into the house of one of the chief Pharisees to eat bread on the sabbath day, that they watched him.

2. And, behold, there was a certain man before him which had the dropsy.

3. And Jesus answering spake unto the lawyers and Pharisees, saying, Is it lawful to heal on the sabbath day?

4. And they held their peace. And he took him, and healed him, and let him go;

5. And answered them, saying, Which of you shall have an ass or an ox fallen into a pit, and will not straightway pull him out on the sabbath day?

6. And they could not answer him again to these things.

7. And he put forth a parable to those which were bidden, when he marked how they chose out the chief rooms; saying unto them.

8. When thou art bidden of any man to a wedding, sit not down in the highest room; lest a more honourable man than thou be bidden of him;

9. And he that bade thee and him come and say to thee, Give this man place; and thou begin with shame to take the lowest room.

10. But when thou art bidden, go and sit down in the lowest room; that when he that bade thee cometh, he may say unto thee, Friend, go up higher: then shalt thou have worship in the presence of them that sit at meat with thee.

11. For whosoever exalteth himself shall be abased; and he that humbleth himself shall be exalted.

12. Then said he also to him that bade him, When thou makest a dinner or a supper, call not thy friends, nor thy brethren, neither thy kinsmen, nor thy rich neighbours; lest they also bid thee again, and a recompence be made thee.

13. But when thou makest a feast, call the poor, the maimed, the lame, the blind:

14. And thou shalt be blessed; for they cannot recompense thee: for thou shalt be recompensed at the resurrection of the just.

15. And when one of them that sat at meat with him heard these things, he said unto him, Blessed is he that shall eat bread in the kingdom of God.

16. Then said he unto him, A certain man made a great supper, and bade many:

17. And sent his servant at supper time to say to them that were bidden, Come; for all things are now ready.

18. And they all with one consent began to make excuse. The first said unto him, I have bought a piece of ground, and I must needs go and see it: I pray thee have me excused.

19. And another said, I have bought five yoke of oxen, and I go to prove them: I pray thee have me excused.

20. And another said, I have married a wife, and therefore I cannot come.

21. So that servant came, and shewed his lord these things. Then the master of the house being angry said to his servant, Go out quickly into the streets and lanes of the city, and bring in hither the poor, and the maimed, and the halt, and the blind.

22. And the servant said, Lord, it is done as thou hast commanded, and yet there is room.

23. And the lord said unto the servant, Go out into the highways and hedges, and compel them to come in, that my house may be filled.

24. For I say unto you, That none of those men which were bidden shall taste of my supper.

25. And there went great multitudes with him: and he turned, and said unto them,

26. If any man come to me, and hate not his father, and mother, and wife, and children, and brethren, and sisters, yea, and his own life also, he cannot be my disciple.

27. And whosoever doth not bear his cross, and come after me, cannot be my disciple.

28. For which of you, intending to build a tower, sitteth not down first, and counteth the cost, whether he have sufficient to finish it?

29. Lest haply, after he hath laid the foundation, and is not able to finish it, all that behold it begin to mock him,

30. Saying, This man began to build, and was not able to finish.

31. Or what king, going to make war against another king, sitteth not down first, and consulteth whether he be able with ten thousand to meet him that cometh against him with twenty thousand?

32. Or else, while the other is yet a great way off, he sendeth an ambassage, and desireth conditions of peace.

33. So likewise, whosoever he be of you that forsaketh not all that he hath, he cannot be my disciple.

34. Salt is good: but if the salt have lost his savour, wherewith shall it be seasoned?

35. It is neither fit for the land, nor yet for the dunghill; but men cast it out. He that hath ears to hear, let him hear.

CHAPTER 15

1. Then drew near unto him all the publicans and sinners for to hear him.

2. And the Pharisees and scribes murmured, saying, This man receiveth sinners, and eateth with them.

3. And he spake this parable unto them, saying,

4. What man of you, having an hundred sheep, if he lose one of them, doth not leave the ninety and nine in the wilderness, and go after that which is lost, until he find it?

5. And when he hath found it, he layeth it on his shoulders, rejoicing.

6. And when he cometh home, he calleth together his friends and neighbours, saying unto them, Rejoice with me; for I have found my sheep which was lost.

7. I say unto you, that likewise joy shall be in heaven over one sinner that repenteth, more than over ninety and nine just persons, which need no repentance.

8. Either what woman having ten pieces of silver, if she lose one piece, doth not light a candle, and sweep the house, and seek diligently till she find it?

9. And when she hath found it, she calleth her friends and her neighbours together, saying, Rejoice with me; for I have found the piece which I had lost.

10. Likewise, I say unto you, there is joy in the presence of the angels of God over one sinner that repenteth.

11. And he said, A certain man had two sons:

12. And the younger of them said to his father, Father, give me the portion of goods that falleth to me. And he divided unto them his living.

13. And not many days after the younger son gathered all together, and took his journey into a far country, and there wasted his substance with riotous living.

14. And when he had spent all, there arose a mighty famine in that land; and he began to be in want.

15. And he went and joined himself to a citizen of that country; and he sent him into his fields to feed swine.

16. And he would fain have filled his belly with the husks that the swine did eat: and no man gave unto him.

17. And when he came to himself, he said, How many hired servants of my father's have bread enough and to spare, and I perish with hunger!

18. I will arise and go to my father, and will say unto him, Father, I have sinned against heaven, and before thee,

19. And am no more worthy to be called thy son: make me as one of thy hired servants.

20. And he arose, and came to his father. But when he was yet a great way off, his father saw him, and had compassion, and ran, and fell on his neck, and kissed him.

21. And the son said unto him, Father, I have sinned against heaven, and in thy sight, and am no more worthy to be called thy son.

22. But the father said to his servants, Bring forth the best robe, and put it on him; and put a ring on his hand, and shoes on his feet:

23. And bring hither the fatted calf, and kill it; and let us eat, and be merry:

24. For this my son was dead, and is alive again; he was lost, and is found. And they began to be merry.

25. Now his elder son was in the field: and as he came and drew nigh to the house, he heard musick and dancing.

26. And he called one of the servants, and asked what these things meant.

27. And he said unto him, Thy brother is come; and thy father hath killed the fatted calf, because he hath received him safe and sound.

28. And he was angry, and would not go in: therefore came his father out, and intreated him.

29. And he answering said to his father, Lo, these many years do I serve thee, neither transgressed I at any time thy commandment: and yet thou never gavest me a kid, that I might make merry with my friends:

30. But as soon as this thy son was come, which hath devoured thy living with harlots, thou hast killed for him the fatted calf.

31. And he said unto him, Son, thou art ever with me, and all that I have is thine.

32. It was meet that we should make merry, and be glad: for this thy brother was dead, and is alive again; and was lost, and is found.

CHAPTER 16

1. And he said also unto his disciples, There was a certain rich man, which had a steward; and the same was accused unto him that he had wasted his goods.

2. And he called him, and said unto him, How is it that I hear this of thee? give an account of thy stewardship; for thou mayest be no longer steward.

3. Then the steward said within himself, What shall I do? for my lord taketh away from me the stewardship: I cannot dig; to beg I am ashamed.

4. I am resolved what to do, that, when I am put out of the stewardship, they may receive me into their houses.

5. So he called every one of his lord's debtors unto him, and said unto the first, How much owest thou unto my lord?

6. And he said, An hundred measures of oil. And he said unto him, Take thy bill, and sit down quickly, and write fifty.

7. Then said he to another, And how much owest thou? And he said, An hundred measures of wheat. And he said unto him, Take thy bill, and write fourscore.

8. And the lord commended the unjust steward, because he had done wisely: for the children of this world are in their generation wiser than the children of light.

9. And I say unto you, Make to yourselves friends of the mammon of unrighteousness; that, when ye fail, they may receive you into everlasting habitations.

10. He that is faithful in that which is least is faithful also in much: and he that is unjust in the least is unjust also in much.

11. If therefore ye have not been faithful in the unrighteous mammon, who will commit to your trust the true riches?

12. And if ye have not been faithful in that which is another man's, who shall give you that which is your own?

13. No servant can serve two masters: for either he will hate the one, and love the other; or else he will hold to the one, and despise the other. Ye cannot serve God and mammon.

14. And the Pharisees also, who were covetous, heard all these things: and they derided him.

15. And he said unto them, Ye are they which justify yourselves before men; but God knoweth your hearts: for that which is highly esteemed among men is abomination in the sight of God.

16. The law and the prophets were until John: since that time the kingdom of God is preached, and every man presseth into it.

17. And it is easier for heaven and earth to pass, than one tittle of the law to fail.

18. Whosoever putteth away his wife, and marrieth another, committeth adultery: and whosoever marrieth her that is put away from her husband committeth adultery.

19. There was a certain rich man, which was clothed in purple and fine linen, and fared sumptuously every day:

20. And there was a certain beggar named Lazarus, which was laid at his gate, full of sores,

21. And desiring to be fed with the crumbs which fell from the rich man's table: moreover the dogs came and licked his sores.

22. And it came to pass, that the beggar died, and was carried by the angels into Abraham's bosom: the rich man also died, and was buried;

23. And in hell he lift up his eyes, being in torments, and seeth Abraham afar off, and Lazarus in his bosom.

24. And he cried and said, Father Abraham, have mercy on me, and send Lazarus, that he may dip the tip of his finger in water, and cool my tongue; for I am tormented in this flame.

25. But Abraham said, Son, remember that thou in thy lifetime receivedst thy good things, and likewise Lazarus evil things: but now he is comforted, and thou art tormented.

26. And beside all this, between us and you there is a great gulf fixed: so that they which would pass from hence to you cannot; neither can they pass to us, that would come from thence.

27. Then he said, I pray thee therefore, father, that thou wouldest send him to my father's house:

28. For I have five brethren; that he may testify unto them, lest they also come into this place of torment.

29. Abraham saith unto him, They have Moses and the prophets; let them hear them.

30. And he said, Nay, father Abraham: but if one went unto them from the dead, they will repent.

31. And he said unto him, If they hear not Moses and the prophets, neither will they be persuaded, though one rose from the dead.

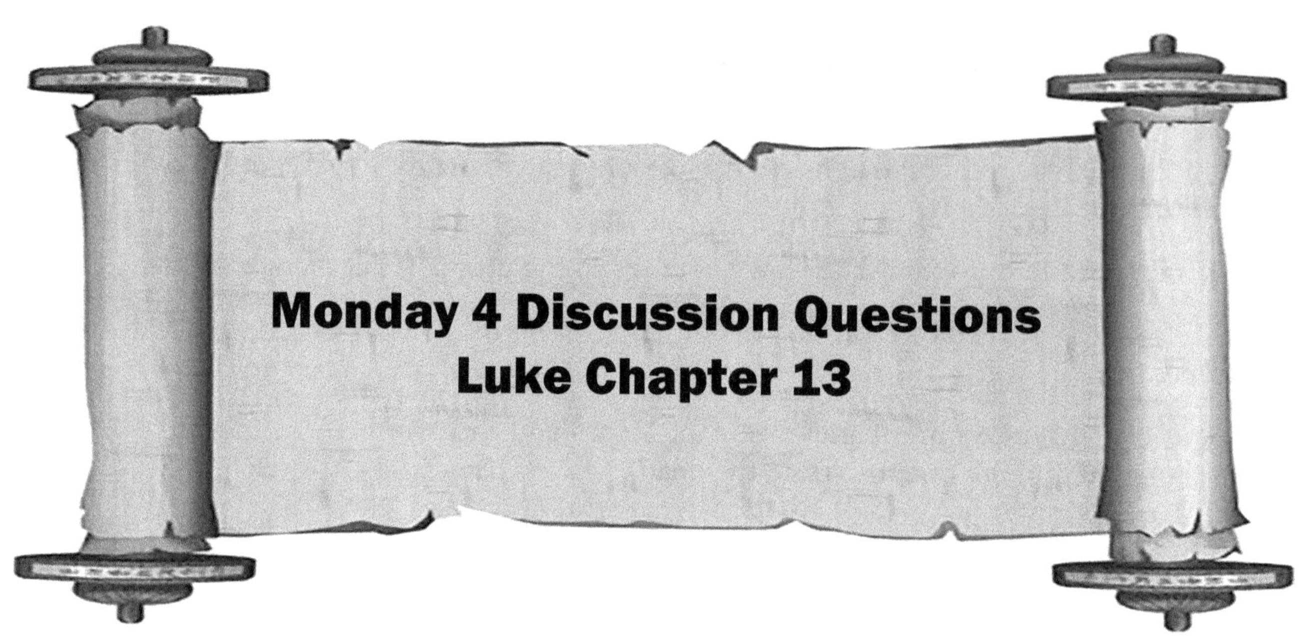

1. What did the people tell Jesus Pilate did? ______________________________

2. What did the Lord tell them? ______________________________

3. What did the Lord say to the woman who was bowed down with an infirmity of 18 years? ______________________________

4. What happened after the Lord laid his hands on her? ______________________________

5. What did the ruler of the synagogue say about it? ______________________________

6. Why did the Lord say to them, Thou hypocrite? ______________________________

7. How did all of his adversaries feel after the Lord said these things? ______________________________

8. Unto what did he resemble the kingdom of God? ______________________________

9. What did he liken the kingdom of heaven to? ______________________________

10. Why did he say, "strive to enter in at the strait gate"? ______________________________

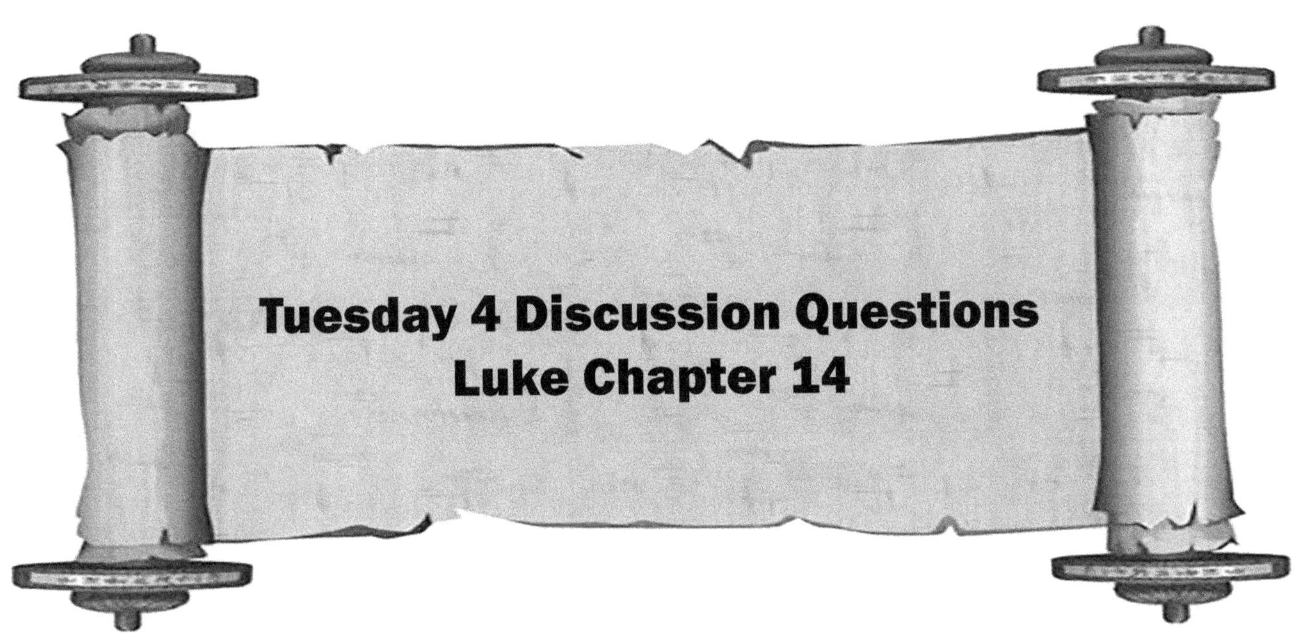

1. What did the Pharisees do when Jesus went into one of the chief Pharisees to eat bread on the Sabbath? ____
2. What disease did the man who came before Jesus have? ______________
3. What did Jesus ask the lawyers and the Pharisees? ______________
4. What was their response? What did Jesus do? ______________
5. Why did he say it's not good to sit in the highest room, when asked to a wedding? Why?
6. Where did he advise that they go? Why? ______________
7. Who did he say to call when you make a feast? Why? ______________
8. What happened when the man invited the people to come to the feast? ______________
9. What did he say a man has to hate to be the Lord's disciple? ______________
10. What did he ask the men that intended to build a tower? ______________
11. What did he ask the kings going to make war against another king? ______________

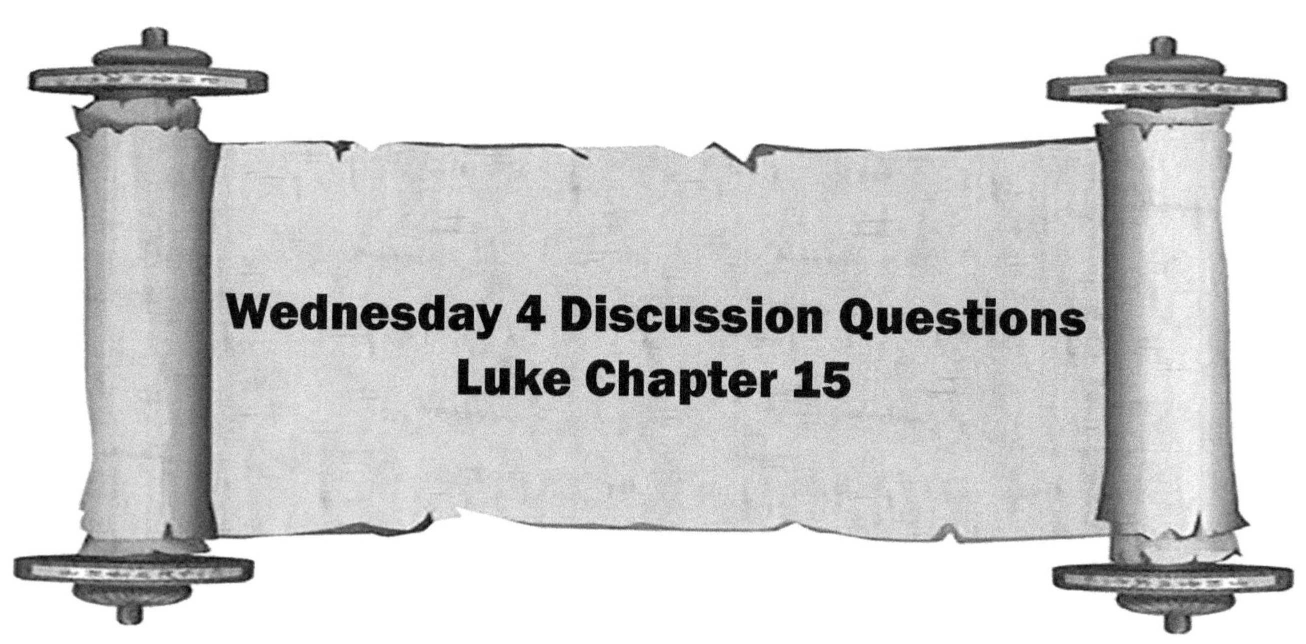

1. Why were the sinners and publicans drawing near to Jesus? What were the scribes and pharisees murmuring about? ______

2. What question did Jesus ask them in the parable? ______

3. What did he compare the joy in heaven over a lost sinner to? ______

4. What is the other parable used in this chapter? ______

5. What did the younger son do with the inheritance his father had given him? ______

6. What job did the citizen of the country give him? ______

7. What did he eat for his meals? ______

8. What did the son say and do, when he came to himself? ______

9. What did the father say and do after the son repented to him? ______

10. What did the elder son say to the father? How did his father respond to him? ______

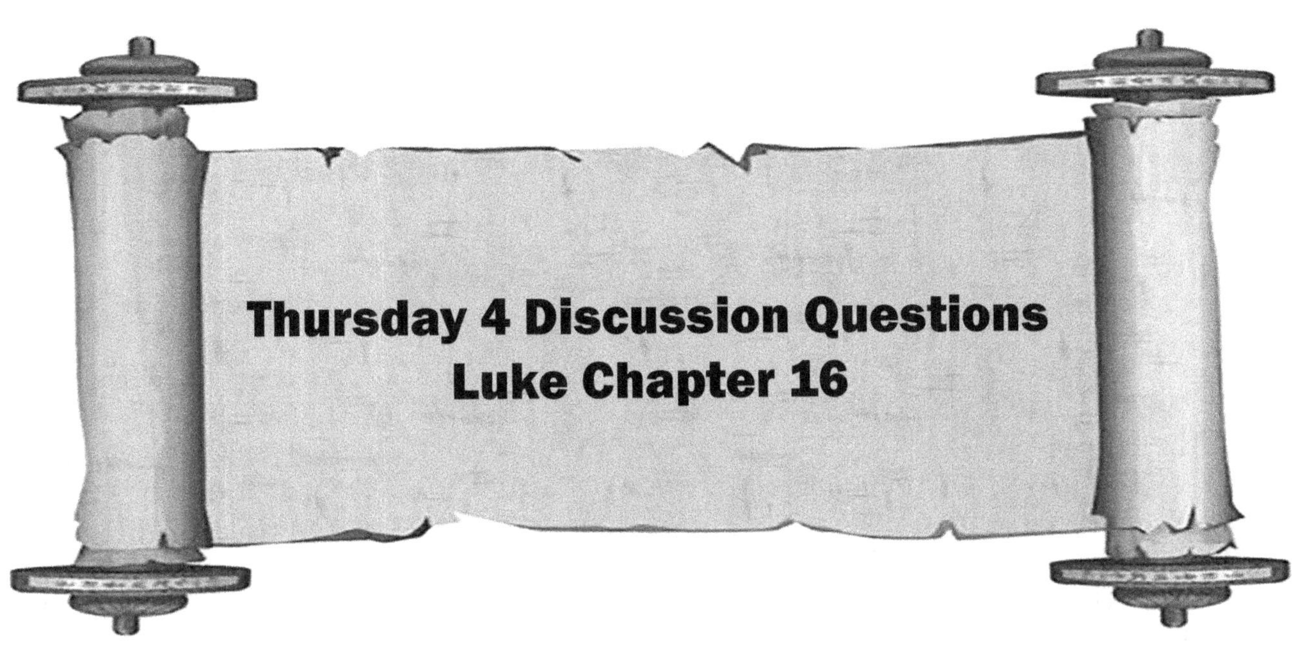

1. What did Jesus say to the rich man that was accused of wasting his goods? ________

2. What did the steward say to himself? ________

3. What did the steward resolve to do? ________

4. How did the Lord feel about what the unjust steward had done? ________

5. What did the Lord say about the faithful, the unfaithful, the just and the unjust? ________

6. What did he say about a servant and serving his master? ________

7. He was angry about the people justifying themselves before men. How does he feel about men who are highly esteemed before men? ________

8. What was the name of the beggar that laid at the rich man's gate? ________

9. What happened to the beggar when he died? What happened to the rich man when he died? ________

10. What was the rich man's cry to Abraham? What was Abraham's response? ________

WEEKLY REVIEW
LUKE CHAPTERS 13-16

NAME THAT CHAPTER

1.______ IN THIS CHAPTER JESUS TEACHES AGAINST JEALOUSY AND TEACHES US TO LOVE ONE ANOTHER AND REJOICE WITH THOSE WHO REJOICE BY GIVING A PARABLE OF A RICH MAN AND HIS TWO SONS.THE YOUNG ONE WHO SQUANDERED HIS INHERITANCE ON WILD WOMEN AND RIOTOUS LIVING, FOUND HIMSELF HUNGRY ENOUGH TO EAT SLOP WITH PIGS. HE WENT HOME AND REPENTED AND HIS FATHER WELCOMED HIM HOME WITH A CELEBRATION, THE FATTED CALF, A RING, ETC. THE OLDER SON WAS JEALOUS AND ANGRILY QUESTIONED HIS FATHER.

2.______ THERE WAS A WOMAN WHO HAD BEEN BOWED OVER WITH INFIRMITY FOR 18 YEARS. JESUS SAW HER AND CALLED HER OVER TO HIM. HE LAID HANDS ON HER AND SAID wOMAN THOU ART LOOSED FROM THOU INFIRMITY AND IMMEDIATELY SHE WAS HEALED. SHE GLORIFIED GOD

3.______ THERE WAS A RICH MAN WHO HAD A STEWARD WHO WAS ACCUSED OF WASTING HIS GOODS. THE RICH MAN CALLED FOR HIM AND TOLD HIM TO GIVE ACCOUNT AND THAT HE MAY NO LONGER BE A STEWARD. THE STEWARD CALLED PEOPLE WHO OWED THEM MONEY. HE FORGAVE A PORTION OF THEIR DEBT, SO THEY OWED LESS. HIS LORD WAS PLEASED WITH WHAT HE HAD DONE.

4.______ WHEN JESUS WENT INTO THE HOUSE OF ONE OF THE CHIEF PHARISEES, HE HEALED A MAN WITH DROPSY (AN UNUSUAL SWELLING OF THE BODY). WHEN JESUS ASKED THE LAWYERS AND PHARISEES IF IT WAS LAWFUL TO HEAL ON THE SABBATH. THEY HELD THEIR PEACE. JESUS GAVE A PARABLE SAYING, "WHICH OF YOU WILL HAVE AN ASS OR OX FALL INTO A PIT ON THE SABBATH AND NOT HELP HIM?" AGAIN, THEY COULD NOT ANSWER HIM.

TRUE OR FALSE

5. IN CHAPTER SIXTEEN WE LEARNED ABOUT A MAN WHO LAID AT A RICH MAN'S GATE TO EAT THE FOOD THAT FELL FROM THE TABLE WHILE DOGS LICKED HIS SORES.

____

LUKE 16:20,21

6. A MAN WAS ASKED TO CUT DOWN A FIG TREE THAT WAS BEARING NO FRUIT. THE MAN REPLIED, "NO LET IT ALONE THIS YEAR TILL I DIG AND DUNG IT."

____

LUKE 13:8

7. IN THE PARABLE WHEN THE MAN MADE A GREAT SUPPER AND BADE MEN TO COME, THE MULTITUDES CAME TILL THERE WAS NO ROOM.

____

LUKE 14:16-18

FILL IN THE BLANKS

8. FOR WHOSOEVER____________HIMSELF SHALL BE ____________; AND HE THAT____________HIMSELF SHALL BE EXALTED

9. AND BRING HITHER THE ____________AND KILL IT; AND LET US____________, AND BE MERRY

10 AND IT IS EASIER FOR____________AND ____________TO PASS, THAN FOR ONE ____________OF THE LAW TO FAIL

MY PRAYER JOURNAL

Please use this space to record your thoughts and feelings as you travel on this spirit led journey through the word of God with us. Please know that you have brothers and sisters in this organization from all over the world praying with and for you. My prayer for you is that you will begin to see the power of God resting in each set of your footprints. As you look back and examine your past in this journal, may you realize that you were never alone and according to Hebrews 13:5, God will never leave nor forsake you. ~LADY FLORA

I THESSALONIANS 5:17

THE STUDY OF THE FOUR GOSPELS VOCABULARY DEFINITIONS FOR LUKE CHAPTERS 17-20

WORD	DEFINITIONS
1) AUSTERE	
2) HUSBANDMAN	
3) REVERENCE	
4) DURST	
5) GIRD	
6) WHENCE	
7) USURY	
8) POUNDS	
9) EXTORTION	
10)MILLSTONE	

DMWW DAILY BIBLE READING
LUKE CHAPTERS 17-20

CHAPTER 17

1. Then said he unto the disciples, It is impossible but that offences will come: but woe unto him, through whom they come!
2. It were better for him that a millstone were hanged about his neck, and he cast into the sea, than that he should offend one of these little ones.
3. Take heed to yourselves: If thy brother trespass against thee, rebuke him; and if he repent, forgive him.
4. And if he trespass against thee seven times in a day, and seven times in a day turn again to thee, saying, I repent; thou shalt forgive him.
5. And the apostles said unto the Lord, Increase our faith.
6. And the Lord said, If ye had faith as a grain of mustard seed, ye might say unto this sycamine tree, Be thou plucked up by the root, and be thou planted in the sea; and it should obey you.
7. But which of you, having a servant plowing or feeding cattle, will say unto him by and by, when he is come from the field, Go and sit down to meat?
8. And will not rather say unto him, Make ready wherewith I may sup, and gird thyself, and serve me, till I have eaten and drunken; and afterward thou shalt eat and drink?
9. Doth he thank that servant because he did the things that were commanded him? I trow not.
10. So likewise ye, when ye shall have done all those things which are commanded you, say, We are unprofitable servants: we have done that which was our duty to do.
11. And it came to pass, as he went to Jerusalem, that he passed through the midst of Samaria and Galilee.
12. And as he entered into a certain village, there met him ten men that were lepers, which stood afar off:
13. And they lifted up their voices, and said, Jesus, Master, have mercy on us.
14. And when he saw them, he said unto them, Go shew yourselves unto the priests. And it came to pass, that, as they went, they were cleansed.
15. And one of them, when he saw that he was healed, turned back, and with a loud voice glorified God,
16. And fell down on his face at his feet, giving him thanks: and he was a Samaritan.

17. And Jesus answering said, Were there not ten cleansed? but where are the nine?

18. There are not found that returned to give glory to God, save this stranger.

19. And he said unto him, Arise, go thy way: thy faith hath made thee whole.

20. And when he was demanded of the Pharisees, when the kingdom of God should come, he answered them and said, The kingdom of God cometh not with observation:

21. Neither shall they say, Lo here! or, lo there! for, behold, the kingdom of God is within you.

22. And he said unto the disciples, The days will come, when ye shall desire to see one of the days of the Son of man, and ye shall not see it.

23. And they shall say to you, See here; or, see there: go not after them, nor follow them.

24. For as the lightning, that lighteneth out of the one part under heaven, shineth unto the other part under heaven; so shall also the Son of man be in his day.

25. But first must he suffer many things, and be rejected of this generation.

26. And as it was in the days of Noe, so shall it be also in the days of the Son of man.

27. They did eat, they drank, they married wives, they were given in marriage, until the day that Noah entered into the ark, and the flood came, and destroyed them all.

28. Likewise also as it was in the days of Lot; they did eat, they drank, they bought, they sold, they planted, they builded;

29. But the same day that Lot went out of Sodom it rained fire and brimstone from heaven, and destroyed them all.

30. Even thus shall it be in the day when the Son of man is revealed.

31. In that day, he which shall be upon the housetop, and his stuff in the house, let him not come down to take it away: and he that is in the field, let him likewise not return back.

32. Remember Lot's wife.

33. Whosoever shall seek to save his life shall lose it; and whosoever shall lose his life shall preserve it.

34. I tell you, in that night there shall be two men in one bed; the one shall be taken, and the other shall be left.

35. Two women shall be grinding together; the one shall be taken, and the other left.

36. Two men shall be in the field; the one shall be taken, and the other left.

37. And they answered and said unto him, Where, Lord? And he said unto them, Wheresoever the body is, thither will the eagles be gathered together.

CHAPTER 18

1. And he spake a parable unto them to this end, that men ought always to pray, and not to faint;

2. Saying, There was in a city a judge, which feared not God, neither regarded man:

3. And there was a widow in that city; and she came unto him, saying, Avenge me of mine adversary.

4. And he would not for a while: but afterward he said within himself, Though I fear not God, nor regard man;

5. Yet because this widow troubleth me, I will avenge her, lest by her continual coming she weary me.

6. And the Lord said, Hear what the unjust judge saith.

7. And shall not God avenge his own elect, which cry day and night unto him, though he bear long with them?

8. I tell you that he will avenge them speedily. Nevertheless when the Son of man cometh, shall he find faith on the earth?

9. And he spake this parable unto certain which trusted in themselves that they were righteous, and despised others:

10. Two men went up into the temple to pray; the one a Pharisee, and the other a publican.

11. The Pharisee stood and prayed thus with himself, God, I thank thee, that I am not as other men are, extortioners, unjust, adulterers, or even as this publican.

12. I fast twice in the week, I give tithes of all that I possess.

13. And the publican, standing afar off, would not lift up so much as his eyes unto heaven, but smote upon his breast, saying, God be merciful to me a sinner.

14. I tell you, this man went down to his house justified rather than the other: for every one that exalteth himself shall be abased; and he that humbleth himself shall be exalted.

15. And they brought unto him also infants, that he would touch them: but when his disciples saw it, they rebuked them.

16. But Jesus called them unto him, and said, Suffer little children to come unto me, and forbid them not: for of such is the kingdom of God.

17. Verily I say unto you, Whosoever shall not receive the kingdom of God as a little child shall in no wise enter therein.

18. And a certain ruler asked him, saying, Good Master, what shall I do to inherit eternal life?

19. And Jesus said unto him, Why callest thou me good? none is good, save one, that is, God.

20. Thou knowest the commandments, Do not commit adultery, Do not kill, Do not steal, Do not bear false witness, Honour thy father and thy mother.

21. And he said, All these have I kept from my youth up.

22. Now when Jesus heard these things, he said unto him, Yet lackest thou one thing: sell all that thou hast, and distribute unto the poor, and thou shalt have treasure in heaven: and come, follow me.

23. And when he heard this, he was very sorrowful: for he was very rich.

24. And when Jesus saw that he was very sorrowful, he said, How hardly shall they that have riches enter into the kingdom of God!

25. For it is easier for a camel to go through a needle's eye, than for a rich man to enter into the kingdom of God.

26. And they that heard it said, Who then can be saved?

27. And he said, The things which are impossible with men are possible with God.

28. Then Peter said, Lo, we have left all, and followed thee.

29. And he said unto them, Verily I say unto you, There is no man that hath left house, or parents, or brethren, or wife, or children, for the kingdom of God's sake,

30. Who shall not receive manifold more in this present time, and in the world to come life everlasting.

31. Then he took unto him the twelve, and said unto them, Behold, we go up to Jerusalem, and all things that are written by the prophets concerning the Son of man shall be accomplished.

32. For he shall be delivered unto the Gentiles, and shall be mocked, and spitefully entreated, and spitted on:

33. And they shall scourge him, and put him to death: and the third day he shall rise again.

34. And they understood none of these things: and this saying was hid from them, neither knew they the things which were spoken.

35. And it came to pass, that as he was come nigh unto Jericho, a certain blind man sat by the way side begging:

36. And hearing the multitude pass by, he asked what it meant.

37. And they told him, that Jesus of Nazareth passeth by.

38. And he cried, saying, Jesus, thou son of David, have mercy on me.

39. And they which went before rebuked him, that he should hold his peace: but he cried so much the more, Thou son of David, have mercy on me.

40. And Jesus stood, and commanded him to be brought unto him: and when he was come near, he asked him,

41. Saying, What wilt thou that I shall do unto thee? And he said, Lord, that I may receive my sight.

42. And Jesus said unto him, Receive thy sight: thy faith hath saved thee.

43. And immediately he received his sight, and followed him, glorifying God: and all the people, when they saw it, gave praise unto God.

CHAPTER 19

1. And Jesus entered and passed through Jericho.

2. And, behold, there was a man named Zacchaeus, which was the chief among the publicans, and he was rich.

3. And he sought to see Jesus who he was; and could not for the press, because he was little of stature.

4. And he ran before, and climbed up into a sycomore tree to see him: for he was to pass that way.

5. And when Jesus came to the place, he looked up, and saw him, and said unto him, Zacchaeus, make haste, and come down; for to day I must abide at thy house.

6. And he made haste, and came down, and received him joyfully.

7. And when they saw it, they all murmured, saying, That he was gone to be guest with a man that is a sinner.

8. And Zacchaeus stood, and said unto the Lord: Behold, Lord, the half of my goods I give to the poor; and if I have taken any thing from any man by false accusation, I restore him fourfold.

9. And Jesus said unto him, This day is salvation come to this house, forsomuch as he also is a son of Abraham.

10. For the Son of man is come to seek and to save that which was lost.

11. And as they heard these things, he added and spake a parable, because he was nigh to Jerusalem, and because they thought that the kingdom of God should immediately appear.

12. He said therefore, A certain nobleman went into a far country to receive for himself a kingdom, and to return.

13. And he called his ten servants, and delivered them ten pounds, and said unto them, Occupy till I come.

14. But his citizens hated him, and sent a message after him, saying, We will not have this man to reign over us.

15. And it came to pass, that when he was returned, having received the kingdom, then he commanded these servants to be called unto him, to whom he had given the money, that he might know how much every man had gained by trading.

16. Then came the first, saying, Lord, thy pound hath gained ten pounds.

17. And he said unto him, Well, thou good servant: because thou hast been faithful in a very little, have thou authority over ten cities.

18. And the second came, saying, Lord, thy pound hath gained five pounds.

19. And he said likewise to him, Be thou also over five cities.

20. And another came, saying, Lord, behold, here is thy pound, which I have kept laid up in a napkin:

21. For I feared thee, because thou art an austere man: thou takest up that thou layedst not down, and reapest that thou didst not sow.

22. And he saith unto him, Out of thine own mouth will I judge thee, thou wicked servant. Thou knewest that I was an austere man, taking up that I laid not down, and reaping that I did not sow:

23. Wherefore then gavest not thou my money into the bank, that at my coming I might have required mine own with usury?

24. And he said unto them that stood by, Take from him the pound, and give it to him that hath ten pounds.

25. (And they said unto him, Lord, he hath ten pounds.)

26. For I say unto you, That unto every one which hath shall be given; and from him that hath not, even that he hath shall be taken away from him.

27. But those mine enemies, which would not that I should reign over them, bring hither, and slay them before me.

28. And when he had thus spoken, he went before, ascending up to Jerusalem.

29. And it came to pass, when he was come nigh to Bethphage and Bethany, at the mount called the mount of Olives, he sent two of his disciples,

30. Saying, Go ye into the village over against you; in the which at your entering ye shall find a colt tied, whereon yet never man sat: loose him, and bring him hither.

31. And if any man ask you, Why do ye loose him? thus shall ye say unto him, Because the Lord hath need of him.

32. And they that were sent went their way, and found even as he had said unto them.

33. And as they were loosing the colt, the owners thereof said unto them, Why loose ye the colt?

34. And they said, The Lord hath need of him.

35. And they brought him to Jesus: and they cast their garments upon the colt, and they set Jesus thereon.

36. And as he went, they spread their clothes in the way.

37. And when he was come nigh, even now at the descent of the mount of Olives, the whole multitude of the disciples began to rejoice and praise God with a loud voice for all the mighty works that they had seen;

38. Saying, Blessed be the King that cometh in the name of the Lord: peace in heaven, and glory in the highest.

39. And some of the Pharisees from among the multitude said unto him, Master, rebuke thy disciples.

40. And he answered and said unto them, I tell you that, if these should hold their peace, the stones would immediately cry out.

41. And when he was come near, he beheld the city, and wept over it,

42. Saying, If thou hadst known, even thou, at least in this thy day, the things which belong unto thy peace! but now they are hid from thine eyes.

43. For the days shall come upon thee, that thine enemies shall cast a trench about thee, and compass thee round, and keep thee in on every side,

44. And shall lay thee even with the ground, and thy children within thee; and they shall not leave in thee one stone upon another; because thou knewest not the time of thy visitation.

45. And he went into the temple, and began to cast out them that sold therein, and them that bought;

46. Saying unto them, It is written, My house is the house of prayer: but ye have made it a den of thieves.

47. And he taught daily in the temple. But the chief priests and the scribes and the chief of the people sought to destroy him,

48. And could not find what they might do: for all the people were very attentive to hear him.

CHAPTER 20

1. And it came to pass, that on one of those days, as he taught the people in the temple, and preached the gospel, the chief priests and the scribes came upon him with the elders,

2. And spake unto him, saying, Tell us, by what authority doest thou these things? or who is he that gave thee this authority?

3. And he answered and said unto them, I will also ask you one thing; and answer me:

4. The baptism of John, was it from heaven, or of men?

5. And they reasoned with themselves, saying, If we shall say, From heaven; he will say, Why then believed ye him not?

6. But and if we say, Of men; all the people will stone us: for they be persuaded that John was a prophet.

7. And they answered, that they could not tell whence it was.

8. And Jesus said unto them, Neither tell I you by what authority I do these things.

9. Then began he to speak to the people this parable; A certain man planted a vineyard, and let it forth to husbandmen, and went into a far country for a long time.

10. And at the season he sent a servant to the husbandmen, that they should give him of the fruit of the vineyard: but the husbandmen beat him, and sent him away empty.

11. And again he sent another servant: and they beat him also, and entreated him shamefully, and sent him away empty.

12. And again he sent a third: and they wounded him also, and cast him out.

13. Then said the lord of the vineyard, What shall I do? I will send my beloved son: it may be they will reverence him when they see him.

14. But when the husbandmen saw him, they reasoned among themselves, saying, This is the heir: come, let us kill him, that the inheritance may be ours.

15. So they cast him out of the vineyard, and killed him. What therefore shall the lord of the vineyard do unto them?

16. He shall come and destroy these husbandmen, and shall give the vineyard to others. And when they heard it, they said, God forbid.

17. And he beheld them, and said, What is this then that is written, The stone which the builders rejected, the same is become the head of the corner?

18. Whosoever shall fall upon that stone shall be broken; but on whomsoever it shall fall, it will grind him to powder.

19. And the chief priests and the scribes the same hour sought to lay hands on him; and they feared the people: for they perceived that he had spoken this parable against them.

20. And they watched him, and sent forth spies, which should feign themselves just men, that they might take hold of his words, that so they might deliver him unto the power and authority of the governor.

21. And they asked him, saying, Master, we know that thou sayest and teachest rightly, neither acceptest thou the person of any, but teachest the way of God truly:

22. Is it lawful for us to give tribute unto Caesar, or no?

23. But he perceived their craftiness, and said unto them, Why tempt ye me?

24. Shew me a penny. Whose image and superscription hath it? They answered and said, Caesar's.

25. And he said unto them, Render therefore unto Caesar the things which be Caesar's, and unto God the things which be God's.

26. And they could not take hold of his words before the people: and they marvelled at his answer, and held their peace.

27. Then came to him certain of the Sadducees, which deny that there is any resurrection; and they asked him,

28. Saying, Master, Moses wrote unto us, If any man's brother die, having a wife, and he die without children, that his brother should take his wife, and raise up seed unto his brother.

29. There were therefore seven brethren: and the first took a wife, and died without children.

30. And the second took her to wife, and he died childless.

31. And the third took her; and in like manner the seven also: and they left no children, and died.

32. Last of all the woman died also.

33. Therefore in the resurrection whose wife of them is she? for seven had her to wife.

34. And Jesus answering said unto them, The children of this world marry, and are given in marriage:

35. But they which shall be accounted worthy to obtain that world, and the resurrection from the dead, neither marry, nor are given in marriage:

36. Neither can they die any more: for they are equal unto the angels; and are the children of God, being the children of the resurrection.

37. Now that the dead are raised, even Moses shewed at the bush, when he calleth the Lord the God of Abraham, and the God of Isaac, and the God of Jacob.

38. For he is not a God of the dead, but of the living: for all live unto him.

39. Then certain of the scribes answering said, Master, thou hast well said.

40. And after that they durst not ask him any question at all.

41. And he said unto them, How say they that Christ is David's son?

42. And David himself saith in the book of Psalms, The Lord said unto my Lord, Sit thou on my right hand,

43. Till I make thine enemies thy footstool.

44. David therefore calleth him Lord, how is he then his son?

45. Then in the audience of all the people he said unto his disciples,

46. Beware of the scribes, which desire to walk in long robes, and love greetings in the markets, and the highest seats in the synagogues, and the chief rooms at feasts;

47. Which devour widows' houses, and for a shew make long prayers: the same shall receive greater damnation.

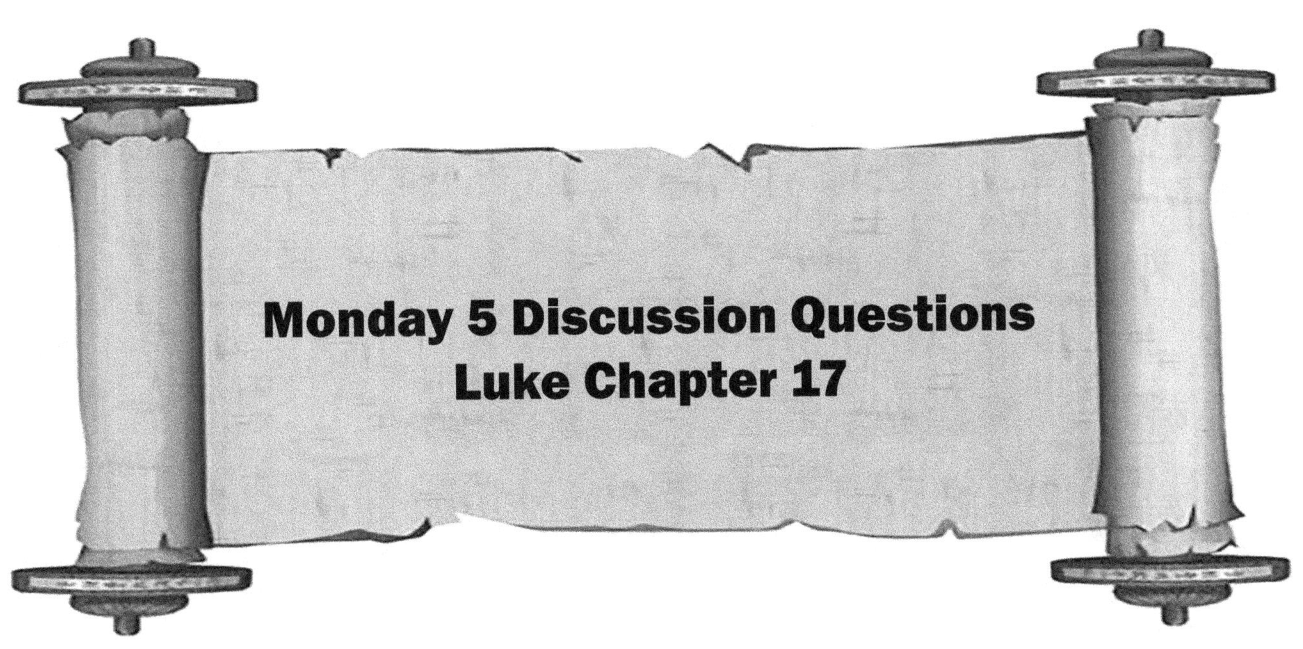

Monday 5 Discussion Questions
Luke Chapter 17

1. What did Jesuus tell his disciples about those who bring about offenses? ____________________

2. What did he say about those who offend the least little one? ____________________

3. If your brother trespasses against you and repents, what should you do? ____________________

4. When the Apostles asked the Lord to increase their faith, what did he say? ____________________

5. What should you do when you have done what was commanded of you? ____________________

6. How many lepers met Jesus when he entered the village? ____________________

7. What did Jesus instruct them to do? ____________________

8. What did the Samaritan do when he saw he was healed? ____________________

9. What was Jesus' response to the Samaritan? ____________________

10. What did the Lord say when the Pharisees asked when the Kingdom of God should come? ____________________

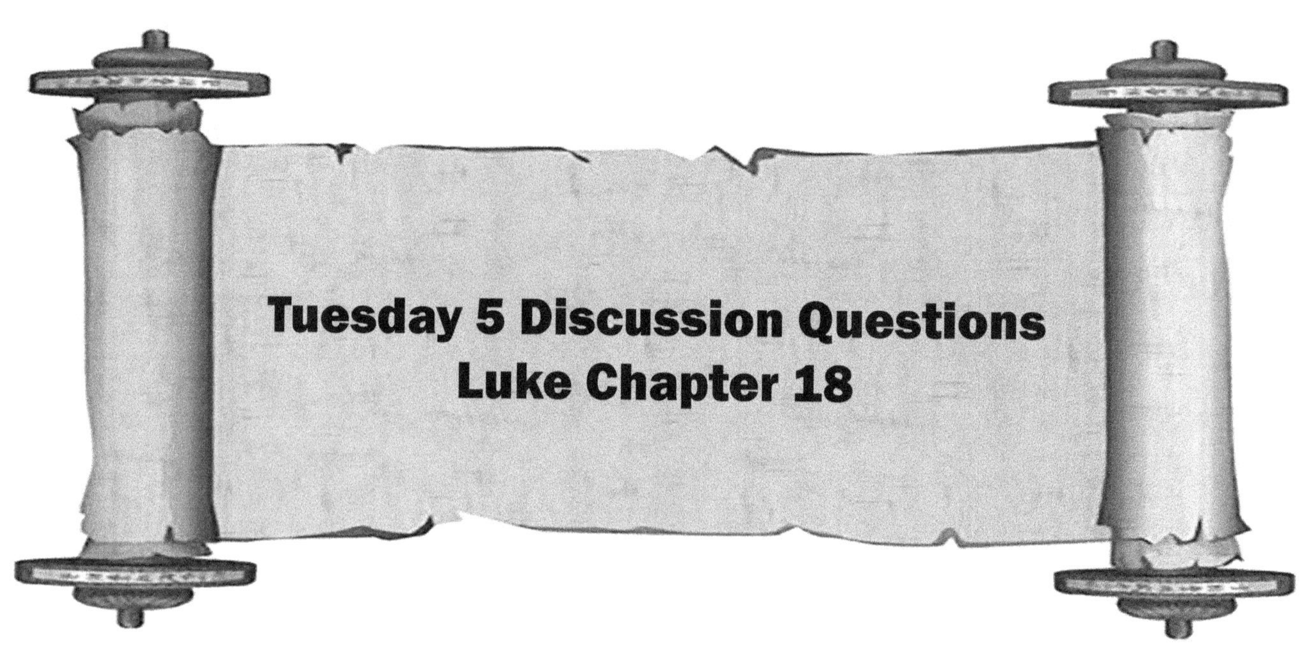

1. What parable is Jesus speaking in this chapter? ____________________
____
____
2. What is the profession of the man who didn't fear God? ____________________
____
____
3. What did the widow woman ask him to do?Did he grant her request? Why? __________
____
____
4. What did he ask about God avenging his own elect? ____________________
____
____
5. What two men went up into the temple to pray? ____________________
____
____
6. What was the Pharisee's prayer? ____________________
____
____
7. What was the publican's prayer? ____________________
____
____
8. What was the Lord's response to the publican's prayer? ____________________
____
____
9. What happens to those who exalt themselves? ____________________
____
____
10. What happens to those who humble themselves? ____________________
____
____

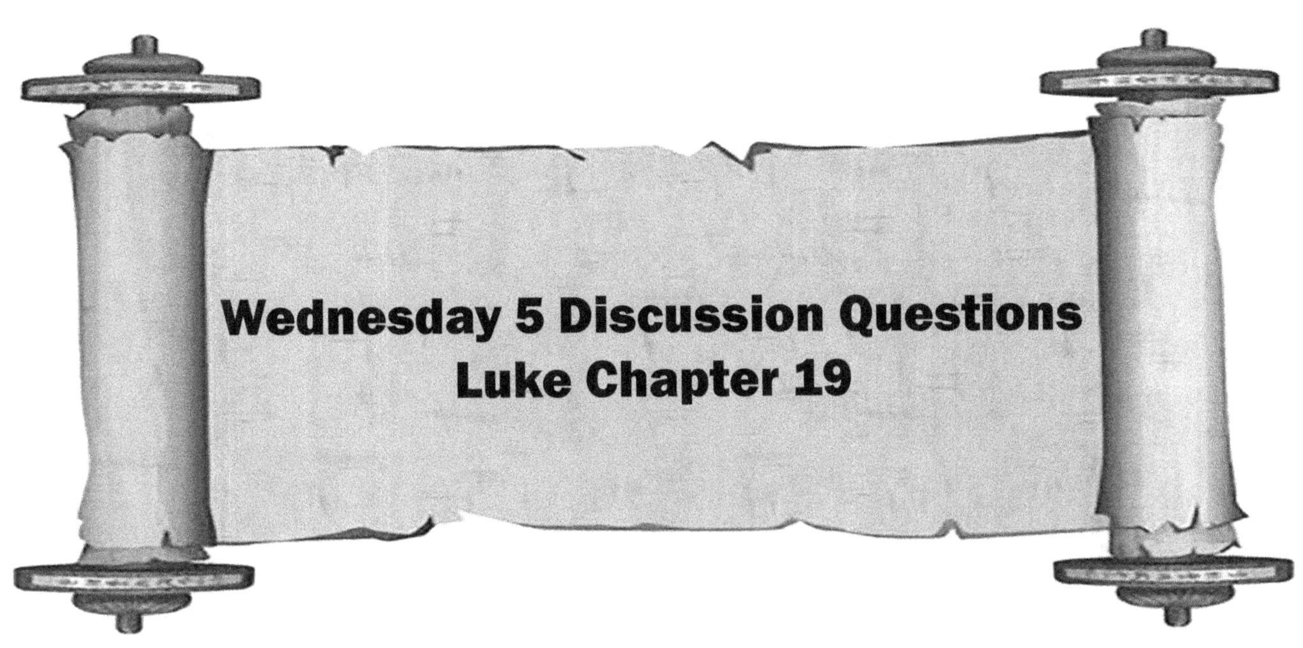

1. What was the name of the rich, chief publican in Jericho? ______________________

2. Why couldn't he see Jesus? ______________________

3. What did he decide to do so he could see Jesus? ______________________

4. Did Jesus see him? What did Jesus say to him? ______________________

5. Did he obey? ______________________

6. What did the people say when they saw them together? ______________________

7. What did Zaccheus say about his goods? ______________________

8. What did the Lord say would come to Zaccheus' house? Why? ______________________

9. What did he give ten servants to occupy until he returned? ______________________

10. What was the message his citizens sent after him saying? ______________________

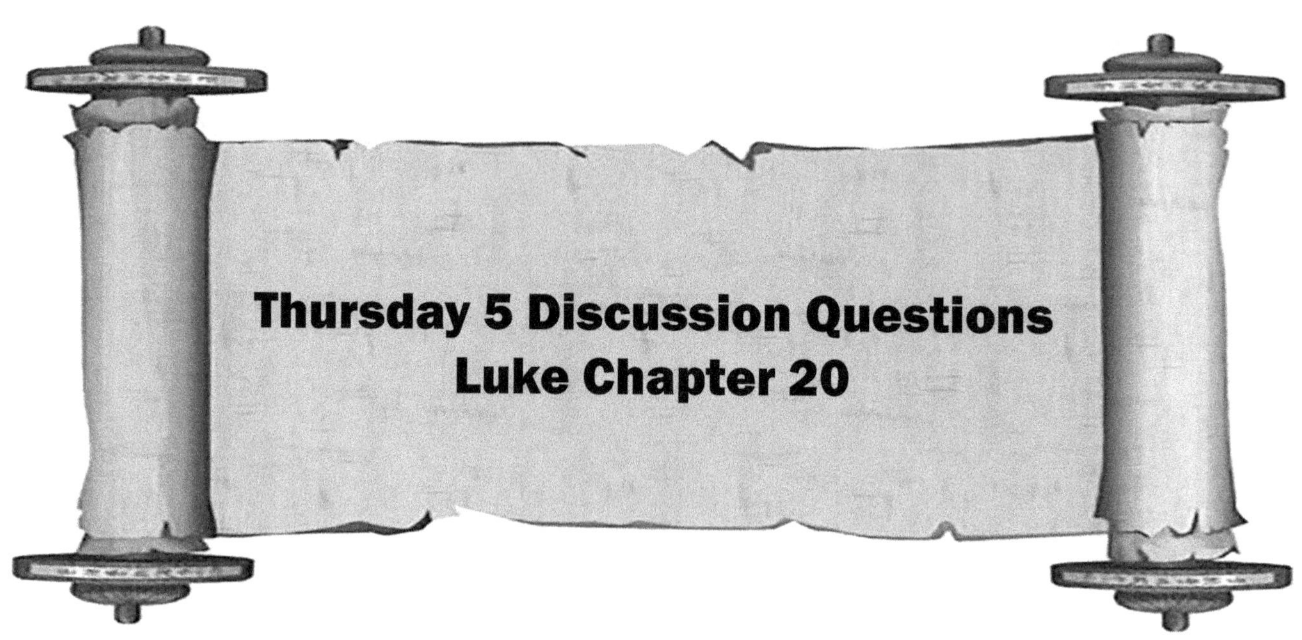

1. When the chief priests and scribes saw Jesus teaching in the temple, what did they say? ______________________________

2. What did the Lord say? ______________________________

3. What was their reasoning within themselves? ______________________________

4. What was their answer? ______________________________

5. What did Jesus say to their response? ______________________________

6. What happened when the first, second and third servant were sent to the husbandmen to get fruit from the vineyard? ______________________________

7. The Lord said, I will send my beloved son: it may be they will reverence him when they see him. What did the husbandmen do? ______________________________

8. What therefore shall the lord of the vineyard do unto them? ______________________________

9. What did he say about the stone that the builders rejected? ______________________________

10. What will happen to the one that falls upon the stone? What shall happen to the one that the stone falls upon? ______________________________

WEEKLY REVIEW
LUKE CHAPTERS 17-20

NAME THAT CHAPTER

1.______ JESUS WAS PREACHING AND TEACHING THE PEOPLE IN THE TEMPLE. THE SCRIBES AND PRIESTS CAME QUESTIONING HIM ASKING, "BY WHAT AUTHORITY ARE YOU DOING THESES THINGS, OR WHO GAVE YOU THE AUTHORITY TO DO THEM.". HE ANSWERED WITH THE RHETORICAL QUESTION, "IF YOU CAN ANSWER THIS I WILL ANSWER YOU. WAS JOHN THE BAPTIST'S BAPTISM FROM HEAVEN OR OF MEN?" THEY REASONED AMONG THEMSELVES AND COULDN'T ANSWER HIM. JESUS KNEW THEY WERE TEMPTING HIM. SO, HE DID NOT ANSWER THEM.

2.______ JESUS WENT TO JERUSALEM THROUGH THE MIDST OF SAMARIA AND GALILEE AND BEGAN TO TEACH THAT DOING WHAT YOU ARE COMMANDED IS REQUIRED,BY GIVING PARABLE OF A MAN WITH A SERVANT WHO PLOWED AS COMMANDED. HE SAID LIKEWISE WHEN YOU OBEY AND JUST DO AS YOU SHOULD, SAY, "WE ARE UNPROFITABLE. wE HAVE DONE THAT WHICH WAS OUR DUTY TO DO."

3.______ JESUS WENT THROUGH JERICHO, WHERE THERE WAS A RICH MAN NAMED ZACHAEUS, WHO WAS A CHIEF PUBLICAN. HE WANTED TO SEE JESUS. BUT, BECAUSE OF THE MULTITUDE HE COULD NOT SEE HIM BECAUSE OF HIS SHORT STATURE OR HEIGHT. THE MAN DECIDED TO CLIMB UP IN A SYCAMORE TREE TO SEE JESUS WHEN HE CAME BY. WHEN JESUS WALKED THROUGH, HE LOOKED UP AND SAW HIM. HE TOLD ZACCHAEUS TO COME DOWN. HE SAID HE WANTED TO GO WITH HIM TO HIS HOUSE. JESUS WENT WITH HIM THAT DAY. THE PEOPLE MURMURED THAT JESUS WENT TO BE THE GUEST OF A SINNER.

4.______ JESUS TAUGHT THAT MEN OUGHT TO ALWAYS PRAY AND NOT FAINT. HE GAVE A PARABLE TO EXPRESS THE MEANING OF WHY THEY SHOULD DO THIS. HE SPOKE OF A JUDGE WHO DID NOT REGARD GOD OR MAN. THERE WAS A WIDOW WOMAN WHO CAME TO HIM TO ASK HIM TO AVENGE HER OF HER ADVERSARY. FOR A WHILE HE DID NOT. BUT AFTER A WHILE OF HER CONTINUOUS REQUEST HE DECIDED TO GRANT HER REQUEST SO SHE COULD STOP BOTHERING HIM. JESUS TAUGHT THAT IS MUCH MORE LIKELY THAT GOD WILL AVENGE HIS OWN ELECT THAT CRY TO HM DAY AND NIGHT. THOUGH HE BEAR LONG WITH THEM.

TRUE OR FALSE

5. THE DISCIPLES WERE EXCITED TO SEE THE CHILDREN BEING BROUGHT TO JESUS TO BE PRAYED FOR.

____

6. WHEN THE MAN SENT HIS SERVANT TO GET FRUIT FROM THE HUSBANDMAN, THE SERVANT WAS BEAT AND SENT AWAY EMPTY.

____

7. WHEN ZACCHAEUS TOLD JESUS HIS REQUEST, JESUS TOLD HIM TO GIVE HALF HIS GOODS TO THE POOR AND RESTORE THE PEOPLE HE HAD CHEATED FOURFOLD.

____

FILL IN THE BLANKS

8. TWO MEN WENT UP INTO THE_____________TO PRAY: THE ONE A_____________ AND THE OTHER A _____________

9. THEN CAME THE_____________, SAYING, LORD THY_____________HATH GAINED _____________ POUNDS.

10. _____________ THEREFORE UNTO_____________THE THINGS WHICH BE CAESAR'S AND UNTO GOD THE THINGS WHICH BE_____________.

MY PRAYER JOURNAL

Please use this space to record your thoughts and feelings as you travel on this spirit led journey through the word of God with us. Please know that you have brothers and sisters in this organization from all over the world praying with and for you. My prayer for you is that you will begin to see the power of God resting in each set of your footprints. As you look back and examine your past in this journal, may you realize that you were never alone and according to Hebrews 13:5, God will never leave nor forsake you. ~LADY FLORA

I THESSALONIANS 5:17

THE STUDY OF THE FOUR GOSPELS VOCABULARY DEFINITIONS FOR LUKE CHAPTERS 21-24

Define the following words. This assignment is worth 200 points when completed ***WITH THE CLASS*** during FB LIVE Weekly Class Discussion for participation grade.

WORD	DEFINITIONS
1) PENURY	
2) ADORNED	
3) GAINSAY	
4) TRODDEN	
5) PERPLEXITY	
6) EXPOUND	
7) SURFEITING	
8) DERIDED	
9) SEDITION	
10) LAMENTED	

DMWW DAILY BIBLE READING
LUKE CHAPTERS 21-24

CHAPTER 21

1. And he looked up, and saw the rich men casting their gifts into the treasury.
2. And he saw also a certain poor widow casting in thither two mites.
3. And he said, Of a truth I say unto you, that this poor widow hath cast in more than they all:
4. For all these have of their abundance cast in unto the offerings of God: but she of her penury hath cast in all the living that she had.
5. And as some spake of the temple, how it was adorned with goodly stones and gifts, he said,
6. As for these things which ye behold, the days will come, in the which there shall not be left one stone upon another, that shall not be thrown down.
7. And they asked him, saying, Master, but when shall these things be? and what sign will there be when these things shall come to pass?
8. And he said, Take heed that ye be not deceived: for many shall come in my name, saying, I am Christ; and the time draweth near: go ye not therefore after them.
9. But when ye shall hear of wars and commotions, be not terrified: for these things must first come to pass; but the end is not by and by.
10. Then said he unto them, Nation shall rise against nation, and kingdom against kingdom:
11. And great earthquakes shall be in divers places, and famines, and pestilences; and fearful sights and great signs shall there be from heaven.
12. But before all these, they shall lay their hands on you, and persecute you, delivering you up to the synagogues, and into prisons, being brought before kings and rulers for my name's sake.
13. And it shall turn to you for a testimony.
14. Settle it therefore in your hearts, not to meditate before what ye shall answer:
15. For I will give you a mouth and wisdom, which all your adversaries shall not be able to gainsay nor resist.
16. And ye shall be betrayed both by parents, and brethren, and kinsfolks, and friends; and some of you shall they cause to be put to death.
17. And ye shall be hated of all men for my name's sake.

18. But there shall not an hair of your head perish.

19. In your patience possess ye your souls.

20. And when ye shall see Jerusalem compassed with armies, then know that the desolation thereof is nigh.

21. Then let them which are in Judaea flee to the mountains; and let them which are in the midst of it depart out; and let not them that are in the countries enter thereinto.

22. For these be the days of vengeance, that all things which are written may be fulfilled.

23. But woe unto them that are with child, and to them that give suck, in those days! for there shall be great distress in the land, and wrath upon this people.

24. And they shall fall by the edge of the sword, and shall be led away captive into all nations: and Jerusalem shall be trodden down of the Gentiles, until the times of the Gentiles be fulfilled.

25. And there shall be signs in the sun, and in the moon, and in the stars; and upon the earth distress of nations, with perplexity; the sea and the waves roaring;

26. Men's hearts failing them for fear, and for looking after those things which are coming on the earth: for the powers of heaven shall be shaken.

27. And then shall they see the Son of man coming in a cloud with power and great glory.

28. And when these things begin to come to pass, then look up, and lift up your heads; for your redemption draweth nigh.

29. And he spake to them a parable; Behold the fig tree, and all the trees;

30. When they now shoot forth, ye see and know of your own selves that summer is now nigh at hand.

31. So likewise ye, when ye see these things come to pass, know ye that the kingdom of God is nigh at hand.

32. Verily I say unto you, This generation shall not pass away, till all be fulfilled.

33. Heaven and earth shall pass away: but my words shall not pass away.

34. And take heed to yourselves, lest at any time your hearts be overcharged with surfeiting, and drunkenness, and cares of this life, and so that day come upon you unawares.

35. For as a snare shall it come on all them that dwell on the face of the whole earth.

36. Watch ye therefore, and pray always, that ye may be accounted worthy to escape all these things that shall come to pass, and to stand before the Son of man.

37. And in the day time he was teaching in the temple; and at night he went out, and abode in the mount that is called the mount of Olives.

38. And all the people came early in the morning to him in the temple, for to hear him.

CHAPTER 22

1. Now the feast of unleavened bread drew nigh, which is called the Passover.
2. And the chief priests and scribes sought how they might kill him; for they feared the people.
3. Then entered Satan into Judas surnamed Iscariot, being of the number of the twelve.
4. And he went his way, and communed with the chief priests and captains, how he might betray him unto them.
5. And they were glad, and covenanted to give him money.
6. And he promised, and sought opportunity to betray him unto them in the absence of the multitude.
7. Then came the day of unleavened bread, when the passover must be killed.
8. And he sent Peter and John, saying, Go and prepare us the passover, that we may eat.
9. And they said unto him, Where wilt thou that we prepare?
10. And he said unto them, Behold, when ye are entered into the city, there shall a man meet you, bearing a pitcher of water; follow him into the house where he entereth in.
11. And ye shall say unto the goodman of the house, The Master saith unto thee, Where is the guestchamber, where I shall eat the passover with my disciples?
12. And he shall shew you a large upper room furnished: there make ready.
13. And they went, and found as he had said unto them: and they made ready the passover.
14. And when the hour was come, he sat down, and the twelve apostles with him.
15. And he said unto them, With desire I have desired to eat this passover with you before I suffer:
16. For I say unto you, I will not any more eat thereof, until it be fulfilled in the kingdom of God.
17. And he took the cup, and gave thanks, and said, Take this, and divide it among yourselves:
18. For I say unto you, I will not drink of the fruit of the vine, until the kingdom of God shall come.
19. And he took bread, and gave thanks, and brake it, and gave unto them, saying, This is my body which is given for you: this do in remembrance of me.
20. Likewise also the cup after supper, saying, This cup is the new testament in my blood, which is shed for you.
21. But, behold, the hand of him that betrayeth me is with me on the table.

22. And truly the Son of man goeth, as it was determined: but woe unto that man by whom he is betrayed!

23. And they began to enquire among themselves, which of them it was that should do this thing.

24. And there was also a strife among them, which of them should be accounted the greatest.

25. And he said unto them, The kings of the Gentiles exercise lordship over them; and they that exercise authority upon them are called benefactors.

26. But ye shall not be so: but he that is greatest among you, let him be as the younger; and he that is chief, as he that doth serve.

27. For whether is greater, he that sitteth at meat, or he that serveth? is not he that sitteth at meat? but I am among you as he that serveth.

28. Ye are they which have continued with me in my temptations.

29. And I appoint unto you a kingdom, as my Father hath appointed unto me;

30. That ye may eat and drink at my table in my kingdom, and sit on thrones judging the twelve tribes of Israel.

31. And the Lord said, Simon, Simon, behold, Satan hath desired to have you, that he may sift you as wheat:

32. But I have prayed for thee, that thy faith fail not: and when thou art converted, strengthen thy brethren.

33. And he said unto him, Lord, I am ready to go with thee, both into prison, and to death.

34. And he said, I tell thee, Peter, the cock shall not crow this day, before that thou shalt thrice deny that thou knowest me.

35. And he said unto them, When I sent you without purse, and scrip, and shoes, lacked ye any thing? And they said, Nothing.

36. Then said he unto them, But now, he that hath a purse, let him take it, and likewise his scrip: and he that hath no sword, let him sell his garment, and buy one.

37. For I say unto you, that this that is written must yet be accomplished in me, And he was reckoned among the transgressors: for the things concerning me have an end.

38. And they said, Lord, behold, here are two swords. And he said unto them, It is enough.

39. And he came out, and went, as he was wont, to the mount of Olives; and his disciples also followed him.

40. And when he was at the place, he said unto them, Pray that ye enter not into temptation.

41. And he was withdrawn from them about a stone's cast, and kneeled down, and prayed,

42. Saying, Father, if thou be willing, remove this cup from me: nevertheless not my will, but thine, be done.

43. And there appeared an angel unto him from heaven, strengthening him.

44. And being in an agony he prayed more earnestly: and his sweat was as it were great drops of blood falling down to the ground.

45. And when he rose up from prayer, and was come to his disciples, he found them sleeping for sorrow,

46. And said unto them, Why sleep ye? rise and pray, lest ye enter into temptation.

47. And while he yet spake, behold a multitude, and he that was called Judas, one of the twelve, went before them, and drew near unto Jesus to kiss him.

48. But Jesus said unto him, Judas, betrayest thou the Son of man with a kiss?

49. When they which were about him saw what would follow, they said unto him, Lord, shall we smite with the sword?

50. And one of them smote the servant of the high priest, and cut off his right ear.

51. And Jesus answered and said, Suffer ye thus far. And he touched his ear, and healed him.

52. Then Jesus said unto the chief priests, and captains of the temple, and the elders, which were come to him, Be ye come out, as against a thief, with swords and staves?

53. When I was daily with you in the temple, ye stretched forth no hands against me: but this is your hour, and the power of darkness.

54. Then took they him, and led him, and brought him into the high priest's house. And Peter followed afar off.

55. And when they had kindled a fire in the midst of the hall, and were set down together, Peter sat down among them.

56. But a certain maid beheld him as he sat by the fire, and earnestly looked upon him, and said, This man was also with him.

57. And he denied him, saying, Woman, I know him not.

58. And after a little while another saw him, and said, Thou art also of them. And Peter said, Man, I am not.

59. And about the space of one hour after another confidently affirmed, saying, Of a truth this fellow also was with him: for he is a Galilaean.

60. And Peter said, Man, I know not what thou sayest. And immediately, while he yet spake, the cock crew.

61. And the Lord turned, and looked upon Peter. And Peter remembered the word of the Lord, how he had said unto him, Before the cock crow, thou shalt deny me thrice.

62. And Peter went out, and wept bitterly.

63. And the men that held Jesus mocked him, and smote him.

64. And when they had blindfolded him, they struck him on the face, and asked him, saying, Prophesy, who is it that smote thee?

65. And many other things blasphemously spake they against him.

66. And as soon as it was day, the elders of the people and the chief priests and the scribes came together, and led him into their council, saying,

67. Art thou the Christ? tell us. And he said unto them, If I tell you, ye will not believe:

68. And if I also ask you, ye will not answer me, nor let me go.

69. Hereafter shall the Son of man sit on the right hand of the power of God.

70. Then said they all, Art thou then the Son of God? And he said unto them, Ye say that I am.

71. And they said, What need we any further witness? for we ourselves have heard of his own mouth.

CHAPTER 23

1. And the whole multitude of them arose, and led him unto Pilate.

2. And they began to accuse him, saying, We found this fellow perverting the nation, and forbidding to give tribute to Caesar, saying that he himself is Christ a King.

3. And Pilate asked him, saying, Art thou the King of the Jews? And he answered him and said, Thou sayest it.

4. Then said Pilate to the chief priests and to the people, I find no fault in this man.

5. And they were the more fierce, saying, He stirreth up the people, teaching throughout all Jewry, beginning from Galilee to this place.

6. When Pilate heard of Galilee, he asked whether the man were a Galilaean.

7. And as soon as he knew that he belonged unto Herod's jurisdiction, he sent him to Herod, who himself also was at Jerusalem at that time.

8. And when Herod saw Jesus, he was exceeding glad: for he was desirous to see him of a long season, because he had heard many things of him; and he hoped to have seen some miracle done by him.

9. Then he questioned with him in many words; but he answered him nothing.

10. And the chief priests and scribes stood and vehemently accused him.

11. And Herod with his men of war set him at nought, and mocked him, and arrayed him in a gorgeous robe, and sent him again to Pilate.

12. And the same day Pilate and Herod were made friends together: for before they were at enmity between themselves.

13. And Pilate, when he had called together the chief priests and the rulers and the people,

14. Said unto them, Ye have brought this man unto me, as one that perverteth the people: and, behold, I, having examined him before you, have found no fault in this man touching those things whereof ye accuse him:

15. No, nor yet Herod: for I sent you to him; and, lo, nothing worthy of death is done unto him.

16. I will therefore chastise him, and release him.

17. (For of necessity he must release one unto them at the feast.)

18. And they cried out all at once, saying, Away with this man, and release unto us Barabbas:

19. (Who for a certain sedition made in the city, and for murder, was cast into prison.)

20. Pilate therefore, willing to release Jesus, spake again to them.

21. But they cried, saying, Crucify him, crucify him.

22. And he said unto them the third time, Why, what evil hath he done? I have found no cause of death in him: I will therefore chastise him, and let him go.

23. And they were instant with loud voices, requiring that he might be crucified. And the voices of them and of the chief priests prevailed.

24. And Pilate gave sentence that it should be as they required.

25. And he released unto them him that for sedition and murder was cast into prison, whom they had desired; but he delivered Jesus to their will.

26. And as they led him away, they laid hold upon one Simon, a Cyrenian, coming out of the country, and on him they laid the cross, that he might bear it after Jesus.

27. And there followed him a great company of people, and of women, which also bewailed and lamented him.

28. But Jesus turning unto them said, Daughters of Jerusalem, weep not for me, but weep for yourselves, and for your children.

29. For, behold, the days are coming, in the which they shall say, Blessed are the barren, and the wombs that never bare, and the paps which never gave suck.

30. Then shall they begin to say to the mountains, Fall on us; and to the hills, Cover us.

31. For if they do these things in a green tree, what shall be done in the dry?

32. And there were also two other, malefactors, led with him to be put to death.

33. And when they were come to the place, which is called Calvary, there they crucified him, and the malefactors, one on the right hand, and the other on the left.

34. Then said Jesus, Father, forgive them; for they know not what they do. And they parted his raiment, and cast lots.

35. And the people stood beholding. And the rulers also with them derided him, saying, He saved others; let him save himself, if he be Christ, the chosen of God.

36. And the soldiers also mocked him, coming to him, and offering him vinegar,

37. And saying, If thou be the king of the Jews, save thyself.

38. And a superscription also was written over him in letters of Greek, and Latin, and Hebrew, This Is The King Of The Jews.

39. And one of the malefactors which were hanged railed on him, saying, If thou be Christ, save thyself and us.

40. But the other answering rebuked him, saying, Dost not thou fear God, seeing thou art in the same condemnation?

41. And we indeed justly; for we receive the due reward of our deeds: but this man hath done nothing amiss.

42. And he said unto Jesus, Lord, remember me when thou comest into thy kingdom.

43. And Jesus said unto him, Verily I say unto thee, Today shalt thou be with me in paradise.

44. And it was about the sixth hour, and there was a darkness over all the earth until the ninth hour.

45. And the sun was darkened, and the veil of the temple was rent in the midst.

46. And when Jesus had cried with a loud voice, he said, Father, into thy hands I commend my spirit: and having said thus, he gave up the ghost.

47. Now when the centurion saw what was done, he glorified God, saying, Certainly this was a righteous man.

48. And all the people that came together to that sight, beholding the things which were done, smote their breasts, and returned.

49. And all his acquaintance, and the women that followed him from Galilee, stood afar off, beholding these things.

50. And, behold, there was a man named Joseph, a counsellor; and he was a good man, and a just:

51. (The same had not consented to the counsel and deed of them;) he was of Arimathaea, a city of the Jews: who also himself waited for the kingdom of God.

52. This man went unto Pilate, and begged the body of Jesus.

53. And he took it down, and wrapped it in linen, and laid it in a sepulchre that was hewn in stone, wherein never man before was laid.

54. And that day was the preparation, and the sabbath drew on.

55. And the women also, which came with him from Galilee, followed after, and beheld the sepulchre, and how his body was laid.

56. And they returned, and prepared spices and ointments; and rested the sabbath day according to the commandment.

CHAPTER 24

1. Now upon the first day of the week, very early in the morning, they came unto the sepulchre, bringing the spices which they had prepared, and certain others with them.
2. And they found the stone rolled away from the sepulchre.
3. And they entered in, and found not the body of the Lord Jesus.
4. And it came to pass, as they were much perplexed thereabout, behold, two men stood by them in shining garments:
5. And as they were afraid, and bowed down their faces to the earth, they said unto them, Why seek ye the living among the dead?
6. He is not here, but is risen: remember how he spake unto you when he was yet in Galilee,
7. Saying, The Son of man must be delivered into the hands of sinful men, and be crucified, and the third day rise again.
8. And they remembered his words,
9. And returned from the sepulchre, and told all these things unto the eleven, and to all the rest.
10. It was Mary Magdalene and Joanna, and Mary the mother of James, and other women that were with them, which told these things unto the apostles.
11. And their words seemed to them as idle tales, and they believed them not.
12. Then arose Peter, and ran unto the sepulchre; and stooping down, he beheld the linen clothes laid by themselves, and departed, wondering in himself at that which was come to pass.
13. And, behold, two of them went that same day to a village called Emmaus, which was from Jerusalem about threescore furlongs.
14. And they talked together of all these things which had happened.
15. And it came to pass, that, while they communed together and reasoned, Jesus himself drew near, and went with them.
16. But their eyes were holden that they should not know him.
17. And he said unto them, What manner of communications are these that ye have one to another, as ye walk, and are sad?
18. And the one of them, whose name was Cleopas, answering said unto him, Art thou only a stranger in Jerusalem, and hast not known the things which are come to pass there in these days?

19. And he said unto them, What things? And they said unto him, Concerning Jesus of Nazareth, which was a prophet mighty in deed and word before God and all the people:

20. And how the chief priests and our rulers delivered him to be condemned to death, and have crucified him.

21. But we trusted that it had been he which should have redeemed Israel: and beside all this, to day is the third day since these things were done.

22. Yea, and certain women also of our company made us astonished, which were early at the sepulchre;

23. And when they found not his body, they came, saying, that they had also seen a vision of angels, which said that he was alive.

24. And certain of them which were with us went to the sepulchre, and found it even so as the women had said: but him they saw not.

25. Then he said unto them, O fools, and slow of heart to believe all that the prophets have spoken:

26. Ought not Christ to have suffered these things, and to enter into his glory?

27. And beginning at Moses and all the prophets, he expounded unto them in all the scriptures the things concerning himself.

28. And they drew nigh unto the village, whither they went: and he made as though he would have gone further.

29. But they constrained him, saying, Abide with us: for it is toward evening, and the day is far spent. And he went in to tarry with them.

30. And it came to pass, as he sat at meat with them, he took bread, and blessed it, and brake, and gave to them.

31. And their eyes were opened, and they knew him; and he vanished out of their sight.

32. And they said one to another, Did not our heart burn within us, while he talked with us by the way, and while he opened to us the scriptures?

33. And they rose up the same hour, and returned to Jerusalem, and found the eleven gathered together, and them that were with them,

34. Saying, The Lord is risen indeed, and hath appeared to Simon.

35. And they told what things were done in the way, and how he was known of them in breaking of bread.

36. And as they thus spake, Jesus himself stood in the midst of them, and saith unto them, Peace be unto you.

37. But they were terrified and affrighted, and supposed that they had seen a spirit.

38. And he said unto them, Why are ye troubled? and why do thoughts arise in your hearts?

39. Behold my hands and my feet, that it is I myself: handle me, and see; for a spirit hath not flesh and bones, as ye see me have.

40. And when he had thus spoken, he shewed them his hands and his feet.

41. And while they yet believed not for joy, and wondered, he said unto them, Have ye here any meat?

42. And they gave him a piece of a broiled fish, and of an honeycomb.

43. And he took it, and did eat before them.

44. And he said unto them, These are the words which I spake unto you, while I was yet with you, that all things must be fulfilled, which were written in the law of Moses, and in the prophets, and in the psalms, concerning me.

45. Then opened he their understanding, that they might understand the scriptures,

46. And said unto them, Thus it is written, and thus it behooved Christ to suffer, and to rise from the dead the third day:

47. And that repentance and remission of sins should be preached in his name among all nations, beginning at Jerusalem.

48. And ye are witnesses of these things.

49. And, behold, I send the promise of my Father upon you: but tarry ye in the city of Jerusalem, until ye be endued with power from on high.

50. And he led them out as far as to Bethany, and he lifted up his hands, and blessed them.

51. And it came to pass, while he blessed them, he was parted from them, and carried up into heaven.

52. And they worshipped him, and returned to Jerusalem with great joy:

53. And were continually in the temple, praising and blessing God. Amen.

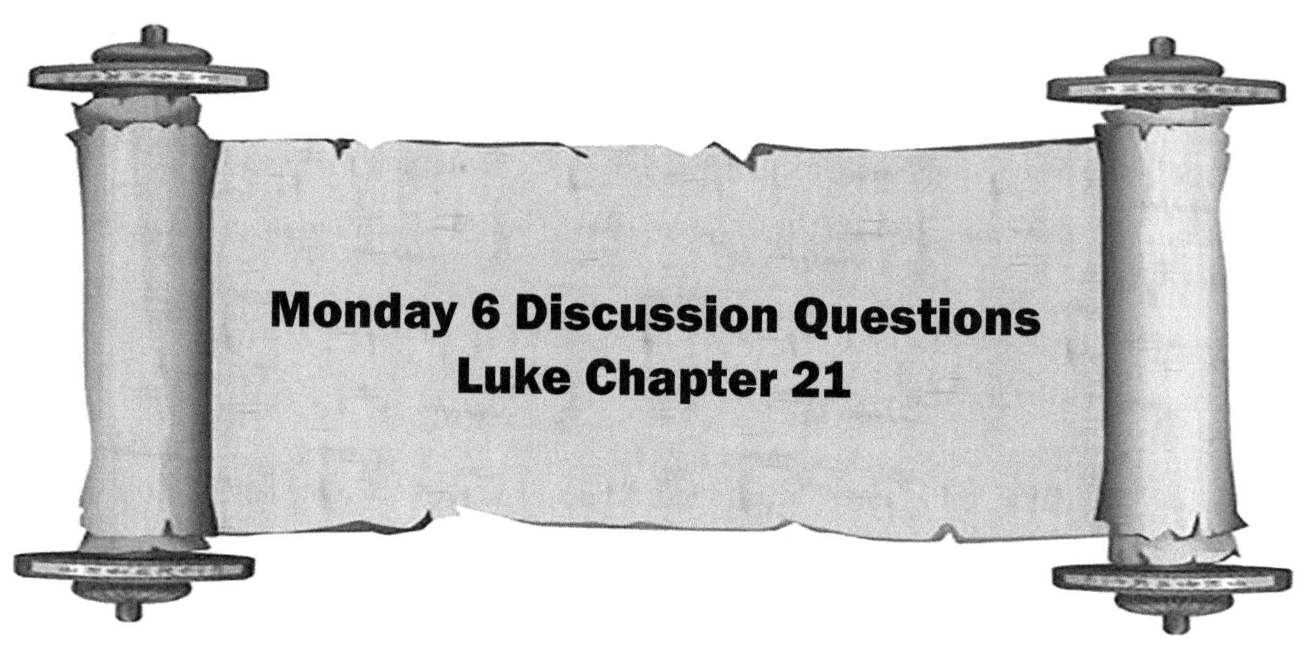

1. What did the Lord see the rich men doing, when he looked up?
2. Who else did he see casting in mites? How much did she cast in?
3. What did the Lord say about what she cast in?
4. How did the Lord answer the question of the people about the beautiful stones of the temple?
5. What did the Lord say to do when we hear of wars and commotions?
6. What did he say about the great signs from heaven?
7. What will happen before the signs for his name's sake, and turn to you for a testimony?
8. He said to settle it in your hearts and not to do what? Why?
9. Why did he say not to worry about what to answer?
10. He warns us that we will be hated. But, what did he promise us? What did he tell us to possess in our souls?

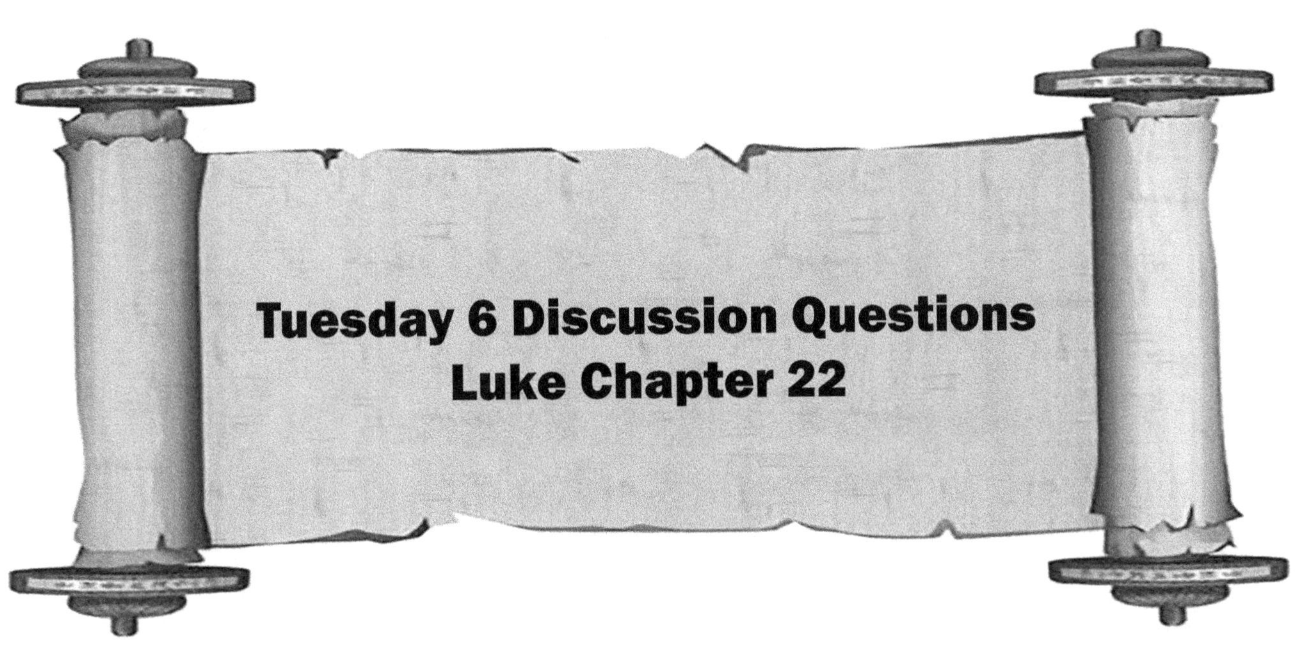

1. What is the feast of the unleavened bread called? __________

2. What were the chief priests and scribes seeking to do? __________

3. Which of the twelve disciples did Satan enter into ? __________

4. When he went to commune with the chief priest, what did they covenant to give him? __________

5. Who did Jesus send to prepare the passover? __________

6. How did Jesus describe the person that would meet the disciples when they enter the city? __________

7. What did Jesus desire to do with the disciples before he suffered? __________

8. What did the Lord tell Simon Satan planned to do to Simon? What did the Lord do for him? __________

9. Peter vowed his allegiance to God. What did the Lord say Peter would do? __________

10. How many swords did they present to the Lord? What did the Lord say to them? __________

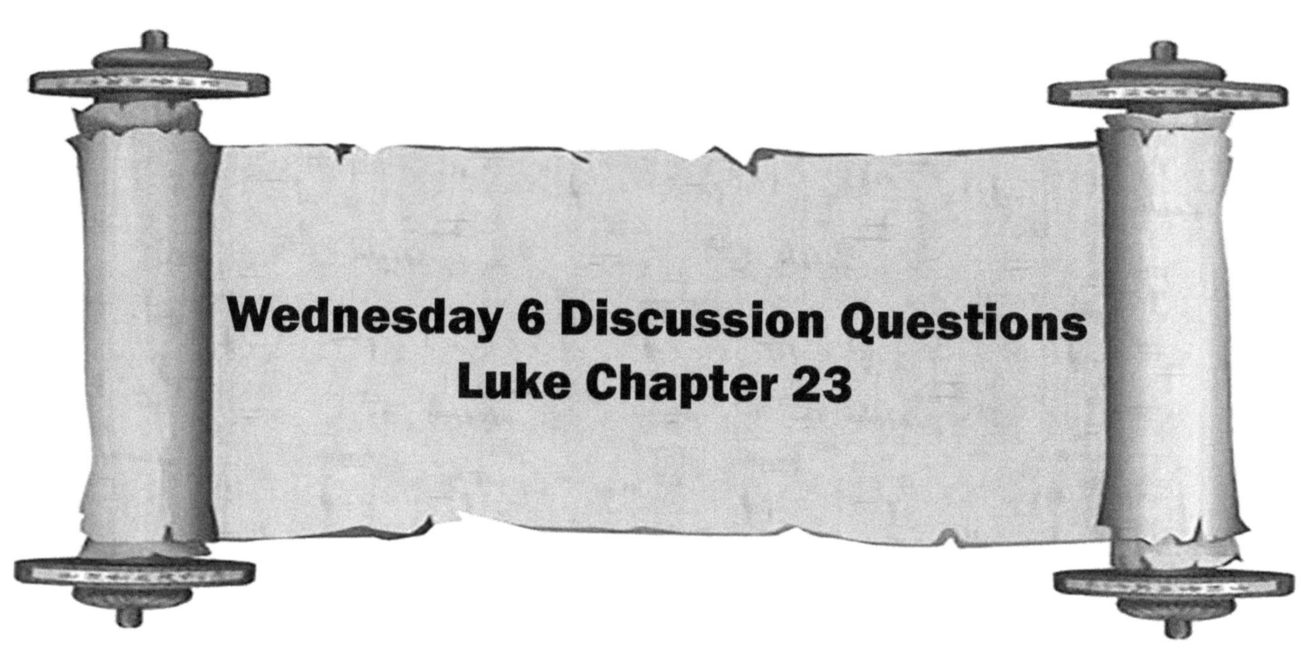

1. How many people led Jesus to Pilate? ______________________________

2. What were the people accusing Jesus of? ______________________________

3. What did Pilate ask Jesus and how did he answer? ______________________________

4. What did Pilate say to the chief priests and the people about Jesus? ______________________________

5. How did they respond? ______________________________

6. What did Pilate do when he found out Jesus was from King Herod's jurisdiction? ______________________________

7. Why was Herod so happy to see Jesus? ______________________________

8. What did Herod and his men do to Jesus before they sent him back to Pilate? ______________________________

9. Why didPilate say he would just chastise Jesus and set him free? ______________________________

10. How did the people respond to the decision Pilate made about Jesus? ______________________________

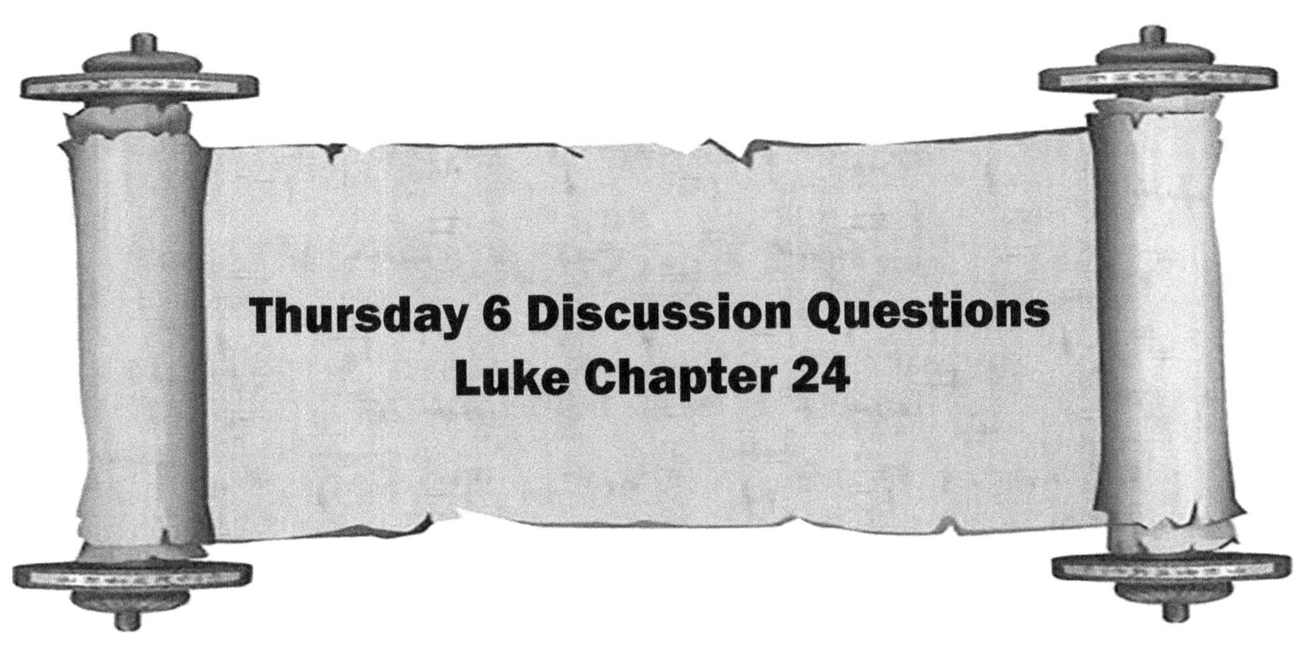

1. What day and time did the women take spices to the sepulcher? ____________________
2. What did they find when they entered the sepulcher? ____________________
3. What did they do and say when they saw the two men dressed in white? ____________________
4. What did they remind the women about what Jesus had told them? Did they remember? ____________________
5. Who was with Mary Magdalene when she went to tell the apostles what happened? ____________________
6. How did the apostles respond to the women's report?What did Peter do? ____________________
7. What was the name of the village the two men went to? ____________________
8. Did they recognize Jesus when he came near? ____________________
9. What did Cleopas tell the people the women did? ____________________

WEEKLY REVIEW
LUKE CHAPTERS 21-24

NAME THAT CHAPTER

1.______ JESUS NOTICED RICH MEN WHO WERE CASTING THEIR GIFTS INTO THE TREASURY AND THEN HE SAW A POOR WIDOW WOMAN CAST IN ONLY TWO MITES. BUT, ALTHOUGH SHE DIDN'T GIVE IN ABUNDANCE AS THEY WERE GIVING, SHE GAVE OUT OF HER PENURY, ALL THAT SHE HAD. JESUS MADE NOTE OF IT AND SAID TO THEM, "OF A TRUTH I SAY UNTO YOU, THAT THIS POOR WIDOW HATH CAST MORE THAN THEY ALL".

2.______ WHEN JESUS SAW THEY WERE AFRAID AND COULDN'T BELIEVE IT WAS HIM, AND THOUGHT THEY WERE SEEING A SPIRIT. HE TOLD THEM TO TOUCH HIS HANDS AND FEET TO SEE THAT HE WAS REAL, BECAUSE SPIRITS ARE NOT MADE OF FLESH AND BONES. THEY DID LOOK. MEANWHILE, HE ASKED FOR SOMETHING TO EAT. THEY GAVE HIM BROILED FISH AND HONEYCOMB. HE ATE AND THEN REMINDED THEM THAT HE WAS GOING TO SUFFER AND RISE ON THE THIRD DAY.

3.______ A GREAT COMPANY OF PEOPLE FOLLOWED THEM AS THEY LED JESUS AWAY. WOMEN BEWAILED AND LAMENTED HIM IN MUCH SORROW. JESUS TURNED TO THEM AND TOLD THEM NOT TO WEEP FOR HIM. HE TOLD THEM TO WEEP FOR THEMSELVES AND THEIR CHILDREN. HE SAID THE DAY WOULD COME THAT THEY WOULD SAY, "BLESSED ARE THE BARREN, AND THE WOMBS THAT NEVER BARE, AND THE PAPS WHICH NEVER GAVE SUCK.

4.______ JESUS ASKED THE CHIEF PRIESTS AND CAPTAINS OF THE TEMPLES WHY THEY WERE COMING AFTER HIM WITH SWORDS AND STAVES AS IF HE WERE A THIEF. HE REMINDED THEM HOW HE WAS WITH THEM DAILY IN THE TEMPLE. AS THEY LED HIM INTO THE HIGH PRIEST'S HOUSE, PETER SAT DOWN BY THE FIRE AND WAS NOTICED BY A MAID, HE DENIED IT. AFTER A WHILE, ANOTHER SAW HIM, HE DENIED IT AGAIN, AFTER AN HOUR HAD PASSED, A THIRD PERSON CONFIDENTLY AFFIRMED THAT HE WAS WITH JESUS. PETER DENIED IT FOR THE THIRD TIME AND IMMEDIATELY THE COCK DID CROW. JESUS LOOKED AT PETER AND PETER REMEMBERED WHAT JESUS HAD SAID. PETER WEPT BITTERLY.

TRUE OR FALSE

5. THE THE MEN SMOTE JESUS AND TOLD HIM TO PROPHECY AND TELL THEM WHO DID IT

____

6. JESUS SAID YOU SHALL BE HATED OF ALL MEN FOR MY SAKE. BUT NOT A HAIR OF YOUR HEAD SHALL PERISH.

____

7. WHEN THEY ENTERED THE TOMB, JESUS WAS GONE AND ANGELS FILLED THE ROOM TO EXPLAIN WHERE JESUS HAD GONE

____

FILL IN THE BLANKS

8. IN YOUR _____________ _____________YE YOUR_____________.
9. THEN SAID_____________TO THE CHIEF PRIESTS, AND TO THE _____________ I FIND NO_____________IN THIS MAN.
10. THIS POOR _____________ HATH _____________ IN MORE THAN _____________ ALL.

LUKE FINAL TEST
PART 1-COMPREHENSION

THERE ARE SEVERAL NEW VOCABULARY DEFINITIONS THAT WE ENCOUNTERED IN THE BOOK OF LUKE. YOUR INSTRUCTOR WILL CHOOSE 30 WORDS FOR YOU TO USE FOR THIS ASSIGNMENT:

To determine your comprehension of the VOCABULARY DEFINITIONS that we have studied in this book, please use the following words in a complete sentence of your own. Then tell what scripture the word occurs in. Please use the King James Version.

1)	16)
2)	17)
3)	18)
4)	19)
5)	20)
6)	21)
7)	22)
8)	23)
9)	24)
10)	25)
11)	26)
12)	27)
13)	28)
14)	29)
15)	30)

HOW TO WRITE A STANDARD SHORT ESSAY FOR DMWW INTERNATIONAL

Discipled Men and Women of Wisdom International practices formal essay writing to develop the art of informed persuasion, by combining two types of essay writings. They are the informative essay and the persuasive essay.

Our goal is to minister to others in a way that persuades them to walk in the truth as we know it, with fact based information from the Holy Bible and our personal experiences which relate to this information. You may also include outside sources that are credible as long as you cite anything you reference.

The element of persuasion according to Romans 8:38,39 ***"For I am persuaded that neither death, nor life, nor angels, nor principalities, nor powers,nor things present nor things to come, nor height, nor depth, nor any other creature shall be able to separate us from the Love of God, which is in Christ Jesus our Lord."*** is what takes place in the mind when one makes a conscious decision to follow Christ.

LUKE Essay
(Due by Midnight)

Write a three page essay that summarizes the book of LUKE. Make sure you check off each thing on the rubric list below, before turning it in, to ensure the best grade possible. This assignment is worth 300 points.

Essay includes a thesis statement and introduction paragraph	/ 50 pts
The student conveys full comprehension of the vocabulary definitions, by using at least 20 of the words correctly in this essay.	/ 50 pts
Student shows understanding and use of weekly discussion question information	/ 50 pts
Student Understands and demonstrates the purpose of the detailed instructions given to the Children of Israel in this book.	/ 50 pts
The student used information from the book of Exodus to show God's undying love for his people.	/ 50 pts
Student's closing includes call to action (salvation or repentance),	/ 50 pts

The following three blank pages are to be used to write your essay.

Name ______________________________
Time ______________________________
Date Due: __________________________

Essay Page 1

Essay Page 2

Essay Page 3

REFLECTIONS PAGE

This page is to keep a diary of how you felt when studying this book and what you learned or discovered in this class that helped you relate the Bible situations to situations in today's world. Jot down notes of spiritual revelations you received while studying the book of Luke that you may want to use in future messages you may preach.

The Study of THE BOOK OF JOHN

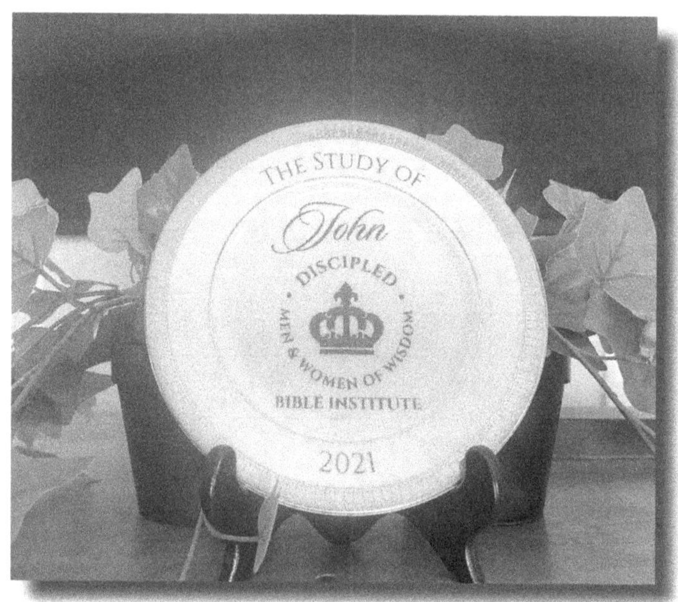

Begin Date______________________________

Course End Date__________________________________

Study Guide Prepared and Distributed by
The Discipled Men & Women of Wisdom, International

INTRODUCTION TO THE BOOK OF JOHN

Welcome to the study of the book of John, the fourth and final book in the volume we call "The Four Gospels". This book has 21 chapters and this class will last 5 weeks. After this class we will close this volume of studies in our journey through the word of God. You will receive a completion certificate from your instructor for "The Study of the Four Gospels" and be invited to join your fellow classmates in a virtual graduation online or in person if you are able to make the commute.

Although John is grouped with this set of books, it is quite different from the other three accounts given in Matthew, Mark and Luke. John is not just a disciple who traveled with the Lord on his journey. John is very apparently called by God to prepare the way of the Lord. This book, unlike the others, begins by giving description of the beginning times, creation and God. It also gives us vivid descriptions of John, what he wore, what he ate, the sound of his voice and what he said and did. It shares the importance of his calling to prepare the way of the Lord. He cried out in the wilderness for people to repent and he went forth baptizing them. John's role was so significant that people thought he was Jesus, although he never took credit for that.

As you continue to study with us, as we travel on this amazing journey through the word of God, you will experience different emotions, have multiple questions, and you may even have responded to certain situations on the travels with the disciples, in your mind. Feel free to examine those thoughts and share them with your class. You will start by using a bible dictionary to complete the vocabulary page. Then you will read one chapter per day Monday through Thursday and answer the corresponding questions. On Fridays, you will complete the weekly review and be prepared to meet with your instructor and classmates online for class participation on Saturday. Ready? Let's Get Started!

MY PRAYER JOURNAL

Please use this space to record your thoughts and feelings as you travel on this spirit led journey through the word of God with us. Please know that you have brothers and sisters in this organization from all over the world praying with and for you. My prayer for you is that you will begin to see the power of God resting in each set of your footprints. As you look back and examine your past in this journal, may you realize that you were never alone and according to Hebrews 13:5, God will never leave nor forsake you. ~LADY FLORA

I THESSALONIANS 5:17

THE STUDY OF THE FOUR GOSPELS VOCABULARY DEFINITIONS FOR JOHN CHAPTERS 1-4

WORD	DEFINITIONS
1) BOSOM	
2) FIRKINS	
3) MANIFEST	
4) PASSOVER	
5) SCOURGE	
6) ZEAL	
7) PERISH	
8) CONDEMNATION	
9) PERCEIVE	
10) MEAT	

DMWW DAILY BIBLE READING
JOHN CHAPTERS 1-4

CHAPTER 1

1. In the beginning was the Word, and the Word was with God, and the Word was God.
2. The same was in the beginning with God.
3. All things were made by him; and without him was not any thing made that was made.
4. In him was life; and the life was the light of men.
5. And the light shineth in darkness; and the darkness comprehended it not.
6. There was a man sent from God, whose name was John.
7. The same came for a witness, to bear witness of the Light, that all men through him might believe.
8. He was not that Light, but was sent to bear witness of that Light.
9. That was the true Light, which lighteth every man that cometh into the world.
10. He was in the world, and the world was made by him, and the world knew him not.
11. He came unto his own, and his own received him not.
12. But as many as received him, to them gave he power to become the sons of God, even to them that believe on his name:
13. Which were born, not of blood, nor of the will of the flesh, nor of the will of man, but of God.
14. And the Word was made flesh, and dwelt among us, (and we beheld his glory, the glory as of the only begotten of the Father,) full of grace and truth.
15. John bare witness of him, and cried, saying, This was he of whom I spake, He that cometh after me is preferred before me: for he was before me.
16. And of his fulness have all we received, and grace for grace.
17. For the law was given by Moses, but grace and truth came by Jesus Christ.
18. No man hath seen God at any time, the only begotten Son, which is in the bosom of the Father, he hath declared him.
19. And this is the record of John, when the Jews sent priests and Levites from Jerusalem to ask him, Who art thou?
20. And he confessed, and denied not; but confessed, I am not the Christ.

21. And they asked him, What then? Art thou Elias? And he saith, I am not. Art thou that prophet? And he answered, No.

22. Then said they unto him, Who art thou? that we may give an answer to them that sent us. What sayest thou of thyself?

23. He said, I am the voice of one crying in the wilderness, Make straight the way of the Lord, as said the prophet Esaias.

24. And they which were sent were of the Pharisees.

25. And they asked him, and said unto him, Why baptizest thou then, if thou be not that Christ, nor Elias, neither that prophet?

26. John answered them, saying, I baptize with water: but there standeth one among you, whom ye know not;

27. He it is, who coming after me is preferred before me, whose shoe's latchet I am not worthy to unloose.

28. These things were done in Bethabara beyond Jordan, where John was baptizing.

29. The next day John seeth Jesus coming unto him, and saith, Behold the Lamb of God, which taketh away the sin of the world.

30. This is he of whom I said, After me cometh a man which is preferred before me: for he was before me.

31. And I knew him not: but that he should be made manifest to Israel, therefore am I come baptizing with water.

32. And John bare record, saying, I saw the Spirit descending from heaven like a dove, and it abode upon him.

33. And I knew him not: but he that sent me to baptize with water, the same said unto me, Upon whom thou shalt see the Spirit descending, and remaining on him, the same is he which baptizeth with the Holy Ghost.

34. And I saw, and bare record that this is the Son of God.

35. Again the next day after John stood, and two of his disciples;

36. And looking upon Jesus as he walked, he saith, Behold the Lamb of God!

37. And the two disciples heard him speak, and they followed Jesus.

38. Then Jesus turned, and saw them following, and saith unto them, What seek ye? They said unto him, Rabbi, (which is to say, being interpreted, Master,) where dwellest thou?

39. He saith unto them, Come and see. They came and saw where he dwelt, and abode with him that day: for it was about the tenth hour.

40. One of the two which heard John speak, and followed him, was Andrew, Simon Peter's brother.

41. He first findeth his own brother Simon, and saith unto him, We have found the Messias, which is, being interpreted, the Christ.

42. And he brought him to Jesus. And when Jesus beheld him, he said, Thou art Simon the son of Jona: thou shalt be called Cephas, which is by interpretation, A stone.

43. The day following Jesus would go forth into Galilee, and findeth Philip, and saith unto him, Follow me.

44. Now Philip was of Bethsaida, the city of Andrew and Peter.

45. Philip findeth Nathanael, and saith unto him, We have found him, of whom Moses in the law, and the prophets, did write, Jesus of Nazareth, the son of Joseph.

46. And Nathanael said unto him, Can there any good thing come out of Nazareth? Philip saith unto him, Come and see.

47. Jesus saw Nathanael coming to him, and saith of him, Behold an Israelite indeed, in whom is no guile!

48. Nathanael saith unto him, Whence knowest thou me? Jesus answered and said unto him, Before that Philip called thee, when thou wast under the fig tree, I saw thee.

49. Nathanael answered and saith unto him, Rabbi, thou art the Son of God; thou art the King of Israel.

50. Jesus answered and said unto him, Because I said unto thee, I saw thee under the fig tree, believest thou? thou shalt see greater things than these.

51. And he saith unto him, Verily, verily, I say unto you, Hereafter ye shall see heaven open, and the angels of God ascending and descending upon the Son of man.

CHAPTER 2

1. And the third day there was a marriage in Cana of Galilee; and the mother of Jesus was there:

2. And both Jesus was called, and his disciples, to the marriage.

3. And when they wanted wine, the mother of Jesus saith unto him, They have no wine.

4. Jesus saith unto her, Woman, what have I to do with thee? mine hour is not yet come.

5. His mother saith unto the servants, Whatsoever he saith unto you, do it.

6. And there were set there six waterpots of stone, after the manner of the purifying of the Jews, containing two or three firkins apiece.

7. Jesus saith unto them, Fill the waterpots with water. And they filled them up to the brim.

8. And he saith unto them, Draw out now, and bear unto the governor of the feast. And they bare it.

9. When the ruler of the feast had tasted the water that was made wine, and knew not whence it was: (but the servants which drew the water knew;) the governor of the feast called the bridegroom,

10. And saith unto him, Every man at the beginning doth set forth good wine; and when men have well drunk, then that which is worse: but thou hast kept the good wine until now.

11. This beginning of miracles did Jesus in Cana of Galilee, and manifested forth his glory; and his disciples believed on him.

12. After this he went down to Capernaum, he, and his mother, and his brethren, and his disciples: and they continued there not many days.

13. And the Jews' passover was at hand, and Jesus went up to Jerusalem.

14. And found in the temple those that sold oxen and sheep and doves, and the changers of money sitting:

15. And when he had made a scourge of small cords, he drove them all out of the temple, and the sheep, and the oxen; and poured out the changers' money, and overthrew the tables;

16. And said unto them that sold doves, Take these things hence; make not my Father's house an house of merchandise.

17. And his disciples remembered that it was written, The zeal of thine house hath eaten me up.

18. Then answered the Jews and said unto him, What sign shewest thou unto us, seeing that thou doest these things?

19. Jesus answered and said unto them, Destroy this temple, and in three days I will raise it up.

20. Then said the Jews, Forty and six years was this temple in building, and wilt thou rear it up in three days?

21. But he spake of the temple of his body.

22. When therefore he was risen from the dead, his disciples remembered that he had said this unto them; and they believed the scripture, and the word which Jesus had said.

23. Now when he was in Jerusalem at the passover, in the feast day, many believed in his name, when they saw the miracles which he did.

24. But Jesus did not commit himself unto them, because he knew all men,

25. And needed not that any should testify of man: for he knew what was in man.

CHAPTER 3

1. There was a man of the Pharisees, named Nicodemus, a ruler of the Jews:

2. The same came to Jesus by night, and said unto him, Rabbi, we know that thou art a teacher come from God: for no man can do these miracles that thou doest, except God be with him.

3. Jesus answered and said unto him, Verily, verily, I say unto thee, Except a man be born again, he cannot see the kingdom of God.

4. Nicodemus saith unto him, How can a man be born when he is old? can he enter the second time into his mother's womb, and be born?

5. Jesus answered, Verily, verily, I say unto thee, Except a man be born of water and of the Spirit, he cannot enter into the kingdom of God.

6. That which is born of the flesh is flesh; and that which is born of the Spirit is spirit.

7. Marvel not that I said unto thee, Ye must be born again.

8. The wind bloweth where it listeth, and thou hearest the sound thereof, but canst not tell whence it cometh, and whither it goeth: so is every one that is born of the Spirit.

9. Nicodemus answered and said unto him, How can these things be?

10. Jesus answered and said unto him, Art thou a master of Israel, and knowest not these things?

11. Verily, verily, I say unto thee, We speak that we do know, and testify that we have seen; and ye receive not our witness.

12. If I have told you earthly things, and ye believe not, how shall ye believe, if I tell you of heavenly things?

13. And no man hath ascended up to heaven, but he that came down from heaven, even the Son of man which is in heaven.

14. And as Moses lifted up the serpent in the wilderness, even so must the Son of man be lifted up:

15. That whosoever believeth in him should not perish, but have eternal life.

16. For God so loved the world, that he gave his only begotten Son, that whosoever believeth in him should not perish, but have everlasting life.

17. For God sent not his Son into the world to condemn the world; but that the world through him might be saved.

18. He that believeth on him is not condemned: but he that believeth not is condemned already, because he hath not believed in the name of the only begotten Son of God.

19. And this is the condemnation, that light is come into the world, and men loved darkness rather than light, because their deeds were evil.

20. For every one that doeth evil hateth the light, neither cometh to the light, lest his deeds should be reproved.

21. But he that doeth truth cometh to the light, that his deeds may be made manifest, that they are wrought in God.

22. After these things came Jesus and his disciples into the land of Judaea; and there he tarried with them, and baptized.

23. And John also was baptizing in Aenon near to Salim, because there was much water there: and they came, and were baptized.

24. For John was not yet cast into prison.

25. Then there arose a question between some of John's disciples and the Jews about purifying.

26. And they came unto John, and said unto him, Rabbi, he that was with thee beyond Jordan, to whom thou barest witness, behold, the same baptizeth, and all men come to him.

27. John answered and said, A man can receive nothing, except it be given him from heaven.

28. Ye yourselves bear me witness, that I said, I am not the Christ, but that I am sent before him.

29. He that hath the bride is the bridegroom: but the friend of the bridegroom, which standeth and heareth him, rejoiceth greatly because of the bridegroom's voice: this my joy therefore is fulfilled.

30. He must increase, but I must decrease.

31. He that cometh from above is above all: he that is of the earth is earthly, and speaketh of the earth: he that cometh from heaven is above all.

32. And what he hath seen and heard, that he testifieth; and no man receiveth his testimony.

33. He that hath received his testimony hath set to his seal that God is true.

34. For he whom God hath sent speaketh the words of God: for God giveth not the Spirit by measure unto him.

35. The Father loveth the Son, and hath given all things into his hand.

36. He that believeth on the Son hath everlasting life: and he that believeth not the Son shall not see life; but the wrath of God abideth on him.

CHAPTER 4

1. When therefore the Lord knew how the Pharisees had heard that Jesus made and baptized more disciples than John,

2. (Though Jesus himself baptized not, but his disciples,)

3. He left Judaea, and departed again into Galilee.

4. And he must needs go through Samaria.

5. Then cometh he to a city of Samaria, which is called Sychar, near to the parcel of ground that Jacob gave to his son Joseph.

6. Now Jacob's well was there. Jesus therefore, being wearied with his journey, sat thus on the well: and it was about the sixth hour.

7. There cometh a woman of Samaria to draw water: Jesus saith unto her, Give me to drink.

8. (For his disciples were gone away unto the city to buy meat.)

9. Then saith the woman of Samaria unto him, How is it that thou, being a Jew, askest drink of me, which am a woman of Samaria? for the Jews have no dealings with the Samaritans.

10. Jesus answered and said unto her, If thou knewest the gift of God, and who it is that saith to thee, Give me to drink; thou wouldest have asked of him, and he would have given thee living water.

11. The woman saith unto him, Sir, thou hast nothing to draw with, and the well is deep: from whence then hast thou that living water?

12. Art thou greater than our father Jacob, which gave us the well, and drank thereof himself, and his children, and his cattle?

13. Jesus answered and said unto her, Whosoever drinketh of this water shall thirst again:

14. But whosoever drinketh of the water that I shall give him shall never thirst; but the water that I shall give him shall be in him a well of water springing up into everlasting life.

15. The woman saith unto him, Sir, give me this water, that I thirst not, neither come hither to draw.

16. Jesus saith unto her, Go, call thy husband, and come hither.

17. The woman answered and said, I have no husband. Jesus said unto her, Thou hast well said, I have no husband:

18. For thou hast had five husbands; and he whom thou now hast is not thy husband: in that saidst thou truly.

19. The woman saith unto him, Sir, I perceive that thou art a prophet.

20. Our fathers worshipped in this mountain; and ye say, that in Jerusalem is the place where men ought to worship.

21. Jesus saith unto her, Woman, believe me, the hour cometh, when ye shall neither in this mountain, nor yet at Jerusalem, worship the Father.

22. Ye worship ye know not what: we know what we worship: for salvation is of the Jews.

23. But the hour cometh, and now is, when the true worshippers shall worship the Father in spirit and in truth: for the Father seeketh such to worship him.

24. God is a Spirit: and they that worship him must worship him in spirit and in truth.

25. The woman saith unto him, I know that Messias cometh, which is called Christ: when he is come, he will tell us all things.

26. Jesus saith unto her, I that speak unto thee am he.

27. And upon this came his disciples, and marvelled that he talked with the woman: yet no man said, What seekest thou? or, Why talkest thou with her?

28. The woman then left her waterpot, and went her way into the city, and saith to the men,

29. Come, see a man, which told me all things that ever I did: is not this the Christ?

30. Then they went out of the city, and came unto him.

31. In the mean while his disciples prayed him, saying, Master, eat.

32. But he said unto them, I have meat to eat that ye know not of.

33. Therefore said the disciples one to another, Hath any man brought him ought to eat?

34. Jesus saith unto them, My meat is to do the will of him that sent me, and to finish his work.

35. Say not ye, There are yet four months, and then cometh harvest? behold, I say unto you, Lift up your eyes, and look on the fields; for they are white already to harvest.

36. And he that reapeth receiveth wages, and gathereth fruit unto life eternal: that both he that soweth and he that reapeth may rejoice together.

37. And herein is that saying true, One soweth, and another reapeth.

38. I sent you to reap that whereon ye bestowed no labour: other men laboured, and ye are entered into their labours.

39. And many of the Samaritans of that city believed on him for the saying of the woman, which testified, He told me all that ever I did.

40. So when the Samaritans were come unto him, they besought him that he would tarry with them: and he abode there two days.

41. And many more believed because of his own word;

42. And said unto the woman, Now we believe, not because of thy saying: for we have heard him ourselves, and know that this is indeed the Christ, the Saviour of the world.

43. Now after two days he departed thence, and went into Galilee.

44. For Jesus himself testified, that a prophet hath no honour in his own country.

45. Then when he was come into Galilee, the Galilaeans received him, having seen all the things that he did at Jerusalem at the feast: for they also went unto the feast.

46. So Jesus came again into Cana of Galilee, where he made the water wine. And there was a certain nobleman, whose son was sick at Capernaum.

47. When he heard that Jesus was come out of Judaea into Galilee, he went unto him, and besought him that he would come down, and heal his son: for he was at the point of death.

48. Then said Jesus unto him, Except ye see signs and wonders, ye will not believe.

49. The nobleman saith unto him, Sir, come down ere my child die.

50. Jesus saith unto him, Go thy way; thy son liveth. And the man believed the word that Jesus had spoken unto him, and he went his way.

51. And as he was now going down, his servants met him, and told him, saying, Thy son liveth.

52. Then enquired he of them the hour when he began to amend. And they said unto him, Yesterday at the seventh hour the fever left him.

53. So the father knew that it was at the same hour, in the which Jesus said unto him, Thy son liveth: and himself believed, and his whole house.

54. This is again the second miracle that Jesus did, when he was come out of Judaea into Galilee.

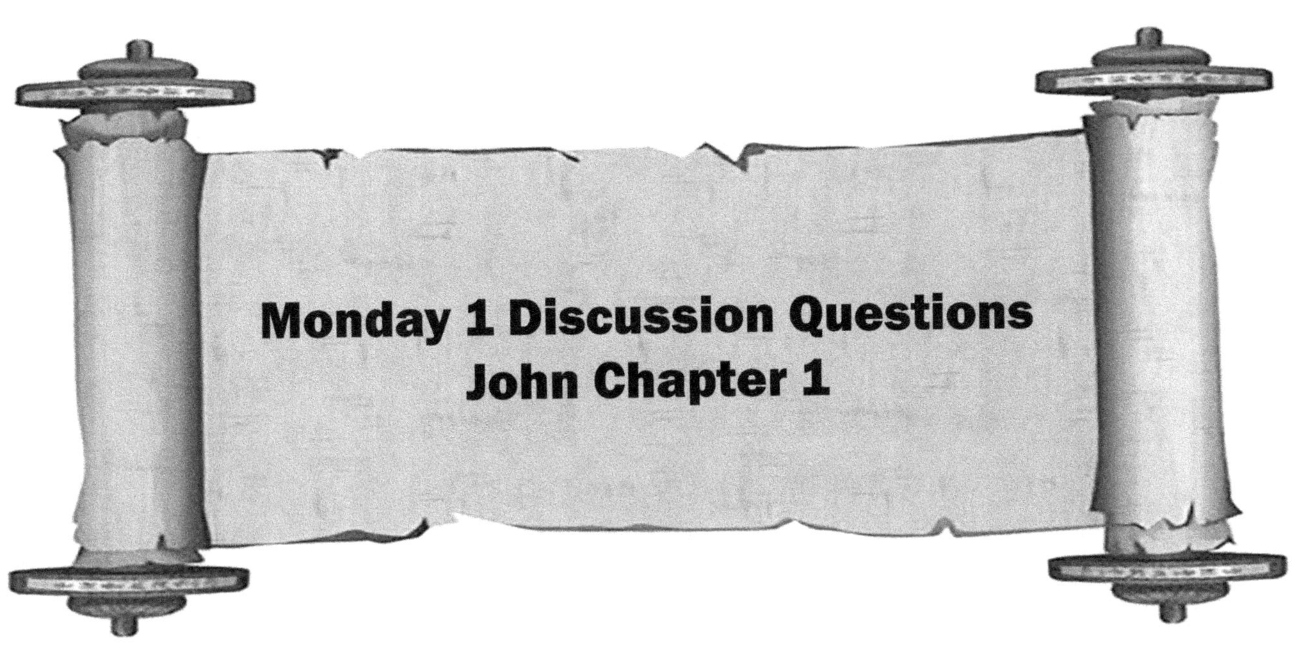

1. What was in the beginning? ______________________________

2. Who made all things? ______________________________

3. What happened when the light shined in the darkness? ______________________________

4. What was the name of the man sent by God in this chapter? ______________________________

5. What did the Lord give to those who received him? ______________________________

6. What was made into flesh? Where did it dwell? ______________________________

7. Who was the law given by? Who did truth and grace come by? ______________________________

8. When the people thought John was Jesus and he said he was not, they asked John who he was, what did he say? ______________________________

9. When John saw Jesus coming, what did he say? ______________________________

10. What happened when the two who were following Jesus asked him where he dwelled?
____

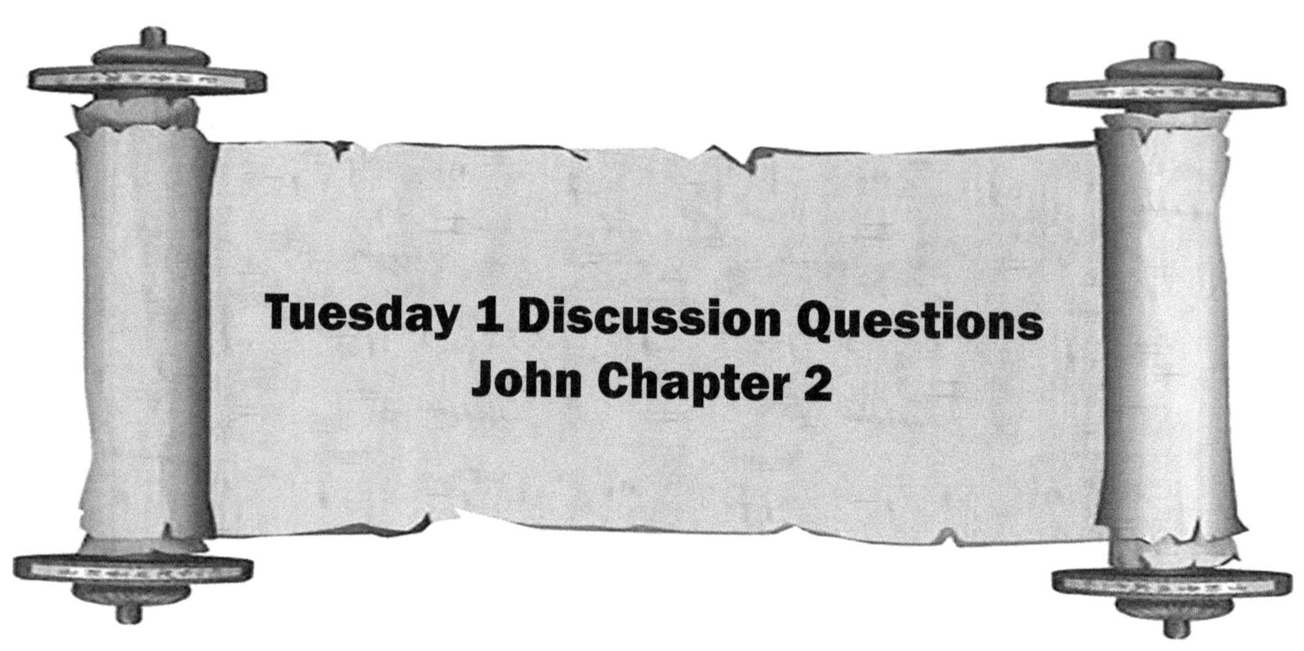

Tuesday 1 Discussion Questions
John Chapter 2

1. What was happening in Cana of Galilee on the third day?
2. Who was called to come with the disciples?
3. What did Jesus' mother say to him when they wanted wine? What was Jesus' response?
4. How many waterpots were there?
5. What did Jesus instruct them to do with the waterpots?
6. Whom did the governor call?
7. What did Jesus find sitting in the temple when he went to Jerusalem?
8. What did Jesus do when he saw them?
9. What did Jesus say to those who sold doves?
10. What did the Jews ask Jesus? What was his response?

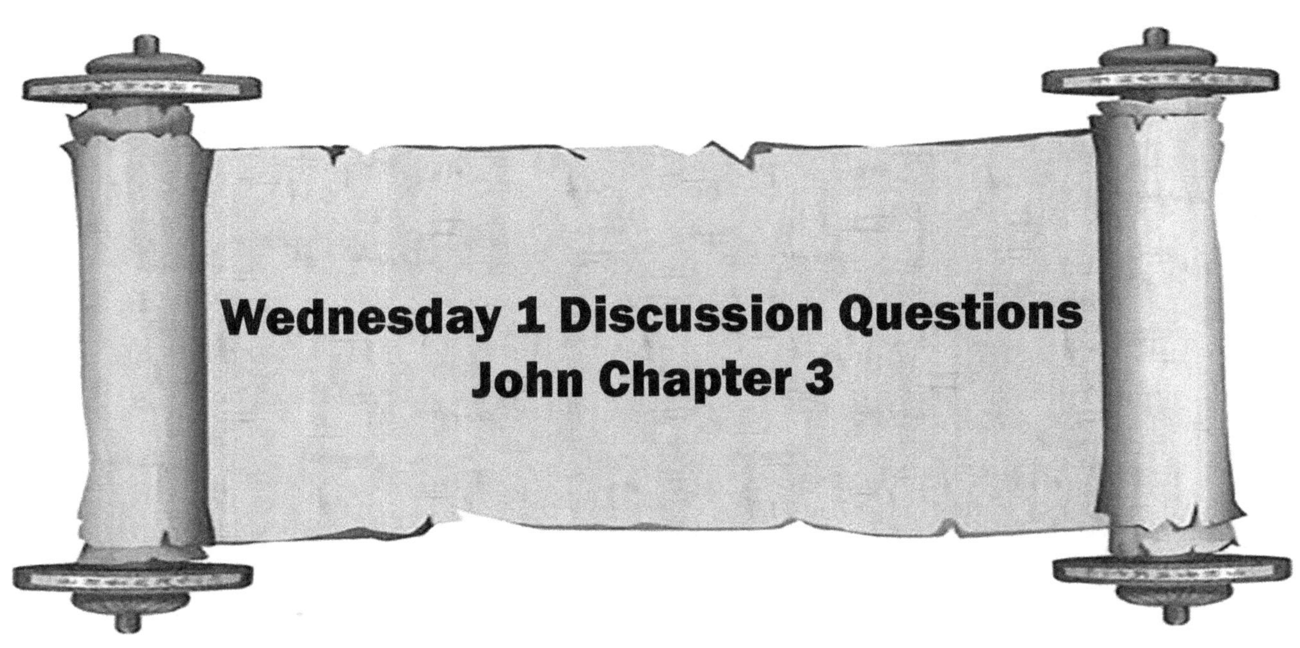

1. What was the name of the Pharisee who was the ruler of the Jews? ______

2. What did he ask Jesus about being born again? ______

3. What was Jesus' answer? ______

4. How did Jesus explain the difference between the flesh and the spirit? ______

5. What is promised to those who believe in Jesus? ______

6. What is the scripture that tells why God gave his son? ______

7. Jesus did not send his son to condemn the world. Why did he send him? ______

8. Who did he say was condemned already? Why? ______

9. What is the condemnation? ______

10. What did he say about those who do evil and those who do truth? ______

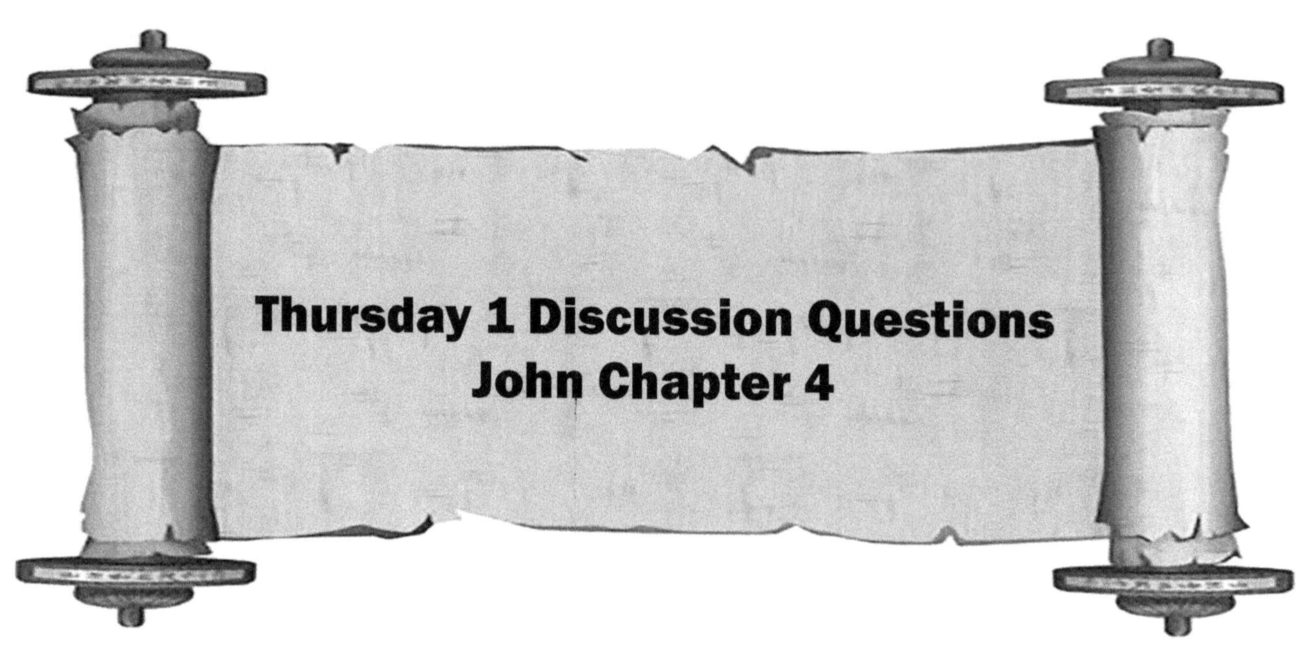

1. What did the Pharisees hear about the amount of people Jesus and John baptized and made disciples? ______________________________
2. Where did Jesus go when he departed from Judea? What town did he need to go through? ______________________________
3. Where was Jesus sitting, wearied from his journey at the sixth hour? ______________________________
4. What did Jesus ask the Samaritan woman to do? Why did he ask her to do it? ______________________________
5. What did Jesus tell the woman about those who drink from that well? ______________________________
6. What did Jesus say about those who drink the water that he gives him? ______________________________
7. What did the woman say when Jesus told her to call her husband and bring him? How did Jesus respond? ______________________________
8. Because God is a Spirit, how must we worship him? ______________________________
9. What did Jesus say when the woman said, "I know that Messias cometh, which is called Christ: when he is come, he will tell us all things? ______________________________
10. Where did the woman go and what did she say when she left the well and went into the city? ______________________________

WEEKLY REVIEW
JOHN CHAPTERS 1-4

NAME THAT CHAPTER

1.______ A RABBI NAMED NICODEMUS, TOLD JESUS HE KNEW THAT JESUS WAS A TEACHER SENT FROM GOD. JESUS TOLD HIM THAT EXCEPT A MAN BE BORN AGAIN, HE COULD NOT SEE THE KINGDOM OF GOD. NICODEMUS WAS CONFUSED AND ASKED HIM HOW A MAN COULD ENTER HIS MOTHER'S WOMB A SECOND TIME. JESUS EXPLAINED WHAT HE MEANT. EXCEPT A MAN BE BORN OF WATER AND OF THE SPIRIT, HE CAN'T ENTER THE KINGDOM OF GOD. THAT WHICH IS BORN OF THE SPIRIT IS OF THE SPIRIT AND THAT WHICH IS BORN OF THE FLESH IS FLESH.

2.______ JESUS'S MOTHER WAS ATTENDING A MARRIAGE IN CANA OF GALILEE. WHEN THEY ASKED FOR MORE WINE, SHE TOLD JESUS. JESUS TOLD HIS MOTHER THAT HIS TIME HAD NOT YET COME. SHE WENT BACK AND TOLD THE SERVANTS TO DO WHATEVER JESUS SAID TO DO. THEY DID. THERE WERE 6 STONE WATERPOTS. HE TOLD THEM TO FILL THEM AND THEY FILLED THEM TO THE BRIM. HE TOLD THEM TO DRAW FROM IT AND TAKE IT TO THE GOVERNOR OF THE FEAST. THE GOVERNOR SAW THAT IT HAD BEEN TURNED TO WINE AND HE WAS PLEASED.

3.______ JESUS CAME TO A PLACE CALLED SYCHAR, SAMARIA NEAR A PLACE JACOB GAVE TO JOSEPH. JESUS SAT DOWN TO REST WHERE JACOB'S WELL WAS LOCATED. IN THE SIXTH HOUR A SAMARITAN CAME THERE TO GET A DRINK. JESUS ASKED HER TO GIVE HIM A DRINK. SHE WAS ASTONISHED BECAUSE NORMALLY JEWS HAD NO DEALINGS WITH THE SAMARITANS. SHE EXPLAINED THAT IF SHE KNEW WHO HE WAS, SHE WOULD BE ASKING HIM FOR A DRINK AND HE WOULD GIVE HER LIVING WATER. SHE MISUNDERSTOOD HIM AND TOLD HIM HE HAD NOTHING TO DRAW WATER WITH. HE EXPLAINED TO HER THAT WHOSOEVER DRINKS OF THE WATER HE GIVES WILL NEVER THIRST AGAIN. BUT THE WATER HE GIVES WILL IN HIM A WELL OF WATER SPRINGING UP INTO EVERLASTING LIFE.

4.______ THIS CHAPTER WENT PRETTY DEEP INTO THE MEATIER THINGS OF GOD. I WANT TO TAKE MY TIME TO BREAK THIS PARTICULAR CHAPTER DOWN SO THAT NONE OF OUR STUDENTS GET CHOKED. IF YOU HAVE QUESTIONS, PLEASE FEEL FREE TO ASK. THAT IS WHAT THIS BIBLE INSTITUTE IS ALL ABOUT.

1) The end of verse 1 clearly says "The Word" so that we understand exactly what and who the Bible is talking about. It says "THE WORD WAS WITH GOD"

2) In verse 2 and 3, John begins to explain more about his statements in verse 1. He is still talking about the word. He is explaining that the word was with God from the beginning. This is to say that "THE WORD WAS ALWAYS WITH GOD" IT WAS THERE WITH GOD FROM THE START AND IT CAME FROM INSIDE GOD. It was always God's intention that it be written. He thought it all out before he began to create.

3) Verse 3 explains how he began to create and that he created everything and without him nothing was created. He knew people would someday question the fact that he created everything. So, he was sure to have it written that he did it and nothing was created without him.

There was no Big Bang and no Evolution. It was all God's doing.

4) Now to clarify further. John would not be telling us Jesus created everything. It would be impossible because Jesus as we know him was not yet introduced to the scene.

He had not yet been born "In the beginning". So, he did not create. Jesus job was not to create. That was God's job. When Jesus came, his whole purpose for coming was to save the lost.

5) The reason God had to take on the form of man by creating himself in a body was because he could not dwell in the uncleanness of this world.

6) In verses 4 and 5, it explains that even after God created himself in the form of man and went down to earth to save man. He was now the light of the world and the darkness of the world didn't understand and accept him.

7) In verses 6 and 7, it tells us that God sent John to be witness of Jesus as the light. So, that a human being of the world could testify of who Jesus really was.

TRUE OR FALSE

5. IN JERUSALEM AT THE FEAST MANY BELIEVED IN JESUS BECAUSE THEY SAW HIS MIRACLES. BUT JESUS DIDN'T COMMIT TO THEM BECAUSE HE DIDN'T NEED ANYONE TO TESTIFY, HE KNEW WHAT WAS IN MAN.

____

6. JESUS TOLD NICODEMUS THAT THE SON OF MAN HAS TO BE LIFTED UP FROM THE EARTH JUST AS MOSES LIFTED UP THE SERPENT IN THE WILDERNESS.

____

7. WHEN THE SAMARITAN WOMAN TOLD JESUS SHE HAD NO HUSBAND, HE SAID YOU HAVE HAD FIVE HUSBANDS AND THE ONE YOU HAVE NOW IS NOT YOURS.

____

FILL IN THE BLANKS

8. And the light ____________ in darkness; and the ____________ ____________ it not.
9. ____________ not that I said unto thee, Ye ____________ be ____________ again.
10. But he ____________ of the ____________ of his ____________.

MY PRAYER JOURNAL

Please use this space to record your thoughts and feelings as you travel on this spirit led journey through the word of God with us. Please know that you have brothers and sisters in this organization from all over the world praying with and for you. My prayer for you is that you will begin to see the power of God resting in each set of your footprints. As you look back and examine your past in this journal, may you realize that you were never alone and according to Hebrews 13:5, God will never leave nor forsake you. ~LADY FLORA

I THESSALONIANS 5:17

THE STUDY OF THE FOUR GOSPELS VOCABULARY DEFINITIONS FOR JOHN CHAPTERS 5-8

WORD	DEFINITIONS
1) LAD	
2) BARLEY	
3) FURLONGS	
4) QUICKEN	
5) DOCTRINE	
6) CIRCUMCISION	
7) DISPERSED	
8) TABERNACLE	
9) SYNAGOGUE	
10)CONVEY	

DMWW DAILY BIBLE READING
JOHN CHAPTERS 5-8

CHAPTER 5

1. After this there was a feast of the Jews; and Jesus went up to Jerusalem.
2. Now there is at Jerusalem by the sheep market a pool, which is called in the Hebrew tongue Bethesda, having five porches.
3. In these lay a great multitude of impotent folk, of blind, halt, withered, waiting for the moving of the water.
4. For an angel went down at a certain season into the pool, and troubled the water: whosoever then first after the troubling of the water stepped in was made whole of whatsoever disease he had.
5. And a certain man was there, which had an infirmity thirty and eight years.
6. When Jesus saw him lie, and knew that he had been now a long time in that case, he saith unto him, Wilt thou be made whole?
7. The impotent man answered him, Sir, I have no man, when the water is troubled, to put me into the pool: but while I am coming, another steppeth down before me.
8. Jesus saith unto him, Rise, take up thy bed, and walk.
9. And immediately the man was made whole, and took up his bed, and walked: and on the same day was the sabbath.
10. The Jews therefore said unto him that was cured, It is the sabbath day: it is not lawful for thee to carry thy bed.
11. He answered them, He that made me whole, the same said unto me, Take up thy bed, and walk.
12. Then asked they him, What man is that which said unto thee, Take up thy bed, and walk? 13 And he that was healed wist not who it was: for Jesus had conveyed himself away, a multitude being in that place.
13. Afterward Jesus findeth him in the temple, and said unto him, Behold, thou art made whole: sin no more, lest a worse thing come unto thee.
14. The man departed, and told the Jews that it was Jesus, which had made him whole.
15. And therefore did the Jews persecute Jesus, and sought to slay him, because he had done these things on the sabbath day.
16. But Jesus answered them, My Father worketh hitherto, and I work.

17. Therefore the Jews sought the more to kill him, because he not only had broken the sabbath, but said also that God was his Father, making himself equal with God.

18. Then answered Jesus and said unto them, Verily, verily, I say unto you, The Son can do nothing of himself, but what he seeth the Father do: for what things soever he doeth, these also doeth the Son likewise.

19. For the Father loveth the Son, and sheweth him all things that himself doeth: and he will shew him greater works than these, that ye may marvel.

20. For as the Father raiseth up the dead, and quickeneth them; even so the Son quickeneth whom he will.

21. For the Father judgeth no man, but hath committed all judgment unto the Son:

22. That all men should honour the Son, even as they honour the Father. He that honoureth not the Son honoureth not the Father which hath sent him.

23. Verily, verily, I say unto you, He that heareth my word, and believeth on him that sent me, hath everlasting life, and shall not come into condemnation; but is passed from death unto life.

24. Verily, verily, I say unto you, The hour is coming, and now is, when the dead shall hear the voice of the Son of God: and they that hear shall live.

25. For as the Father hath life in himself; so hath he given to the Son to have life in himself;

26. And hath given him authority to execute judgment also, because he is the Son of man.

27. Marvel not at this: for the hour is coming, in the which all that are in the graves shall hear his voice,

28. And shall come forth; they that have done good, unto the resurrection of life; and they that have done evil, unto the resurrection of damnation.

29. I can of mine own self do nothing: as I hear, I judge: and my judgment is just; because I seek not mine own will, but the will of the Father which hath sent me.

30. If I bear witness of myself, my witness is not true.

31. There is another that beareth witness of me; and I know that the witness which he witnesseth of me is true.

32. Ye sent unto John, and he bare witness unto the truth.

33. But I receive not testimony from man: but these things I say, that ye might be saved.

34. He was a burning and a shining light: and ye were willing for a season to rejoice in his light. 36 But I have greater witness than that of John: for the works which the Father hath given me to finish, the same works that I do, bear witness of me, that the Father hath sent me.

35. And the Father himself, which hath sent me, hath borne witness of me. Ye have neither heard his voice at any time, nor seen his shape.

36. And ye have not his word abiding in you: for whom he hath sent, him ye believe not.

37. Search the scriptures; for in them ye think ye have eternal life: and they are they which testify of me.

38. And ye will not come to me, that ye might have life.

39. I receive not honour from men.

40. But I know you, that ye have not the love of God in you.

41. I am come in my Father's name, and ye receive me not: if another shall come in his own name, him ye will receive.

42. How can ye believe, which receive honour one of another, and seek not the honour that cometh from God only?

43. Do not think that I will accuse you to the Father: there is one that accuseth you, even Moses, in whom ye trust.

44. For had ye believed Moses, ye would have believed me; for he wrote of me.

45. But if ye believe not his writings, how shall ye believe my words?

CHAPTER 6

1. After these things Jesus went over the sea of Galilee, which is the sea of Tiberias.

2. And a great multitude followed him, because they saw his miracles which he did on them that were diseased.

3. And Jesus went up into a mountain, and there he sat with his disciples.

4. And the passover, a feast of the Jews, was nigh.

5. When Jesus then lifted up his eyes, and saw a great company come unto him, he saith unto Philip, Whence shall we buy bread, that these may eat?

6. And this he said to prove him: for he himself knew what he would do.

7. Philip answered him, Two hundred pennyworth of bread is not sufficient for them, that every one of them may take a little.

8. One of his disciples, Andrew, Simon Peter's brother, saith unto him,

9. There is a lad here, which hath five barley loaves, and two small fishes: but what are they among so many?

10. And Jesus said, Make the men sit down. Now there was much grass in the place. So the men sat down, in number about five thousand.

11. And Jesus took the loaves; and when he had given thanks, he distributed to the disciples, and the disciples to them that were set down; and likewise of the fishes as much as they would.

12. When they were filled, he said unto his disciples, Gather up the fragments that remain, that nothing be lost.

13. Therefore they gathered them together, and filled twelve baskets with the fragments of the five barley loaves, which remained over and above unto them that had eaten.

14. Then those men, when they had seen the miracle that Jesus did, said, This is of a truth that prophet that should come into the world.

15. When Jesus therefore perceived that they would come and take him by force, to make him a king, he departed again into a mountain himself alone.

16. And when even was now come, his disciples went down unto the sea,

17. And entered into a ship, and went over the sea toward Capernaum. And it was now dark, and Jesus was not come to them.

18. And the sea arose by reason of a great wind that blew.

19. So when they had rowed about five and twenty or thirty furlongs, they see Jesus walking on the sea, and drawing nigh unto the ship: and they were afraid.

20. But he saith unto them, It is I; be not afraid.

21. Then they willingly received him into the ship: and immediately the ship was at the land whither they went.

22. The day following, when the people which stood on the other side of the sea saw that there was none other boat there, save that one whereinto his disciples were entered, and that Jesus went not with his disciples into the boat, but that his disciples were gone away alone;

23. (Howbeit there came other boats from Tiberias nigh unto the place where they did eat bread, after that the Lord had given thanks:)

24. When the people therefore saw that Jesus was not there, neither his disciples, they also took shipping, and came to Capernaum, seeking for Jesus.

25. And when they had found him on the other side of the sea, they said unto him, Rabbi, when camest thou hither?

26. Jesus answered them and said, Verily, verily, I say unto you, Ye seek me, not because ye saw the miracles, but because ye did eat of the loaves, and were filled.

27. Labour not for the meat which perisheth, but for that meat which endureth unto everlasting life, which the Son of man shall give unto you: for him hath God the Father sealed.

28. Then said they unto him, What shall we do, that we might work the works of God?

29. Jesus answered and said unto them, This is the work of God, that ye believe on him whom he hath sent.

30. They said therefore unto him, What sign shewest thou then, that we may see, and believe thee? what dost thou work?

31. Our fathers did eat manna in the desert; as it is written, He gave them bread from heaven to eat.

32. Then Jesus said unto them, Verily, verily, I say unto you, Moses gave you not that bread from heaven; but my Father giveth you the true bread from heaven.

33. For the bread of God is he which cometh down from heaven, and giveth life unto the world.

34. Then said they unto him, Lord, evermore give us this bread.

35. And Jesus said unto them, I am the bread of life: he that cometh to me shall never hunger; and he that believeth on me shall never thirst.

36. But I said unto you, That ye also have seen me, and believe not.

37. All that the Father giveth me shall come to me; and him that cometh to me I will in no wise cast out.

38. For I came down from heaven, not to do mine own will, but the will of him that sent me.

39. And this is the Father's will which hath sent me, that of all which he hath given me I should lose nothing, but should raise it up again at the last day.

40. And this is the will of him that sent me, that every one which seeth the Son, and believeth on him, may have everlasting life: and I will raise him up at the last day.

41. The Jews then murmured at him, because he said, I am the bread which came down from heaven.

42. And they said, Is not this Jesus, the son of Joseph, whose father and mother we know? how is it then that he saith, I came down from heaven?

43. Jesus therefore answered and said unto them, Murmur not among yourselves.

44. No man can come to me, except the Father which hath sent me draw him: and I will raise him up at the last day.

45. It is written in the prophets, And they shall be all taught of God. Every man therefore that hath heard, and hath learned of the Father, cometh unto me.

46. Not that any man hath seen the Father, save he which is of God, he hath seen the Father.

47. Verily, verily, I say unto you, He that believeth on me hath everlasting life.

48. I am that bread of life.

49. Your fathers did eat manna in the wilderness, and are dead.

50. This is the bread which cometh down from heaven, that a man may eat thereof, and not die.

51. I am the living bread which came down from heaven: if any man eat of this bread, he shall live for ever: and the bread that I will give is my flesh, which I will give for the life of the world.

52. The Jews therefore strove among themselves, saying, How can this man give us his flesh to eat?

53. Then Jesus said unto them, Verily, verily, I say unto you, Except ye eat the flesh of the Son of man, and drink his blood, ye have no life in you.

54. Whoso eateth my flesh, and drinketh my blood, hath eternal life; and I will raise him up at the last day.

55. For my flesh is meat indeed, and my blood is drink indeed.

56. He that eateth my flesh, and drinketh my blood, dwelleth in me, and I in him.

57. As the living Father hath sent me, and I live by the Father: so he that eateth me, even he shall live by me.

58. This is that bread which came down from heaven: not as your fathers did eat manna, and are dead: he that eateth of this bread shall live for ever.

59. These things said he in the synagogue, as he taught in Capernaum.

60. Many therefore of his disciples, when they had heard this, said, This is an hard saying; who can hear it?

61. When Jesus knew in himself that his disciples murmured at it, he said unto them, Doth this offend you?

62. What and if ye shall see the Son of man ascend up where he was before?

63. It is the spirit that quickeneth; the flesh profiteth nothing: the words that I speak unto you, they are spirit, and they are life.

64. But there are some of you that believe not. For Jesus knew from the beginning who they were that believed not, and who should betray him.

65. And he said, Therefore said I unto you, that no man can come unto me, except it were given unto him of my Father.

66. From that time many of his disciples went back, and walked no more with him.

67. Then said Jesus unto the twelve, Will ye also go away?

68. Then Simon Peter answered him, Lord, to whom shall we go? thou hast the words of eternal life.

69. And we believe and are sure that thou art that Christ, the Son of the living God.

70. Jesus answered them, Have not I chosen you twelve, and one of you is a devil?

71. He spake of Judas Iscariot the son of Simon: for he it was that should betray him, being one of the twelve.

CHAPTER 7

1. After these things Jesus walked in Galilee: for he would not walk in Jewry, because the Jews sought to kill him.

2. Now the Jew's feast of tabernacles was at hand.

3. His brethren therefore said unto him, Depart hence, and go into Judaea, that thy disciples also may see the works that thou doest.

4. For there is no man that doeth any thing in secret, and he himself seeketh to be known openly. If thou do these things, shew thyself to the world.

5. For neither did his brethren believe in him.

6. Then Jesus said unto them, My time is not yet come: but your time is alway ready.

7. The world cannot hate you; but me it hateth, because I testify of it, that the works thereof are evil.

8. Go ye up unto this feast: I go not up yet unto this feast: for my time is not yet full come.

9. When he had said these words unto them, he abode still in Galilee.

10. But when his brethren were gone up, then went he also up unto the feast, not openly, but as it were in secret.

11. Then the Jews sought him at the feast, and said, Where is he?

12. And there was much murmuring among the people concerning him: for some said, He is a good man: others said, Nay; but he deceiveth the people.

13. Howbeit no man spake openly of him for fear of the Jews.

14. Now about the midst of the feast Jesus went up into the temple, and taught.

15. And the Jews marvelled, saying, How knoweth this man letters, having never learned?

16. Jesus answered them, and said, My doctrine is not mine, but his that sent me.

17. If any man will do his will, he shall know of the doctrine, whether it be of God, or whether I speak of myself.

18. He that speaketh of himself seeketh his own glory: but he that seeketh his glory that sent him, the same is true, and no unrighteousness is in him.

19. Did not Moses give you the law, and yet none of you keepeth the law? Why go ye about to kill me?

20. The people answered and said, Thou hast a devil: who goeth about to kill thee?

21. Jesus answered and said unto them, I have done one work, and ye all marvel.

22. Moses therefore gave unto you circumcision; (not because it is of Moses, but of the fathers;) and ye on the sabbath day circumcise a man.

23. If a man on the sabbath day receive circumcision, that the law of Moses should not be broken; are ye angry at me, because I have made a man every whit whole on the sabbath day?

24. Judge not according to the appearance, but judge righteous judgment.

25. Then said some of them of Jerusalem, Is not this he, whom they seek to kill?

26. But, lo, he speaketh boldly, and they say nothing unto him. Do the rulers know indeed that this is the very Christ?

27. Howbeit we know this man whence he is: but when Christ cometh, no man knoweth whence he is.

28. Then cried Jesus in the temple as he taught, saying, Ye both know me, and ye know whence I am: and I am not come of myself, but he that sent me is true, whom ye know not.

29. But I know him: for I am from him, and he hath sent me.

30. Then they sought to take him: but no man laid hands on him, because his hour was not yet come.

31. And many of the people believed on him, and said, When Christ cometh, will he do more miracles than these which this man hath done?

32. The Pharisees heard that the people murmured such things concerning him; and the Pharisees and the chief priests sent officers to take him.

33. Then said Jesus unto them, Yet a little while am I with you, and then I go unto him that sent me.

34. Ye shall seek me, and shall not find me: and where I am, thither ye cannot come.

35. Then said the Jews among themselves, Whither will he go, that we shall not find him? will he go unto the dispersed among the Gentiles, and teach the Gentiles?

36. What manner of saying is this that he said, Ye shall seek me, and shall not find me: and where I am, thither ye cannot come?

37. In the last day, that great day of the feast, Jesus stood and cried, saying, If any man thirst, let him come unto me, and drink.

38. He that believeth on me, as the scripture hath said, out of his belly shall flow rivers of living water.

39. (But this spake he of the Spirit, which they that believe on him should receive: for the Holy Ghost was not yet given; because that Jesus was not yet glorified.)

40. Many of the people therefore, when they heard this saying, said, Of a truth this is the Prophet.

41. Others said, This is the Christ. But some said, Shall Christ come out of Galilee?

42. Hath not the scripture said, That Christ cometh of the seed of David, and out of the town of Bethlehem, where David was?

43. So there was a division among the people because of him.

44. And some of them would have taken him; but no man laid hands on him.

45. Then came the officers to the chief priests and Pharisees; and they said unto them, Why have ye not brought him?

46. The officers answered, Never man spake like this man.

47. Then answered them the Pharisees, Are ye also deceived?

48. Have any of the rulers or of the Pharisees believed on him?

49. But this people who knoweth not the law are cursed.

50. Nicodemus saith unto them, (he that came to Jesus by night, being one of them,)

51. Doth our law judge any man, before it hear him, and know what he doeth?

52. They answered and said unto him, Art thou also of Galilee? Search, and look: for out of Galilee ariseth no prophet.

53. And every man went unto his own house.

CHAPTER 8

1. Jesus went unto the mount of Olives.

2. And early in the morning he came again into the temple, and all the people came unto him; and he sat down, and taught them.

3. And the scribes and Pharisees brought unto him a woman taken in adultery; and when they had set her in the midst,

4. They say unto him, Master, this woman was taken in adultery, in the very act.

5. Now Moses in the law commanded us, that such should be stoned: but what sayest thou?

6. This they said, tempting him, that they might have to accuse him. But Jesus stooped down, and with his finger wrote on the ground, as though he heard them not.

7. So when they continued asking him, he lifted up himself, and said unto them, He that is without sin among you, let him first cast a stone at her.

8. And again he stooped down, and wrote on the ground.

9. And they which heard it, being convicted by their own conscience, went out one by one, beginning at the eldest, even unto the last: and Jesus was left alone, and the woman standing in the midst.

10. When Jesus had lifted up himself, and saw none but the woman, he said unto her, Woman, where are those thine accusers? hath no man condemned thee?

11. She said, No man, Lord. And Jesus said unto her, Neither do I condemn thee: go, and sin no more.

12. Then spake Jesus again unto them, saying, I am the light of the world: he that followeth me shall not walk in darkness, but shall have the light of life.

13. The Pharisees therefore said unto him, Thou bearest record of thyself; thy record is not true.

14. Jesus answered and said unto them, Though I bear record of myself, yet my record is true: for I know whence I came, and whither I go; but ye cannot tell whence I come, and whither I go.

15. Ye judge after the flesh; I judge no man.

16. And yet if I judge, my judgment is true: for I am not alone, but I and the Father that sent me.

17. It is also written in your law, that the testimony of two men is true.

18. I am one that bear witness of myself, and the Father that sent me beareth witness of me.

19. Then said they unto him, Where is thy Father? Jesus answered, Ye neither know me, nor my Father: if ye had known me, ye should have known my Father also.

20. These words spake Jesus in the treasury, as he taught in the temple: and no man laid hands on him; for his hour was not yet come.

21. Then said Jesus again unto them, I go my way, and ye shall seek me, and shall die in your sins: whither I go, ye cannot come.

22. Then said the Jews, Will he kill himself? because he saith, Whither I go, ye cannot come.

23. And he said unto them, Ye are from beneath; I am from above: ye are of this world; I am not of this world.

24. I said therefore unto you, that ye shall die in your sins: for if ye believe not that I am he, ye shall die in your sins.

25. Then said they unto him, Who art thou? And Jesus saith unto them, Even the same that I said unto you from the beginning.

26. I have many things to say and to judge of you: but he that sent me is true; and I speak to the world those things which I have heard of him.

27. They understood not that he spake to them of the Father.

28. Then said Jesus unto them, When ye have lifted up the Son of man, then shall ye know that I am he, and that I do nothing of myself; but as my Father hath taught me, I speak these things.

29. And he that sent me is with me: the Father hath not left me alone; for I do always those things that please him.

30. As he spake these words, many believed on him.

31. Then said Jesus to those Jews which believed on him, If ye continue in my word, then are ye my disciples indeed;

32. And ye shall know the truth, and the truth shall make you free.

33. They answered him, We be Abraham's seed, and were never in bondage to any man: how sayest thou, Ye shall be made free?

34. Jesus answered them, Verily, verily, I say unto you, Whosoever committeth sin is the servant of sin.

35. And the servant abideth not in the house for ever: but the Son abideth ever.

36. If the Son therefore shall make you free, ye shall be free indeed.

37. I know that ye are Abraham's seed; but ye seek to kill me, because my word hath no place in you.

38. I speak that which I have seen with my Father: and ye do that which ye have seen with your father.

39. They answered and said unto him, Abraham is our father. Jesus saith unto them, If ye were Abraham's children, ye would do the works of Abraham.

40. But now ye seek to kill me, a man that hath told you the truth, which I have heard of God: this did not Abraham.

41. Ye do the deeds of your father. Then said they to him, We be not born of fornication; we have one Father, even God.

42. Jesus said unto them, If God were your Father, ye would love me: for I proceeded forth and came from God; neither came I of myself, but he sent me.

43. Why do ye not understand my speech? even because ye cannot hear my word.

44. Ye are of your father the devil, and the lusts of your father ye will do. He was a murderer from the beginning, and abode not in the truth, because there is no truth in him. When he speaketh a lie, he speaketh of his own: for he is a liar, and the father of it.

45. And because I tell you the truth, ye believe me not.

46. Which of you convinceth me of sin? And if I say the truth, why do ye not believe me?

47. He that is of God heareth God's words: ye therefore hear them not, because ye are not of God.

48. Then answered the Jews, and said unto him, Say we not well that thou art a Samaritan, and hast a devil?

49. Jesus answered, I have not a devil; but I honour my Father, and ye do dishonour me.

50. And I seek not mine own glory: there is one that seeketh and judgeth.

51. Verily, verily, I say unto you, If a man keep my saying, he shall never see death.

52. Then said the Jews unto him, Now we know that thou hast a devil. Abraham is dead, and the prophets; and thou sayest, If a man keep my saying, he shall never taste of death.

53. Art thou greater than our father Abraham, which is dead? and the prophets are dead: whom makest thou thyself?

54. Jesus answered, If I honour myself, my honour is nothing: it is my Father that honoureth me; of whom ye say, that he is your God:

55. Yet ye have not known him; but I know him: and if I should say, I know him not, I shall be a liar like unto you: but I know him, and keep his saying.

56. Your father Abraham rejoiced to see my day: and he saw it, and was glad.

57. Then said the Jews unto him, Thou art not yet fifty years old, and hast thou seen Abraham?

58. Jesus said unto them, Verily, verily, I say unto you, Before Abraham was, I am.

59. Then took they up stones to cast at him: but Jesus hid himself, and went out of the temple, going through the midst of them, and so passed by.

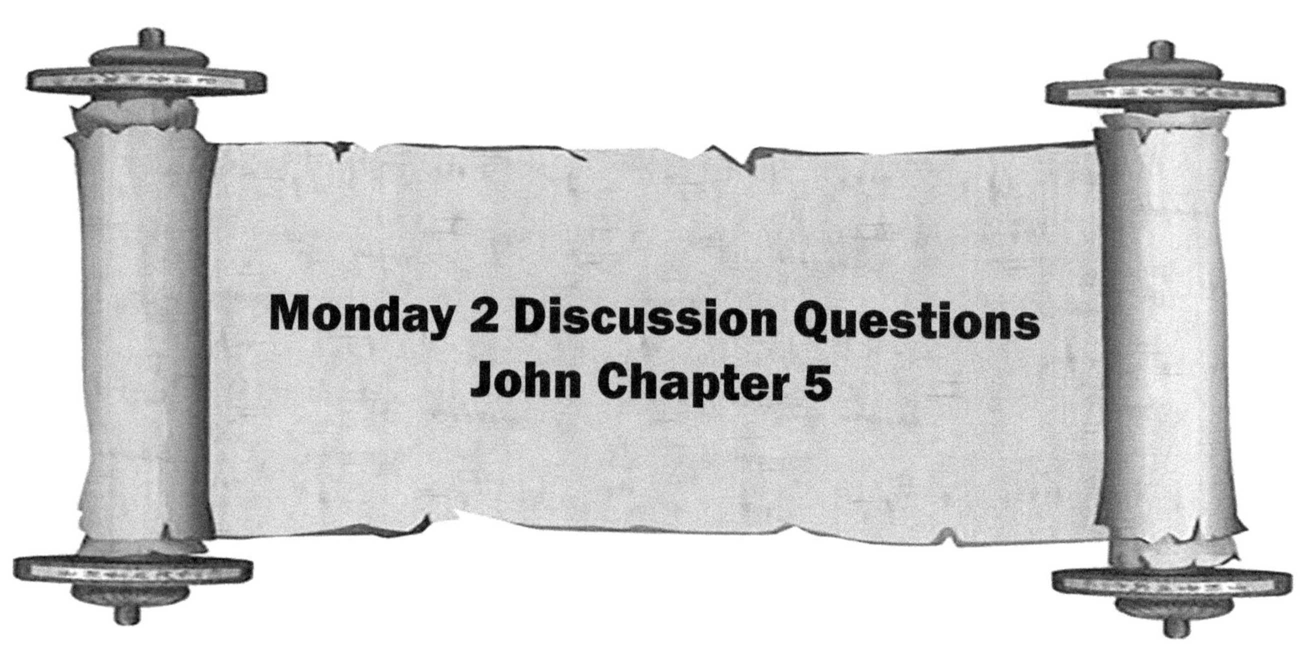

1. What is the name of the pool beside the sheep market? How many porches did it have? ______

2. Who was laying at the pool? Why? ______

3. At a certain season, an angel went down and troubled the water. What happened after the troubling of the water? ______

4. How long had the man with the infirmity been waiting by the pool? ______

5. What was his infirmity? ______

6. What did Jesus say about those who drink the water that he gives him? ______

7. What did the woman say when Jesus told her to call her husband and bring him? How did Jesus respond? ______

8. What was Jesus' response? ______

9. After Jesus healed him and found him in the temple, what did he say to him? ______

10. What did the man do when he departed? ______

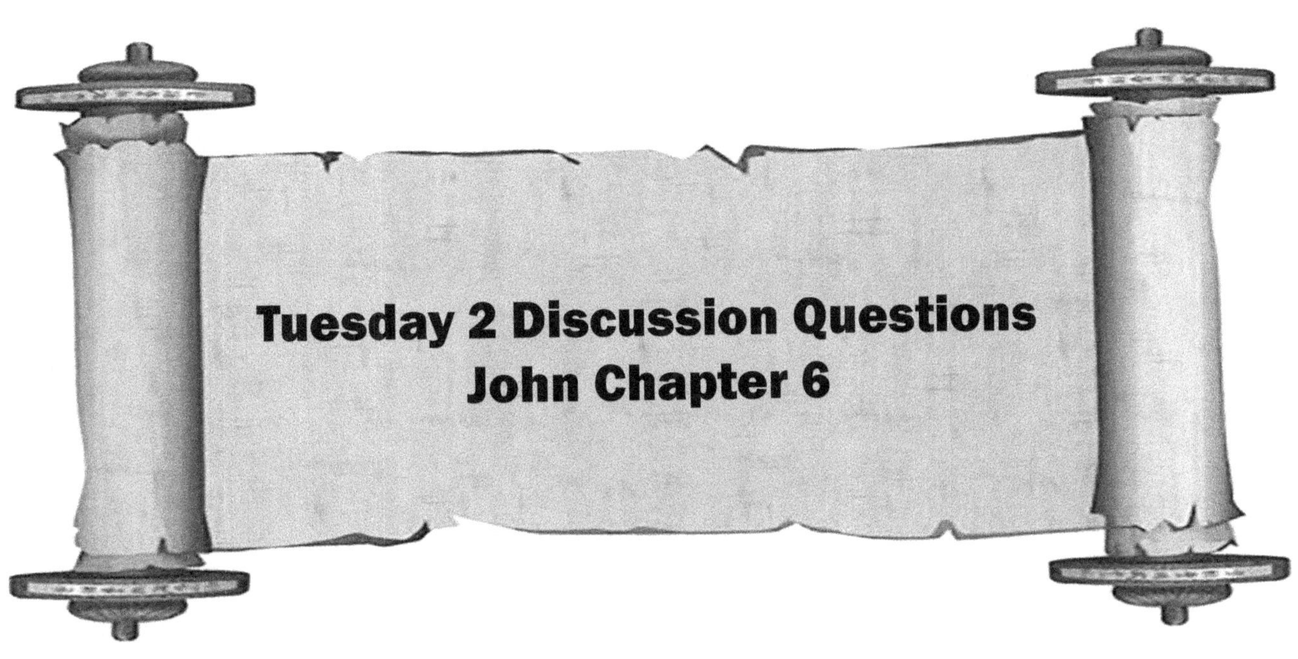

1. What sea did Jesus go over in the beginning of this chapter? What was this sea also called? ______

2. Why was the multitude following Jesus? ______

3. Where did Jesus go to sit with his disciples? ______

4. When Jesus looked up and saw the multitude, what did he ask Philip? Why did he ask him that? ______

5. What did Andrew suggest? What did he ask about his suggestion? ______

6. What did Jesus tell Andrew and the disciples to do? ______

7. How many men sat down? ______

8. What did Jesus do when the 5,000 sat down on the grass? ______

9. Were they able to feed everyone with the boy's lunch? How much was leftover after feeding everyone? ______

10. What did the men say when they witnessed this miracle? ______

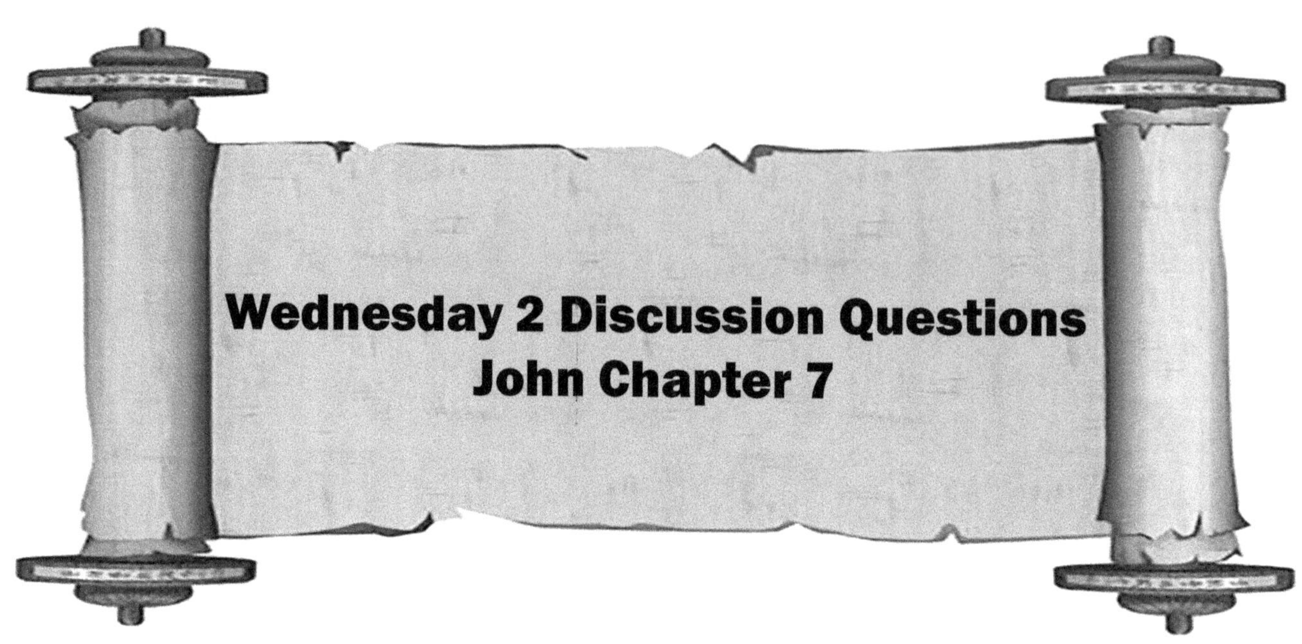

1. Why did Jesus walk in Galilee and not in Jewry? ______________________________

2. Where did his brethren tell him to depart and go into Judea? ______________________________

3. What was Jesus' response? ______________________________

4. Why did the Lord say the world hated him? ______________________________

5. Why did the jews marvel when they saw Jesus in the temple teaching? ______________________________

6. How did Jesus respond to their question? ______________________________

7. What is the difference in one who seeks his own glory and one who is true to the one who sent him? ______________________________

8. How did he tell them to judge rather than by appearance? ______________________________

9. What did Jesus cry out on the day of the feast? ______________________________

10. What did he promise for those who believe on him as the scripture has said it? ______________________________

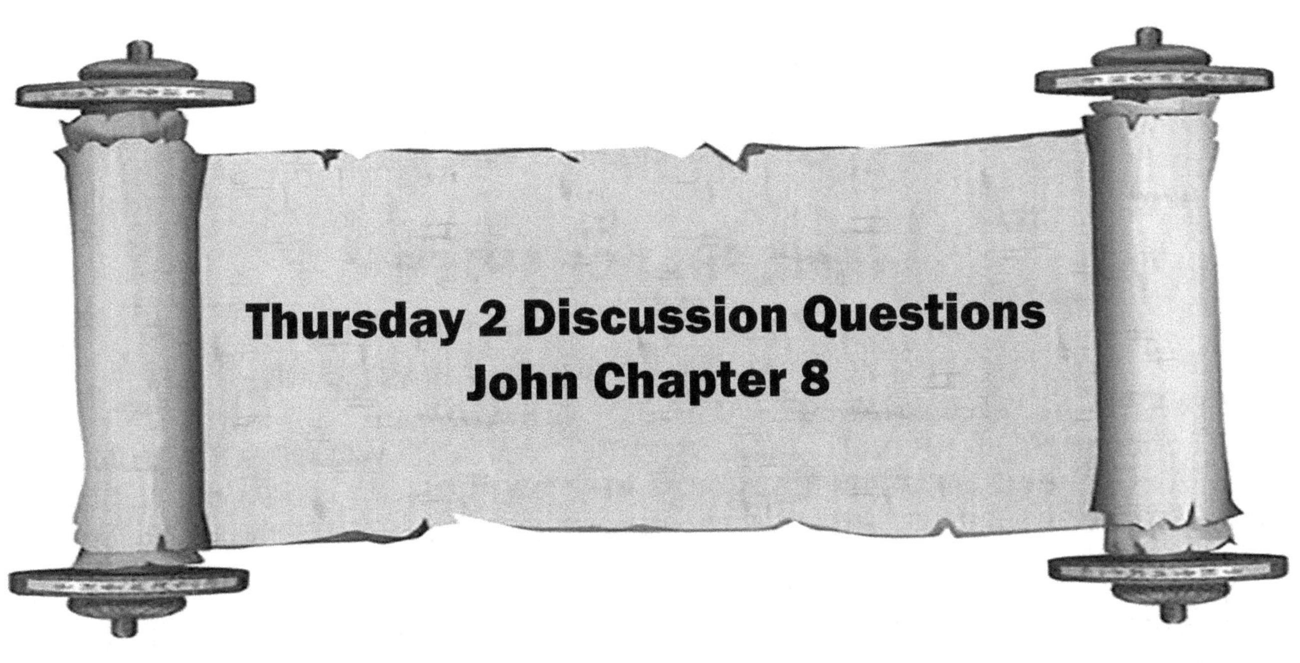

Thursday 2 Discussion Questions
John Chapter 8

1. Where did Jesus go in this chapter?

2. What happened early in the morning when he went into the temple?

3. Who did the scribes and Pharisees take in to him?

4. Why did they say to Jesus, "Now Moses in the law commanded us, that such should be stoned: but what sayest thou"?

5. How did Jesus respond to them?

6. What did Jesus say when they continued asking him?

7. What did the accusers do when Jesus wrote on the ground a second time?

8. What did the woman say when Jesus told her to call her husband and bring him? How did Jesus respond?

9. When Jesus stood up what did he ask the woman?

10. When she answered Jesus, what did he say to her and command her to do?

WEEKLY REVIEW
JOHN CHAPTERS 5-8

NAME THAT CHAPTER

1.______ A WOMAN WHO WAS TAKEN IN ADULTERY WAS BROUGHT TO JESUS BY THE SCRIBES AND THE PHARISEES. THEY TOLD HIM MOSES COMMANDMENT WAS THAT SHE MUST BE STONED. JESUS KNELT DOWN AND WROTE SOMETHING IN THE SAND AS IF HE DID NOT HEAR THEM. THEY KEPT ASKING JESUS WHAT TO DO. JESUS SAID TO THEM, LET HIM WHO IS WITHOUT SIN CAST THE FIRST STONE.

2.______ THERE WAS A GREAT MURMURING AMONG THE PEOPLE ABOUT JESUS. THEY DID NOT AGREE ON WHO HE WAS. SOME SAID HE WAS A GREAT MAN, BUT SOME SAID HE WAS A DECEIVER. JESUS BEGAN TO TEACH IN THE TEMPLE IN THE MIDST OF THE FEAST. PEOPLE STARTED TO ASK HOW HE KNEW LETTERS WHEN HE NEVER HAD BEEN TAUGHT. HE EXPLAINED THAT THE DOCTRINE WAS NOT HIS OWN. IT WAS FROM GOD.

3.______ JESUS EXPLAINS WHO HE IS AND SAYS, "I am the living bread which came down from heaven: if any man eat of this bread, he shall live forever: and the bread that I will give is my flesh, which I will give for the life of the world." THE JEWS WERE CONFUSED SAYING HOW CAN THIS MAN GIVE US HIS FLESH TO EAT. JESUS ANSWERED THEM SAYING, "Verily, verily, I say unto you, Except ye eat the flesh of the Son of man, and drink his blood, ye have no life in you. Whoso eateth my flesh, and drinketh my blood, hath eternal life; and I will raise him up at the last day."

4.______ THERE WAS A POOL BY THE SHEEP MARKET IN JERUSALEM. MANY PEOPLE WITH INFIRMITIES AND AFFLICTIONS WENT THERE TO BE HEALED WHEN THE ANGEL WOULD COME TO TROUBLE THE WATERS. WHEN JESUS CAME BY HE SAW A BLIND MAN WHO HAD BEEN INFIRMITY 38 YEARS LAYING THERE. HE ASKED HIM, "WILT THOU BE MADE WHOLE?" HE TOLD JESUS HE HAD NO MAN TO PUT HIM IN THE WATER WHEN IT IS TROUBLED. JESUS TOLD HIM TO TAKE UP HIS BED AND WALK. HE WAS IMMEDIATELY HEALED.

TRUE OR FALSE

5. THE POOL WITH 5 PORCHES WAS CALLED BETHESDA

____

6. WHEN THE PHARISEES TOLD JESUS MOSES COMMANDED THEM TO STONE THE WOMAN FOR ADULTERY, THEY WANTED TO TEMPT JESUS TO ACCUSE HIM.

____

7. WHEN THE MAN FROM THE POOL AND TOOK UP HIS BED TO WALK, HE WAS TOLD IT WAS NOT LAWFUL FOR HIM TO CARRY HIS BED.

FILL IN THE BLANKS

8. Then Jesus said unto them, My _____________ is not yet_____________: but your time is alway_____________.

9. And_____________went up into a_____________, and there he sat with his_____________.

10. As he_____________these words, many _____________on_____________.

MY PRAYER JOURNAL

Please use this space to record your thoughts and feelings as you travel on this spirit led journey through the word of God with us. Please know that you have brothers and sisters in this organization from all over the world praying with and for you. My prayer for you is that you will begin to see the power of God resting in each set of your footprints. As you look back and examine your past in this journal, may you realize that you were never alone and according to Hebrews 13:5, God will never leave nor forsake you. ~LADY FLORA

I THESSALONIANS 5:17

THE STUDY OF THE FOUR GOSPELS VOCABULARY DEFINITIONS FOR JOHN CHAPTERS 9-12

WORD	DEFINITIONS
1) MANIFEST	
2) SILOAM	
3) CONFESS	
4) REVILE	
5) SHEEPFOLD	
6) HIRELING	
7) DIDYMUS	
8) PREVAIL	
9) EXPEDIENT	
10) SPIKENARD	

DMWW DAILY BIBLE READING
JOHN CHAPTERS 9-12

CHAPTER 9

1. And as Jesus passed by, he saw a man which was blind from his birth.
2. And his disciples asked him, saying, Master, who did sin, this man, or his parents, that he was born blind?
3. Jesus answered, Neither hath this man sinned, nor his parents: but that the works of God should be made manifest in him.
4. I must work the works of him that sent me, while it is day: the night cometh, when no man can work.
5. As long as I am in the world, I am the light of the world.
6. When he had thus spoken, he spat on the ground, and made clay of the spittle, and he anointed the eyes of the blind man with the clay,
7. And said unto him, Go, wash in the pool of Siloam, (which is by interpretation, Sent.) He went his way therefore, and washed, and came seeing.
8. The neighbours therefore, and they which before had seen him that he was blind, said, Is not this he that sat and begged?
9. Some said, This is he: others said, He is like him: but he said, I am he.
10. Therefore said they unto him, How were thine eyes opened?
11. He answered and said, A man that is called Jesus made clay, and anointed mine eyes, and said unto me, Go to the pool of Siloam, and wash: and I went and washed, and I received sight.
12. Then said they unto him, Where is he? He said, I know not.
13. They brought to the Pharisees him that aforetime was blind.
14. And it was the sabbath day when Jesus made the clay, and opened his eyes.
15. Then again the Pharisees also asked him how he had received his sight. He said unto them, He put clay upon mine eyes, and I washed, and do see.
16. Therefore said some of the Pharisees, This man is not of God, because he keepeth not the sabbath day. Others said, How can a man that is a sinner do such miracles? And there was a division among them.
17. They say unto the blind man again, What sayest thou of him, that he hath opened thine eyes? He said, He is a prophet.

18. But the Jews did not believe concerning him, that he had been blind, and received his sight, until they called the parents of him that had received his sight.

19. And they asked them, saying, Is this your son, who ye say was born blind? how then doth he now see?

20. His parents answered them and said, We know that this is our son, and that he was born blind:

21. But by what means he now seeth, we know not; or who hath opened his eyes, we know not: he is of age; ask him: he shall speak for himself.

22. These words spake his parents, because they feared the Jews: for the Jews had agreed already, that if any man did confess that he was Christ, he should be put out of the synagogue.

23. Therefore said his parents, He is of age; ask him.

24. Then again called they the man that was blind, and said unto him, Give God the praise: we know that this man is a sinner.

25. He answered and said, Whether he be a sinner or no, I know not: one thing I know, that, whereas I was blind, now I see.

26. Then said they to him again, What did he to thee? how opened he thine eyes?

27. He answered them, I have told you already, and ye did not hear: wherefore would ye hear it again? will ye also be his disciples?

28. Then they reviled him, and said, Thou art his disciple; but we are Moses' disciples.

29. We know that God spake unto Moses: as for this fellow, we know not from whence he is.

30. The man answered and said unto them, Why herein is a marvellous thing, that ye know not from whence he is, and yet he hath opened mine eyes.

31. Now we know that God heareth not sinners: but if any man be a worshipper of God, and doeth his will, him he heareth.

32. Since the world began was it not heard that any man opened the eyes of one that was born blind.

33. If this man were not of God, he could do nothing.

34. They answered and said unto him, Thou wast altogether born in sins, and dost thou teach us? And they cast him out.

35. Jesus heard that they had cast him out; and when he had found him, he said unto him, Dost thou believe on the Son of God?

36. He answered and said, Who is he, Lord, that I might believe on him?

37. And Jesus said unto him, Thou hast both seen him, and it is he that talketh with thee.

38. And he said, Lord, I believe. And he worshipped him.

39. And Jesus said, For judgment I am come into this world, that they which see not might see; and that they which see might be made blind.

40. And some of the Pharisees which were with him heard these words, and said unto him, Are we blind also?

41. Jesus said unto them, If ye were blind, ye should have no sin: but now ye say, We see; therefore your sin remaineth.

CHAPTER 10

1. Verily, verily, I say unto you, He that entereth not by the door into the sheepfold, but climbeth up some other way, the same is a thief and a robber.

2. But he that entereth in by the door is the shepherd of the sheep.

3. To him the porter openeth; and the sheep hear his voice: and he calleth his own sheep by name, and leadeth them out.

4. And when he putteth forth his own sheep, he goeth before them, and the sheep follow him: for they know his voice.

5. And a stranger will they not follow, but will flee from him: for they know not the voice of strangers.

6. This parable spake Jesus unto them: but they understood not what things they were which he spake unto them.

7. Then said Jesus unto them again, Verily, verily, I say unto you, I am the door of the sheep.

8. All that ever came before me are thieves and robbers: but the sheep did not hear them.

9. I am the door: by me if any man enter in, he shall be saved, and shall go in and out, and find pasture.

10. The thief cometh not, but for to steal, and to kill, and to destroy: I am come that they might have life, and that they might have it more abundantly.

11. I am the good shepherd: the good shepherd giveth his life for the sheep.

12. But he that is an hireling, and not the shepherd, whose own the sheep are not, seeth the wolf coming, and leaveth the sheep, and fleeth: and the wolf catcheth them, and scattereth the sheep.

13. The hireling fleeth, because he is an hireling, and careth not for the sheep.

14. I am the good shepherd, and know my sheep, and am known of mine.

15. As the Father knoweth me, even so know I the Father: and I lay down my life for the sheep.

16. And other sheep I have, which are not of this fold: them also I must bring, and they shall hear my voice; and there shall be one fold, and one shepherd.

17. Therefore doth my Father love me, because I lay down my life, that I might take it again.

18. No man taketh it from me, but I lay it down of myself. I have power to lay it down, and I have power to take it again. This commandment have I received of my Father.

19. There was a division therefore again among the Jews for these sayings.

20. And many of them said, He hath a devil, and is mad; why hear ye him?

21. Others said, These are not the words of him that hath a devil. Can a devil open the eyes of the blind?

22. And it was at Jerusalem the feast of the dedication, and it was winter.

23. And Jesus walked in the temple in Solomon's porch.

24. Then came the Jews round about him, and said unto him, How long dost thou make us to doubt? If thou be the Christ, tell us plainly.

25. Jesus answered them, I told you, and ye believed not: the works that I do in my Father's name, they bear witness of me.

26. But ye believe not, because ye are not of my sheep, as I said unto you.

27. My sheep hear my voice, and I know them, and they follow me:

28. And I give unto them eternal life; and they shall never perish, neither shall any man pluck them out of my hand.

29. My Father, which gave them me, is greater than all; and no man is able to pluck them out of my Father's hand.

30. I and my Father are one.

31. Then the Jews took up stones again to stone him.

32. Jesus answered them, Many good works have I shewed you from my Father; for which of those works do ye stone me?

33. The Jews answered him, saying, For a good work we stone thee not; but for blasphemy; and because that thou, being a man, makest thyself God.

34. Jesus answered them, Is it not written in your law, I said, Ye are gods?

35. If he called them gods, unto whom the word of God came, and the scripture cannot be broken;

36. Say ye of him, whom the Father hath sanctified, and sent into the world, Thou blasphemest; because I said, I am the Son of God?

37. If I do not the works of my Father, believe me not.

38. But if I do, though ye believe not me, believe the works: that ye may know, and believe, that the Father is in me, and I in him.

39. Therefore they sought again to take him: but he escaped out of their hand,

40. And went away again beyond Jordan into the place where John at first baptized; and there he abode.

41. And many resorted unto him, and said, John did no miracle: but all things that John spake of this man were true.

42. And many believed on him there.

CHAPTER 11

1. Now a certain man was sick, named Lazarus, of Bethany, the town of Mary and her sister Martha.

2. (It was that Mary which anointed the Lord with ointment, and wiped his feet with her hair, whose brother Lazarus was sick.)

3. Therefore his sisters sent unto him, saying, Lord, behold, he whom thou lovest is sick.

4. When Jesus heard that, he said, This sickness is not unto death, but for the glory of God, that the Son of God might be glorified thereby.

5. Now Jesus loved Martha, and her sister, and Lazarus.

6. When he had heard therefore that he was sick, he abode two days still in the same place where he was.

7. Then after that saith he to his disciples, Let us go into Judaea again.

8. His disciples say unto him, Master, the Jews of late sought to stone thee; and goest thou thither again?

9. Jesus answered, Are there not twelve hours in the day? If any man walk in the day, he stumbleth not, because he seeth the light of this world.

10. But if a man walk in the night, he stumbleth, because there is no light in him.

11. These things said he: and after that he saith unto them, Our friend Lazarus sleepeth; but I go, that I may awake him out of sleep.

12. Then said his disciples, Lord, if he sleep, he shall do well.

13. Howbeit Jesus spake of his death: but they thought that he had spoken of taking of rest in sleep.

14. Then said Jesus unto them plainly, Lazarus is dead.

15. And I am glad for your sakes that I was not there, to the intent ye may believe; nevertheless let us go unto him.

16. Then said Thomas, which is called Didymus, unto his fellowdisciples, Let us also go, that we may die with him.

17. Then when Jesus came, he found that he had lain in the grave four days already.

18. Now Bethany was nigh unto Jerusalem, about fifteen furlongs off:

19. And many of the Jews came to Martha and Mary, to comfort them concerning their brother.

20. Then Martha, as soon as she heard that Jesus was coming, went and met him: but Mary sat still in the house.

21. Then said Martha unto Jesus, Lord, if thou hadst been here, my brother had not died.

22. But I know, that even now, whatsoever thou wilt ask of God, God will give it thee.

23. Jesus saith unto her, Thy brother shall rise again.

24. Martha saith unto him, I know that he shall rise again in the resurrection at the last day.

25. Jesus said unto her, I am the resurrection, and the life: he that believeth in me, though he were dead, yet shall he live:

26. And whosoever liveth and believeth in me shall never die. Believest thou this?

27. She saith unto him, Yea, Lord: I believe that thou art the Christ, the Son of God, which should come into the world.

28. And when she had so said, she went her way, and called Mary her sister secretly, saying, The Master is come, and calleth for thee.

29. As soon as she heard that, she arose quickly, and came unto him.

30. Now Jesus was not yet come into the town, but was in that place where Martha met him.

31. The Jews then which were with her in the house, and comforted her, when they saw Mary, that she rose up hastily and went out, followed her, saying, She goeth unto the grave to weep there.

32. Then when Mary was come where Jesus was, and saw him, she fell down at his feet, saying unto him, Lord, if thou hadst been here, my brother had not died.

33. When Jesus therefore saw her weeping, and the Jews also weeping which came with her, he groaned in the spirit, and was troubled.

34. And said, Where have ye laid him? They said unto him, Lord, come and see.

35. Jesus wept.

36. Then said the Jews, Behold how he loved him!

37. And some of them said, Could not this man, which opened the eyes of the blind, have caused that even this man should not have died?

38. Jesus therefore again groaning in himself cometh to the grave. It was a cave, and a stone lay upon it.

39. Jesus said, Take ye away the stone. Martha, the sister of him that was dead, saith unto him, Lord, by this time he stinketh: for he hath been dead four days.

40. Jesus saith unto her, Said I not unto thee, that, if thou wouldest believe, thou shouldest see the glory of God?

41. Then they took away the stone from the place where the dead was laid. And Jesus lifted up his eyes, and said, Father, I thank thee that thou hast heard me.

42. And I knew that thou hearest me always: but because of the people which stand by I said it, that they may believe that thou hast sent me.

43. And when he thus had spoken, he cried with a loud voice, Lazarus, come forth.

44. And he that was dead came forth, bound hand and foot with graveclothes: and his face was bound about with a napkin. Jesus saith unto them, Loose him, and let him go.

45. Then many of the Jews which came to Mary, and had seen the things which Jesus did, believed on him.

46. But some of them went their ways to the Pharisees, and told them what things Jesus had done.

47. Then gathered the chief priests and the Pharisees a council, and said, What do we? for this man doeth many miracles.

48. If we let him thus alone, all men will believe on him: and the Romans shall come and take away both our place and nation.

49. And one of them, named Caiaphas, being the high priest that same year, said unto them, Ye know nothing at all,

50. Nor consider that it is expedient for us, that one man should die for the people, and that the whole nation perish not.

51. And this spake he not of himself: but being high priest that year, he prophesied that Jesus should die for that nation;

52. And not for that nation only, but that also he should gather together in one the children of God that were scattered abroad.

53. Then from that day forth they took counsel together for to put him to death.

54. Jesus therefore walked no more openly among the Jews; but went thence unto a country near to the wilderness, into a city called Ephraim, and there continued with his disciples.

55. And the Jews' passover was nigh at hand: and many went out of the country up to Jerusalem before the passover, to purify themselves.

56. Then sought they for Jesus, and spake among themselves, as they stood in the temple, What think ye, that he will not come to the feast?

57. Now both the chief priests and the Pharisees had given a commandment, that, if any man knew where he were, he should shew it, that they might take him.

CHAPTER 12

1. Then Jesus six days before the passover came to Bethany, where Lazarus was, which had been dead, whom he raised from the dead.
2. There they made him a supper; and Martha served: but Lazarus was one of them that sat at the table with him.
3. Then took Mary a pound of ointment of spikenard, very costly, and anointed the feet of Jesus, and wiped his feet with her hair: and the house was filled with the odour of the ointment.
4. Then saith one of his disciples, Judas Iscariot, Simon's son, which should betray him,
5. Why was not this ointment sold for three hundred pence, and given to the poor?
6. This he said, not that he cared for the poor; but because he was a thief, and had the bag, and bare what was put therein.
7. Then said Jesus, Let her alone: against the day of my burying hath she kept this.
8. For the poor always ye have with you; but me ye have not always.
9. Much people of the Jews therefore knew that he was there: and they came not for Jesus' sake only, but that they might see Lazarus also, whom he had raised from the dead.
10. But the chief priests consulted that they might put Lazarus also to death;
11. Because that by reason of him many of the Jews went away, and believed on Jesus.
12. On the next day much people that were come to the feast, when they heard that Jesus was coming to Jerusalem,
13. Took branches of palm trees, and went forth to meet him, and cried, Hosanna: Blessed is the King of Israel that cometh in the name of the Lord.
14. And Jesus, when he had found a young ass, sat thereon; as it is written,
15. Fear not, daughter of Sion: behold, thy King cometh, sitting on an ass's colt.
16. These things understood not his disciples at the first: but when Jesus was glorified, then remembered they that these things were written of him, and that they had done these things unto him.
17. The people therefore that was with him when he called Lazarus out of his grave, and raised him from the dead, bare record.
18. For this cause the people also met him, for that they heard that he had done this miracle.

19. The Pharisees therefore said among themselves, Perceive ye how ye prevail nothing? behold, the world is gone after him.

20. And there were certain Greeks among them that came up to worship at the feast:

21. The same came therefore to Philip, which was of Bethsaida of Galilee, and desired him, saying, Sir, we would see Jesus.

22. Philip cometh and telleth Andrew: and again Andrew and Philip tell Jesus.

23. And Jesus answered them, saying, The hour is come, that the Son of man should be glorified.

24. Verily, verily, I say unto you, Except a corn of wheat fall into the ground and die, it abideth alone: but if it die, it bringeth forth much fruit.

25. He that loveth his life shall lose it; and he that hateth his life in this world shall keep it unto life eternal.

26. If any man serve me, let him follow me; and where I am, there shall also my servant be: if any man serve me, him will my Father honour.

27. Now is my soul troubled; and what shall I say? Father, save me from this hour: but for this cause came I unto this hour.

28. Father, glorify thy name. Then came there a voice from heaven, saying, I have both glorified it, and will glorify it again.

29. The people therefore, that stood by, and heard it, said that it thundered: others said, An angel spake to him.

30. Jesus answered and said, This voice came not because of me, but for your sakes.

31. Now is the judgment of this world: now shall the prince of this world be cast out.

32. And I, if I be lifted up from the earth, will draw all men unto me.

33. This he said, signifying what death he should die.

34. The people answered him, We have heard out of the law that Christ abideth for ever: and how sayest thou, The Son of man must be lifted up? who is this Son of man?

35. Then Jesus said unto them, Yet a little while is the light with you. Walk while ye have the light, lest darkness come upon you: for he that walketh in darkness knoweth not whither he goeth.

36. While ye have light, believe in the light, that ye may be the children of light. These things spake Jesus, and departed, and did hide himself from them.

37. But though he had done so many miracles before them, yet they believed not on him:

38. That the saying of Esaias the prophet might be fulfilled, which he spake, Lord, who hath believed our report? and to whom hath the arm of the Lord been revealed?

39. Therefore they could not believe, because that Esaias said again,

40. He hath blinded their eyes, and hardened their heart; that they should not see with their eyes, nor understand with their heart, and be converted, and I should heal them.

41. These things said Esaias, when he saw his glory, and spake of him.

42. Nevertheless among the chief rulers also many believed on him; but because of the Pharisees they did not confess him, lest they should be put out of the synagogue:

43. For they loved the praise of men more than the praise of God.

44. Jesus cried and said, He that believeth on me, believeth not on me, but on him that sent me.

45. And he that seeth me seeth him that sent me.

46. I am come a light into the world, that whosoever believeth on me should not abide in darkness.

47. And if any man hear my words, and believe not, I judge him not: for I came not to judge the world, but to save the world.

48. He that rejecteth me, and receiveth not my words, hath one that judgeth him: the word that I have spoken, the same shall judge him in the last day.

49. For I have not spoken of myself; but the Father which sent me, he gave me a commandment, what I should say, and what I should speak.

50. And I know that his commandment is life everlasting: whatsoever I speak therefore, even as the Father said unto me, so I speak.

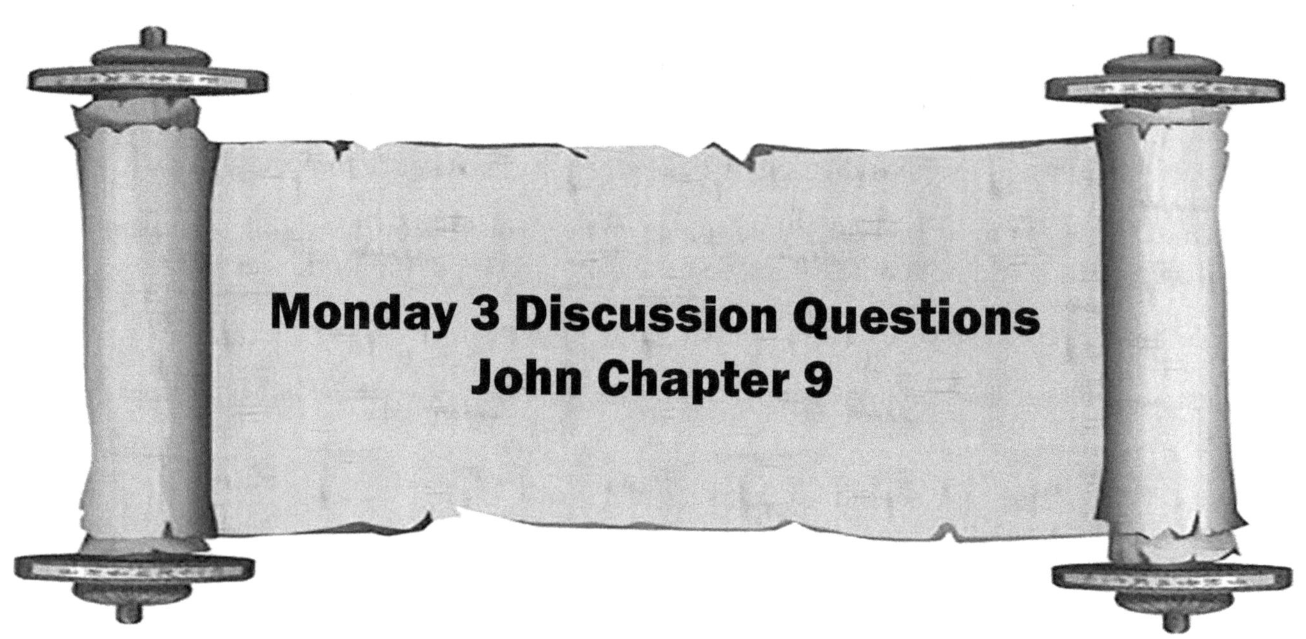

1. What did the disciples ask Jesus about the blind man they saw? ____________________
2. What was Jesus' answer? ____________________
3. What did Jesus tell the disciples about him working, the night and the day? ____________________
4. What would be as long as he was in the world"? ____________________
5. What did Jesus do after he spit on the ground? ____________________
6. What did Jesus command the man to go and do? What happened when he obeyed? ____________________
7. What did the man say when the people asked him how he was blind and now he could see? ____________________
8. What day was it when Jesus healed the blind man? ____________________
9. The Jews didn't believe he was healed from blindness. Who did they call to ask if he had been blind? ____________________
10. What was the conversation between Jesus and the blind man after they had cast the blind man out? ____________________

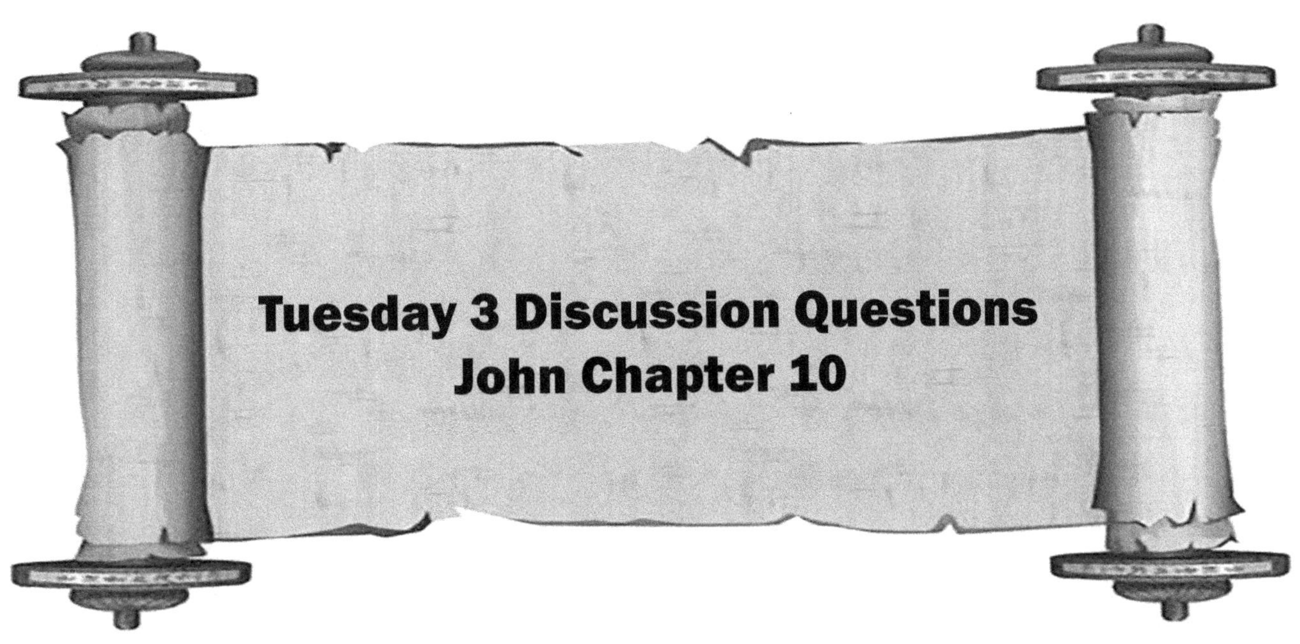

1. What did the Lord say about those who tried to enter the sheepfold, by some other way than the door? ______

2. What did he call those who enter by way of the door? ______

3. Whose voice will the sheep know and whose voice will they not follow? ______

4. Did the people understand the parables Jesus spoke? ______

5. Who is the door? How shall man be saved and find pasture? ______

6. Why did the thief come? Why did Jesus come? ______

7. What does a good shepherd give? ______

8. What does a hireling do when he sees the wolf coming? ______

9. What did Jesus say he must do with other sheep which were not of that fold? ______

10. The Lord informed them that no man could take his life. What did he say he had the power to do? Who commanded him to do so? ______

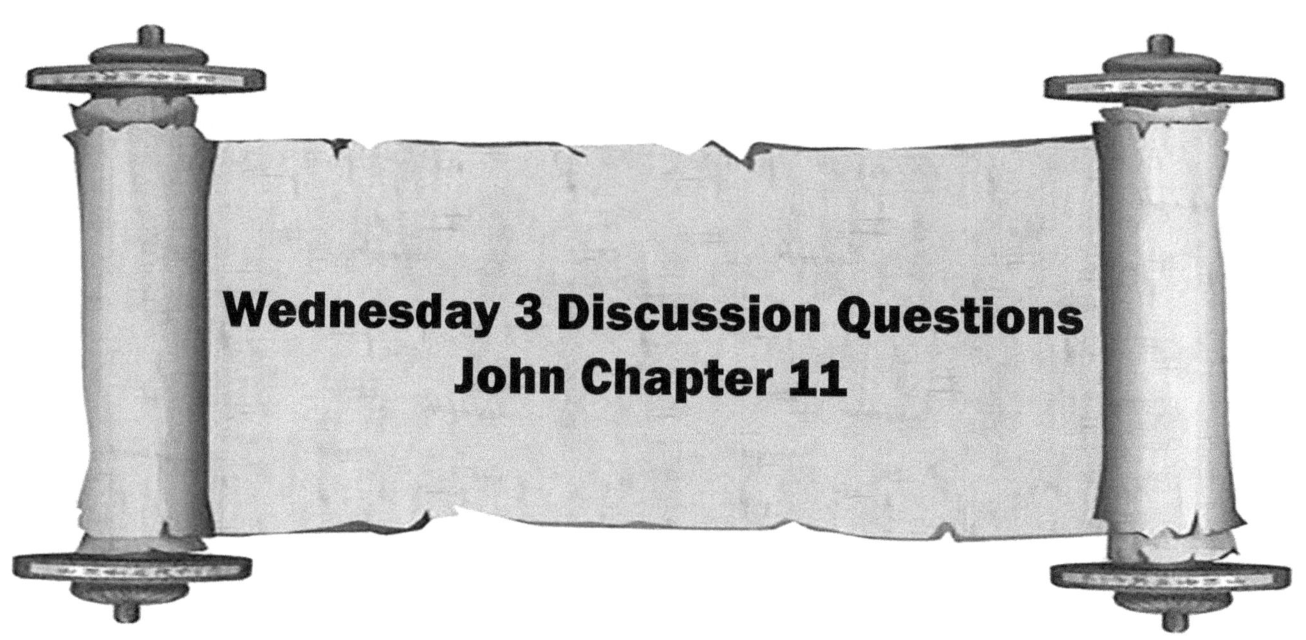

1. What was the name of the man who was sick? Where did he live? ____________________

2. What did Jesus say when Mary and Martha sent word that Lazarus was sick? ________

3. How long did Jesus stay where he was after he heard Lazarus was sick? ____________

4. What did the disciples say to Jesus when he decided to go see about Lazarus? ________

5. How did Jesus respond to them? Are there not twelve hours in the day? ____________

6. What did the disciples think when he told them he needed to go and wake Lazarus from sleeping? What was their conversation with Jesus about it? ________________

7. How long had Lazarus laid in the grave by the time Jesus got there? ______________

8. What did Martha say to Jesus when she saw him coming after her brother had already been dead for days? ______________________________

9. How did Jesus respond to her? What else did he explain to her about resurrection and life? ______________________________

10. What did Jesus do when he saw Mary and the Jews weeping? ________________

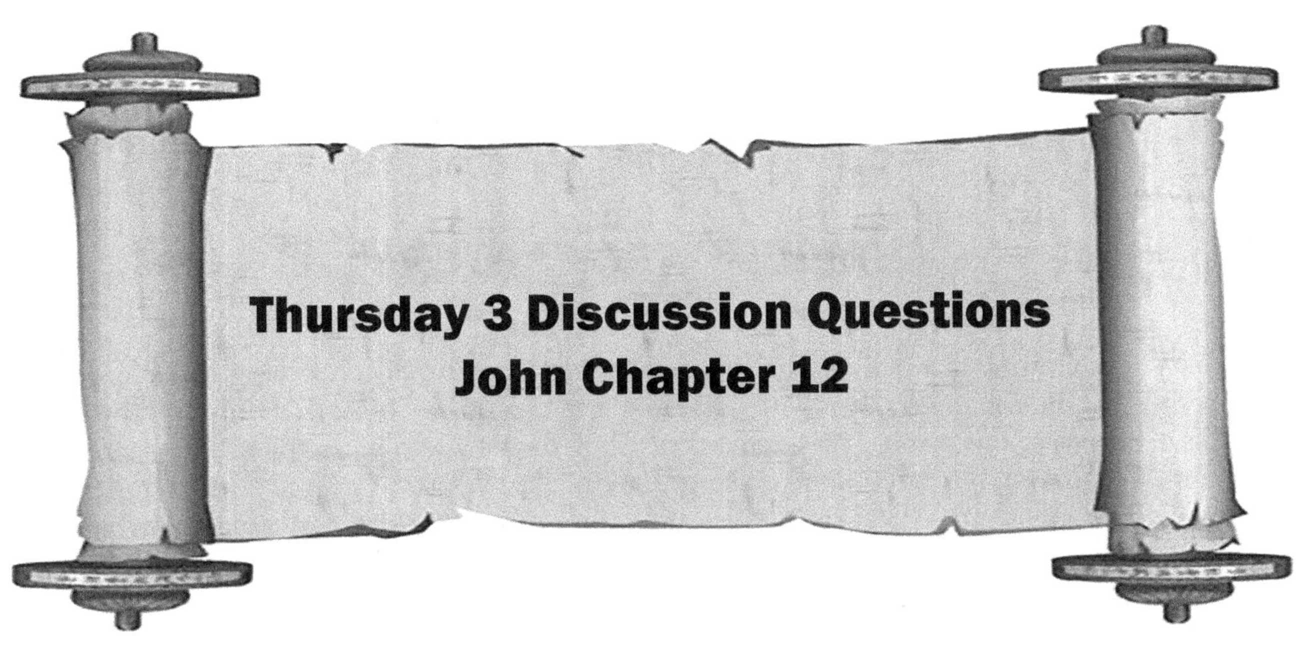

Thursday 3 Discussion Questions
John Chapter 12

1. Where did Jesus go six days before the passover? ______

2. Who was there? ______

3. Mary, Martha and Lazarus prepared a meal for Jesus. What did each of them do? ______

4. Who complained about what Mary did? What did he ask her? ______

5. Did Judas Iscariot care for the poor? ______

6. What did Jesus tell him to do? Why? ______

7. Why did the chief priests want to put Lazarus to death? ______

8. What did the people do when they heard Jesus was coming? ______

9. What parable did Jesus use about the corn of wheat, to explain the purpose of his death? ______

10. What did Jesus promise any man who serves him? ______

11. When she answered Jesus, what did he say to her and command her to do? ______

WEEKLY REVIEW
JOHN CHAPTERS 9-12

NAME THAT CHAPTER

1.______ This chapter teaches that he that entereth not by the door into the sheepfold, but climbeth up some other way, the same is a thief and a robber. Those that enter by the door are the shepherd of the sheep. The sheep follow him: for they know his voice. And a stranger they will not follow, but will flee from him: for they know not the voice of strangers. This parable spoke Jesus unto them: but they understood not what things they were which he spoke unto them. I am the door: by me if any man enters, he shall be saved, and shall go in and out, and find pasture. The thief cometh not, but for to steal, and to kill, and to destroy: I am come that they might have life, and that they might have it more abundantly. I am the good shepherd: the good shepherd giveth his life for the sheep. But he that is a hireling, and not the shepherd, whose own the sheep are not, seeth the wolf coming, and leaveth the sheep, and fleeth: and the wolf catcheth them, and scattereth the sheep.

2.______ Mary, Martha and Lazarus prepared a meal for Jesus. What did each of them do? Martha served: but Lazarus was one of them that sat at the table with him.Then Mary took a pound of ointment of spikenard, very costly, and anointed the feet of Jesus, and wiped his feet with her hair: and the house was filled with the odor of the ointment. Judas Iscariot, Simon's son asked, "Why wasn't this ointment sold for three hundred pence, and given to the poor?" This he said, not that he cared for the poor; but because he was a thief, and had the bag, and bare what was put therein. Jesus told Judas to let her alone: against the day of my burying hath she kept this. For the poor always ye have with you; but me ye have not always. The chief priests consulted that they might put Lazarus also to death because by reason of him many of the Jews went away, and believed in Jesus. The people took branches of palm trees, and went forth to meet him, and cried, Hosanna: Blessed is the King of Israel that cometh in the name of the Lord.

3.______ The disciples and Jesus came across a blind man. His disciples asked him, saying, Master, who did sin, this man, or his parents, that he was born blind? Neither hath this man sinned, nor his parents: but that the works of God should be made manifest in him. I must work the works of him that sent me, while it is day: the night cometh, when no man can work. Jesus spat on the ground, and made clay of the spittle, and he anointed the eyes of the blind man with the clay. Jesus commanded the man to go and wash in the pool of Siloam, (which is by interpretation, Sent.) He went his way therefore, and washed, and came seeing. He answered and said, A man that is called Jesus made clay, and anointed mine eyes, and said unto me, Go to the pool of Siloam, and wash: and I went and washed, and I received sight.

4.______ Now a certain man was sick, named Lazarus, of Bethany, the town of Mary and her sister Martha. When Jesus heard that he was sick, he abode two days still in the same place where he was. Master, the Jews of late sought to stone thee; and goest thou thither again? Are there not twelve hours in the day? If any man walks in the day, he stumbleth not, because he seeth the light of this world. But if a man walks in the night, he stumbleth, because there is no light in him. Then the disciples said, Lord, if he sleeps, he shall do well. Howbeit Jesus spoke of his death: but they thought that he had spoken of rest in sleep. Then said Jesus unto them plainly, Lazarus is dead. Then when Jesus came, he found that he had lain in the grave four days already. Then said Martha unto Jesus, Lord, if thou hadst been here, my brother had not died. But I know, that even now, whatsoever thou wilt ask of God, God will give it thee.

TRUE OR FALSE

5. The blind man was blind as a generational curse, because of the sins of his father.

____

JEREMIAH 9

6. In order to come to Jesus you must confess your sins to a Rabbi to be forgiven.

____

JEREMIAH 10

7. Mary took a pound of ointment of spikenard, very costly, and anointed the feet of Jesus, and wiped his feet with her hair: and the house was filled with the odor of the ointment

____

FILL IN THE BLANKS

8. Those that ____________ by the ____________ are the shepherd of the____________.
9. They took branches of____________ trees, and went forth to ____________ him, and cried,____________.
10. For the ____________ always ye have with____________; but me ye have not____________.

MY PRAYER JOURNAL

Please use this space to record your thoughts and feelings as you travel on this spirit led journey through the word of God with us. Please know that you have brothers and sisters in this organization from all over the world praying with and for you. My prayer for you is that you will begin to see the power of God resting in each set of your footprints. As you look back and examine your past in this journal, may you realize that you were never alone and according to Hebrews 13:5, God will never leave nor forsake you. ~LADY FLORA

I THESSALONIANS 5:17

THE STUDY OF THE FOUR GOSPELS VOCABULARY DEFINITIONS FOR JOHN CHAPTERS 13-16

WORD	DEFINITIONS
1) GIRT	
2) SILOAM	
3) CONFESS	
4) REVILE	
5) SHEEPFOLD	
6) HIRELING	
7) DIDYMUS	
8) PREVAIL	
9) EXPEDIENT	
10) SPIKENARD	

DMWW DAILY BIBLE READING
JOHN CHAPTERS 13-16

CHAPTER 13

1. Now before the feast of the passover, when Jesus knew that his hour was come that he should depart out of this world unto the Father, having loved his own which were in the world, he loved them unto the end.
2. And supper being ended, the devil having now put into the heart of Judas Iscariot, Simon's son, to betray him;
3. Jesus knowing that the Father had given all things into his hands, and that he was come from God, and went to God;
4. He riseth from supper, and laid aside his garments; and took a towel, and girded himself.
5. After that he poureth water into a bason, and began to wash the disciples' feet, and to wipe them with the towel wherewith he was girded.
6. Then cometh he to Simon Peter: and Peter saith unto him, Lord, dost thou wash my feet?
7. Jesus answered and said unto him, What I do thou knowest not now; but thou shalt know hereafter.
8. Peter saith unto him, Thou shalt never wash my feet. Jesus answered him, If I wash thee not, thou hast no part with me.
9. Simon Peter saith unto him, Lord, not my feet only, but also my hands and my head.
10. Jesus saith to him, He that is washed needeth not save to wash his feet, but is clean every whit: and ye are clean, but not all.
11. For he knew who should betray him; therefore said he, Ye are not all clean.
12. So after he had washed their feet, and had taken his garments, and was set down again, he said unto them, Know ye what I have done to you?
13. Ye call me Master and Lord: and ye say well; for so I am.
14. If I then, your Lord and Master, have washed your feet; ye also ought to wash one another's feet.
15. For I have given you an example, that ye should do as I have done to you.
16. Verily, verily, I say unto you, The servant is not greater than his lord; neither he that is sent greater than he that sent him.
17. If ye know these things, happy are ye if ye do them.

18. I speak not of you all: I know whom I have chosen: but that the scripture may be fulfilled, He that eateth bread with me hath lifted up his heel against me.

19. Now I tell you before it come, that, when it is come to pass, ye may believe that I am he.

20. Verily, verily, I say unto you, He that receiveth whomsoever I send receiveth me; and he that receiveth me receiveth him that sent me.

21. When Jesus had thus said, he was troubled in spirit, and testified, and said, Verily, verily, I say unto you, that one of you shall betray me.

22. Then the disciples looked one on another, doubting of whom he spake.

23. Now there was leaning on Jesus' bosom one of his disciples, whom Jesus loved.

24. Simon Peter therefore beckoned to him, that he should ask who it should be of whom he spake.

25. He then lying on Jesus' breast saith unto him, Lord, who is it?

26. Jesus answered, He it is, to whom I shall give a sop, when I have dipped it. And when he had dipped the sop, he gave it to Judas Iscariot, the son of Simon.

27. And after the sop Satan entered into him. Then said Jesus unto him, That thou doest, do quickly.

28. Now no man at the table knew for what intent he spake this unto him.

29. For some of them thought, because Judas had the bag, that Jesus had said unto him, Buy those things that we have need of against the feast; or, that he should give something to the poor.

30. He then having received the sop went immediately out: and it was night.

31. Therefore, when he was gone out, Jesus said, Now is the Son of man glorified, and God is glorified in him.

32. If God be glorified in him, God shall also glorify him in himself, and shall straightway glorify him.

33. Little children, yet a little while I am with you. Ye shall seek me: and as I said unto the Jews, Whither I go, ye cannot come; so now I say to you.

34. A new commandment I give unto you, That ye love one another; as I have loved you, that ye also love one another.

35. By this shall all men know that ye are my disciples, if ye have love one to another.

36. Simon Peter said unto him, Lord, whither goest thou? Jesus answered him, Whither I go, thou canst not follow me now; but thou shalt follow me afterwards.

37. Peter said unto him, Lord, why cannot I follow thee now? I will lay down my life for thy sake.

38. Jesus answered him, Wilt thou lay down thy life for my sake? Verily, verily, I say unto thee, The cock shall not crow, till thou hast denied me thrice.

CHAPTER 14

1. Let not your heart be troubled: ye believe in God, believe also in me.
2. In my Father's house are many mansions: if it were not so, I would have told you. I go to prepare a place for you.
3. And if I go and prepare a place for you, I will come again, and receive you unto myself; that where I am, there ye may be also.
4. And whither I go ye know, and the way ye know.
5. Thomas saith unto him, Lord, we know not whither thou goest; and how can we know the way?
6. Jesus saith unto him, I am the way, the truth, and the life: no man cometh unto the Father, but by me.
7. If ye had known me, ye should have known my Father also: and from henceforth ye know him, and have seen him.
8. Philip saith unto him, Lord, show us the Father, and it sufficeth us.
9. Jesus saith unto him, Have I been so long time with you, and yet hast thou not known me, Philip? he that hath seen me hath seen the Father; and how sayest thou then, Show us the Father?
10. Believest thou not that I am in the Father, and the Father in me? the words that I speak unto you I speak not of myself: but the Father that dwelleth in me, he doeth the works.
11. Believe me that I am in the Father, and the Father in me: or else believe me for the very works' sake.
12. Verily, verily, I say unto you, He that believeth on me, the works that I do shall he do also; and greater works than these shall he do; because I go unto my Father.
13. And whatsoever ye shall ask in my name, that will I do, that the Father may be glorified in the Son.
14. If ye shall ask any thing in my name, I will do it.
15. If ye love me, keep my commandments.
16. And I will pray the Father, and he shall give you another Comforter, that he may abide with you for ever;
17. Even the Spirit of truth; whom the world cannot receive, because it seeth him not, neither knoweth him: but ye know him; for he dwelleth with you, and shall be in you.
18. I will not leave you comfortless: I will come to you.

19. Yet a little while, and the world seeth me no more; but ye see me: because I live, ye shall live also.

20. At that day ye shall know that I am in my Father, and ye in me, and I in you.

21. He that hath my commandments, and keepeth them, he it is that loveth me: and he that loveth me shall be loved of my Father, and I will love him, and will manifest myself to him.

22. Judas saith unto him, not Iscariot, Lord, how is it that thou wilt manifest thyself unto us, and not unto the world?

23. Jesus answered and said unto him, If a man love me, he will keep my words: and my Father will love him, and we will come unto him, and make our abode with him.

24. He that loveth me not keepeth not my sayings: and the word which ye hear is not mine, but the Father's which sent me.

25. These things have I spoken unto you, being yet present with you.

26. But the Comforter, which is the Holy Ghost, whom the Father will send in my name, he shall teach you all things, and bring all things to your remembrance, whatsoever I have said unto you.

27. Peace I leave with you, my peace I give unto you: not as the world giveth, give I unto you. Let not your heart be troubled, neither let it be afraid.

28. Ye have heard how I said unto you, I go away, and come again unto you. If ye loved me, ye would rejoice, because I said, I go unto the Father: for my Father is greater than I.

29. And now I have told you before it come to pass, that, when it is come to pass, ye might believe.

30. Hereafter I will not talk much with you: for the prince of this world cometh, and hath nothing in me.

31. But that the world may know that I love the Father; and as the Father gave me commandment, even so I do. Arise, let us go hence.

CHAPTER 15

1. I am the true vine, and my Father is the husbandman.

2. Every branch in me that beareth not fruit he taketh away: and every branch that beareth fruit, he purgeth it, that it may bring forth more fruit.

3. Now ye are clean through the word which I have spoken unto you.

4. Abide in me, and I in you. As the branch cannot bear fruit of itself, except it abide in the vine; no more can ye, except ye abide in me.

5. I am the vine, ye are the branches: He that abideth in me, and I in him, the same bringeth forth much fruit: for without me ye can do nothing.

6. If a man abide not in me, he is cast forth as a branch, and is withered; and men gather them, and cast them into the fire, and they are burned.

7. If ye abide in me, and my words abide in you, ye shall ask what ye will, and it shall be done unto you.

8. Herein is my Father glorified, that ye bear much fruit; so shall ye be my disciples.

9. As the Father hath loved me, so have I loved you: continue ye in my love.

10. If ye keep my commandments, ye shall abide in my love; even as I have kept my Father's commandments, and abide in his love.

11. These things have I spoken unto you, that my joy might remain in you, and that your joy might be full.

12. This is my commandment, That ye love one another, as I have loved you.

13. Greater love hath no man than this, that a man lay down his life for his friends.

14. Ye are my friends, if ye do whatsoever I command you.

15. Henceforth I call you not servants; for the servant knoweth not what his lord doeth: but I have called you friends; for all things that I have heard of my Father I have made known unto you.

16. Ye have not chosen me, but I have chosen you, and ordained you, that ye should go and bring forth fruit, and that your fruit should remain: that whatsoever ye shall ask of the Father in my name, he may give it you.

17. These things I command you, that ye love one another.

18. If the world hate you, ye know that it hated me before it hated you.

19. If ye were of the world, the world would love his own: but because ye are not of the world, but I have chosen you out of the world, therefore the world hateth you.

20. Remember the word that I said unto you, The servant is not greater than his lord. If they have persecuted me, they will also persecute you; if they have kept my saying, they will keep yours also.

21. But all these things will they do unto you for my name's sake, because they know not him that sent me.

22. If I had not come and spoken unto them, they had not had sin: but now they have no cloak for their sin.

23. He that hateth me hateth my Father also.

24. If I had not done among them the works which none other man did, they had not had sin: but now have they both seen and hated both me and my Father.

25. But this cometh to pass, that the word might be fulfilled that is written in their law, They hated me without a cause.

26. But when the Comforter is come, whom I will send unto you from the Father, even the Spirit of truth, which proceedeth from the Father, he shall testify of me:

27. And ye also shall bear witness, because ye have been with me from the beginning.

CHAPTER 16

1. These things have I spoken unto you, that ye should not be offended.

2. They shall put you out of the synagogues: yea, the time cometh, that whosoever killeth you will think that he doeth God service.

3. And these things will they do unto you, because they have not known the Father, nor me.

4. But these things have I told you, that when the time shall come, ye may remember that I told you of them. And these things I said not unto you at the beginning, because I was with you.

5. But now I go my way to him that sent me; and none of you asketh me, Whither goest thou?

6. But because I have said these things unto you, sorrow hath filled your heart.

7. Nevertheless I tell you the truth; It is expedient for you that I go away: for if I go not away, the Comforter will not come unto you; but if I depart, I will send him unto you.

8. And when he is come, he will reprove the world of sin, and of righteousness, and of judgment:

9. Of sin, because they believe not on me;

10. Of righteousness, because I go to my Father, and ye see me no more;

11. Of judgment, because the prince of this world is judged.

12. I have yet many things to say unto you, but ye cannot bear them now.

13. Howbeit when he, the Spirit of truth, is come, he will guide you into all truth: for he shall not speak of himself; but whatsoever he shall hear, that shall he speak: and he will shew you things to come.

14. He shall glorify me: for he shall receive of mine, and shall shew it unto you.

15. All things that the Father hath are mine: therefore said I, that he shall take of mine, and shall shew it unto you.

16. A little while, and ye shall not see me: and again, a little while, and ye shall see me, because I go to the Father.

17. Then said some of his disciples among themselves, What is this that he saith unto us, A little while, and ye shall not see me: and again, a little while, and ye shall see me: and, Because I go to the Father?

18. They said therefore, What is this that he saith, A little while? we cannot tell what he saith.

19. Now Jesus knew that they were desirous to ask him, and said unto them, Do ye enquire among yourselves of that I said, A little while, and ye shall not see me: and again, a little while, and ye shall see me?

20. Verily, verily, I say unto you, That ye shall weep and lament, but the world shall rejoice: and ye shall be sorrowful, but your sorrow shall be turned into joy.

21. A woman when she is in travail hath sorrow, because her hour is come: but as soon as she is delivered of the child, she remembereth no more the anguish, for joy that a man is born into the world.

22. And ye now therefore have sorrow: but I will see you again, and your heart shall rejoice, and your joy no man taketh from you.

23. And in that day ye shall ask me nothing. Verily, verily, I say unto you, Whatsoever ye shall ask the Father in my name, he will give it you.

24. Hitherto have ye asked nothing in my name: ask, and ye shall receive, that your joy may be full.

25. These things have I spoken unto you in proverbs: but the time cometh, when I shall no more speak unto you in proverbs, but I shall shew you plainly of the Father.

26. At that day ye shall ask in my name: and I say not unto you, that I will pray the Father for you:

27. For the Father himself loveth you, because ye have loved me, and have believed that I came out from God.

28. I came forth from the Father, and am come into the world: again, I leave the world, and go to the Father.

29. His disciples said unto him, Lo, now speakest thou plainly, and speakest no proverb.

30. Now are we sure that thou knowest all things, and needest not that any man should ask thee: by this we believe that thou camest forth from God.

31. Jesus answered them, Do ye now believe?

32. Behold, the hour cometh, yea, is now come, that ye shall be scattered, every man to his own, and shall leave me alone: and yet I am not alone, because the Father is with me.

33. These things I have spoken unto you, that in me ye might have peace. In the world ye shall have tribulation: but be of good cheer; I have overcome the world.

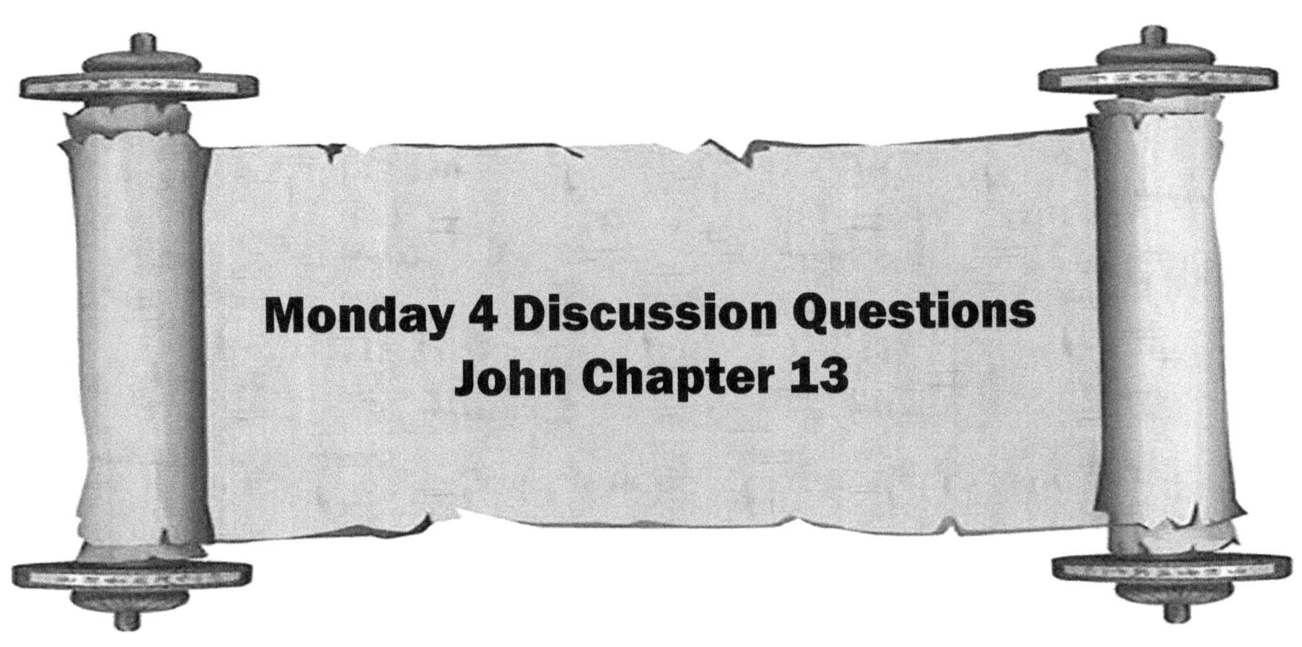

1. What was Judas Iscariot's father's name? ____________________

2. What did the devil put in his heart to do after supper? ____________________

3. What did Jesus do after supper? ____________________

4. When Jesus began to wash the disciples' feet, what was the conversation between Jesus and Peter? ____________________

5. What did the Lord say to the disciples about what he had done after washing their feet?

6. What did Jesus tell them they should do since their Lord and master washed their feet? Why? ____________________

7. What were the words he used to describe the servant and the one that is sent? ______

8. Who did Jesus say lifted his heel against him? ____________________

9. What happened when Jesus told the disciples he knew one of them would betray him?

10. What did Jesus say when Peter laid on him and asked who would betray him? ______

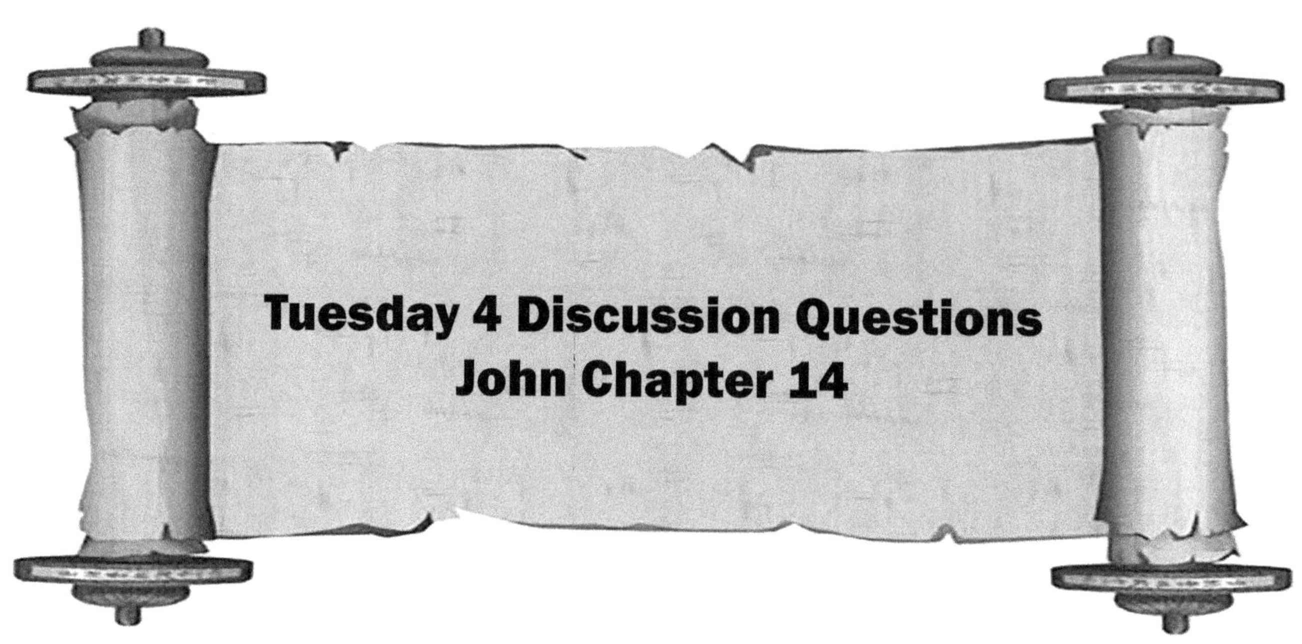

1. What did Jesus say to believe in if you believe in God?

2. What did Jesus say is in his father's house?

3. Where did he say he was going?

4. What did the Lord say he would do when he went to prepare a place for us?

5. What did Philip ask the Lord to show them?

6. What did Jesus ask them if they believed? Whose words did he say these were?

7. What did Jesus promise would happen when you ask anything in his name? Why?

8. What did the Lord say you will keep if you love the Lord?

9. What did Jesus say about those who didn't love him?

10. Who is the comforter that the father sent in Jesus' name? What will the comforter do?

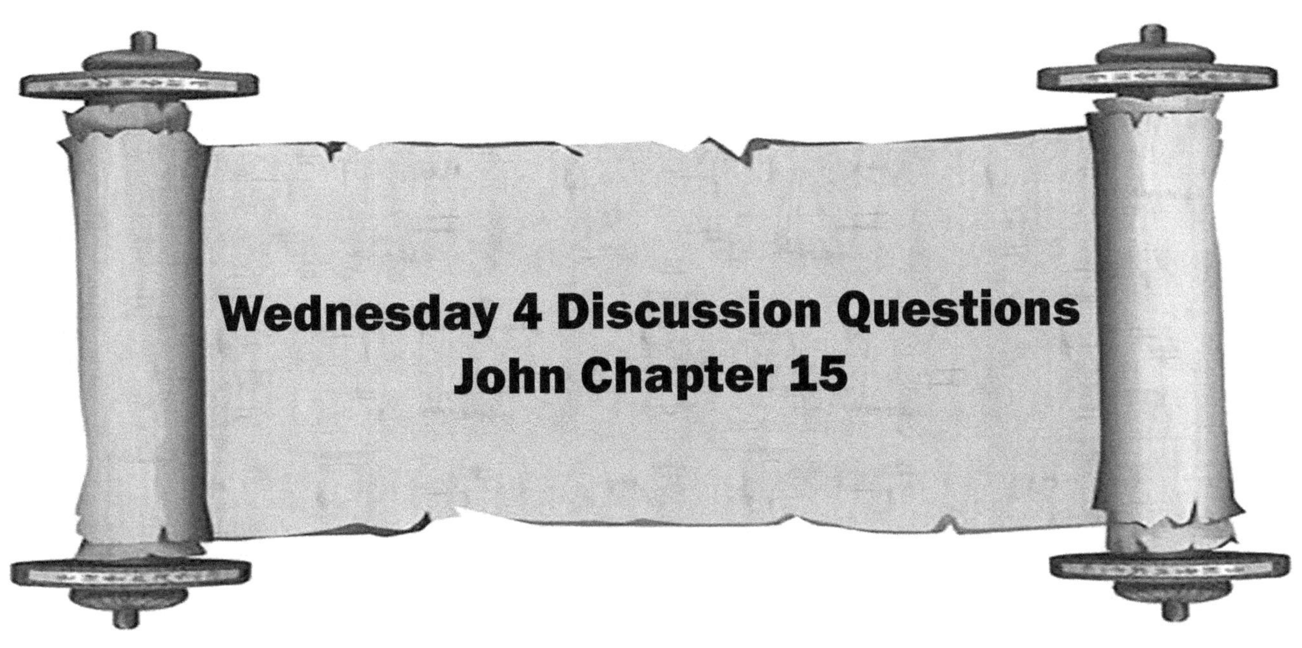

1. Who is the true vine? ____

2. Who did Jesus say is the husbandman? ____

3. What happens to every branch that bears no fruit? What happens with the ones that do bear fruit? ____

4. How does Jesus explain the possibility of bearing fruit? ____

5. Wherein did Jesus say his father is glorified? ____

6. What words did Jesus speak about joy remaining? ____

7. What did Jesus say about his commandment about love? ____

8. Jesus said, Ye are my friends if you do what? ____

9. Why did Jesus say he calls us friends and not servants? ____

10. What did Jesus say you should know if the world hates you? ____

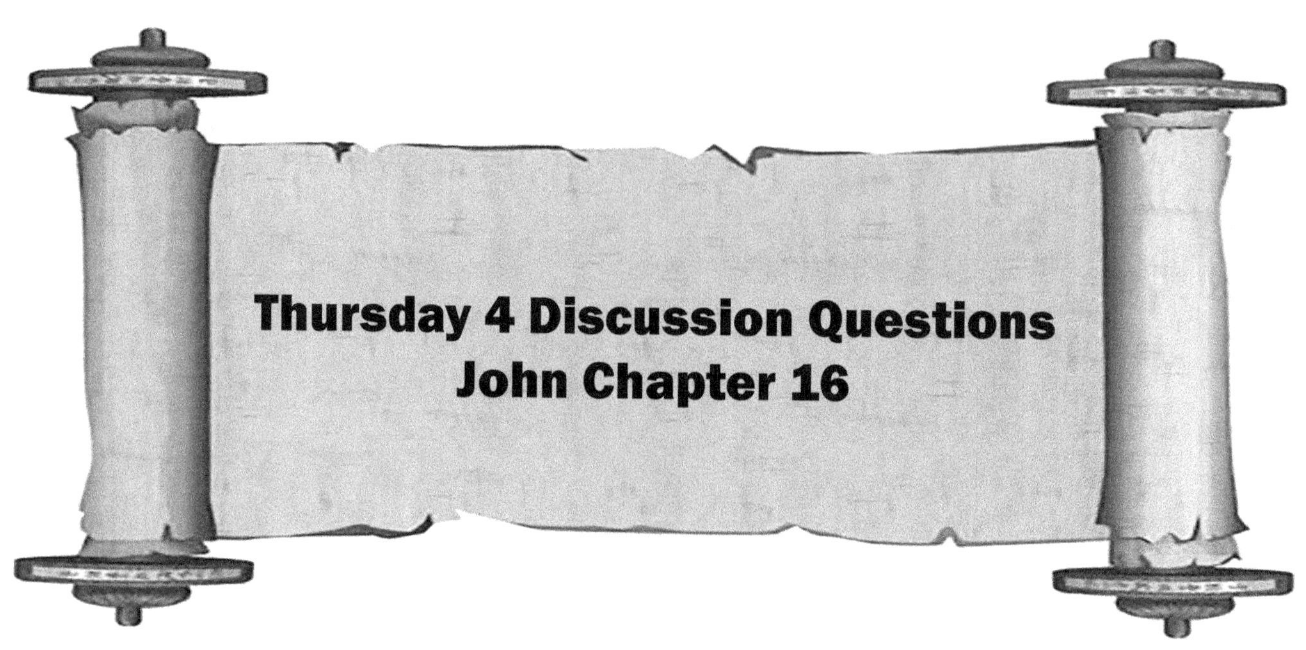

1. What did Jesus say you should not be? ______

2. What did he say they will put you out of? ______

3. What will the people who kill you think? ______

4. Why will they do these things? ______

5. What filled the peoples' hearts when Jesus told them he was returning to his father? ______

6. What did Jesus say the spirit of truth will guide us into? ______

7. What shall he speak and show us? ______

8. What did Jesus ask the disciples when he heard them asking about what he meant by "in a little while…? ______

9. Jesus comforted the disciples who were sad he was leaving. What did he say about their sorrow and joy? ______

10. Why did Jesus say he had spoken these things? He said there would be tribulation in the world. But what? ______

WEEKLY REVIEW
JOHN CHAPTERS 13-16

NAME THAT CHAPTER

1.______ Yea, the time cometh, that whosoever killeth you will think that he doeth God service. These things will they do unto you, because they have not known the Father, nor me. Jesus said, because I have said these things unto you, sorrow hath filled your heart. When he, the Spirit of truth, is come, he will guide you into all truth: for he shall not speak of himself. Whatsoever he shall hear, that shall he speak: and he will shew you things to come. He said, And ye now therefore have sorrow: but I will see you again, and your heart shall rejoice, and your joy no man taketh from you

2.______ After supper, Jesus laid aside his garments; and took a towel, and girded himself. Peter saith unto him, Lord, dost thou wash my feet? Jesus answered and said unto him, What I do thou knowest not now; but thou shalt know hereafter. Peter saith unto him, Thou shalt never wash my feet. Jesus answered him, If I wash thee not, thou hast no part with me. Simon Peter saith unto him, Lord, not my feet only, but also my hands and my head. After he had washed their feet, and had taken his garments, and was set down again, he said unto them, Know ye what I have done to you? Ye call me Master and Lord: and ye say well; for so I am If I then, your Lord and Master, have washed your feet; ye also ought to wash one another's feet. For I have given you an example, that ye should do as I have done to you.

3.______ The Lord said, Let not your heart be troubled: ye believe in God, believe also in me. Philip saith unto him, Lord, show us the Father, and it sufficeth us. Believest thou not that I am in the Father, and the Father in me? the words that I speak unto you I speak not of myself: but the Father that dwelleth in me, he doeth the works. Whatsoever ye shall ask in my name, that will I do, that the Father may be glorified in the Son. If ye shall ask anything in my name, I will do it. He said, "If ye love me, keep my commandments". He that loveth me not keepeth not my sayings: and the word which ye hear is not mine, but the Father's which sent me. But the Comforter, which is the Holy Ghost, whom the Father will send in my name, he shall teach you all things, and bring all things to your remembrance, whatsoever I have said unto you.

4.______ Jesus said, I am the true vine. God is the husbandman(vine dresser). Every branch in me that beareth not fruit he taketh away: and every branch that beareth fruit, he purgeth it, that it may bring forth more fruit. Abide in me, and I in you. As the branch cannot bear fruit of itself, except it abides in the vine; no more can ye, except ye abide in me. He said, These things have I spoken unto you, that my joy might remain in you, and that your joy might be full. Henceforth I call you not servants; for the servant knoweth not what his lord doeth: but I have called you friends; for all thing

TRUE OR FALSE

5. There are many mansions in heaven.

____

John 14

6. Jesus said the world hated him.

____

John 15

7. The Lord said to be of good cheer because he had overcome the world.

____

John 16

FILL IN THE BLANKS

8. He said, "I will ____________ to __________ a ____________ for____________

9.This is my __________, That ye ________ one________, as I have loved_____________.

10. _________ in me, and I in you. As the ________ cannot bear_____________of itself, except it abides in the___________; no more can ye, except ye abide in me.

MY PRAYER JOURNAL

Please use this space to record your thoughts and feelings as you travel on this spirit led journey through the word of God with us. Please know that you have brothers and sisters in this organization from all over the world praying with and for you. My prayer for you is that you will begin to see the power of God resting in each set of your footprints. As you look back and examine your past in this journal, may you realize that you were never alone and according to Hebrews 13:5, God will never leave nor forsake you. ~LADY FLORA

I THESSALONIANS 5:17

THE STUDY OF THE FOUR GOSPELS VOCABULARY DEFINITIONS FOR JOHN CHAPTERS 17-21

WORD	DEFINITIONS
1) PERDITION	
2) RESORT	
3) SHEATH	
4) SYNAGOGUE	
5) CRUCIFY	
6) RAIMENT	
7) HYSSOP	
8) REMIT	
9) GIRT	
10) CUBIT	

DMWW DAILY BIBLE READING
JOHN CHAPTERS 17-21

CHAPTER 17

1. These words spake Jesus, and lifted up his eyes to heaven, and said, Father, the hour is come; glorify thy Son, that thy Son also may glorify thee:

2. As thou hast given him power over all flesh, that he should give eternal life to as many as thou hast given him.

3. And this is life eternal, that they might know thee the only true God, and Jesus Christ, whom thou hast sent.

4. I have glorified thee on the earth: I have finished the work which thou gavest me to do.

5. And now, O Father, glorify thou me with thine own self with the glory which I had with thee before the world was.

6. I have manifested thy name unto the men which thou gavest me out of the world: thine they were, and thou gavest them me; and they have kept thy word.

7. Now they have known that all things whatsoever thou hast given me are of thee.

8. For I have given unto them the words which thou gavest me; and they have received them, and have known surely that I came out from thee, and they have believed that thou didst send me.

9. I pray for them: I pray not for the world, but for them which thou hast given me; for they are thine.

10. And all mine are thine, and thine are mine; and I am glorified in them.

11. And now I am no more in the world, but these are in the world, and I come to thee. Holy Father, keep through thine own name those whom thou hast given me, that they may be one, as we are.

12. While I was with them in the world, I kept them in thy name: those that thou gavest me I have kept, and none of them is lost, but the son of perdition; that the scripture might be fulfilled.

13. And now come I to thee; and these things I speak in the world, that they might have my joy fulfilled in themselves.

14. I have given them thy word; and the world hath hated them, because they are not of the world, even as I am not of the world.

15. I pray not that thou shouldest take them out of the world, but that thou shouldest keep them from the evil.

16. They are not of the world, even as I am not of the world.

17. Sanctify them through thy truth: thy word is truth.

18. As thou hast sent me into the world, even so have I also sent them into the world.

19. And for their sakes I sanctify myself, that they also might be sanctified through the truth.

20. Neither pray I for these alone, but for them also which shall believe on me through their word;

21. That they all may be one; as thou, Father, art in me, and I in thee, that they also may be one in us: that the world may believe that thou hast sent me.

22. And the glory which thou gavest me I have given them; that they may be one, even as we are one:

23. I in them, and thou in me, that they may be made perfect in one; and that the world may know that thou hast sent me, and hast loved them, as thou hast loved me.

24. Father, I will that they also, whom thou hast given me, be with me where I am; that they may behold my glory, which thou hast given me: for thou lovedst me before the foundation of the world.

25. O righteous Father, the world hath not known thee: but I have known thee, and these have known that thou hast sent me.

26. And I have declared unto them thy name, and will declare it: that the love wherewith thou hast loved me may be in them, and I in them.

CHAPTER 18

1. When Jesus had spoken these words, he went forth with his disciples over the brook Cedron, where was a garden, into the which he entered, and his disciples.

2. And Judas also, which betrayed him, knew the place: for Jesus ofttimes resorted thither with his disciples.

3. Judas then, having received a band of men and officers from the chief priests and Pharisees, cometh thither with lanterns and torches and weapons.

4. Jesus therefore, knowing all things that should come upon him, went forth, and said unto them, Whom seek ye?

5. They answered him, Jesus of Nazareth. Jesus saith unto them, I am he. And Judas also, which betrayed him, stood with them.

6. As soon then as he had said unto them, I am he, they went backward, and fell to the ground.

7. Then asked he them again, Whom seek ye? And they said, Jesus of Nazareth.

8. Jesus answered, I have told you that I am he: if therefore ye seek me, let these go their way:

9. That the saying might be fulfilled, which he spake, Of them which thou gavest me have I lost none.

10. Then Simon Peter having a sword drew it, and smote the high priest's servant, and cut off his right ear. The servant's name was Malchus.

11. Then said Jesus unto Peter, Put up thy sword into the sheath: the cup which my Father hath given me, shall I not drink it?

12. Then the band and the captain and officers of the Jews took Jesus, and bound him,

13. And led him away to Annas first; for he was father in law to Caiaphas, which was the high priest that same year.

14. Now Caiaphas was he, which gave counsel to the Jews, that it was expedient that one man should die for the people.

15. And Simon Peter followed Jesus, and so did another disciple: that disciple was known unto the high priest, and went in with Jesus into the palace of the high priest.

16. But Peter stood at the door without. Then went out that other disciple, which was known unto the high priest, and spake unto her that kept the door, and brought in Peter.

17. Then saith the damsel that kept the door unto Peter, Art not thou also one of this man's disciples? He saith, I am not.

18. And the servants and officers stood there, who had made a fire of coals; for it was cold: and they warmed themselves: and Peter stood with them, and warmed himself.

19. The high priest then asked Jesus of his disciples, and of his doctrine.

20. Jesus answered him, I spake openly to the world; I ever taught in the synagogue, and in the temple, whither the Jews always resort; and in secret have I said nothing.

21. Why askest thou me? ask them which heard me, what I have said unto them: behold, they know what I said.

22. And when he had thus spoken, one of the officers which stood by struck Jesus with the palm of his hand, saying, Answerest thou the high priest so?

23. Jesus answered him, If I have spoken evil, bear witness of the evil: but if well, why smitest thou me?

24. Now Annas had sent him bound unto Caiaphas the high priest.

25. And Simon Peter stood and warmed himself. They said therefore unto him, Art not thou also one of his disciples? He denied it, and said, I am not.

26. One of the servants of the high priest, being his kinsman whose ear Peter cut off, saith, Did not I see thee in the garden with him?

27. Peter then denied again: and immediately the cock crew.

28. Then led they Jesus from Caiaphas unto the hall of judgment: and it was early; and they themselves went not into the judgment hall, lest they should be defiled; but that they might eat the passover.

29. Pilate then went out unto them, and said, What accusation bring ye against this man?

30. They answered and said unto him, If he were not a malefactor, we would not have delivered him up unto thee.

31. Then said Pilate unto them, Take ye him, and judge him according to your law. The Jews therefore said unto him, It is not lawful for us to put any man to death:

32. That the saying of Jesus might be fulfilled, which he spake, signifying what death he should die.

33. Then Pilate entered into the judgment hall again, and called Jesus, and said unto him, Art thou the King of the Jews?

34. Jesus answered him, Sayest thou this thing of thyself, or did others tell it thee of me?

35. Pilate answered, Am I a Jew? Thine own nation and the chief priests have delivered thee unto me: what hast thou done?

36. Jesus answered, My kingdom is not of this world: if my kingdom were of this world, then would my servants fight, that I should not be delivered to the Jews: but now is my kingdom not from hence.

37. Pilate therefore said unto him, Art thou a king then? Jesus answered, Thou sayest that I am a king. To this end was I born, and for this cause came I into the world, that I should bear witness unto the truth. Every one that is of the truth heareth my voice.

38. Pilate saith unto him, What is truth? And when he had said this, he went out again unto the Jews, and saith unto them, I find in him no fault at all.

39. But ye have a custom, that I should release unto you one at the passover: will ye therefore that I release unto you the King of the Jews?

40. Then cried they all again, saying, Not this man, but Barabbas. Now Barabbas was a robber.

CHAPTER 19

1. Then Pilate therefore took Jesus, and scourged him.

2. And the soldiers platted a crown of thorns, and put it on his head, and they put on him a purple robe,

3. And said, Hail, King of the Jews! and they smote him with their hands.

4. Pilate therefore went forth again, and saith unto them, Behold, I bring him forth to you, that ye may know that I find no fault in him.

5. Then came Jesus forth, wearing the crown of thorns, and the purple robe. And Pilate saith unto them, Behold the man!

6. When the chief priests therefore and officers saw him, they cried out, saying, Crucify him, crucify him. Pilate saith unto them, Take ye him, and crucify him: for I find no fault in him.

7. The Jews answered him, We have a law, and by our law he ought to die, because he made himself the Son of God.

8. When Pilate therefore heard that saying, he was the more afraid;

9. And went again into the judgment hall, and saith unto Jesus, Whence art thou? But Jesus gave him no answer.

10. Then saith Pilate unto him, Speakest thou not unto me? knowest thou not that I have power to crucify thee, and have power to release thee?

11. Jesus answered, Thou couldest have no power at all against me, except it were given thee from above: therefore he that delivered me unto thee hath the greater sin.

12. And from thenceforth Pilate sought to release him: but the Jews cried out, saying, If thou let this man go, thou art not Caesar's friend: whosoever maketh himself a king speaketh against Caesar.

13. When Pilate therefore heard that saying, he brought Jesus forth, and sat down in the judgment seat in a place that is called the Pavement, but in the Hebrew, Gabbatha.

14. And it was the preparation of the passover, and about the sixth hour: and he saith unto the Jews, Behold your King!

15. But they cried out, Away with him, away with him, crucify him. Pilate saith unto them, Shall I crucify your King? The chief priests answered, We have no king but Caesar.

16. Then delivered he him therefore unto them to be crucified. And they took Jesus, and led him away.

17. And he bearing his cross went forth into a place called the place of a skull, which is called in the Hebrew Golgotha:

18. Where they crucified him, and two other with him, on either side one, and Jesus in the midst.

19. And Pilate wrote a title, and put it on the cross. And the writing was Jesus Of Nazareth The King Of The Jews.

20. This title then read many of the Jews: for the place where Jesus was crucified was nigh to the city: and it was written in Hebrew, and Greek, and Latin.

21. Then said the chief priests of the Jews to Pilate, Write not, The King of the Jews; but that he said, I am King of the Jews.

22. Pilate answered, What I have written I have written.

23. Then the soldiers, when they had crucified Jesus, took his garments, and made four parts, to every soldier a part; and also his coat: now the coat was without seam, woven from the top throughout.

24. They said therefore among themselves, Let us not rend it, but cast lots for it, whose it shall be: that the scripture might be fulfilled, which saith, They parted my raiment among them, and for my vesture they did cast lots. These things therefore the soldiers did.

25. Now there stood by the cross of Jesus his mother, and his mother's sister, Mary the wife of Cleophas, and Mary Magdalene.

26. When Jesus therefore saw his mother, and the disciple standing by, whom he loved, he saith unto his mother, Woman, behold thy son!

27. Then saith he to the disciple, Behold thy mother! And from that hour that disciple took her unto his own home.

28. After this, Jesus knowing that all things were now accomplished, that the scripture might be fulfilled, saith, I thirst.

29. Now there was set a vessel full of vinegar: and they filled a spunge with vinegar, and put it upon hyssop, and put it to his mouth.

30. When Jesus therefore had received the vinegar, he said, It is finished: and he bowed his head, and gave up the ghost.

31. The Jews therefore, because it was the preparation, that the bodies should not remain upon the cross on the sabbath day, (for that sabbath day was an high day,) besought Pilate that their legs might be broken, and that they might be taken away.

32. Then came the soldiers, and brake the legs of the first, and of the other which was crucified with him.

33. But when they came to Jesus, and saw that he was dead already, they brake not his legs:

34. But one of the soldiers with a spear pierced his side, and forthwith came there out blood and water.

35. And he that saw it bare record, and his record is true: and he knoweth that he saith true, that ye might believe.

36. For these things were done, that the scripture should be fulfilled, A bone of him shall not be broken.

37. And again another scripture saith, They shall look on him whom they pierced.

38. And after this Joseph of Arimathaea, being a disciple of Jesus, but secretly for fear of the Jews, besought Pilate that he might take away the body of Jesus: and Pilate gave him leave. He came therefore, and took the body of Jesus.

39. And there came also Nicodemus, which at the first came to Jesus by night, and brought a mixture of myrrh and aloes, about an hundred pound weight.

40. Then took they the body of Jesus, and wound it in linen clothes with the spices, as the manner of the Jews is to bury.

41. Now in the place where he was crucified there was a garden; and in the garden a new sepulchre, wherein was never man yet laid.

42. There laid they Jesus therefore because of the Jews' preparation day; for the sepulchre was nigh at hand.

CHAPTER 20

1. The first day of the week cometh Mary Magdalene early, when it was yet dark, unto the sepulchre, and seeth the stone taken away from the sepulchre.

2. Then she runneth, and cometh to Simon Peter, and to the other disciple, whom Jesus loved, and saith unto them, They have taken away the Lord out of the sepulchre, and we know not where they have laid him.

3. Peter therefore went forth, and that other disciple, and came to the sepulchre.

4. So they ran both together: and the other disciple did outrun Peter, and came first to the sepulchre.

5. And he stooping down, and looking in, saw the linen clothes lying; yet went he not in.

6. Then cometh Simon Peter following him, and went into the sepulchre, and seeth the linen clothes lie,

7. And the napkin, that was about his head, not lying with the linen clothes, but wrapped together in a place by itself.

8. Then went in also that other disciple, which came first to the sepulchre, and he saw, and believed.

9. For as yet they knew not the scripture, that he must rise again from the dead.

10. Then the disciples went away again unto their own home.

11. But Mary stood without at the sepulchre weeping: and as she wept, she stooped down, and looked into the sepulchre,

12. And seeth two angels in white sitting, the one at the head, and the other at the feet, where the body of Jesus had lain.

13. And they say unto her, Woman, why weepest thou? She saith unto them, Because they have taken away my Lord, and I know not where they have laid him.

14. And when she had thus said, she turned herself back, and saw Jesus standing, and knew not that it was Jesus.

15. Jesus saith unto her, Woman, why weepest thou? whom seekest thou? She, supposing him to be the gardener, saith unto him, Sir, if thou have borne him hence, tell me where thou hast laid him, and I will take him away.

16. Jesus saith unto her, Mary. She turned herself, and saith unto him, Rabboni; which is to say, Master.

17. Jesus saith unto her, Touch me not; for I am not yet ascended to my Father: but go to my brethren, and say unto them, I ascend unto my Father, and your Father; and to my God, and your God.

18. Mary Magdalene came and told the disciples that she had seen the Lord, and that he had spoken these things unto her.

19. Then the same day at evening, being the first day of the week, when the doors were shut where the disciples were assembled for fear of the Jews, came Jesus and stood in the midst, and saith unto them, Peace be unto you.

20. And when he had so said, he shewed unto them his hands and his side. Then were the disciples glad, when they saw the Lord.

21. Then said Jesus to them again, Peace be unto you: as my Father hath sent me, even so send I you.

22. And when he had said this, he breathed on them, and saith unto them, Receive ye the Holy Ghost:

23. Whose soever sins ye remit, they are remitted unto them; and whose soever sins ye retain, they are retained.

24. But Thomas, one of the twelve, called Didymus, was not with them when Jesus came.

25. The other disciples therefore said unto him, We have seen the Lord. But he said unto them, Except I shall see in his hands the print of the nails, and put my finger into the print of the nails, and thrust my hand into his side, I will not believe.

26. And after eight days again his disciples were within, and Thomas with them: then came Jesus, the doors being shut, and stood in the midst, and said, Peace be unto you.

27. Then saith he to Thomas, Reach hither thy finger, and behold my hands; and reach hither thy hand, and thrust it into my side: and be not faithless, but believing.

28. And Thomas answered and said unto him, My Lord and my God.

29. Jesus saith unto him, Thomas, because thou hast seen me, thou hast believed: blessed are they that have not seen, and yet have believed.

30. And many other signs truly did Jesus in the presence of his disciples, which are not written in this book:

31. But these are written, that ye might believe that Jesus is the Christ, the Son of God; and that believing ye might have life through his name.

CHAPTER 21

1. After these things Jesus shewed himself again to the disciples at the sea of Tiberias; and on this wise shewed he himself.

2. There were together Simon Peter, and Thomas called Didymus, and Nathanael of Cana in Galilee, and the sons of Zebedee, and two other of his disciples.

3. Simon Peter saith unto them, I go a fishing. They say unto him, We also go with thee. They went forth, and entered into a ship immediately; and that night they caught nothing.

4. But when the morning was now come, Jesus stood on the shore: but the disciples knew not that it was Jesus.

5. Then Jesus saith unto them, Children, have ye any meat? They answered him, No.

6. And he said unto them, Cast the net on the right side of the ship, and ye shall find. They cast therefore, and now they were not able to draw it for the multitude of fishes.

7. Therefore that disciple whom Jesus loved saith unto Peter, It is the Lord. Now when Simon Peter heard that it was the Lord, he girt his fisher's coat unto him, (for he was naked,) and did cast himself into the sea.

8. And the other disciples came in a little ship; (for they were not far from land, but as it were two hundred cubits,) dragging the net with fishes.

9. As soon then as they were come to land, they saw a fire of coals there, and fish laid thereon, and bread.

10. Jesus saith unto them, Bring of the fish which ye have now caught.

11. Simon Peter went up, and drew the net to land full of great fishes, an hundred and fifty and three: and for all there were so many, yet was not the net broken.

12. Jesus saith unto them, Come and dine. And none of the disciples durst ask him, Who art thou? knowing that it was the Lord.

13. Jesus then cometh, and taketh bread, and giveth them, and fish likewise.

14. This is now the third time that Jesus shewed himself to his disciples, after that he was risen from the dead.

15. So when they had dined, Jesus saith to Simon Peter, Simon, son of Jonas, lovest thou me more than these? He saith unto him, Yea, Lord; thou knowest that I love thee. He saith unto him, Feed my lambs.

16. He saith to him again the second time, Simon, son of Jonas, lovest thou me? He saith unto him, Yea, Lord; thou knowest that I love thee. He saith unto him, Feed my sheep.

17. He saith unto him the third time, Simon, son of Jonas, lovest thou me? Peter was grieved because he said unto him the third time, Lovest thou me? And he said unto him, Lord, thou knowest all things; thou knowest that I love thee. Jesus saith unto him, Feed my sheep.

18. Verily, verily, I say unto thee, When thou wast young, thou girdest thyself, and walkedst whither thou wouldest: but when thou shalt be old, thou shalt stretch forth thy hands, and another shall gird thee, and carry thee whither thou wouldest not.

19. This spake he, signifying by what death he should glorify God. And when he had spoken this, he saith unto him, Follow me.

20. Then Peter, turning about, seeth the disciple whom Jesus loved following; which also leaned on his breast at supper, and said, Lord, which is he that betrayeth thee?

21. Peter seeing him saith to Jesus, Lord, and what shall this man do?

22. Jesus saith unto him, If I will that he tarry till I come, what is that to thee? follow thou me.

23. Then went this saying abroad among the brethren, that that disciple should not die: yet Jesus said not unto him, He shall not die; but, If I will that he tarry till I come, what is that to thee?

24. This is the disciple which testifieth of these things, and wrote these things: and we know that his testimony is true.

25. And there are also many other things which Jesus did, the which, if they should be written every one, I suppose that even the world itself could not contain the books that should be written. Amen.

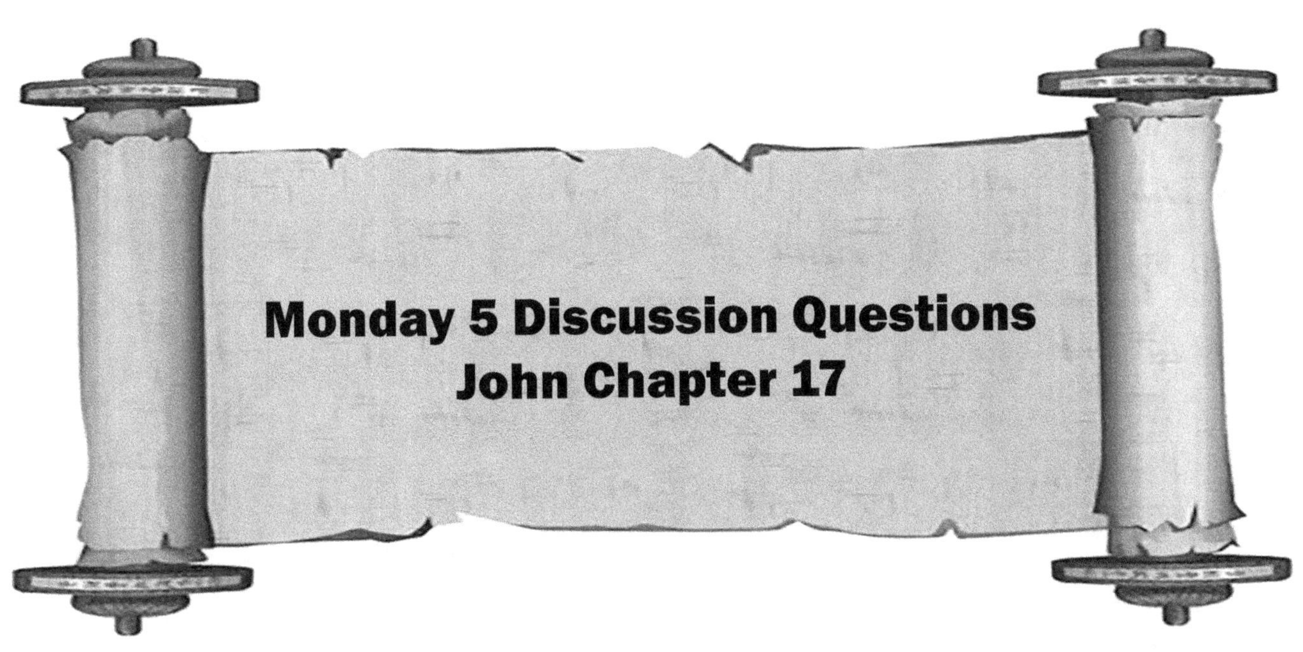

1. What did Jesus ask his father to do when his hour had come? ______________________

2. What did Jesus desire to have like he had before the world was? ______________________

3. What did Jesus say he did and did not pray for? ______________________

4. Who did he ask the father to keep through his own name? ______________________

5. When Jesus prayed for the people, what are some comparisons he made between God sending him and himself sending the people? ______________________

6. Because we are also believers today, he also prayed for us. Which scripture tells us this is true? ______________________

7. What part of his prayer shows that we will all be as one with the father and the son? ______________________

8. What did Jesus say he gave them, like the father had given him? ______________________

9. What did Jesus tell the father he wanted for the ones he had given him? Why? ______________________

10. At the end of this chapter, how did Jesus connect himself to the father and to the people of the world although the world had not known the father directly? ______________________

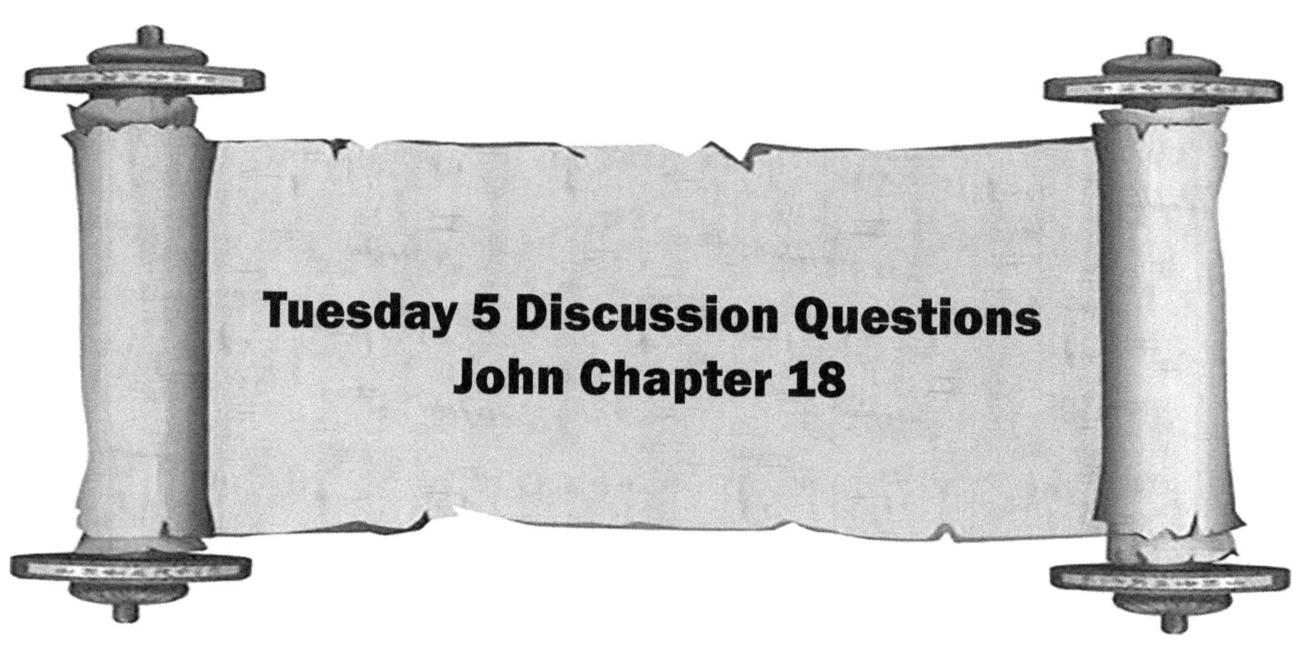

1. What is the name of the brook Jesus and the disciples crossed over? ______________

2. After they crossed the brook, what did they enter? ______________

3. What did Judas do? Who did he bring with him? ______________

4. What did Jesus ask them? ______________

5. What did they answer when he asked them twice? ______________

6. What did Simon Peter do to Malchus? ______________

7. What did Peter say when one of the servants of the high priest, being his kinsman whose ear Peter cut off, saith, Did not I see thee in the garden with Jesus? What happened immediately? ______________

8. When Pilate asked Jesus if he was a king, what did Jesus say…? ______________

9. What did Pilate say to the people after questioning Jesus? ______________

10. What did the people cry out when Pilate asked if they wanted him to release the king of the Jews? ______________

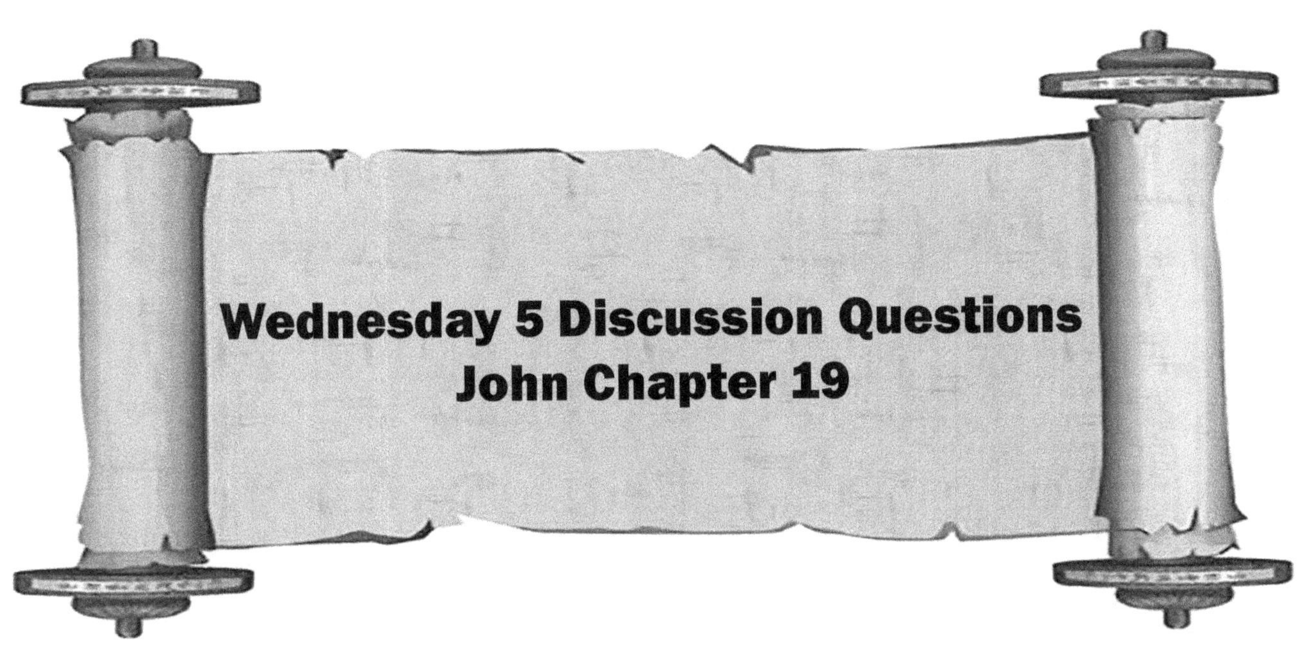

1. What did Pilate do to Jesus? ______

2. What did the soldiers put on Jesus? ______

3. What did Pilate say when he brought Jesu forth? Why did he say he brought him out that way? ______

4. What did Jesus come forth wearing? ______

5. What did the chief priests and officers cry out when they saw him? ______

6. What did Jesus say when Pilate asked him if he knew he had the power to crucify? ______

7. What title did Pilate put on the cross? ______

8. Who stood by the cross with Jesus' mother? ______

9. What did Jesus say to his mother and a disciple standing by? ______

10. What did they serve Jesus when he said he was thirsty? ______

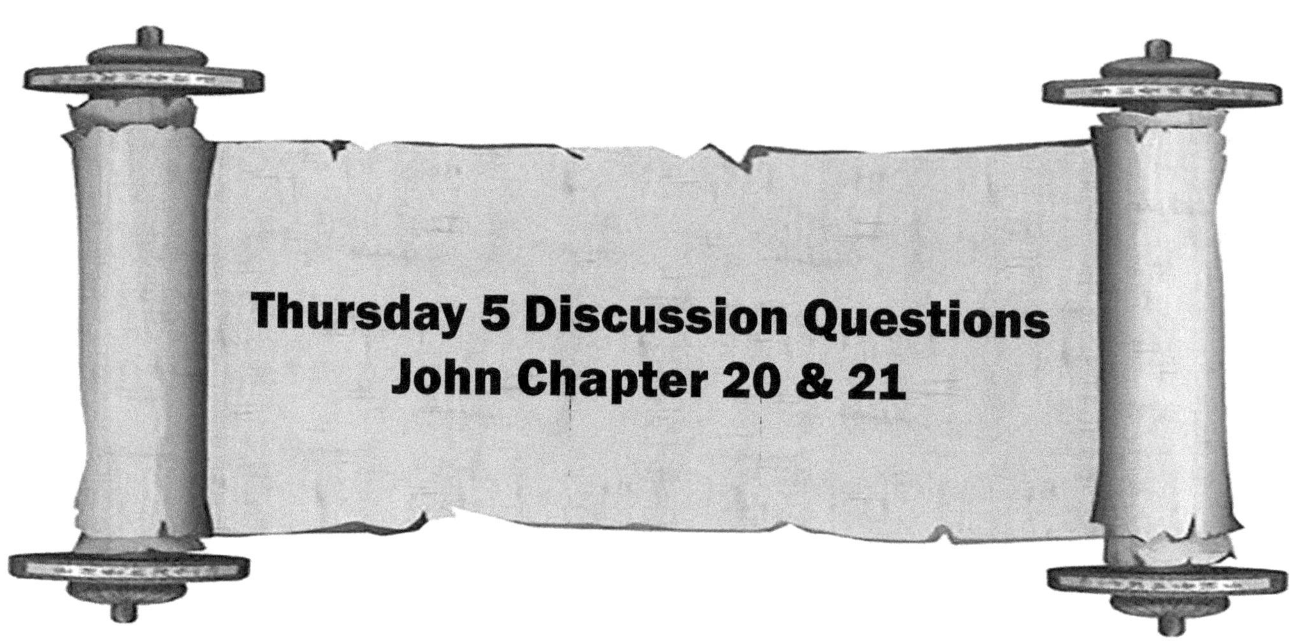

CHAPTER 20

1. What did Mary Magdalene see when she arrived at the sepulcher on the sixth day? ____

2. What happened when Mary went to tell Peter and the disciples? ____

3. What did the angels ask Mary, when they saw her weeping? Woman, why weepest thou? ____

4. When she saw Jesus appear, whom did she think he was? What did she ask him? ____

5. When she realized who Jesus was, why did he ask her not to touch him? ____

CHAPTER 21

6. Where did Jesus show himself to the disciples again? Who was there? ____

7. Did the disciples know who Jesus was when they saw him standing on the shore the next morning? ____

8. What did Jesus ask them to do? What happened when they did? ____

9. What happened with the other disciples in the little ship? ____

10. What did John say would be if every miracle were to be written? ____

WEEKLY REVIEW
JOHN CHAPTERS 17-21

NAME THAT CHAPTER

1.______ Judas then, having received a band of men and officers from the chief priests and Pharisees, went with lanterns and torches and weapons.

Jesus asked them, Whom seek ye? They ended up taking Jesus to Pilate. When Pilate asked Jesus if he was a king, and Jesus said, "Thou sayest that I am a king. To this end was I born, and for this cause came I into the world, that I should bear witness unto the truth. Every one that is of the truth heareth my voice". Pilate went out again unto the Jews, and saith unto them, I find in him no fault at all. Then they all cried again, saying, No, not this man, but release Barabbas the robber.

2.______ Mary Magdalene arrived at the sepulcher on the sixth day. The stone was taken away from the sepulcher. They ran both together: and the other disciple did outrun Peter, and came first to the sepulcher. Jesus appeared but said to her, Touch me not; for I am not yet ascended to my Father. Jesus shewed himself again to the disciples at the sea of Tiberias; and on this wise shewed he himself.There were together Simon Peter, and Thomas called Didymus, and Nathanael of Cana in Galilee, and the sons of Zebedee, and two other of his disciples. Jesus stood on the shore: but the disciples knew not that it was Jesus. Jesus told them to cast the net on the right side of the ship, and ye shall find. They cast therefore, and now they were not able to draw it for the multitude of fishes. The other disciples came in a little ship; dragging the net with fishes.

3.______ Pilate therefore took Jesus, and scourged him. The soldiers platted a crown of thorns, and put it on his head, and they put on him a purple robe. Jesus came forth, wearing the crown of thorns, and the purple robe. And Pilate saith unto them, Behold the man! Pilate wrote a title, and put it on the cross. And the writing was Jesus Of Nazareth The King Of The Jews. His mother's sister, Mary the wife of Cleophas, and Mary Magdalene. When Jesus saw his mother, and the disciple standing by her, he said to his mother, Woman, behold thy son! Then he said to the disciple, Behold thy mother! And from that hour that disciple took her to his own home. Jesus said he was thirsty. Then they filled a sponge with vinegar, and put it on hyssop, and put it in his mouth. When Jesus received the vinegar, he said, It is finished: and he bowed his head, and gave up the ghost.

4.______ When the hour had come, Jesus said, glorify thy Son, that thy Son also may glorify thee. He said, O Father, glorify thou me with thine own self with the glory which I had with thee before the world was. Jesus said, I pray for them: I pray not for the world, but for them which thou hast given me; for they are thine. He said, Holy Father, keep through thine own name those whom thou hast given me, that they may be one, as we are. Jesus said,They are not of the world, even as I am not of the world. Sanctify them through thy truth: thy word is truth. As thou hast sent me into the world, even so have I also sent them into the world. And for their sakes I sanctify myself, that they also might be sanctified through the truth

TRUE OR FALSE

5. Jesus prayed that God would take them out of the world

____

John 17:15

6. Judas knew where to find Jesus because he had gone there several times with the disciples.

____

John 18:2

7. The Jews told Pilate their law said Jesus should die because he made himself the son of God

____

John 19:7

FILL IN THE BLANKS

8. Jesus_____________, I have told you that I am_____________: if therefore ye_____________ me, let these go their _____________.

9. _____________, the hour is come;_____________thy Son, that thy_____________also may glorify _____________.

10. There are also many other_____________which Jesus did, which, if every one should be_____________, even the_____________itself could not_____________the books that should be written. Amen.

The Study of The Four Gospels
POST-Test

Students will take this quiz before and after studying in this class to determine what they know before and what they have learned after taking our course.

How many weeks will it take to complete the class? How many chapters will this study cover in all? ______________________________

What four books of the bible are considered the Four Gospels? How many chapters are in the book of Matthew? ______________________________

How many chapters are in the book of Mark? How many chapters are in the book of Luke? How many chapters are in the book of John? ______________________________

Which author(s) told about the step-daughter dancing and being rewarded with John's head on a platter for her mother? ______________________________

What was her name? ______________________________

Which author(s) told the people to repent and be baptized? ______________________________

Which author(s) told in detail about fishermen's nets breaking full of fish after obeying God's instructions? ______________________________

Which author(s) told about the woman with the issue of blood? ______________________________

Which author(s) told about the demons being cast out of a man and into swine? ______________________________

Which author(s) told about Jesus raising the dead man, Lazarus? Which three (3) gospels are the most similar in their storyline? ______________________________

Who is the most different? What makes one author stand out from the rest in his particular gospel? ______________________________

Where can you find our daily lessons online? ______________________________

What day and time do we meet together each week for class discussion and participation grades? ______________________________

What is the objective of this study of The Four Gospels? ______________________________

Give a specific parable that you recall from the book of Matthew? ______________________________

Tell of a lesson you learned in Mark that you did not learn in Matthew? ______________________________

Tell a story or lesson that was given in Luke that is not given in Matthew or Mark. ______________________________

Which particular parables were told by all four disciples, Matthew, Mark, Luke, and John.

____

What is something significant about the book of John that is very different from the books of Matthew, Mark, and Luke? ______________________________

THE BOOK OF JOHN
FINAL PART 1

Word Comprehension

Your instructor will choose 30 words from the lesson for you to use for this assignment from our study of JOHN in a sentence to show your understanding of the vocabulary word given. This assignment is worth 500 points when completed.

WORD		PERSONAL SENTENCE
1)		
2)		
3)		
4)		
5)		
6)		
7)		
8)		
9)		
10)		
11)		
12)		
13)		
14)		
15)		
16)		
17)		
18)		
19)		
20)		
21)		
22)		

23)		
24)		
25)		
26)		
27)		
28)		
29)		
30)		

NAME ______________________________

DATE COMPLETED ______________________________

TIME COMPLETED ______________________________

FINAL PART 2 - ESSAY JOHN

HOW TO WRITE A STANDARD SHORT ESSAY FOR DMWW INTERNATIONAL

Discipled Men and Women of Wisdom International practices formal essay writing to develop the art of informed persuasion, by combining two types of essay writings. They are the informative essay and the persuasive essay.

Our goal is to minister to others in a way that persuades them to walk in the truth as we know it, with fact based information from the Holy Bible and our personal experiences which relate to this information. You may also include outside sources that are credible as long as you cite anything you reference.

The element of persuasion according to Romans 8:38,39 ***"For I am persuaded that neither death, nor life, nor angels, nor principalities, nor powers,nor things present nor things to come, nor height, nor depth, nor any other creature shall beable to separate us from the Love of God, which is in Christ Jesus our Lord."*** is what takes place in the mind when one makes a conscious decision to follow Christ.

This week your final is a short essay. We will keep it simple.

Your essay will contain three parts, separated into three paragraphs. Use the following steps to write a 3 paragraph essay about any new information you learned in John that you did not learn in Matthew, Mark, or Luke.

PARAGRAPH 1	INTRODUCTION	Thesis Statement and Opening
PARAGRAPH 2	BODY	Supporting Statements
PARAGRAPH 3	CONCLUSION	Summary of the Information Given

REFLECTIONS PAGE

This page is to keep a diary of how you felt when studying this book and what you learned or discovered in this class that helped you relate the Bible situations to situations in today's world. Jot down notes of spiritual revelations you received while studying that you may want to use in future messages you may preach.

Certificate of Completion

This is to certify that

has successfully completed The Study of The Four Gospels, Matthew, Mark, Luke & John

Instructor Signature

Date

President, DMWW Bible Institute

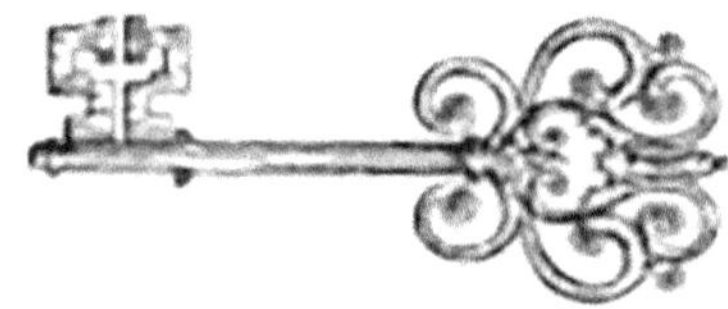

The Study of Matthew Chapters 1-4
VOCABULARY DEFINITIONS

WORD	DEFINITIONS
1) GENERATION	A people born and living at about the same time relatively
2) BEGAT	Bringing a child into existence by the process of reproduction
3) ESPOUSED	To adopt, embrace or make one's own
4) PRIVILY	Done in a private or secret manner
5) DILIGENT	Showing care in doing one's duties
6) LAMENTATION	A passionate expression of grief or sorrow
7) LEATHERN	Something that is made of leather
8) PURGE	An abrupt or violent removal or riddance of people or things
9) LUNATIC(K)	Person affected with a severely disordered state of mind.
10) PALSY	Person affected with paralysis and involuntary tremors

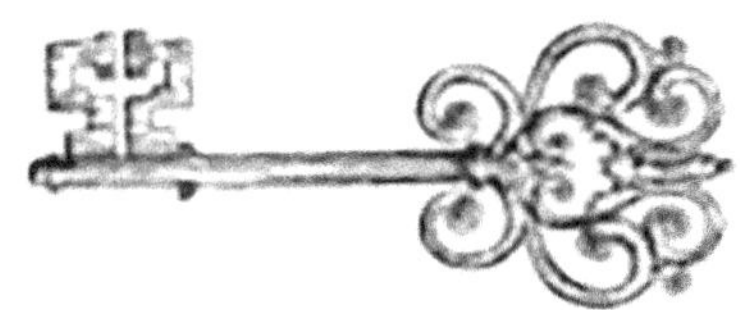

THE STUDY OF THE FOUR GOSPELS VOCABULARY DEFINITIONS FOR MATTHEW CHAPTERS 5-8

WORD	DEFINITIONS
1) REVILE	TO ABUSE OR ATTACK WITH EVIL WORDS
2) RACA	EMPTY HEADED, FOOLISH, VAIN
3) OUGHT	DUTY OR MORAL OBLIGATION
4) FORSWEAR	TO COMMIT PERJURY OR SWEAR FALSELY
5) TWAIN	TWO SEPARATE PARTS
6) ALMS	FOOD OR MONEY GIVEN TO RELIEVE THE POOR
7) MAMMON	EARTHLY GOODS, PROPERTY, AND RICHES,
8) METE	TO MEASURE OUT, OR PORTION OUT
9) MOTE	A SMALL SPOT OR PARTICLE
10) SCRIBES	A MEMBER OF A LEARNED CLASS OF PEOPLE IN ANCIENT ISRAEL

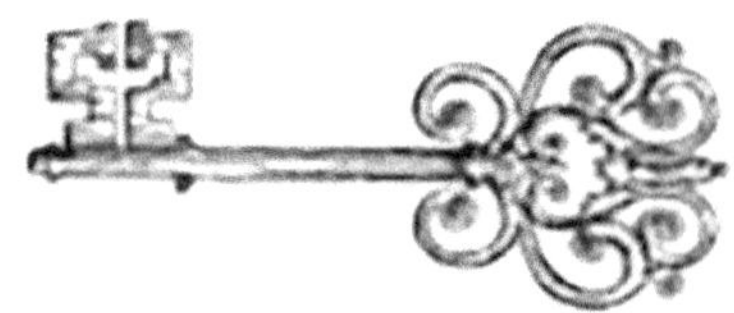

The Study of The Four Gospels
Matthew Chapters 9-12
VOCABULARY DEFINITIONS

WORD	DEFINITIONS
1. BLASPHEMY	OFFENSE OF SPEAKING SACRILEGIOUSLY ABOUT GOD OR SACRED THINGS, SYNONYMOUS WITH IRREVERENCE AND DISRESPECT OF GOD.
2. MARVEL	WONDERFUL, STRANGE, EXCITING WONDER
3. PUBLICANS	A JEWISH TAX COLLECTOR FOR THE ANCIENT ROMANS
4. BRIDECHAMBER	THE ROOM IN WHICH THE MARRIAGE CEREMONIES WERE HELD
5. SURNAME	A NAME ADDED TO THE CHRISTIAN NAME, WHICH BECOMES A FAMILY NAME
6. SCOURGE	TO FLOG, WHIP, PUNISH SEVERELY
7. BEELZEBUB	THE PRINCE OF THE DEVILS THE NAME GIVEN TO THE GOD OF THE PHILISTINE CITY OF EKRON
.8. FARTHING	A SMALL COIN WORTH A FOURTH OF A PENNY IN VALUE
9. GLUTTONOUS	EATING TO EXCESS, EATING TO INDULGE THE APPETITE EXCESSIVELY
10. FLAX	A PLANT OF THE GENUS LINUM, CONSISTING OF A SINGLE SLENDER STALK, THE SKIN OF HERL USED TO MAKE THREAD AND CLOTH CALLED LINEN

THE STUDY OF THE FOUR GOSPELS VOCABULARY DEFINITIONS FOR MATTHEW CHAPTERS 13-16

WORD	DEFINITIONS
1) PARABLES	A story that has two meanings TOLD TO TEACH A LESSON, something like a metaphor
2) SOW	To plant seeds, also a metaphor of a person's actions
3) PERCEIVE	To obtain knowledge of, through the senses
4) DURETH	To continue, last, hold on in time or endure
5) WAILING	To mourn, lament, express great sorrow
6) GNASHING	Grinding or striking together in rage
7) TETRARCH	A ruler of one fourth of a province
8) VICTUALS	Food or provisions
9) VEXEN	Troubled, distressed, or tormented
10) TRANSGRESS	To break or violate a law or rule

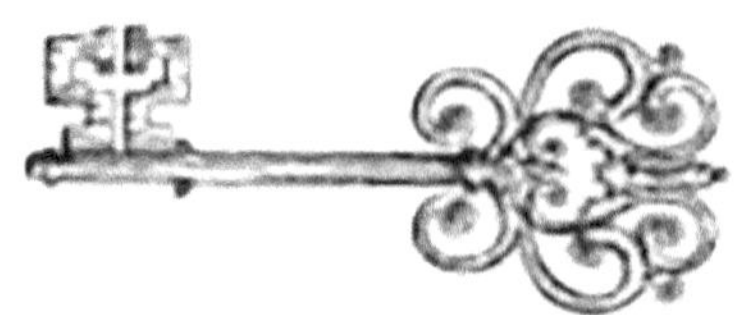

THE STUDY OF THE FOUR GOSPELS VOCABULARY DEFINITIONS FOR MATTHEW CHAPTERS 17-20

WORD	DEFINITIONS
1) TRANSFIGURED	CHANGED INTO SOMETHING MORE BEAUTIFUL
2) PERVERSE	AN OBSTINATE DESIRE TO BEHAVE IN AN UNACCEPTABLE MANNER REGARDLESS OF CONSEQUENCE
3) CONVERTED	TO BE BROUGHT OVER FROM ONE VIEW OR BELIEF TO ANOTHER
4) MILLSTONE	TWO CIRCULAR STONES USED FOR GRINDING GRAIN
5) RECKON	TO CONSIDER OR REGARD IN A SPECIFIED WAY
6) TALENTS	A WEIGHT OR GOLD COIN
7) TWAIN	A PAIR OR A COUPLE
8) ASUNDER	SEPARATED, DIVIDED, PULLED APART
9) EUNUCHS	A CASTRATED MAN, OFTEN ORDERED TO GUARD THE BEDROOM DOOR OF A ROYAL WOMAN
10) EYE OF A NEEDLE	A NARROW GATEWAY INTO THE CITY OF JERUSALEM CALLED "THE EYE OF A NEEDLE"

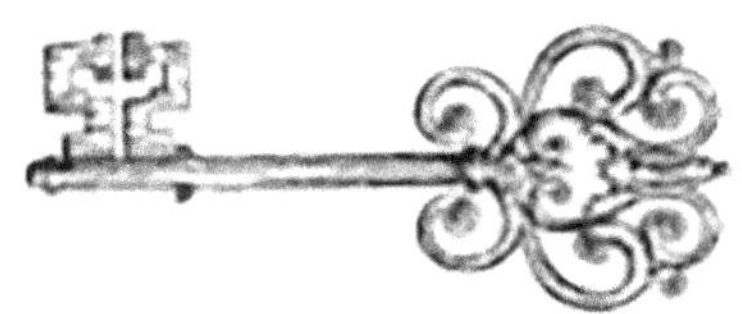

The Study of The Four Gospels
Matthew Chapters 21-24
VOCABULARY DEFINITIONS

WORD	DEFINITIONS
1. NIGH	CLOSE OR NEAR
2. OUGHT	TO BE UNDER OBLIGATION TO DO SOMETHING
3. MONEYCHANGERS	PEOPLE WHO EXCHANGED ROMAN MONEY TO MONEY ACCEPTED IN THE TEMPLE WORSHIP
4. HOSANNA	ANCIENT HEBREW WORD MEANING TO SAVE OR RESCUE
5. HUSBANDMAN	ONE PLOWS AND CULTIVATES THE FIELDS
6. SUPERSCRIPTION	SOMETHING WRITTEN OR ENGRAVED ON THE SURFACE OF SOMETHING
7. PHYLACTERIES	SMALL, SQUARE, LEATHER BOXES THAT CONTAINED SCRIPTURES
8. ABASED	LOWERED OR CAST DOWN
9. PESTILENCE	A DISEASE THAT AFFECTS AN ENTIRE COMMUNITY
10. GOODMAN	A GREEK WORD MEANING "HEAD OF THE FAMILY"

THE STUDY OF THE FOUR GOSPELS VOCABULARY DEFINITIONS FOR MATTHEW CHAPTERS 25-28

WORD	DEFINITIONS
1) LIKENED	TO POINT OUT THE RESEMBLANCE OF SOMEONE OR SOMETHING
2) TALENTS	ANCIENT ROMAN UNIT OF MEASURE
3) RECKON	CONSIDER
4) STRAWED	SPREAD OR SCATTERED
5) USURY	LENDING MONEY AT UNUSUALLY HIGH RATES OF INTEREST
6) SUBTILITY	THIN, FINE, LIGHT
7) ALABASTER	FINE GRAINED TRANSLUCENT GYPSUM
8) WROUGHT	BEAT INTO SHAPE
9) SMITE	TO STRIKE OR HIT HARD
10)BEWRAY	TO EXPOSE OR BETRAY

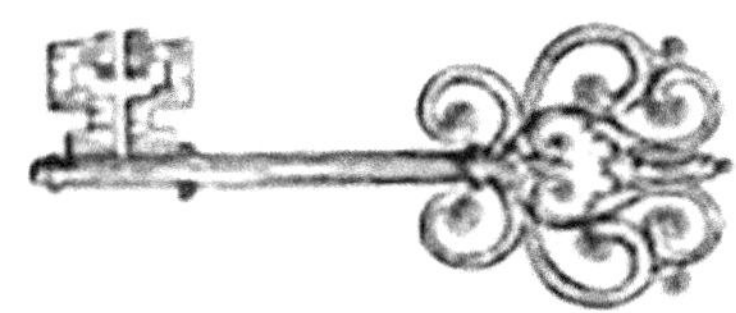

THE STUDY OF THE FOUR GOSPELS VOCABULARY DEFINITIONS FOR MARK CHAPTERS 1-4

WORD	DEFINITIONS
1) REMISSION	EXEMPTION FROM CONSEQUENCE FOR AN OFFENSE, FORGIVENESS
2) GIRDLE	A BAND OR BELT DRAWN AROUND THE WAIST, SYMBOL OF STRENGTH
3) ASTONISHED	BEING STARTLED OR STUNNED BY A WONDERFUL THING
4) BESEECH	TO REQUEST URGENTLY OR ANXIOUSLY
5) LEPROSY	A DISEASE THAT EATS AWAY AT THE FLESH, IT REPRESENTS SIN EATING AWAY AT OUR LIVES
6) RENT	TORN, RIPPED BY FORCE
7) MAR	TO DAMAGE, DISFIGURE, OR DESTROY
8) SHEWBREAD	TWELVE LOAVES PLACED IN THE JEWISH TEMPLE ON THE SABBATH, FOR THE PRIESTS TO EAT AT THE END OF THE WEEK.
9) SYNAGOGUE	A JEWISH HOUSE OF WORSHIP
10) PARABLES	AN ILLUSTRATIVE STORY BY WHICH A FAMILIAR IDEA IS CAST

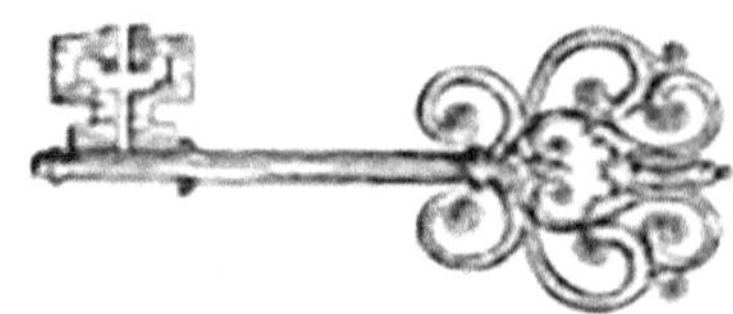

THE STUDY OF THE FOUR GOSPELS VOCABULARY DEFINITIONS FOR MARK CHAPTERS 5-8

WORD	DEFINITIONS
1) GADARENE	Involved in a potentially disastrous rush
2) FETTERS	Ankle chains used to restrain prisoners
3) LEGION	A vast multitude of people or things
4) VIRTUE	Behavior of high moral value
5) ADO	A state of agitation
6) DAMSEL	A young unmarried woman
7) TALITHA	A little girl
8) CUMI	Arise, get up
9) SHOD	Wearing foot gear
10)LASCIVIOUS	Lewd, lustful acts and thoughts

THE STUDY OF THE FOUR GOSPELS VOCABULARY DEFINITIONS FOR MARK CHAPTERS 9-12

WORD	DEFINITIONS
1) WINEFAT	A VESSEL, VAT, OR TROUGH BENEATH A WINEPRESS
2) HAPLY	BY CHANCE, BY LUCK, OR BY ACCIDENT
3) EVENTIDE	THE END OF THE DAY
4) PINE	TO DESIRE SOMETHING THAT IS DIFFICULT TO OBTAIN
5) WONT	TO BE ACCUSTOMED TO
6) PRECEPT	A GENERAL RULE INTENDED TO REGULATE BEHAVIOR
7) SALUTE	A GESTURE OF RESPECT
8) NOUGHT	NOTHING
9) VERILY	TRULY, CERTAINLY
10)ERR	TO MAKE A MISTAKE

THE STUDY OF THE MINOR PROPHETS VOCABULARY DEFINITIONS FOR MARK CHAPTERS 13-16

WORD	DEFINITIONS
1) GOODMAN	MASTER OF THE HOUSE OR FAMILY
2) SPIKENARD	AN EXPENSIVE PERFUME
3) DESOLATION	DEPOPULATION OR DESTRUCTION OF POPULATION
4) ABOMINATION	SOMETHING THAT CAUSES HATE OR DISGUST
5) PORTER	A GATE KEEPER
6) UTTERMOST	THE GREATEST OR HIGHEST DEGREE OF
7) UNLEAVENED	ROUND FLAT CAKES OF BREAD MADE WITH FLOUR AND WATER WITHOUT YEAST
8) GUESTCHAMBER	SPARE ROOM ON THE UPPER FLOOR WHERE ENTERTAINMENTS WERE PREPARED
9) STAVES	PLURAL WORD FOR MORE THAN ONE STAFF
10) BLASPHEMY	SHOWING CONTEMPT OR A LACK OF REVERENCE FOR GOD

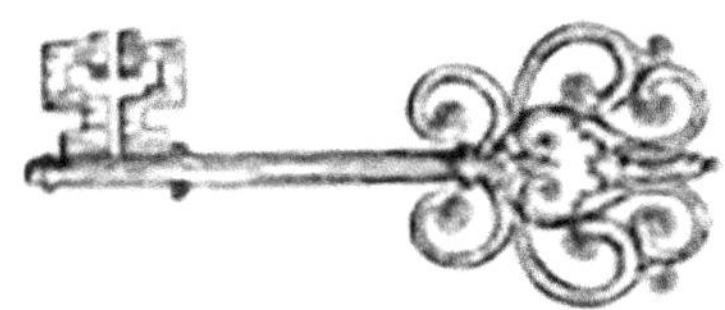

THE STUDY OF THE FOUR GOSPELS VOCABULARY DEFINITIONS FOR LUKE CHAPTERS 1-4

WORD	DEFINITIONS
1) VEHEMENTLY	VIOLENTLY, INTENSELY
2) BECKON	TO SUMMON BY A MOTION OF THE HAND
3) TOILED	TO WORK LONG AND HARD
4) COMMUNE	TO CONVERSE CONFIDENTIALLY AND SYMPATHETICALLY
5) CONSOLE	TO COMFORT
6) PARABLE	A REPRESENTATION OF SOMETHING IN REAL LIFE
7) CONDEMN	TO PASS JUDGMENT AGAINST
8) PERCEIVE	TO OBTAIN KNOWLEDGE OF THROUGH THE SENSES.
9) MOTE	A SMALL PIECE OF ANYTHING LIGHT
10) GLUTTONOUS	THE OVERINDULGENCE OF EATING FOOD

THE STUDY OF THE FOUR GOSPELS VOCABULARY DEFINITIONS FOR LUKE CHAPTERS 5-8

WORD	DEFINITIONS
1) MURMUR	TO COMPLAIN AND GRUMBLE IN LOW TONES
2) DRAUGHT	THE ACT OF BEING DRAWN
3) BLASPHEMIES	SHOWING A LACK OF REVERENCE FOR GOD
4) PUBLICAN	A JEWISH TAX COLLECTOR
5) BRIDECHAMBER	THE ROOM WHERE MARRIAGE CEREMONIES WERE HELD
6) COMMUNE	INTIMATE INTENSE COMMUNICATION
7) VEX	TO TORMENT, TROUBLE, DISTRESS
8) REPROACH	TO EXPRESS DISAPPOINTMENT OR DISPLEASURE IN A PERSON
9) VIRTUE	LIFE CONFORMED BY PRINCIPLES OF MORALITY
10) BRAMBLE	SHARP, PRICKLY ARCHING STEMS

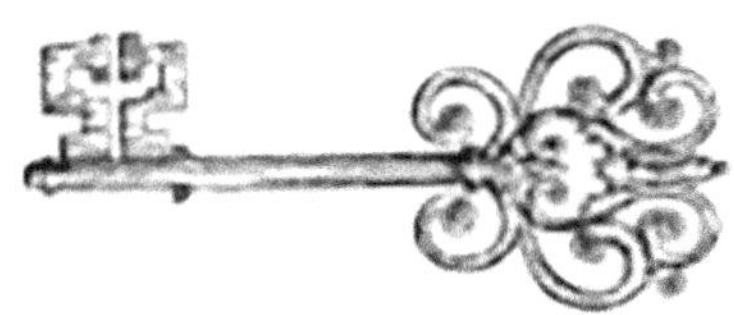

THE STUDY OF THE FOUR GOSPELS VOCABULARY DEFINITIONS FOR LUKE CHAPTERS 9-12

WORD	DEFINITIONS
1) PERPLEXED	FILLED WITH CONFUSION, DIFFICULTY, DOUBT
2) TETRARCH	THE RULER OVER A FOURTH PART OF A PROVINCE
3) VICTUALS	SUPPLY OF FOOD
4) COUNTENANCE	TO ENCOURAGE, FAVOR OR APPROVE
5) GLISTERING	TO SHINE, SPARKLE, BE BRIGHT (THE WHITE OF CHRIST'S GARMENTS)
6) PRUDENT	DISCREET, CAREFUL, WISE DISCERNMENT
7) CUMBERED	TO BE HINDERED BY OBSTRUCTION OR INTERFERENCE
8) HALLOWED	EXALTED, ESTEEMED WORTHY OF COMPLETE DEVOTION
9) PAPS	TEAT, NIPPLE, FEMALE BREAST
10) RAVENING	DEVOURING FOOD IN LARGE QUANTITIES

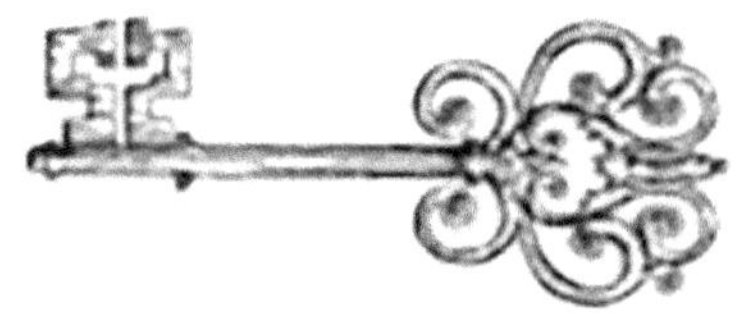

THE STUDY OF THE FOUR GOSPELS VOCABULARY DEFINITIONS FOR LUKE CHAPTERS 13-16

WORD	DEFINITIONS
1) SILOAM	IT MEANS "SENT" IT IS ALSO THE NAME OF A POOL LOCATED BY A TOWER THAT FELLON 18 UNJUST MEN
2) DUNG	MANURE USED AS FERTILIZER
3) ADVERSARIES	ENEMY OR FOE, ONE WHO HAS ENMITY AT HEART
4) STRAIT GATE	NARROW, TIGHT OR DIFFICULT PATH
5) CURES	REPAIRING OR HEALING OF THE MIND OR SPIRIT
6) BROOD	YOUNG COVERED BY WINGS, INCUBATION
7) ABASE	TO BRING LOW TO HUMBLE
8) RECOMPENSE	PAY FOR SOMETHING DAMAGED OR RETURN IN KIND
9) AMBASSAGE	A MESSAGE BROUGHT BY A GROUP OF AMBASSADORS
10)MAMMON	RICHES, WEALTH

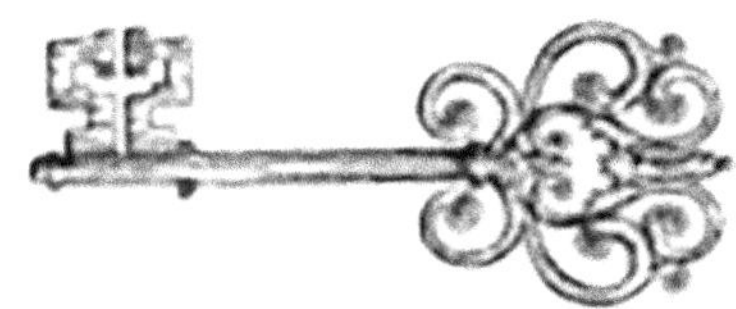

THE STUDY OF THE FOUR GOSPELS VOCABULARY DEFINITIONS FOR LUKE CHAPTERS 17-20

WORD	DEFINITIONS
1) AUSTERE	HARSH ROUGH RIGID
2) HUSBANDMAN	ONE WHO PLOWS OR CULTIVATES LAND
3) REVERENCE	TO SHOW DEEP FEAR OR RESPECT FOR
4) DURST	PAST TENSE OF DARE
5) GIRD	TO EQUIP OR PREPARE
6) WHENCE	FROM WHAT PLACE
7) USURY	LENDING MONEY AT OUTRAGEOUS INTEREST RATES
8) POUNDS	HEBREW SILVER (WORTH 25 DOLLARS)
9) EXTORTION	TAKING SOMETHING FROM SOMEONE BY ILLEGAL MEANS
10)MILLSTONE	A STONE USED FOR GRINDING GRAIN

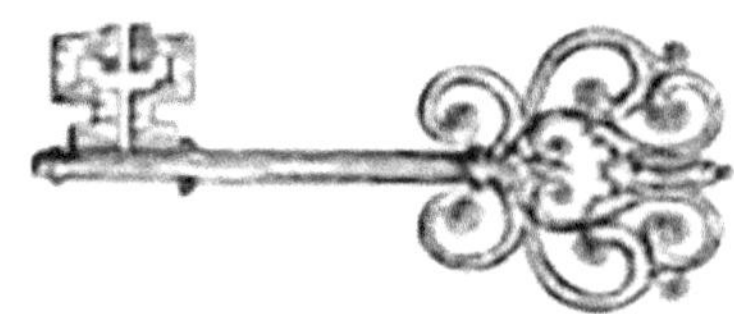

THE STUDY OF THE FOUR GOSPELS VOCABULARY DEFINITIONS FOR LUKE CHAPTERS 21-24

WORD	DEFINITIONS
1) PENURY	EXTREME POVERTY
2) ADORNED	TO MAKE MORE BEAUTIFUL OR ATTRACTIVE
3) GAINSAY	TO CONTRADICT OR OPPOSE
4) TRODDEN	TRAMPLED OR STOMPED DOWN
5) PERPLEXITY	COMPLICATED, DIFFICULT, ENTANGLED
6) EXPOUND	TO EXPLAIN
7) SURFEITING	HAVING AN EXCESS OR OVERABUNDANCE OF SOMETHING
8) DERIDED	RIDICULED OR SCORN
9) SEDITION	DEFIANCE, RESISTANCE TO LAWFUL AUTHORITY
10) LAMENTED	TO FEEL LOSS, SORROW OR GRIEF

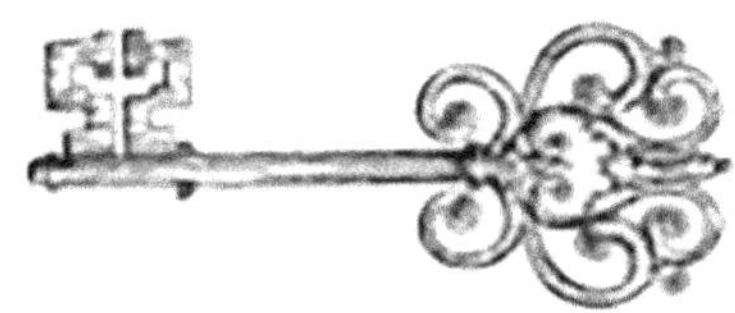

THE STUDY OF THE FOUR GOSPELS VOCABULARY DEFINITIONS FOR JOHN CHAPTERS 1-4

WORD	DEFINITIONS
1) BOSOM	The breast or area between the arms
2) FIRKINS	Hebrew unit of measure that is equal to 9 gallons
3) MANIFEST	To appear or make openly known
4) PASSOVER	A Jewish feast to commemorate the escape of the Hebrews in Egypt
5) SCOURGE	To punish severely
6) ZEAL	Great energy for a cause or objective
7) PERISH	The loss of life
8) CONDEMNATION	To declare as wrong
9) PERCEIVE	To become aware of, by way of the senses
10) MEAT	Suitable, fit, proper (as in "help meet"

THE STUDY OF THE FOUR GOSPELS VOCABULARY DEFINITIONS FOR JOHN CHAPTERS 5-8

WORD	DEFINITIONS
1) LAD	A boy or young man
2) BARLEY	A grain used to feed horses, also cultivated to make malt liquor
3) FURLONGS	Measures ⅛ of a mile
4) QUICKEN	To stimulate or make alive
5) DOCTRINE	Teaching
6) CIRCUMCISION	The surgical removal of the foreskin of males
7) DISPERSED	scattered
8) TABERNACLE	Tent structures used by the Israelites during the exodus
9) SYNAGOGUE	Place where Jews gathered for worship
10)CONVEY	To transport from one place to another

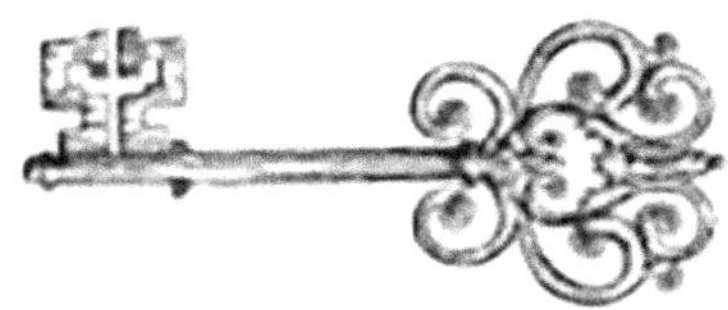

THE STUDY OF THE FOUR GOSPELS VOCABULARY DEFINITIONS FOR JOHN CHAPTERS 9-12

WORD	DEFINITIONS
1) MANIFEST	TO BECOME CLEARLY VISIBLE
2) SILOAM	SENT (IT IS ALSO THE NAME OF A POOL WHERE JESUS HEALED A BLIND MAN)
3) CONFESS	TO TELL OR MAKE KNOWN
4) REVILE	TO SCOLD ABUSIVELY AND ANGRILY
5) SHEEPFOLD	A SHELTER FOR SHEEP
6) HIRELING	A MERCENARY, ONE PAID WAGES FOR SHORT TERM WORK
7) DIDYMUS	TWIN (DIDYMUS IS ALSO WHAT THEY CALLED THOMAS.)
8) PREVAIL	OVERCOME, SUCCEED, TRIUMPH
9) EXPEDIENT	PRACTICAL, OPPORTUNE, FEASIBLE
10) SPIKENARD	AN ANCIENT FRAGRANT OINTMENT

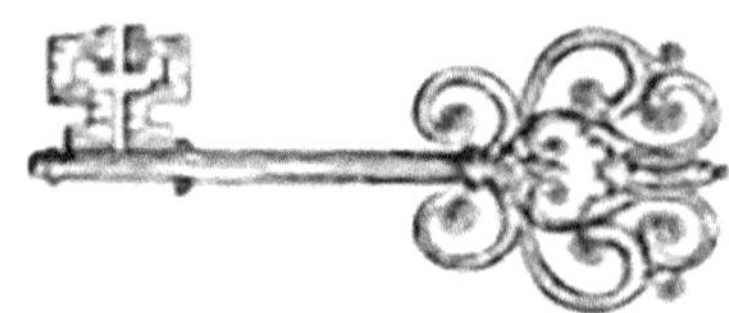

THE STUDY OF THE FOUR GOSPELS VOCABULARY DEFINITIONS FOR JOHN CHAPTERS 13-16

WORD	DEFINITIONS
1) GIRT	To surround, band, strap or saddle
2) SILOAM	A pool in Jerusalem. The name means "sent"
3) CONFESS	The acknowledgement of sin
4) REVILE	To abuse or attack with words
5) SHEEPFOLD	Strong fenced enclosure, used to protect sheep
6) HIRELING	A laborer employed for a limited time and paid as soon as work is finished
7) DIDYMUS	Double, twofold, or twins
8) PREVAIL	To overcome, to gain the victory
9) EXPEDIENT	Suitable to a purpose, hastening, urging forward
10) SPIKENARD	A very valuable perfume

THE STUDY OF THE FOUR GOSPELS VOCABULARY DEFINITIONS FOR JOHN CHAPTERS 17-21

WORD	DEFINITIONS
1) PERDITION	Total destruction, entire loss or ruin
2) RESORT	To apply, betake, or have recourse
3) SHEATH	A casing for a sword
4) SYNAGOGUE	Place where Jews gather for worship and instruction
5) CRUCIFY	To be put to death by hanging from a cross
6) RAIMENT	Clothing or garments
7) HYSSOP	A plant used for ritualistic cleansing purposes
8) REMIT	To release from guilt or penalty of something
9) GIRT	To encircle band or strap
10) CUBIT	Ancient unit of measure based on the distance between the elbow and the tip of the middle finger

www.ingramcontent.com/pod-product-compliance
Lightning Source LLC
Chambersburg PA
CBHW080835120626
46553CB00009B/2438

* 9 7 9 8 8 9 3 3 0 7 2 8 3 *